VISUAL QUICKSTART GUIDE

WordPerfect 3.5

FOR MACINTOSH

Rita Lewis

Peachpit Press

Visual QuickStart Guide
WordPerfect 3.5 for Macintosh

Rita Lewis

Peachpit Press

2414 Sixth Street
Berkeley, CA 94710
510/548-4393
510/548-5991 (fax)

Find us on the World Wide Web at: http://www.peachpit.com

Peachpit Press is a division of Addison-Wesley Publishing Company.

Editor: Jeremy Judson

Copyeditors: Irene Lea Taylor and Gina King

Technical Editor: Douglas Lewis

Cover design and illustration: The Visual Group

Interior design: Elaine Weinmann

ISBN 0-201-88355-4

9 8 7 6 5 4 3 2 1

Printed and bound in the United States of America

Printed on Recycled Paper.

Printed and bound in the United States of America.

Thank You.

Ted Nace, Peachpit Press publisher, who introduced the Visual QuickStart Guide series that makes learning the Mac that much easier and fun.

Roslyn Bullas, Mimi Heft, Hannah Onstad, and all the other staff at Peachpit Press who were so helpful and resourceful in getting this book out on time and publicizing it so well. Without you all (and anyone I may have missed), the book production would not have run so smoothly.

Dan Hoffman, owner of Business Direct. Thank you for your accurate and timely printing job. You run the most helpful service bureau I have ever worked with.

Jeremy Judson, editor at Peachpit Press. Thanks for your tireless patience with my sputtering, your gracious suggestions, and your humor. As usual, I am in your debt. The weather here is fine, I guess you got all the rain.

Steve Rath, indexer. Thank you for taking on the thankless task of indexing the book on such short notice. Your pleasant manner and thoroughness are much appreciated.

Irene Lea Taylor, copy editor. As usual, you made a hard task easier with your humor and professionalism. Thank you for your quick eye, colorful pens, and helpful suggestions.

Gina King, copy-editor. You stepped in at the last minute and cheerfully and professionally took over the ugly task of editing the updated chapters. To say thank you is not enough.

Douglas Lewis, technical editor and husband extraordinaire. We make a great team, you and I, in all of our endeavors. Thank you for your wonderful suggestions and accurate technical editing. And thank you for graciously giving me the time to work on this book and on all my past writing efforts. Thank you also for your confidence in me.

To all of the dinners prepared late, baby-sitting I foisted on your wide shoulders, and all of the chaos that reigns while books are produced, thanks for being there for me.

Lastly, thank you to my two beautiful daughters, *Lisa* and *Hannah,* who so patiently played while their mommy furiously typed and moused.

This book is dedicated to my father,

H. Richard Freidin

who taught me that the gold ring is worth it in the reaching...

TABLE OF CONTENTS

Table of Contents

INTRODUCTION 1

Novell's WordPerfect 3.5 offers a world of word processing features. The Visual QuickStart Guide serves as your introduction to the program's power.

YOU HAVE just unwrapped the next wave in word processors. WordPerfect 3 for Macintosh is the first word processor compiled to run native on Apple's PowerMac. As such, it supports a whole slew of features designed to work seamlessly with Macintosh System 7.5 to make your writing efforts easier and more efficient. WordPerfect lends a silent hand to smooth even the most complicated tasks via such features as:

- **Button Bars**—perform common tasks, such as applying bullets or indenting text quickly without the use of dialog boxes.
- **Ruler and Control Bars**—use the Ruler bar to display common or advanced features and the Control bar to expand this accessibility.
- **Drag and Drop**—rearrange text and paragraphs in documents without using cut and paste.
- **Powerful graphics tools**—create fully realized graphic objects using bézier curves, freehand shapes, and other polygons with the built-in drawing package.
- **QuickCorrect**—catch common typos on-the-fly and expand acronyms and abbreviations with the click of your keyboard.
- **Document Experts**—lets WordPerfect layout and design documents to fit your every need.

The above list doesn't exhaust the numerous functions provided by WordPerfect. For instance, WordPerfect automates the design and formatting of tables, the creation of pull quotes, the adding of borders and fills to text, the entering and consistent numbering of figure captions, the adding of annotations to text, the creation of multiple or mixing columns, and on and on... The trouble with all of these multitudinous features is that they are all there on the desktop at once. You need a hand to guide you into using the proper tool for the proper job. That's where this book comes into play.

About This Book

As with all of the previous *Visual QuickStart Guides*, this one is task-based, meaning that rather than a boring description of each command and where it's found on what menu, the *WordPerfect 3.5 for Macintosh Visual QuickStart Guide* uses a practical approach to teach you WordPerfect that applies your work habits to the program.

Use this book's many screen shots and step-by-step instructions as a hands-on manual to ease your way into WordPerfect's powerful tools. Each instruction is illustrated with the appropriate picture to let you visualize how to approach a task.

This book assumes that you have a rudimentary knowledge of basic Mac terminology, such as Open, Cut, Paste, and so forth. Yet, how WordPerfect performs these Mac-isms is clearly explained.

Beginners will feel comfortable with the basic orientation to word processing and WordPerfect provided by the first few chapters. Use these introductions to get comfortable with the characteristics of WordPerfect's menus and toolbars. Read the first chapters to also learn how to perform basic typing tasks and to ease your way into more advanced features.

Tips and recommendations are provided along the way to enhance your work. Later chapters discuss more adventurous WordPerfect features, such as the art of table creation and graphics. Try to read the book in its chapter order to get a feel for how WordPerfect operates; then use the handy sidebars to find instructions for the exact task you want to perform.

There are many complex things, such as the writing of scripts and macros to automate repetitious tasks or the merging of databases into forms, that can't be covered in a book this size. When you are ready to use these features, Peachpit Press has more comprehensive books covering these topics.

Tip

In this chapter (and all subsequent chapters), each formatting concept is described from the Menu bar. Buttons, Ruler bars, and keyboard shortcuts are displayed in sidebars, where appropriate.

Hardware and Software Requirements

Macintosh

- Mac Plus or later with a hard disk. At least 11MB of hard disk space free for the standard installation. You may need an additional 8 to 10MB if you install all of the templates and macros.
- 2MB of available RAM for System 6.0.x or 4MB of RAM for System 7.0 or later.
- System 6.0.7 or later. If you want to use Apple's Balloon Help, Publish/Subscribe, PowerTalk, or QuickTime, you must have at least System 7.0 installed. If you want to use WordPerfect Guide, QuickCorrect, or QuickDraw GX, you should be running System 7.5.

PowerMac

- 12MB free on your hard disk.
- 4.5MB of available RAM.
- System 7.1.2 or later. Note that the same System 7.5 requirements for advanced features apply to the PowerMac as to other Macs.

How WordPerfect Works

Every word processing program has an underlying theme—a way of working, that if understood, makes working in that program more efficient and easier.

Some word processors are based upon outlines—series of headings and hierarchies, where formatting is based on where you are in relation to other paragraphs in your document.

WordPerfect is more free-form and relies on changing *states*, in other words how each individual character is allowed to behave and appear. States are controlled through the use of *codes*, tiny commands that turn the look or activities of your text on or off.

When you select text and apply a font style or paragraph tab, codes are placed at the beginning and ending of where you want to apply that format. The codes delineate the boundaries of the formatting and specify its content for each format choice. Codes include bold, underline, italic, paragraph indents, hard returns, page breaks, and so on.

Now you see them, now you don't...

Although all codes are embedded directly into your document, some are available for view directly in the Document Editor window. These codes, such as paragraph marks, tab marks, and spaces, are made visible by using the **Show ¶** or **Hide ¶** commands on the Edit menu (**Figure 1**). Another type of code records font styles and paragraph information. These codes also reside in your document, but WordPerfect segregates their visibility into their own little world. You can view how your document is coded by selecting **Show Codes** from the Edit menu (**Figure 2**).

One neat thing about WordPerfect is its flexibility. You can literally format the document by manipulating these codes—adding, moving, or deleting them as necessary to achieve your formatting aims. When you click the mouse anywhere in your document with the code window open (as shown in **Figure 2**), your cursor goes to the same location among the coded version. Move the cursor to delete or add codes, and change how the selection is formatted.

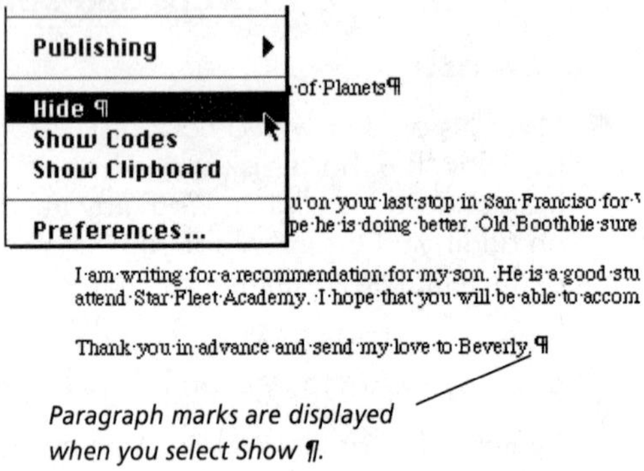

Figure 1: When you select **Show ¶**, paragraph marks and spaces are displayed and the command changes to **Hide ¶**.

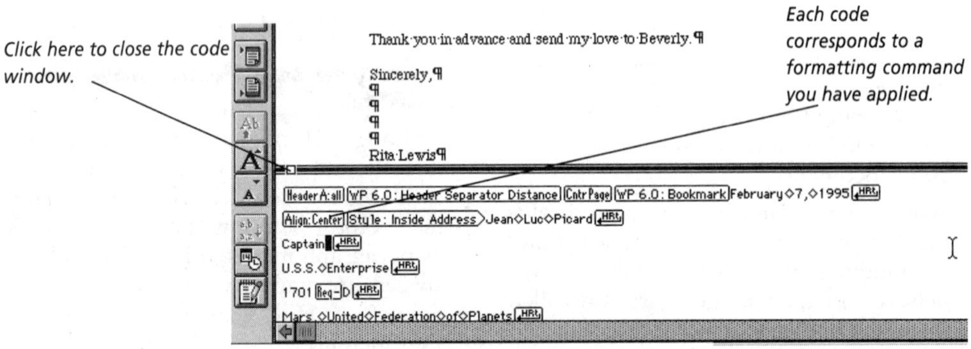

Figure 2: When you select **Show Codes** from the Edit menu, the hidden codes are displayed in their own window.

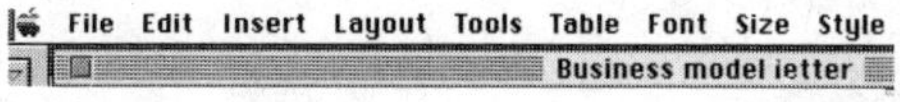

Figure 3: The Menu bar.

Menus and WordPerfect

WordPerfect adheres closely to Macintosh rules. Menus therefore function like they do in most Mac programs. WordPerfect organizes its desktop like all Mac programs with a Menu bar covering the top of the screen (**Figure 3**). WordPerfect adds seven menus to the Menu bar in addition to the two standard Mac menus (File and Edit): Insert, Layout, Tools, Table, Font, Size, and Style. *These menus are described in detail in Chapter 2: "Basics."*

Menus are used to perform tasks within WordPerfect. Each menu contains a list of commands organized under the menu name. Some menu items can contain other menus or open dialog boxes where you can make additional choices about how you want the command to behave. These commands are displayed with either an arrow (indicating the existence of a sub-menu) or an ellipse (indicating that the command opens a dialog box) (**Figure 4a**). Menus can exist in several environments. Menus that drop down or pop up when you click an item are called *pop-up menus* (shown in **Figure 4b**) and offer subsets of commands or other options within a command. Pop-up menus are found in both menus and dialog boxes (as shown in **Figure 5**).

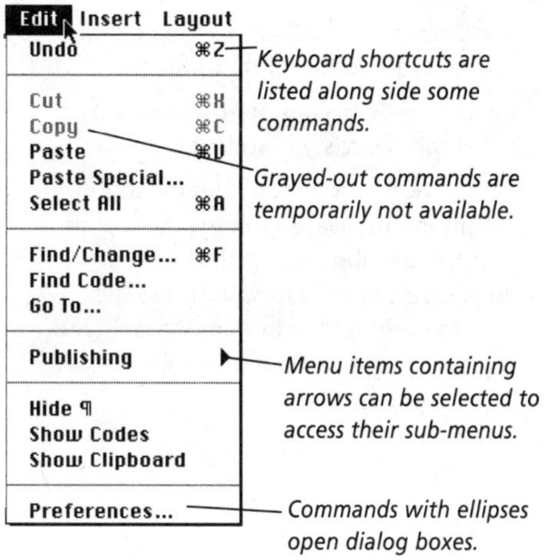

Figure 4a: A typical menu in WordPerfect.

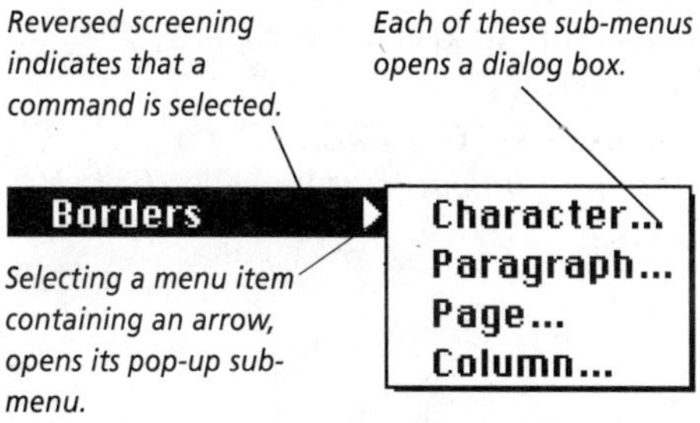

Figure 4b: Some menu items open sub-menus, called pop-up menus.

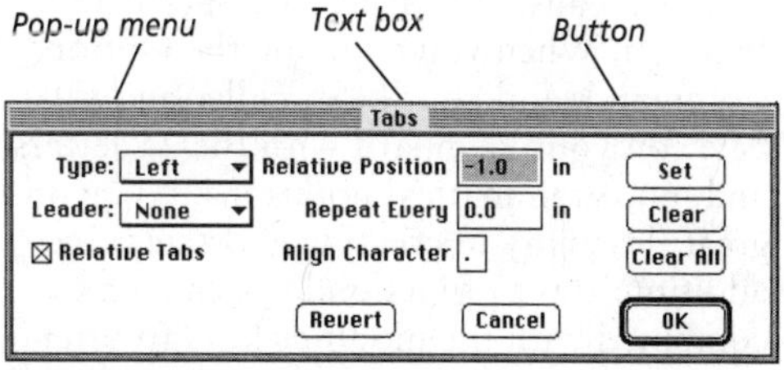

Figure 5: Commands with ellipses open dialog boxes where more control over commands is provided.

Using the Mouse

To...	Do This...
Pull down a menu	Click and hold the mouse cursor on the menu name to open the menu.
Select	Click and drag the mouse across your target item. For instance, on a menu, drag the mouse cursor down the menu list. Stop at the command you want to invoke. Note that this command is outlined in a reversed screen (see **Figure 4b**).
Highlight	Another term for "select." The "reversed screen" effect is called "highlighting."
Click	Press the mouse button once. Use clicks to pull down menus or select buttons, icons, or any other time you want to highlight an item.
Double-click	Press and release the mouse button twice. Use double-clicks to select items in dialog box lists, or select single words within text.
Drag and Drop	Select the item you want to move to another location. The cursor changes to a left-facing arrow. With the mouse button pressed, slide the cursor to the new location and release the mouse. The item is placed at the new location when you release the mouse. Press the Option key while selecting the text to copy rather than move an item. This is an alternative way to copy and paste without using the Clipboard.

Keyboard Shortcuts and WordPerfect

When you gain proficiency with WordPerfect you will want to speed up your progress by avoiding pulling down menus, clicking buttons, and juggling dialog boxes. One way WordPerfect increases your efficiency is by providing *keyboard shortcuts* for common commands. Keyboard shortcuts are key combinations, which when pressed together, cause WordPerfect to perform a function. When you combine the Option, Command, and Shift keys, called *modifier keys,* on your keyboard with the 26 letters and nine grammatical notations, you gain great flexibility in creating shortcuts. In addition, the 15 function keys can be combined with the modifier keys to offer even more combinations.

WordPerfect offers preset keyboard shortcuts next to many of its menu commands. As shown in **Figure 4a**, keyboard shortcuts for commands are indicated next to many commands on the Menu bar. You can customize WordPerfect's commands to assign more shortcuts or change existing defaults to shortcuts more in keeping with your working style.

See Chapter 15: "Customizing" for a description of how to customize keyboard shortcuts.

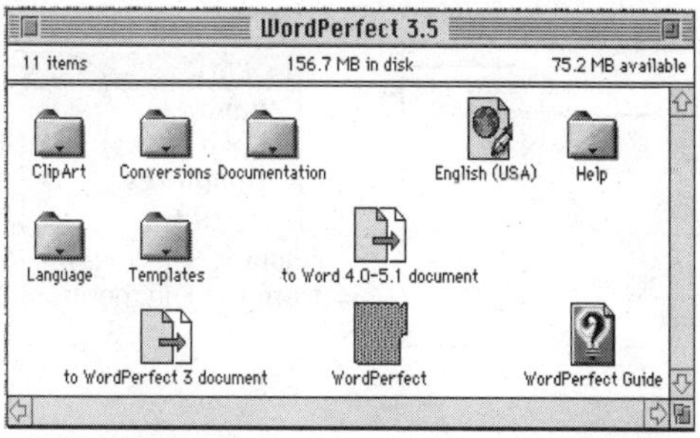

Figure 6a: WordPerfect creates its own folder on your hard disk.

Figure 6b: Double-click the application's icon to start the program.

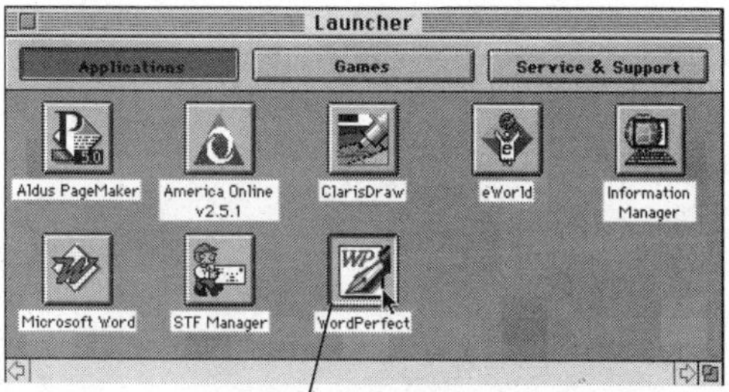

The WordPerfect icon appears on the Launcher when you insert its alias into the Launcher Items folder in the Systems folder. If you install System 7.5 Update 1, drag the icon on to the Launcher window or press Option and drag on to a Title bar button.

Figure 7: Click WordPerfect's icon on the Launcher window.

Getting Started

When you install WordPerfect on to your hard disk it makes its own folder, called appropriately enough, WordPerfect 3.5 (**Figure 6a**). WordPerfect stores its tools within this folder. Also in this folder is the application's icon. The Mac offers many ways to open applications and documents. Under System 7.5, you can open WordPerfect or one of its documents in the following ways:

- Double-click the program's icon (**Figure 6b**) or select it and use the File menu's Open command.
- Click the application's icon on the Launcher (**Figure** 7). (*Hint:* This only works if you have made an alias of the application and placed the alias in the Launcher Items folder in the System folder.)
- Double-click the document's icon on the Mac's Desktop.
- Drag a document's icon on top of the program's icon either on the Desktop or if you install System 7.5 Upgrade 1, on to the icon's Launcher button.
- Select the application from the Recent Applications pop-up menu on the Apple menu. (*Hint:* This only works if you have recently opened the application.)
- Select the document from the Recent Documents pop-up menu on the Apple menu. (*Hint:* This only works if you have previously opened the document.)

Tip

Make an alias of the WordPerfect program icon (Command+M under System 7.5) and place the alias on the Apple menu. Then, any time you want to open the program, select it from the Apple menu.

To open a new document from within WordPerfect:

1. Pull down the File menu and select New (**Figure 8**).
2. WordPerfect displays a blank Document Editor window (**Figure 9**).

Shortcuts

Figure 8: Select **New** from the File menu.

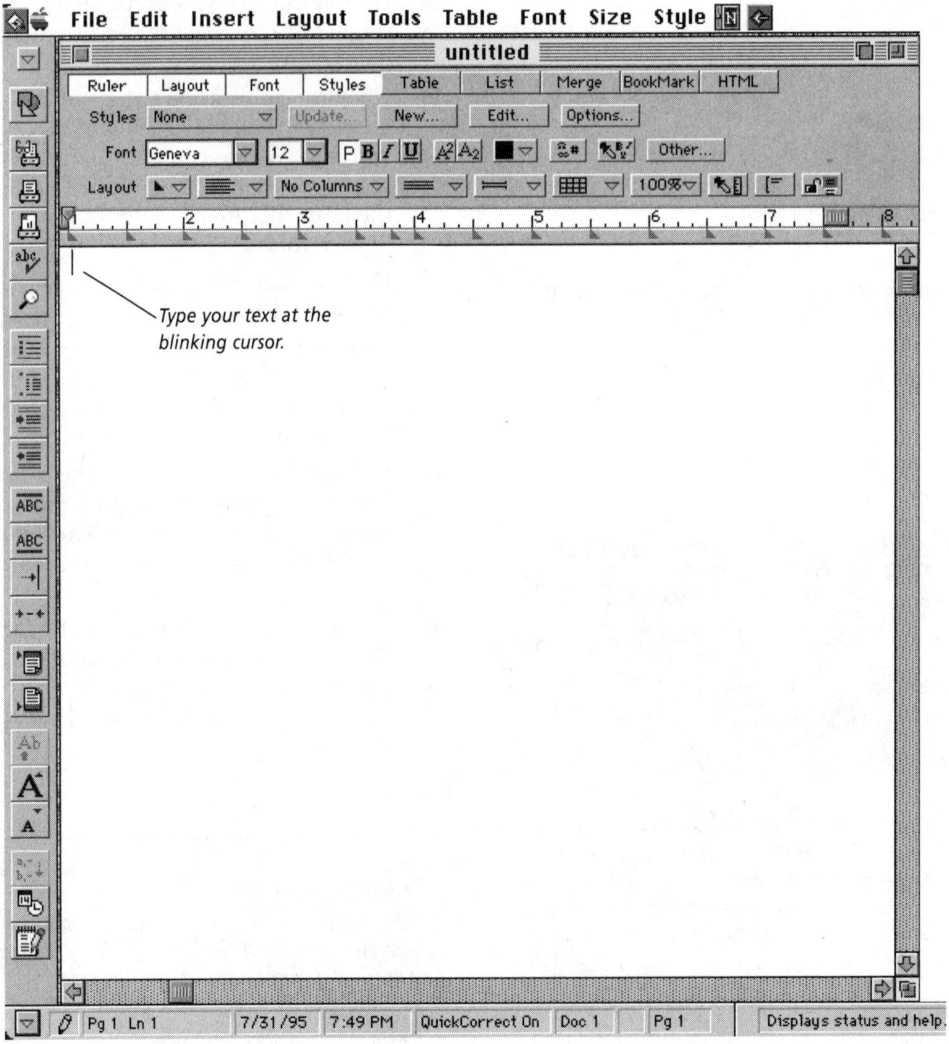

Figure 9: A new Document Editor window is displayed. An I-beam indicates where the type will appear.

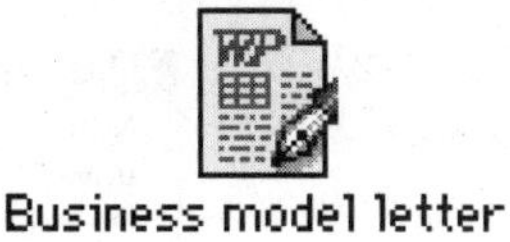

Figure 10: Double-click the document icon that you want to open or drag it on top of WordPerfect's icon or alias.

Figure 11: Select **Open** from the File menu.

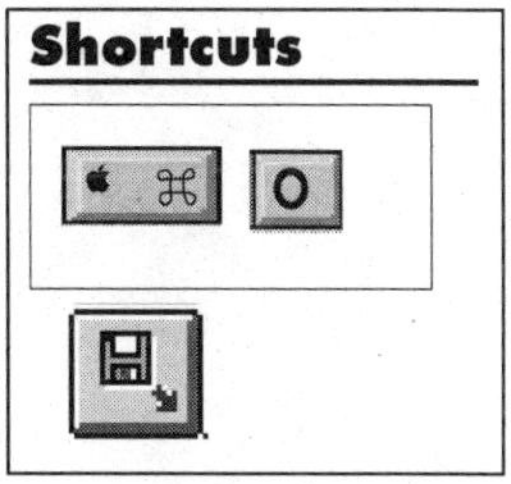

To open an existing document from the desktop:

Double-click the document's icon (**Figure 10**).

You can also drag the document's icon on top of the WordPerfect icon (if you are running System 7.x).

To open an existing document from within WordPerfect:

1. Pull down the File menu and select Open (**Figure 11**).
2. In the resulting Open dialog box, (**Figure 12**) select the document you want to open from the Directory list box. You can use the title bar's pop-up menu to change folders or volumes. Use the WordPerfect menu to open the last-opened document, a Templates file, or search for a document.
3. Click Open.
4. *Optional:* If you decide to open a new document, click New.

An optional menu bar appears if you have Now Utilities' Super Boomerang installed.

Use the Title bar's pop-up menu to select another folder or volume.

Select a document from the list box. Double-click on folders to select their contents. Shift-click to select more than one document at a time.

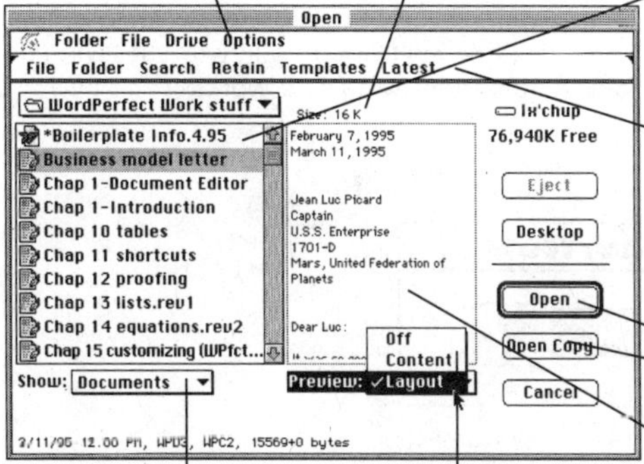

Use WordPerfect's menu bar to select other folders or Templates documents. Search for a specific document or open your latest document by selecting it from a pop-up menu.

Click Open to open the file or New to open a blank Document Editor window.

Select a document from the list box and its contents is displayed in the Preview box here.

You can change the types of documents displayed by selecting another criteria from this pop-up menu.

You can change what is displayed in the Preview window by selecting another option from this pop-up menu.

Figure 12: Select your file from the Open dialog box.

Quitting WordPerfect

Once you are inside WordPerfect, you might sometimes need to leave the program. There are two types of closure you can do: *quitting* and *closing*. Quitting totally leaves the program, whereas closing simply exits the currently active document but leaves the program open.

It is important to exit correctly so that you do not lose any of your work or corrupt the program. WordPerfect makes it very hard to lose data, because if you made any changes to a document, it asks you if you want to save the document before it quits. Since you can open more than one document at a time, these alerts are a very handy way of performing a quick save on more than one file at a time. Use the more formal Save or Save As commands if you want to save new or specific documents or rename a document.

The following tasks describe how to safely quit WordPerfect. *See Chapter 3: "Working" for more details on how to save your document.*

To quit after saving your work:

1. Pull down the File menu and select Quit (**Figure** 13).
2. In the resulting alert box, (**Figure** 14) click Save.

To quit without saving:

1. Pull down the File menu and select Quit (see **Figure** 13).
2. In the resulting alert box, click Don't Save (**Figure** 14).

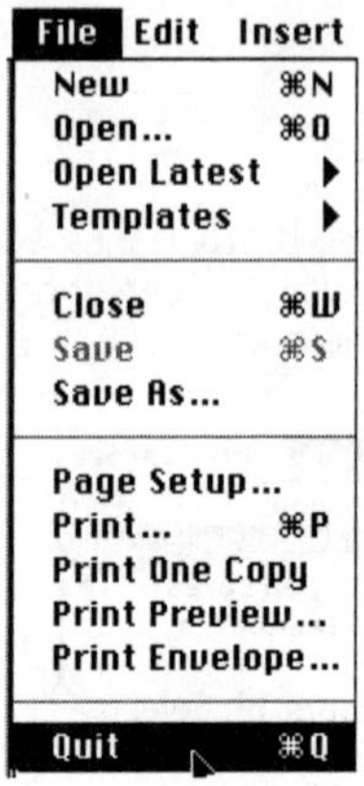

Figure 13: Select **Quit** from the File menu.

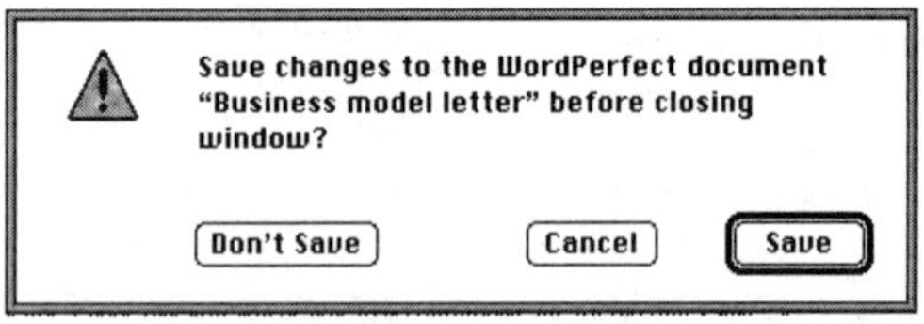

Figure 14: Click **Don't Save** to quit without saving or **Save** to quit after saving your work.

Shortcuts

Figure 15: Select **Close** to close a document without quitting.

Shortcuts

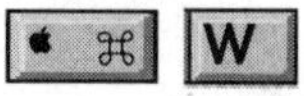

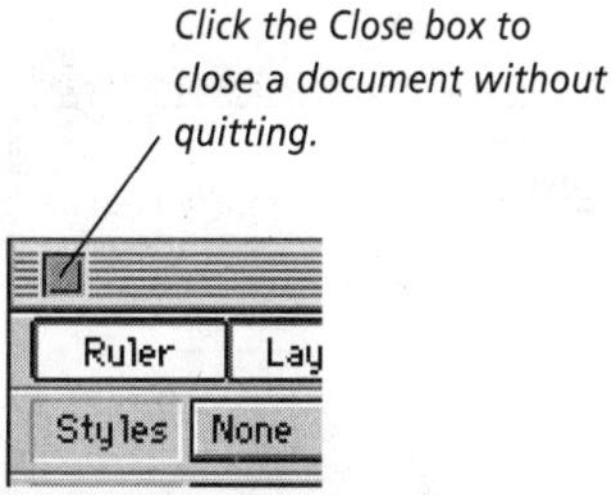

Figure 16: You can also click the close box on the Document Editor's window to close a document without quitting.

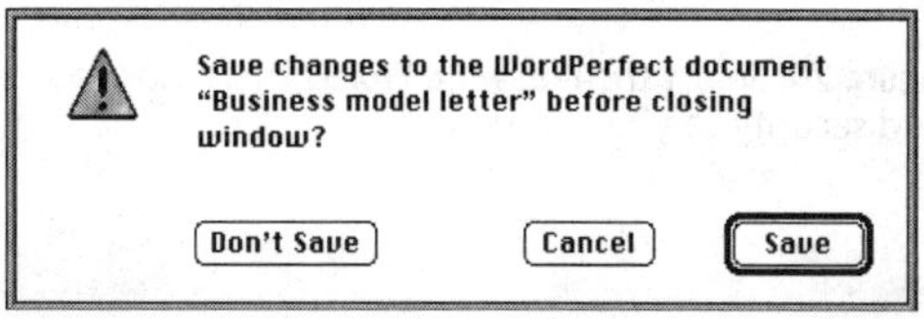

Figure 17: Click **Save** or **Don't Save** to close a document window.

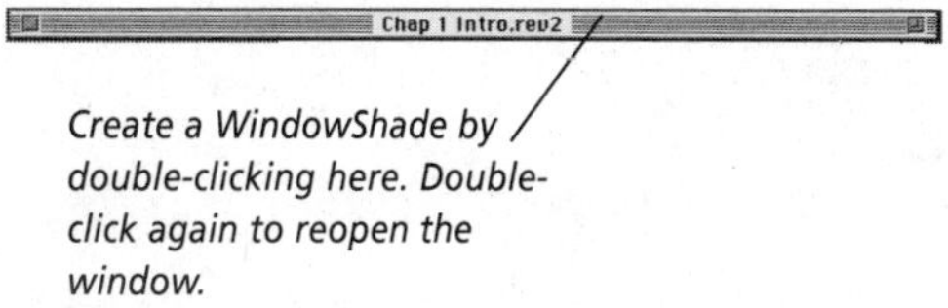

Figure 18: Double-click the document's title-bar to temporarily close its window without quitting the program.

To close a document without exiting WordPerfect:

1. Pull down the File menu and select Close (**Figure 15**).

   You can also click the close box on the Document Editor window (**Figure 16**).

2. If you have not saved the document, WordPerfect displays an alert box (**Figure 17**) asking if you want to save. Click either Save or Don't Save. (*See the previous task for an explanation of the alert box.*)

Tip

You can also hide a window without exiting the document or WordPerfect by double-clicking the window's title bar (**Figure 18**). (*Hint:* This only works if you are running System 7.5 and have turned on WindowShade in the Control Panels folder.)

Protecting Your Work

Because we work in a world that is not altogether trusting or secure from prying eyes, we sometimes need a way to protect our work. One of the simplest ways to prevent unauthorized people from reading your documents is to assign a password to each document. In this way, if a person wants to open or print one of your files, they will need to know how to unlock the file by typing the correct word. You will know who opened the file (in theory) because you limit the number of people to whom you give this password.

Figure 19: Select **Save As** from the File menu.

To add password protection to a document:

1. Pull down the File menu and select Save As (**Figure 19**).
2. *Optional*: In the resulting Save As dialog box (**Figure 20**), if you are saving the document for the first time, type a name for the document in the Save Document As text box and select a location where you want to store the file from the Directory list box and title bar.

   (*See Chapter 3: "Working" for a more detailed description of how to save your document.*)
3. Select the Password Protect checkbox (**Figure 20**) and click the Save button.

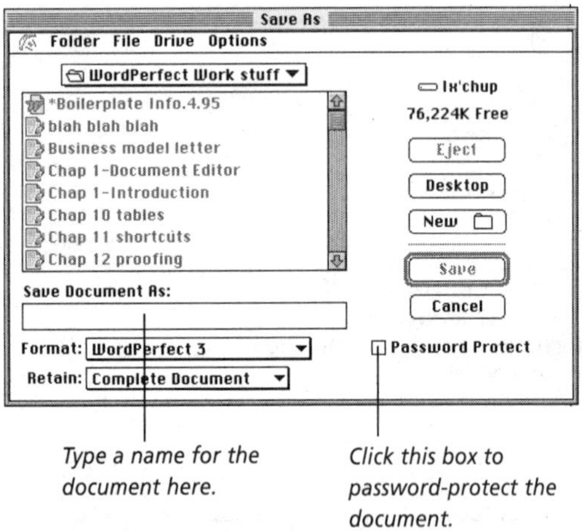

Figure 20: Select the **Password Protect** check box to add security to your document.

Tip

Select a password that is difficult to figure out, yet easy for you to remember, such as a unique birth date, anniversary, address, and so forth. In WordPerfect, passwords can be up to 59 characters or spaces in length and can include combinations of numbers, symbols, and letters (except the colon (:) that is reserved for the Mac's use). WordPerfect passwords are not case sensitive (meaning that it doesn't matter if you use capital letters or not).

Figure 21: Add a password up to 59 characters in length to your document.

Figure 22: Use the **Open** command to open a password-protected document.

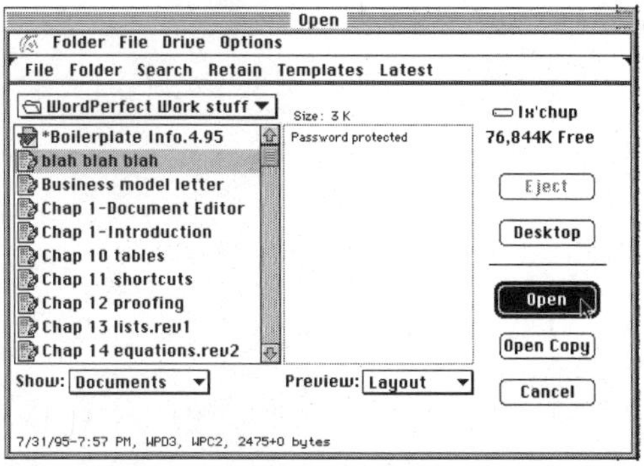

Figure 23 Select the document you want to open and click **Open**.

Figure 24: If the document is protected, the Password dialog box will be displayed.

4. In the resulting Password dialog box, type a password in the Password text box (**Figure 21**).
5. Click the OK button.
6. Type the password again a second time to verify its correctness.
7. Click the OK button.

To open a password-protected document:

1. Pull down the File menu and select Open (or press the key combination Command+O) (**Figure 22**).
2. In the resulting Open dialog box, select the document you want to open from the Directory list box and click the Open button (**Figure 23**).

   (See Chapter 3: "Working" for a description of how to open a document from within WordPerfect.)
3. If the document is password protected, WordPerfect displays the Password dialog box (**Figure 24**). Type the password in the Enter Password for Document text box. Should you type the password wrong, WordPerfect gives you another chance to enter it correctly.
4. Click the OK button.

Tip

When you type out the password, WordPerfect does not print it on the screen, but types apples in the place of the characters you enter. Be sure that you have spelled the password the way you want, since you will not be able to view the results on the screen, and WordPerfect is not forgiving, should you not type the password correctly after creating it in the Password dialog box.

To remove a password from a document:

1. Open the password protected document using the steps listed in the previous task. You will have to type in the password when asked.
2. With the document opened, pull down the File menu and select Save As.
3. In the resulting Save As dialog box shown in **Figure 23**, deselect the Password Protect check box.
4. Click the Save button.
5. WordPerfect will display the Replace alert box (**Figure 25**). Click the Replace button.

Figure 25: The Replace alert box lets you change your mind about overwriting a document. In this case, you want to replace the password-protected version with the non-secure version, so click **Replace.**

> **Tip**
>
> Be sure the document name is not changed so that WordPerfect replaces the password-protected version with one that is not password-protected and does not create a totally new document.

Getting Help Online

If you find that this book does not have the information you are seeking (hard to believe!), then look for help under the question mark (called the *Help menu*) on the Menu bar. WordPerfect provides an extensive array of online help in this location via three methods:

- **WordPerfect Guide.** Apple's new System 7.5 AppleGuide technology provides spoken and automated quick answers to basic questions about WordPerfect (with Apple Guide's System Extensions and MacInTalk installed). The guide literally walks you through the process of performing basic tasks in WordPerfect.
- **WordPerfect Help.** WordPerfect provides a large online help system equipped with bookmarks, keyword index, and interconnected descriptions for most of WordPerfect's commands.
- **Balloon Help.** Apple's System 7.0 balloon help technology lets you glide the cursor over a WordPerfect object to display a short description of what that item does. Balloon help offers limited support in WordPerfect (in fact, only the bullet bars offer balloon descriptions) and thus is not covered in this book.

To turn WordPerfect Guide on:

1. Pull down the Help menu and select WordPerfect Guide (**Figure 26**).
2. WordPerfect alerts you to "One moment, please..." and then displays the WordPerfect Guide dialog box (**Figure 27**).
3. Select a topic category from the left-hand list box. Each topic selected displays a series of related questions, such as "How do I" and "Why does this happen" in the right-hand list box.
4. Select the question you want answered from the right-hand Directory list box.

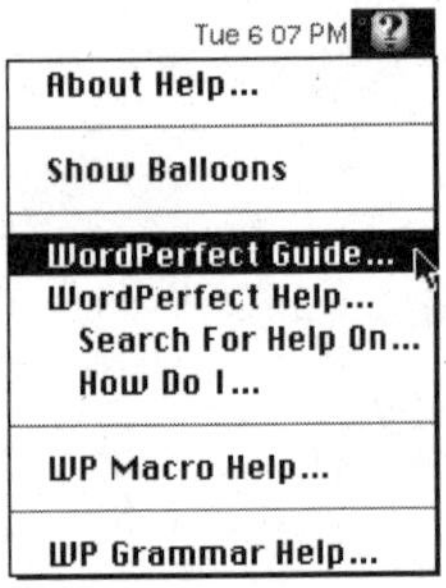

Figure 26: Select **WordPerfect Guide** from the Help menu to invoke the Guide.

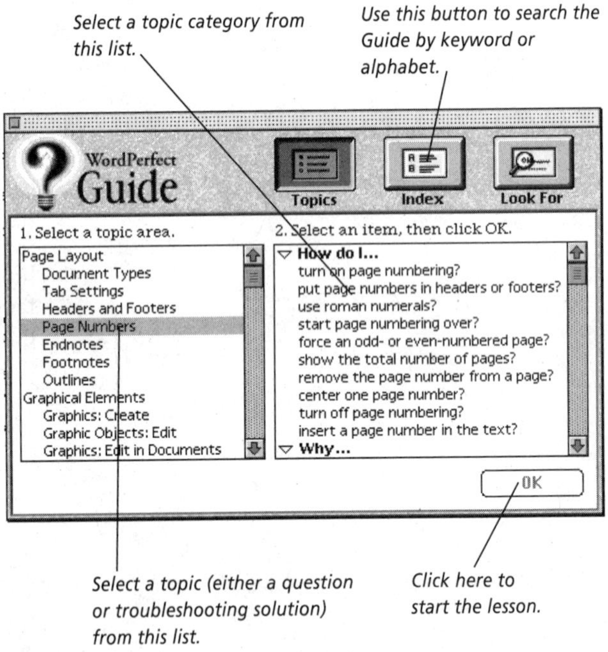

Figure 27: The WordPerfect Guide dialog box with a topic selected.

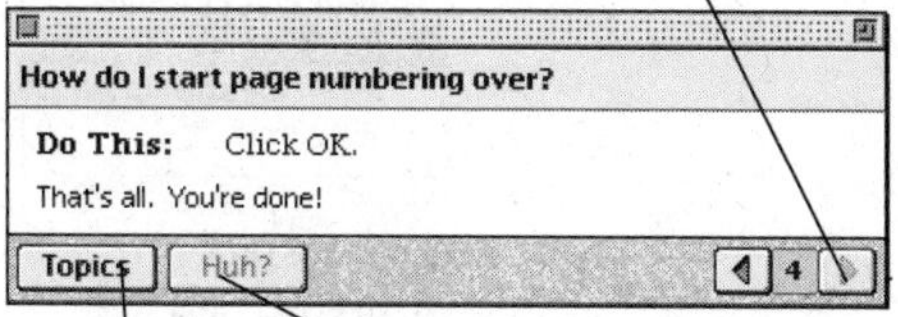

Figure 28: The Guide window tells you what to do, step by step. Each move is illustrated with a red marker on the screen (as shown in the next figure).

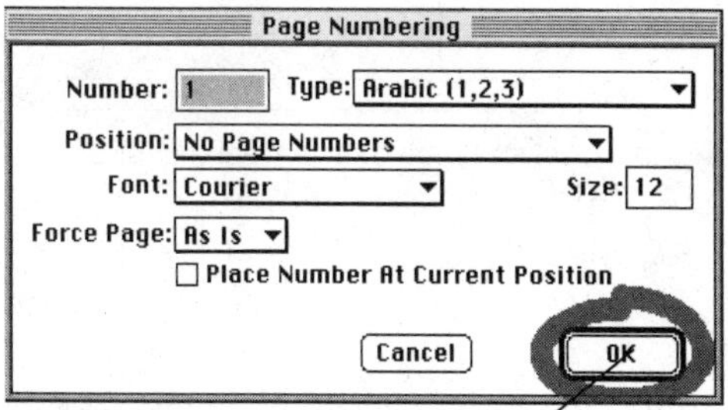

Figure 29: The Guide (shown in **Figure 28** above) said to select the **Page Numbering** command and then click **OK** in the resulting dialog box.

5. Click the **OK** button.
6. WordPerfect displays the guide in the lower left-hand corner of your screen (**Figure 28**).
7. Follow the prompts provided in the Guide dialog box and animated marker on your screen to complete the task (**Figure 29**).

Tip

You can click the **Index** and **Look For** buttons in the Main WordPerfect Guide dialog box to search for a specific question.

The **Index** is an alphabetical scrolling list of subjects contained in the Guide.

The **Look For** feature lets you use keywords to search for subjects.

To access Online Help:

1. Pull down the Help menu and select WordPerfect Help (**Figure 30**). You can also access WordPerfect Help from the Apple menu or click the Help key on an extended keyboard.
2. In the resulting Main WordPerfect Help dialog box (**Figure 31**), select a category from the list of Help Topics.
3. In the resulting list of topics, select a subject from the solidly underlined sub-items (**Figure 32**).
4. WordPerfect Help displays information on the topic selected (**Figure 33**).

Figure 30: Select **WordPerfect Help** from the Help or Apple menu to invoke the online help system.

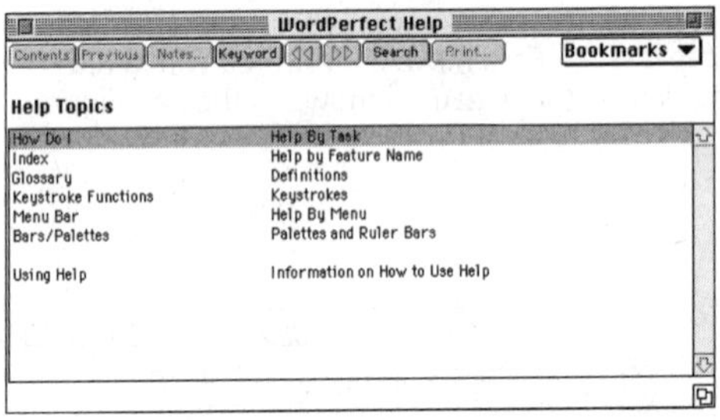

Figure 31: Select a type of help from the list of categories.

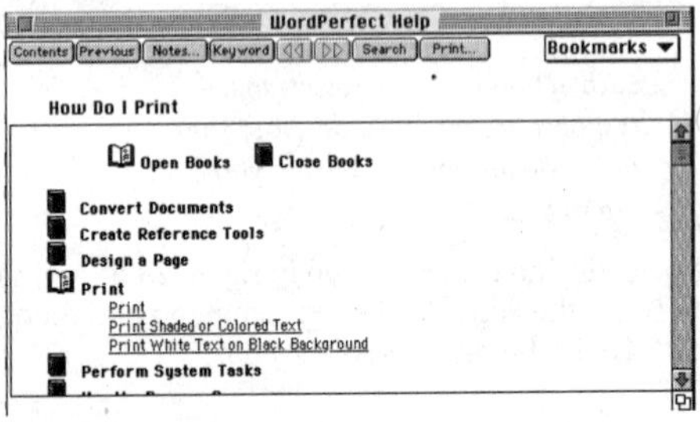

Figure 32 Select a topic from the underlined list for each category.

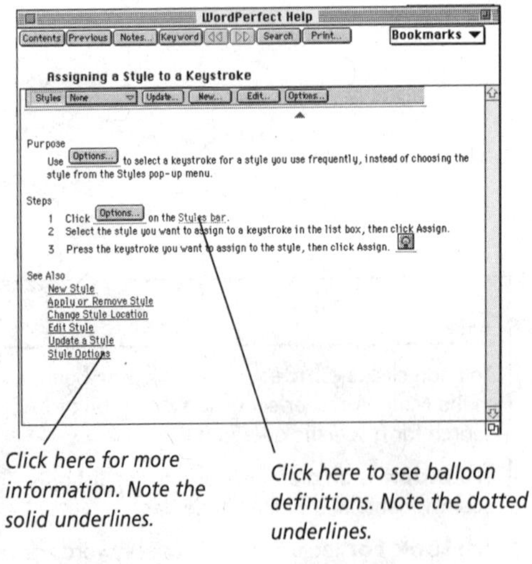

Figure 33: WordPerfect displays step-by-step instructions how to accomplish the task in question.

BASICS 2

WORDPERFECT OFFERS three different working environments: the Document Editor, the Graphics Editor, and the Equation Editor. Each window provides a different set of button bars and toolbars offering a specific set of features.

The following pages dissects the components of the Document Editor. We discuss the Control bar, various toolbars, the Ruler, the Button bar, and the Status bar, as well as identify the uses of the various menus on the Menu bar.

Later chapters describe the other available working environments, namely the Print Preview window (Chapter 7: "Printing"), the Graphics Editor (Chapter 8: "Graphics" and Chapter 9: "Layout"), and the Equations Editor (Chapter 14: "Equations ").

Mini-Glossary

Document The basic place where you do your work in WordPerfect. The term *file* and *document* are used interchangeably.

Icon A pictorial representation of a command. Click or double-click the cursor on an icon to perform that function it symbolizes. Icons are used to represent applications, documents, folders, and volumes, as well as specific features within a program. If you are running System 7, you can also drag a document icon on top of its associated application's icon to open and display its contents.

Buttons Three-dimensional icons representing specific features in a program. Click the cursor on a button to perform a task.

Tools Button icons located on bars used as shortcuts to perform WordPerfect commands.

The Document Editor

When you first open a new WordPerfect document, an empty Document Editor window is displayed (**Figure 1**). The Document Editor provides tools and an environment to perform the basic functions of word processing.

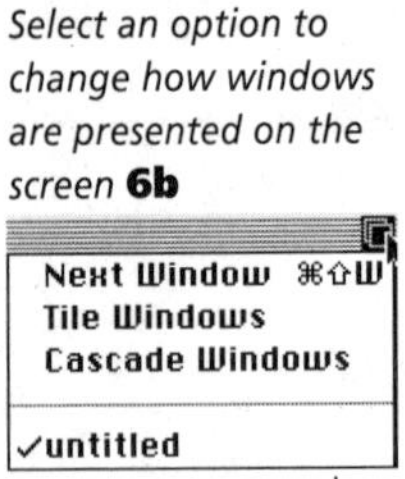

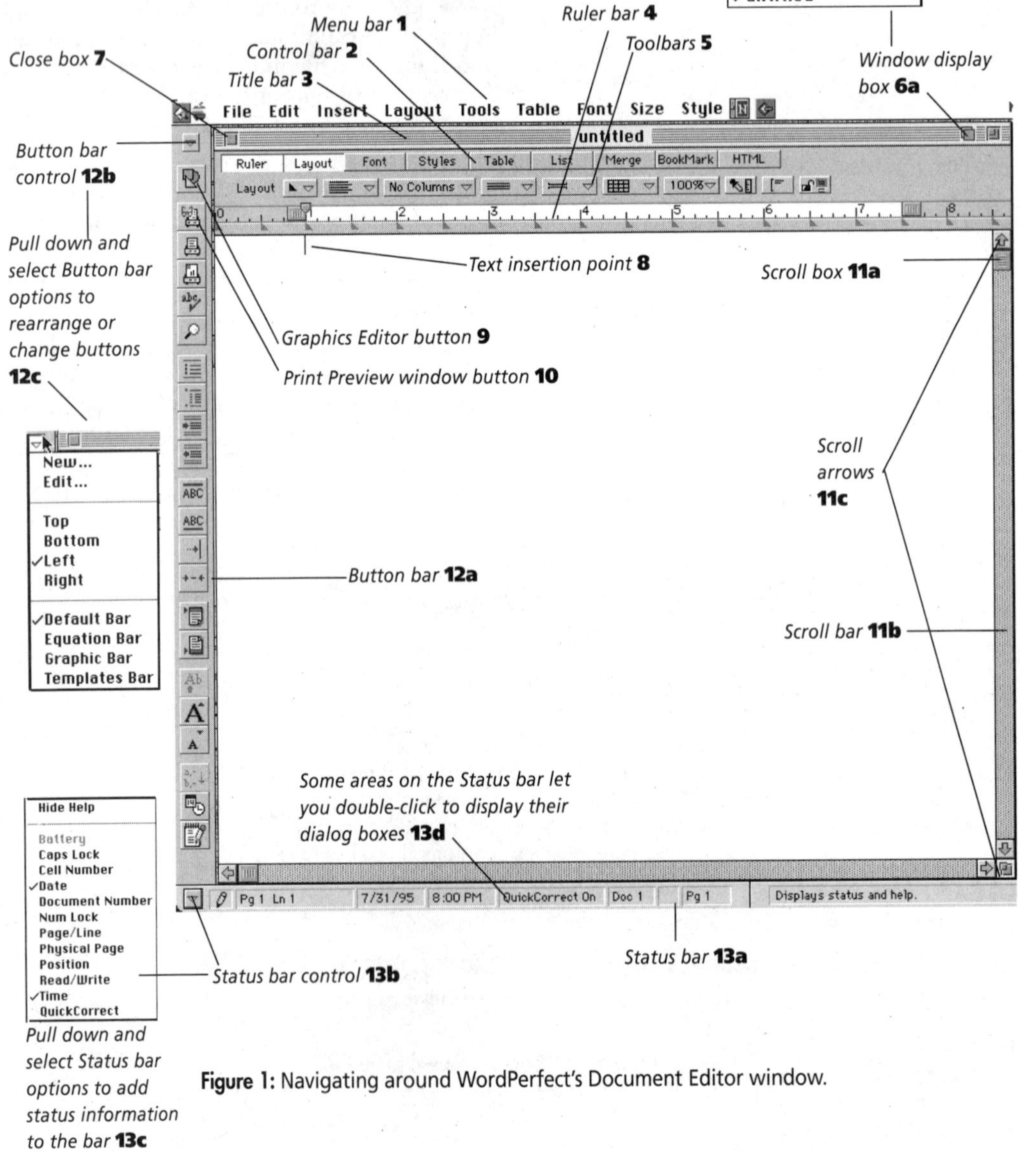

Figure 1: Navigating around WordPerfect's Document Editor window.

The Document Editor Window Explained

1 *Menu bar*

Pull down the menus on the Menu bar and select WordPerfect commands. *(See "WordPerfect's Menus Explained" on page 25 for a description of the different menu options.)*

2 *Control bar*

Click the buttons on the bar to open or shut the Ruler bars. Buttons appear white to connote open Ruler bars or grey to connote closed bars.

3 *Title bar*

Displays the document's name. If you are running System 7.5 and have Window shade on, double-click the Title bar to temporarily hide the window. Holding the Option button while clicking the Title bar displays the folder location of your current document.

4 *The Ruler bar*

Display or hide the Ruler bar by selecting Show/Hide Ruler from the Layout menu. The Ruler bar displays WordPerfect's ruler with the current tab and indentation settings as well as your margin settings.

5 *Toolbars*

The Toolbars provide a shortcut for applying formatting, font attributes, Styles, table layouts, print merging options, and list options. You can turn other bars on or off from the Control bar to control the display of the toolbars. Open or close the Styles, Layout, Fonts, Tables, Lists, Print Merge, and if Apple PowerTalk is installed, Mail bars. *(More about the Ruler and Tabs in Chapter 4: "Formatting.")*

6a, b *Window Display box*

Clicking and holding the Window Display box opens its menu. Select a different way to display windows from the Tile, Cascade, and Next options.

- **Tile** causes all of the open windows to appear simultaneously laid out like mosaic tiles on the desktop. All but the currently active window appear grey.
- **Cascade** causes all of the windows to be displayed one on top of another so that only their Title bars are visible. The currently active window is displayed on top and all other windows are grey.
- **Next Window** causes the currently active window to disappear and the next document window to be displayed and activated.

Click on any window in either view to make its window the currently active one. You can also select a window by name from the list at the bottom of the menu.

7 *The Close box*

Click the Close box to close the currently active document editor but keep WordPerfect active. Many dialog boxes also use close boxes. Clicking these boxes closes their dialog boxes and returns you to the Editor window.

The Document Editor Window continued...

8 *Text Insertion Point*

The insertion point is a blinking bar that indicates where text will appear.

9 *Graphics Editor button*

Click the New Graphics button to open the Graphics Editor window and replace the Document Editor's bars with those of the Graphics Editor. Click the Graphics Editor window's close bar to return to the Document Editor window. *(See Chapter 8: "Graphics" for more information on using the Graphics Editor.)*

10 *Print Preview Window button*

Click the Print Preview button to open the Print Preview window. The Print Preview window provides tools to view your document exactly (almost) like it will look when printed. Click the Print Preview window's close button to return to the Document Editor window. (*See Chapter 7: "Printing" for further details about using the Print Preview window.*)

11a, b, c *Scrolling tools: Scroll box, bar, and arrows*

Click inside the slider bar to scroll through a document one screen at a time. Drag the Scroll box to go to different parts of your document. Click the Scroll up or down arrow to move through your document up or down one line at a time.

12a, b, c *Button bar*

Click the buttons on this bar to perform common WordPerfect commands. The Button bar can be customized with command icons to fit your working style. You can also relocate the button bar to other areas of the screen.

Pull down the Button bar control pop-up menu to customize the Button bar or relocate it elsewhere on the screen. You can also open the other two Editor windows (Graphics Editor (9) and Print Preview (10)) using this menu. *(See "Working with the Button bar" on page 23 for further details.)*

13a, b, c, d *Status bar*

Show or hide the Status bar by pressing the key combination Command+ Option+W. Use the Status bar to display status information about your document, such as the location of the cursor on the screen, the current page count and page location in the document, the status of toggled commands such as QuickCorrect, and helpful hints. Double-clicking on some of the Status bar buttons opens their associated dialog boxes. Pull down the Status Bar's pop-up menu to customize the bar to suit your needs.

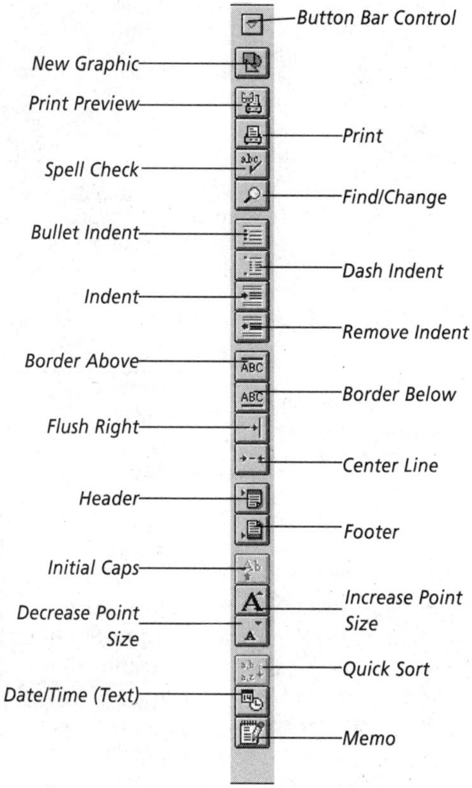

Figure 2a: The Document Editor's Default Button bar.

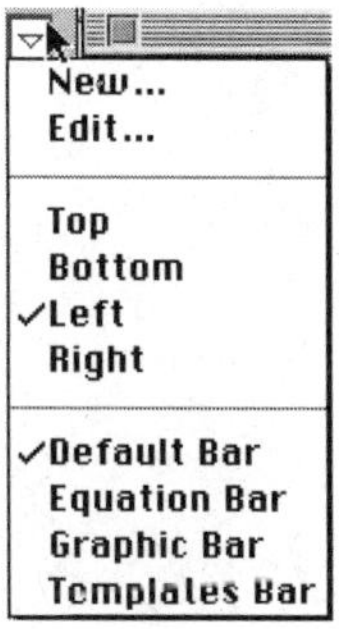

Figure 2b: Use the Button bar Control pop-up menu to manage your button bars.

Figure 2c: The Help box of the Status bar displays descriptions of tools when you pass your cursor over a button or icon in a WordPerfect window.

Working with the Button Bar

WordPerfect's button bars provide easy shortcuts to the word processors voluminous commands. When you open the box, WordPerfect offers four button bars: the Default Button bar, the Graphics Button bar, and the Equation Editor Button bar.

Figure 2a displays the Default Button bar that is used in the Document Editor. Press the Button bar Control pop-up menu (**Figure 2b**) to customize the Button bar by adding existing or new buttons or by removing unused buttons. (*See Chapter 15: "Customizing" for more discussion of customizing button bars.*)

The Graphics and Equation Editor Button bars appear when you invoke their Editors. These latter button bars are described later in the book.

Tip

If you cannot remember what each button does (and who can with so many?), pass your cursor over a button to display a short description of its function on the status bar (**Figure 2c**).

The Button Bar Explained

Button bars (see **Figure 2a**) provide easy access to WordPerfect's commands and dialog boxes. Click once on a button to activate it. Some buttons perform a since function, such as adding an indent to a paragraph, while others, such as the Find/ Change button, perform complex tasks using dialog boxes.

Figure 3: The Button Bar Control menu lets you relocate and organize your buttons.

To change the location of the Button bar on the desktop:

1. Click the Button bar control button on the top of the Button bar (**Figure 3**).
2. Select Top, Bottom, Left, or Right from the resulting pop-up menu (**Figure 4**).

To display a different Button bar:

1. Click the Button Bar Control button from the top of the Button bar (see **Figure 3**).
2. Select the Button bar you want to display from the bottom of the menu (Default, Equation, or Graphic bars) (see **Figure 4**).
3. *Optional:* Select the New command to create a new, customized Button bar.

   See Chapter 15: "Customizing" for a discussion of creating new buttons and Button bars.

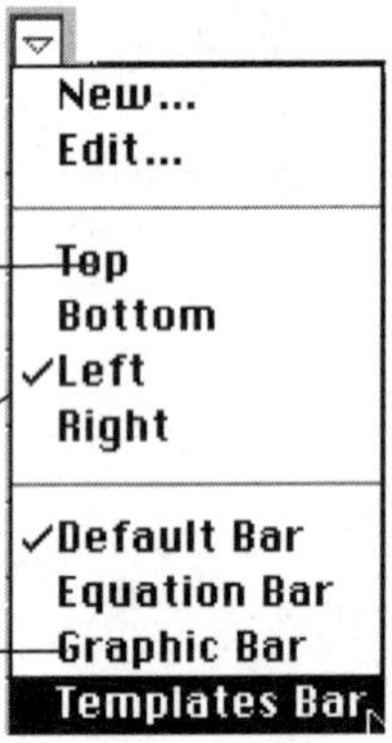

Figure 4: The Button bar Control pop-up menu.

Tip

If you are using a small monitor (such as a PowerBook or Mac Classic), you may not be able to see all of the buttons on the button bar until you move the bar to the top or bottom of the screen. See the section above on "To change the location of the Button bar on the desktop" for a description of how to move around the bars.

Figure 5a: Use the Status bar to learn about the current activity of your document.

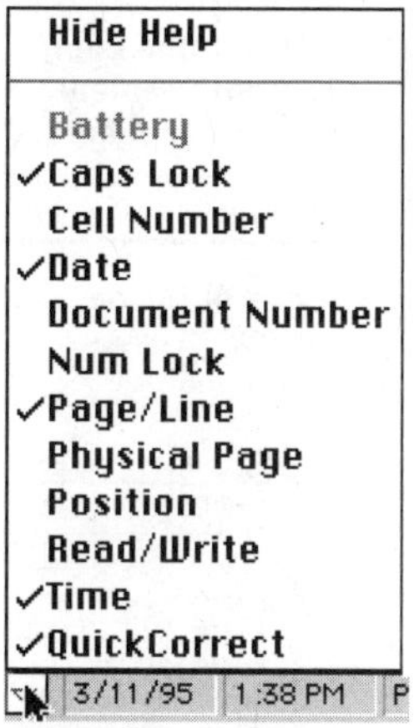

Figure 5b: Change the information displayed on the Status bar by pulling down the Status bar Control pop-up menu and selecting other options.

The Status Bar Explained

The Status bar (**Figure 5a**) is a useful addition to WordPerfect's information arsenal. You can display data about your document, such as your current page, the date and time, what automatic features such as QuickCorrect, are currently operating, the position of your insertion point, your current line, and so forth.

Use the Status Bar Control pop-up menu (**Figure 5b**) to add or subtract items fro the Status bar display. For example, if you do not want the help bar displayed, select Hide Help from the pop-up menu. You can also rearrange how items are displayed by dragging them into new positions on the bar. Delete items fro the bar by selecting them and dragging them off the bar.

Some items, such as the current page, will display dialog boxes if double-clicked.

WordPerfect's Menus Explained

As described earlier in Chapter 1, WordPerfect follows Apple's Macintosh rules very closely. This adherence to Apple's specifications results in menus that are functionally very intuitive. WordPerfect offers nine menus on its Menu bar, each used to manipulate a different part of your document.

To review how to access a menu, see Chapter 1: "Introduction" and the section called "Menus and WordPerfect."

The following pages describe WordPerfect menus and the functions of their commands.

The File menu

File menu (**Figure 6**) commands are used to create, open, close, save, print, and quit your documents. In addition, File contains special subsets of these commands that let you open the latest documents you previously used, insert existing documents into your current document (such as graphics, spreadsheets, or other word processed documents), open pre-formatted templates, print a single copy of your document, and set up the document for printing.

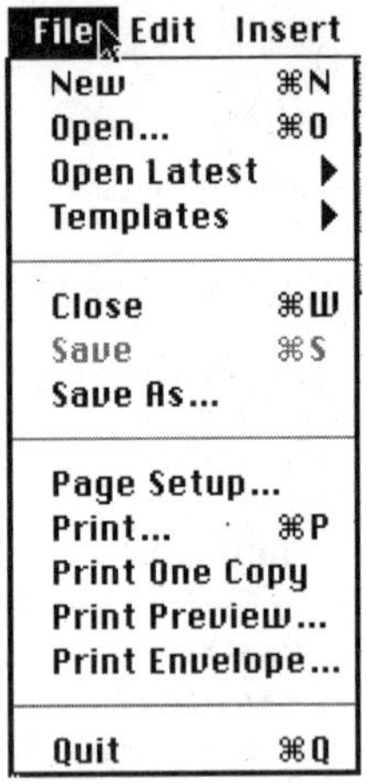

Figure 6: The **File** menu.

The Edit menu

The Edit menu (**Figure 7**) is the basic workhorse of Macintosh software, and WordPerfect's Edit menu is no different.

The Edit menu's commands include Undo, which undoes your last modification; cut, copy, and paste that let you move and replicate items via the Clipboard; Select All that provides the ability to select all of the text and graphics in your document at the same time to perform some universal action; Find/Change that lets you search for text or attributes, including codes, and replace them with some other item; Go To that lets you move around your document; Show/Hide ¶ markings and other codes and the Clipboard; and lastly, the ability to modify how you use WordPerfect via the Preferences command.

Figure 7: The **Edit** menu.

The Insert menu

Commands under this menu (**Figure 8**) let you insert codes into your document that break to another page or column, insert a blank line in front of a paragraph, insert different types of indents into paragraphs, and insert automatically updated or fixed-time and -date stamps into your document.

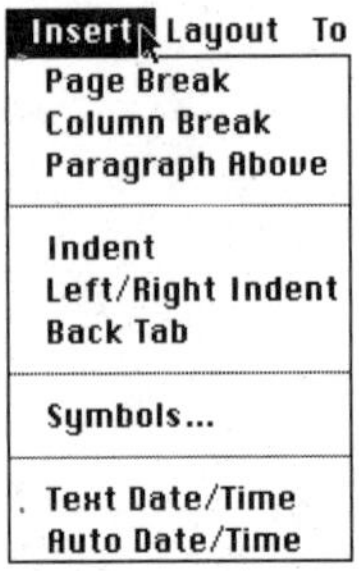

Figure 8: The **Insert** menu.

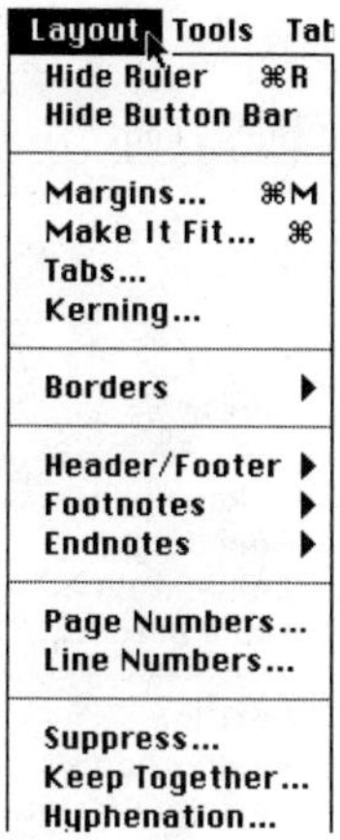

Figure 9: The **Layout** menu.

The Layout menu

The Layout menu (**Figure 9**) contains commands used to manipulate text at the paragraph level. Commands include those that set margins, tabs, and kerning rules; allow you to enter header or footer information, insert footnotes or endnotes, as well as page numbers; and display or hide the ruler and Button bars. The Layout menu also contains commands that let you group blocks of lines to prevent widowed and orphaned lines of text; and commands to set hyphenation criteria for a document.

The Tools menu

The Tools menu (**Figure 10**) is a catchall menu containing commands that make your document more professional and ease your work flow. For example, this menu contains the spell checker and grammar checker commands, as well as the handy QuickCorrect feature where you can set WordPerfect to correct spelling and grammatical errors on the fly, as well as spell out acronyms that you inadvertently (or purposely) type.

The List commands used to generate indexes and Tables of Contents, are also located on this menu, as are the sorting and line numbering commands. Tools to open the Graphic Editor and Equation Editor windows also are located in this menu, as well as the command to insert or play QuickTime movies (should you be running WordPerfect under System 7 and the QuickTime extension). Other tools let you direct where you want a graphic placed (whether over or under the text).

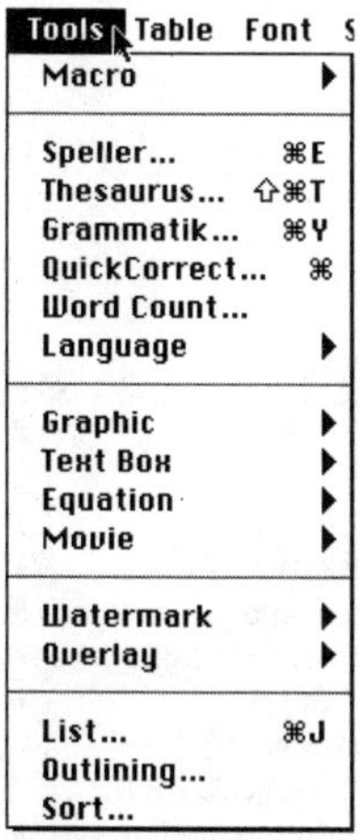

Figure 10: The **Tools** menu.

The Table menu

This is a specialized menu (**Figure 11**) for use when you want to build and manipulate tables of text or numbers. Table menu commands are used when you assign text to tables to insert rows or columns, merge rows or columns, and adjust row or column widths and heights. You can also perform mathematical calculations on tabular information and add fills and borders to table cells.

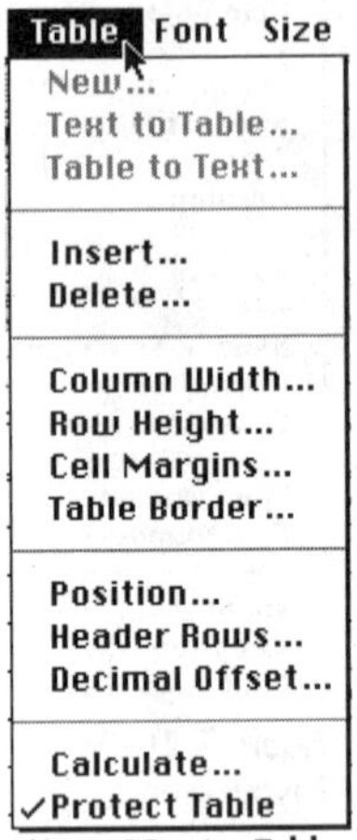

Figure 11: The **Table** menu.

The Font menu

All fonts that you have currently installed in your Fonts folder (under System 7) or in your System folder (under System 6) are listed on this menu (**Figure 12**). Use the menu to change the type of font you are using. On smaller screens, basic font sizes (for example 9, 10,12, 14, 18, and 24 points) are also displayed on this menu.

> **Tip**
>
> Note that the menu displayed in Figure 12 displays the fonts by family and in their actual type face. This enhancement is available if you install Now Utilities' Now WYSIWYG System extension and Now Menus. You can also display fonts grouped by family by installing Adobe Type Reunion or Fifth Generation's Suitecase 2.

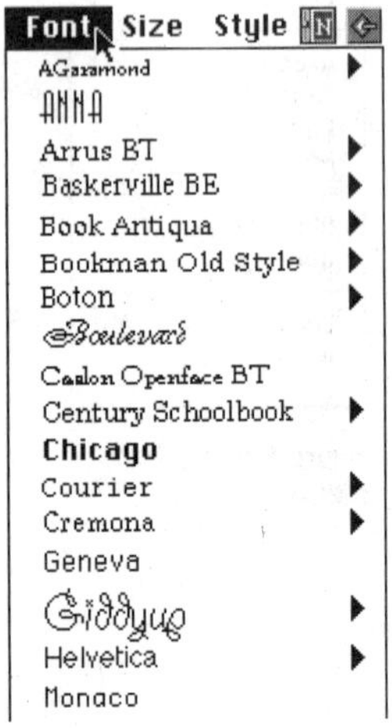

Figure 12: The **Font** menu.

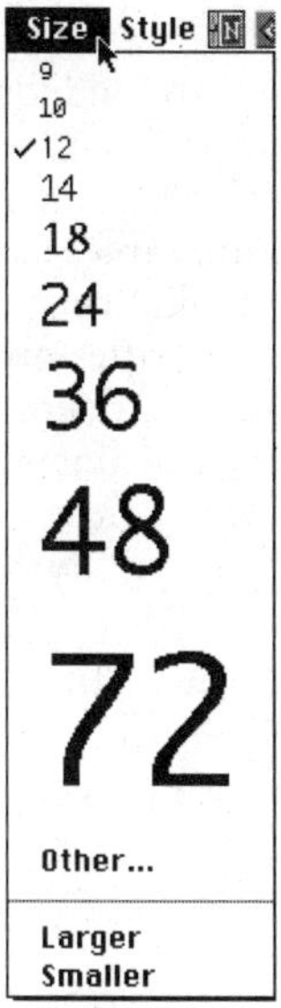

Figure 13: The **Size** menu.

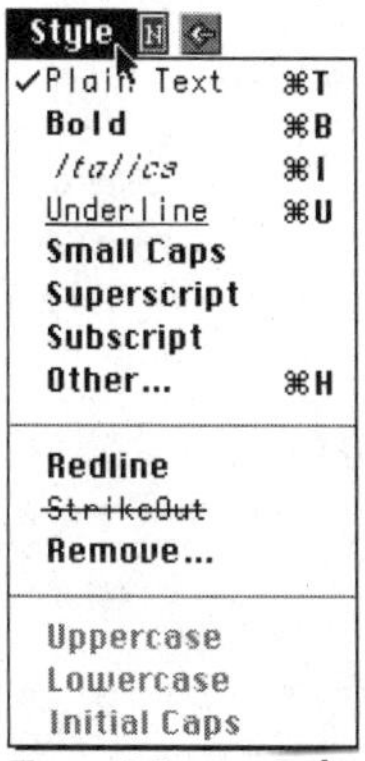

Figure 14: The **Style** menu.

The Size menu

Set the size of the font you are using by selecting a point size from this menu (**Figure 13**). Standard font sizes are displayed as well as Other, Larger, and Smaller. Use the latter three commands to make your fonts one point larger or smaller than currently displayed, or to set the font size to a nonstandard size. Note that because Now WYSIWYG is installed, font sizes are displayed at their actual sizes on the menu. On some smaller monitors, the Other, Larger, and Smaller commands appear beneath the fonts on the Font menu and there is no Size menu.

The Style menu

This menu (**Figure 14**) lets you set the formatting style for your font. Standard styles are displayed, including plain text, bold, italics, and underline. In addition, nonstandard character formats are included, such as small caps, superscript/ subscript, redline (that marks newly added text with a line in the margin), strikeout (that indicates deleted text with a line through the middle), uppercase/ lowercase (that changes the case of selected text), and Initial caps. The menu also includes a useful command called Remove, that allows you to delete both text marked with a strikeout as well as the redline markings next to inserted text.

Tip

If you have Type 1 printer fonts installed that include variations for italics and bold, use these rather than Apple's styles. PostScript printers will not treat screen-printed bold and italics with the same precision as when it actually draws the font's versions of these styles.

Working with Ruler Bars

When you have worked with WordPerfect for a short time, you will find yourself relying less and less on the commands contained on the Menu bar and more and more on their shortcut versions contained on the Ruler bars accessed at the top of your screen (Figure 15). WordPerfect lets you control which Ruler bars are displayed by turning them on or off using the Control bar. The Control bar features seven buttons, one for each Ruler bar: Layout, Fonts, Styles, Formatting, Tables, List, and Merge. (An optional eighth Control bar for electronic mail will appear if you have PowerTalk installed on your Mac under System 7.5.)

Each Ruler bar offers common commands to set such things as font style, size, and type; to set or edit a paragraph or character style sheet; to set up and modify tables as well as perform math within tables; to create tables or contents or authorities on the fly; and to generate a database document (also called a print merge document). The following paragraphs describe how these Ruler bars can be used to simplify your work.

In addition to these seven bars, WordPerfect uses a Ruler to set tabs, margins, and indents (Figure 16). You can turn the Ruler on or off using the Control bar.

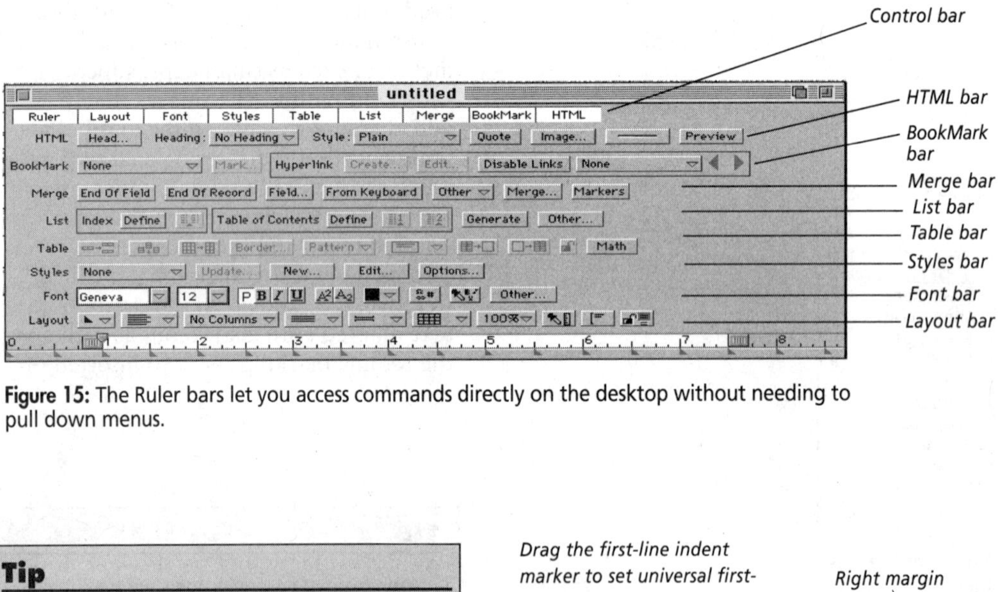

Figure 15: The Ruler bars let you access commands directly on the desktop without needing to pull down menus.

> **Tip**
>
> You can see what each item on a bar does by passing the mouse cursor across a bar's icon and reading the description displayed in the Status bar at the bottom of the Document Editor's window.

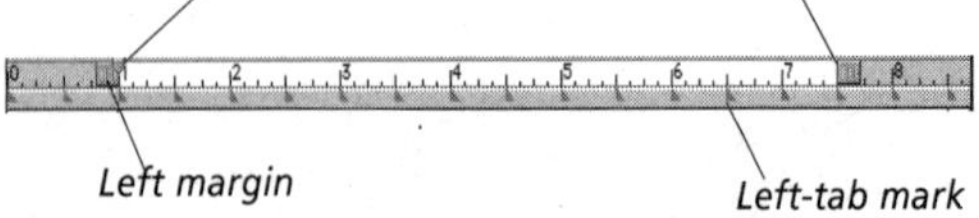

Figure 16: The Ruler bar. *See Chapter 4: "Formatting Documents" for a discussion of how to use the Ruler bar.*

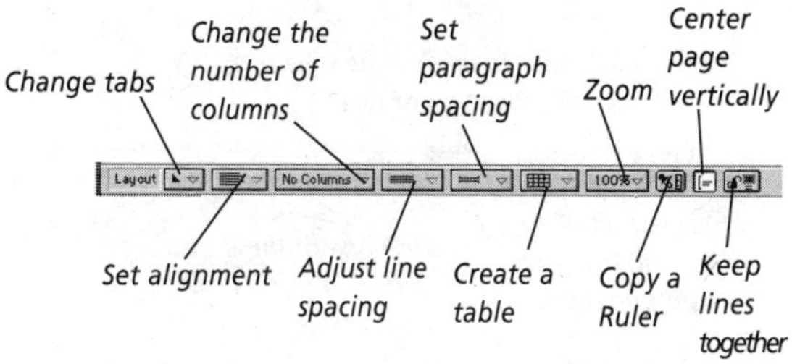

Figure 17: The Layout bar.

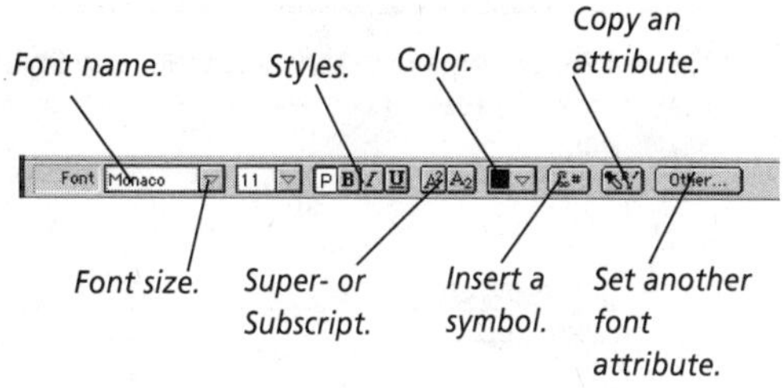

Figure 18a: The Font bar.

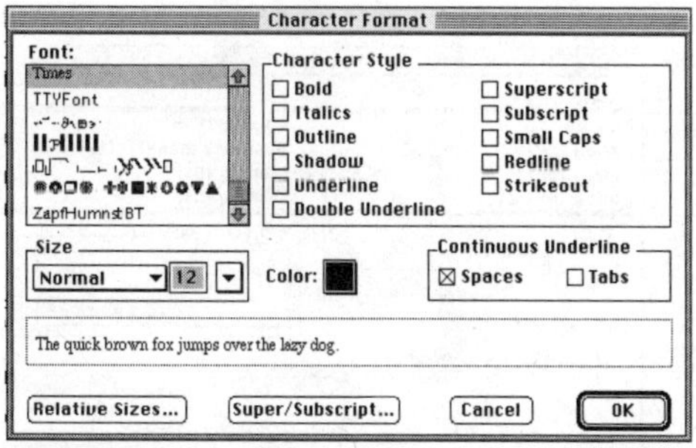

Figure 18b: Click **Other** on the Font toolbar to open the Character Format dialog box.

The Layout bar

Use the Layout bar (**Figure 17**) to change the layout attributes of paragraphs. For example, you can change the tab types from left- to right-justified tabs or clear them all together from the Ruler; change the alignment of paragraphs from left-justified to full-justified; change the line spacing from single- to double-spaced lines; or the paragraph spacing from no points to 12 points between paragraphs; or center a line of text vertically on a page. In addition, this ruler lets you place paragraphs of text into tables, change the view size by zooming in or out, and copy the ruler settings from one paragraph to another.

See Chapter 4: "Formatting" for further descriptions of how each button works.

The Font bar

Use the Font bar (**Figure 18a**) to set how characters of text appears on the page. You can use this bar to change the font type, size, and style, (for example change text to bold, underline, italic, and so forth, or increase or decrease its size or tracking level). You can also set a character's placement on a line (for example superscript or subscript), change the color of text, insert a special character or symbol, and copy font attributes from one set of selected text to another.

If you don't find the specific criteria you want to set directly on the Font bar, you can also open the Character Format dialog box (**Figure 18b**) by clicking the Other tool on the Font toolbar.

For more information on setting character-level styles, see Chapter 4: "Formatting."

The Styles bar

The Styles bar offers command shortcuts to create, edit, and link styles for paragraphs and characters (**Figures 19a, b, c, and d**). The Styles bar provides three buttons that open the three different Styles command dialog boxes.

See Chapter 6: "Styles" for more discussion about using these dialog boxes and the Styles bar.

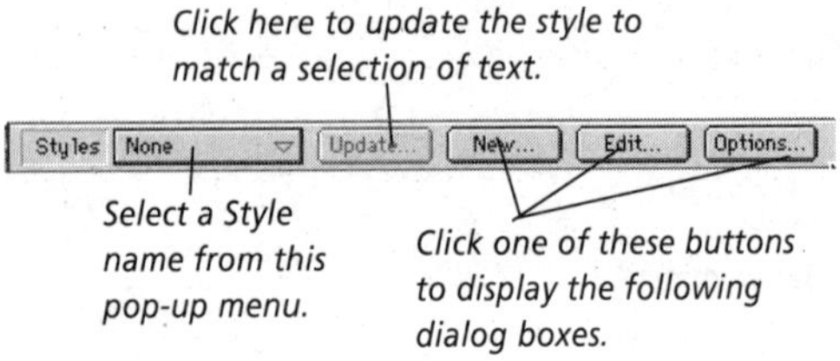

Figure 19a: The Styles bar.

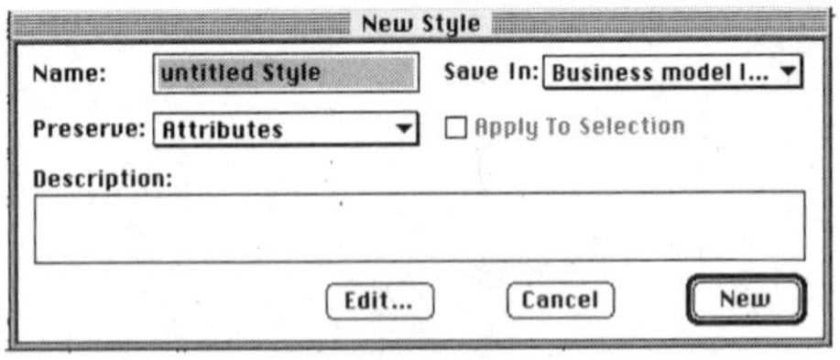

Figure 19b: Create a new style with the New Style dialog box by pressing the **New** button on the Styles bar.

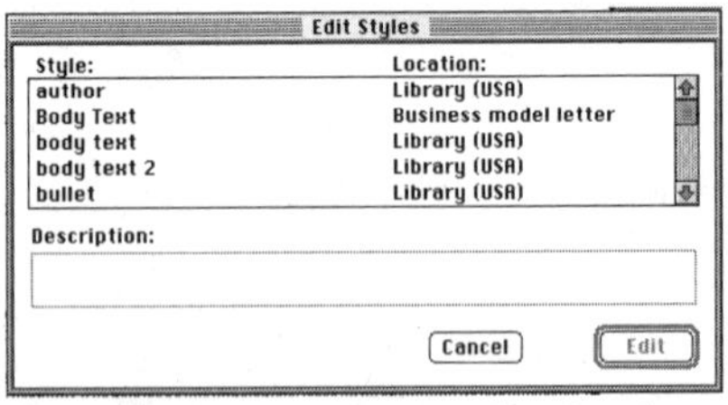

Figure 19c: Edit an existing style using the Edit Styles dialog box accessed via the **Edit** button on the Styles bar.

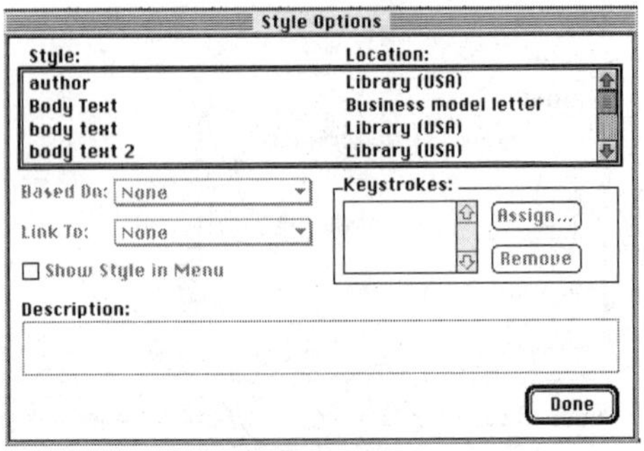

Figure 19d: Link styles together and set keyboard shortcuts using the Style Options dialog box.

Mini-Glossary

Attributes: Those elements of style that help to define how a character appears on the page. Examples include bold, 10-point size, and Normal tracking.

Formatting: Those elements that define how a page of text appears. Examples include margins, indents, alignment, and so forth.

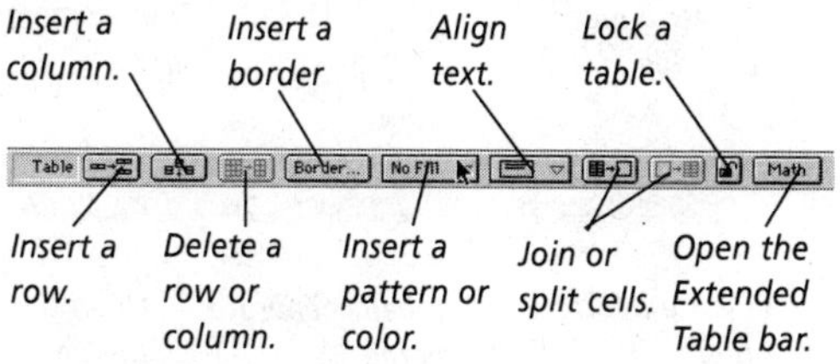

Figure 20a: The Table bar.

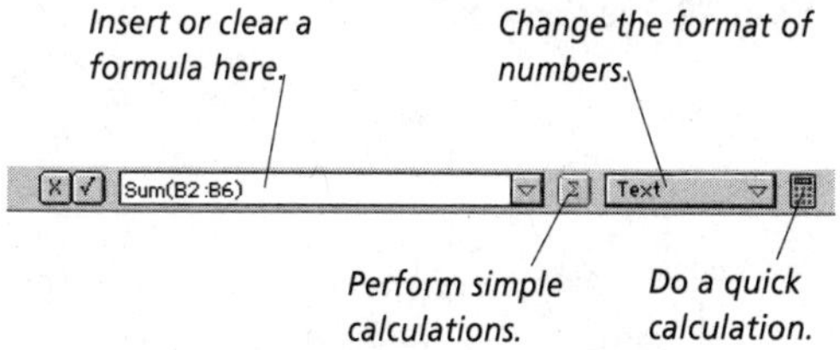

Figure 20b: Click the **Math** button to access the calculation tools on the Extended Table bar.

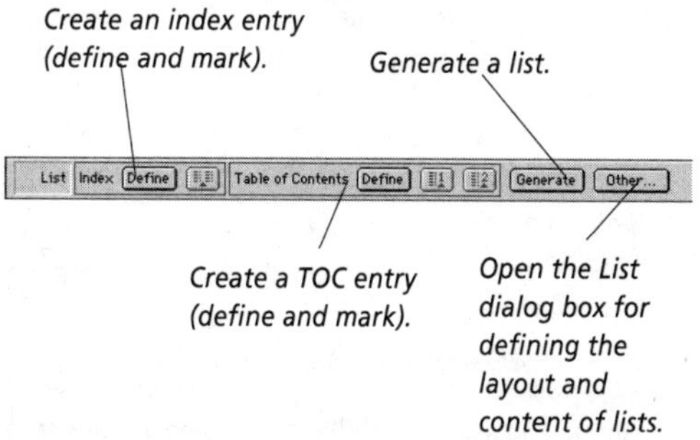

Figure 21: The List bar.

The Table bar

After creating a table using the Create Table command on the Table menu, you can modify the cells using the Table bar's tools (**Figure 20a**). Use the Table bar to insert or delete rows or columns, place borders or fills into cells, change the vertical alignment of text, merge or split cells, or lock the table so that it cannot be inadvertently changed.

The Table bar also offers a subsidiary toolbar that offers a place to perform mathematics on the contents of the table. Use the Math button to turn on the Extended Table bar (**Figure 20b**). Use the Extended Table bar to perform formulas that you type or select on the Formula text box, do basic calculations, or change the format of numbers in the table.

See Chapter 10: "Tables" for more information on creating and modifying tabular materials.

The List bar

Use the List bar (**Figure 21**) to generate different types of Lists, such as Tables of Contents, Tables of Authorities (for legal use), indices, or cross-references between information in lists. You can both create and modify lists using the List bar.

See Chapter 13: "Lists" for a discussion of creating and modifying Tables of Contents and indices.

The Merge bar

WordPerfect lets you create mini-databases to automate form letters. Use the Merge commands located on the Merge bar (**Figure 22**) to merge such databases as lists of addresses into form letters or a labels template. This is an advanced use of WordPerfect that is beyond the scope of this book. Check with WordPerfect Online Help (*see Chapter 1: "Introduction," for information on accessing help files*) for information on how to use the merge features.

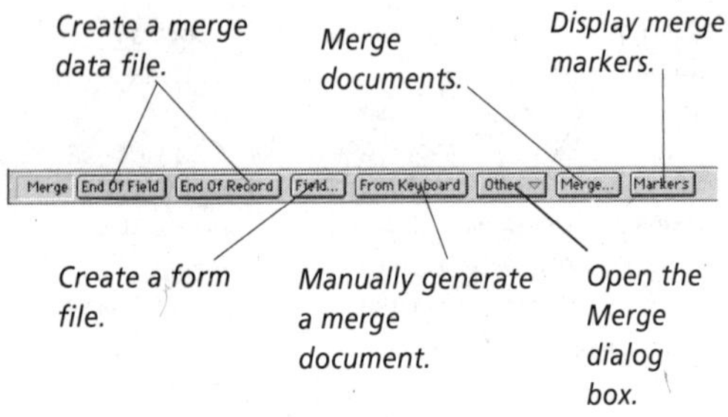

Figure 22: The **Merge** bar.

The BookMark bar

Use the BookMark bar (**Figure 23**) to link text or paragraphs in either other areas of your document to your current location; or to link your current document to a completely different document. Documents can reside on your computer, a different computer on a network, or even on the Internet. Bookmarks use hyperlinks that when saved as Hypertext Markup Language format (HTML) let you pull information from World Wide Web pages into your document.

See Chapter 16: "Internet" for a discussion of bookmarks and HTML.

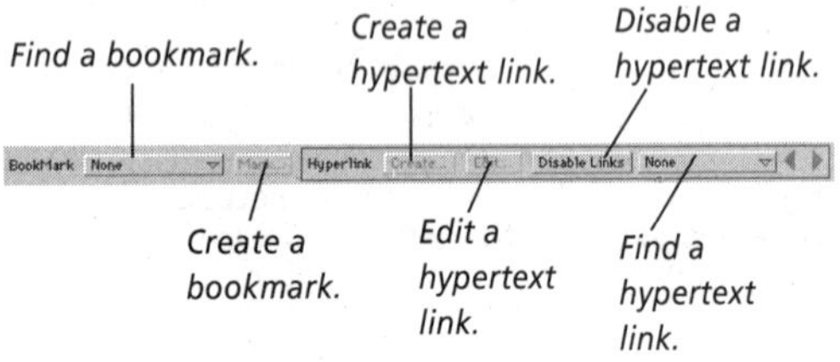

Figure 23: The **BookMark** bar.

The HTML bar

WordPerfect 3.5 introduces the first word processing program that lets you publish Web documents directly from your word processor. The HTML bar (**Figure 24**) provides access to HyperText Markup Language tools to automatically convert your document into one that can be published on the Internet.

See Chapter 16: "Internet" for a discussion of markup languages, and a description of how to generate and edit HTML documents.

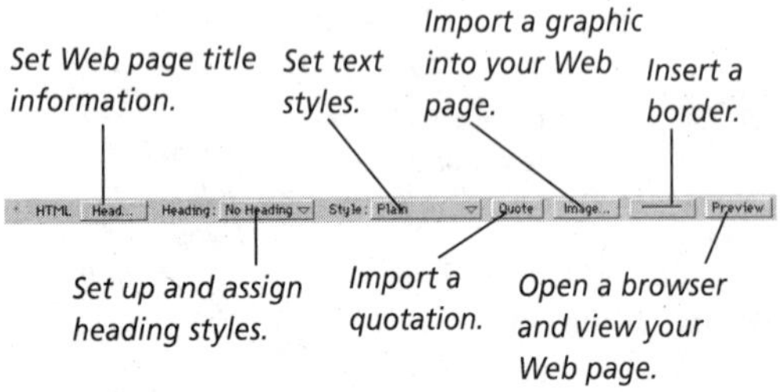

Figure 24: The **Hypertext Markup Language (HTML)** bar.

WORKING 3

YOU HAVE NOW learned your way around WordPerfect's desktop—twiddled with buttons and Ruler bars, learned about menus and commands, and played with keyboard shortcuts and codes. You have also learned how to open and close WordPerfect's program and documents. It is now time to get down tothe work of a word processing program—writing. This chapter covers the basics of typing in WordPerfect. Included in this chapter are the following tasks:

- Entering text
- Selecting text
- Recovering from an error using the Undo command
- Saving a document
- Naming a new document
- Copying and moving text in several ways
- Deleting text in several ways
- Shortcuts for entering dates and times

After finishing this chapter you will be well on your way to being proficient at WordPerfect. Later chapters will build on your new skills to add pizzazz to documents by changing font attributes, page formats, and adding graphics. You will also learn to automate portions of your work via macros and style sheets.

Mini-Glossary

Arrow cursor. The cursor changes to a left-facing arrow when you pass the cursor over a button on the Button bar, the Ruler, or any toolbar. The left-hand arrow also appears after you select text to enable you to drag and drop the text to another location.

I-beam cursor. The I-beam appears on the desktop when you are inputting text. Use the I-beam to guide you where to type and where to insert text.

Blinking cursor. This cursor is always located in front of text you type to indicate where the next text will appear.

Entering Text in WordPerfect

After opening a WordPerfect document, you have before you a blank window with an I-beam cursor blinking and blinking, waiting for you to type your first line (**Figure 1a**). All you do now is type.

To type a line of text:

Hint: Prior to performing the next task, select **Show ¶** from the Edit menu so that you can see the paragraph and space markings as you type.

1. Type the following text, "Now is the time for all good men to come to the aid of their country."
2. WordPerfect will wrap the text to the next line if you continue typing. If you want to start a new paragraph, press the Return key (**Figure 1b**).

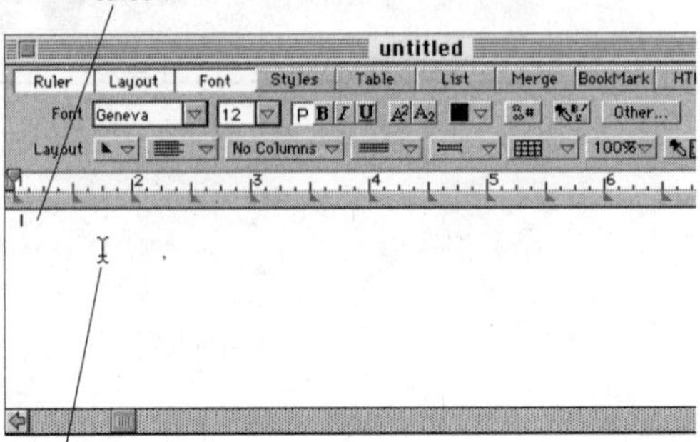

Figure 1a: When you open a new document, WordPerfect offers a blank window for your work.

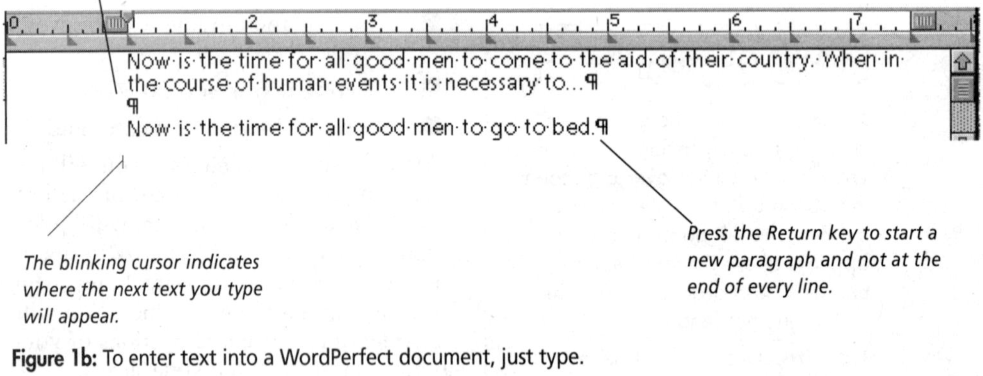

Figure 1b: To enter text into a WordPerfect document, just type.

Tip

When you type, do not press the Return key at the end of each line, but let WordPerfect wrap the text to the next line when the cursor comes to the end of a line. Use the Return key to indicate the end of a paragraph and the start of a new one. Let WordPerfect perform all of the "scut" work of typing, such as word wrapping, page breaking, and so forth, whenever possible. This leaves you free to think about what you are writing and not about the physical functions of the word processor. As Robin Williams says, "The Mac is Not a Typewriter!"© Other old-fashioned typewriter-type rules no longer apply, for example:

1. Press the space bar only once at the end of a sentence. You'll find that WordPerfect's QuickCorrect will assist you in this by automatically correcting any inadvertent double-spaces after periods. See Chapter 11: "Shortcuts," for a description of how to use QuickCorrect.
2. Use the Paragraph Space commands on the Layout bar to insert the proper space between paragraphs. Do not press Return twice at the end of a paragraph.
3. Use the Tab key to indicate indents or tabs. Do not use the space bar to vertically align text.

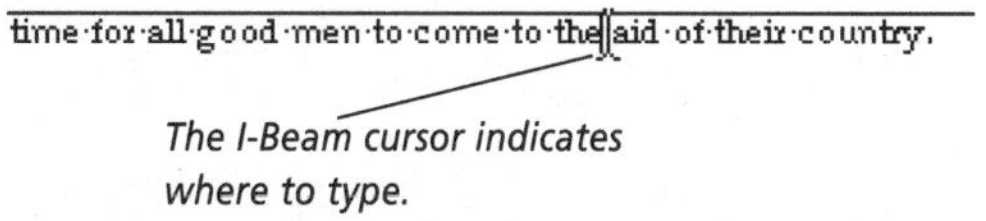

Figure 2a: Move the cursor and click where you want to insert a word.

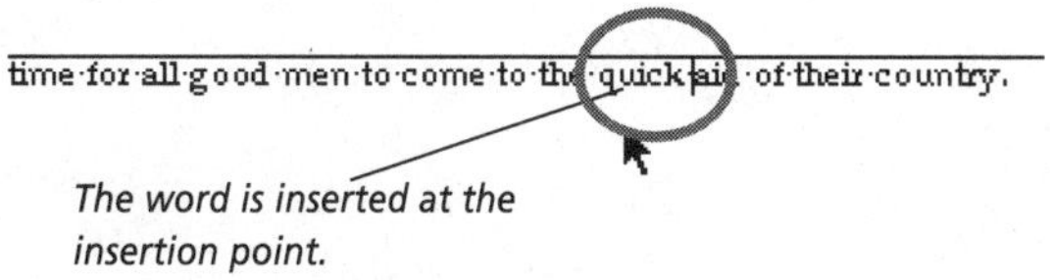

Figure 2b: Type the word at the insertion point.

To insert a word into a line:

1. Move the cursor to where you want to insert the word. (In this case, we are inserting the word "quick" in front of the word "aid," so move the cursor in front of the word "aid.")
2. Click the mouse button once (**Figure 2a**). Notice that the I-Beam moves to where you want to insert the new word. This is called the insertion point.
3. Type the word "quick." Notice that in **Figure 2b**, the word is typed in front of "aid," exactly where you want it.

Manipulating Words in WordPerfect

The beauty of a word processing program is that you can manipulate text on the screen, and thus create on the fly. Manipulating text entails selecting characters, words, or lines of text and moving them around, copying them, or deleting them at will. The following tasks describe how to perform these important functions.

To select text:

1. Place the I-beam in front of the word you want to select (**Figure 3a**), in this case "quick."
2. Drag the cursor across the word while holding down the mouse button (**Figure 3b**).
3. Release the mouse button when you have reached the end of the text you want to select.

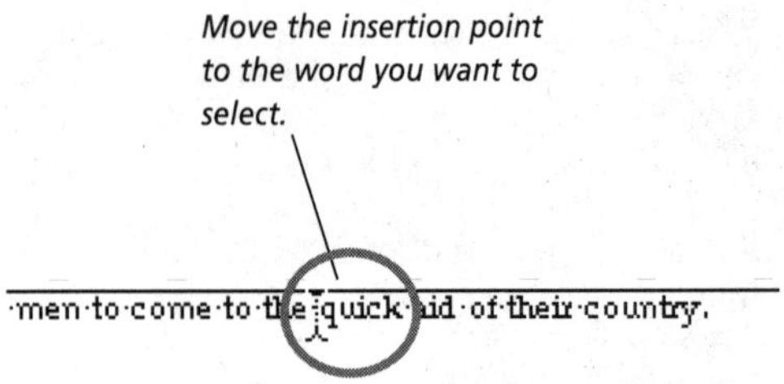

Figure 3a: Move the cursor to the word you want to select.

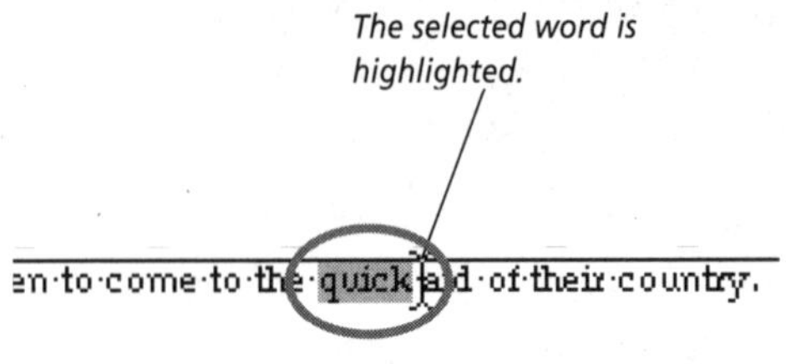

Figure 3b: Drag the mouse across the word and release the mouse.

Correcting Your Errors

WordPerfect add value to the Mac's built-in ability to undo errors and provides many other ways to delete text or undo mistaken uses of commands. The two basic commands that let you reverse a command or action are the Undo and Cancel commands. The Undo command reverses the last action you made in WordPerfect. The Cancel command halts an action. In addition, various levels of delete let you erase textual or graphic mistakes. The following pages describe these procedures.

Selection Shortcuts

To...	Do This...
Select a word	Double-click in front of the word.
Select a sentence	Press Command+Shift+U, or press F6.
Select a paragraph	Triple-click inside the paragraph, press Command+Shift+Y, or press Command+F6.
Select an entire document	Select All from the Edit menu or press Command+A.
Extend a selection	Press the Shift key while clicking where you want the selection to end.
Extend one character at a time	Press Shift+Right arrow or Left arrow.
Extend up or down one line at a time	Press Shift+Up arrow or Down arrow.
Extend one word at a time	Press Option+Shift+Right arrow or Left arrow.
Extend to the end of a document	Press Shift+End key.

To undo a command:

Select Undo from the Edit menu (**Figure 4**). You can reverse an undo by selecting Undo again.

Hint: Any text that had been accidentally deleted and is restored after performing an Undo is restored and selected by the command.

Or, if you want to stop a command such as Print, the selection of an item, or close a dialog box without saving changes made from the box. Press the key combination Command+. (Period), the Clear command on the Edit menu, or the Escape key. This is called the Cancel command.

Figure 4: The **Undo** command.

Shortcuts

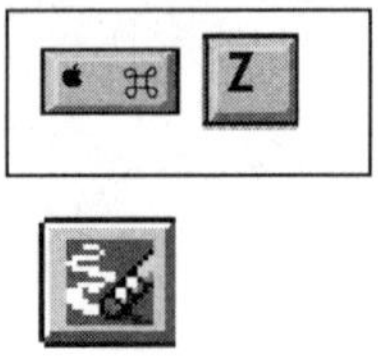

Tip

Undo will not reverse an action that made no change to your document. For example, you cannot undo scrolling, moving an insertion point, or selecting a tool.

You cannot use the **Cancel** command to stop recording a macro. To halt a macro, select **Stop Recording** from the Macro pop-up menu on the Tools menu.

To delete an item:

1. Select the item you want to delete (**Figure 5a**).
2. Press the Backspace key (or the Delete key on extended keyboards) (**Figure 5b**).

Hint: If you delete a selection that contains either a text box or figure box code, WordPerfect displays an alert box asking you if you really want to perform this delete. If you select Yes, the text box or graphic is deleted along with the rest of the selection.

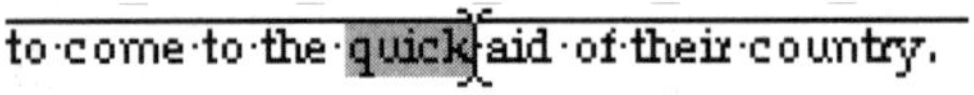

Figure 5a: Select the item you want to delete...

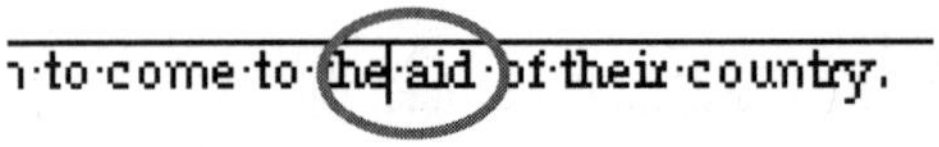

Figure 5b:...and press the Delete or Backspace key.

Shortcuts

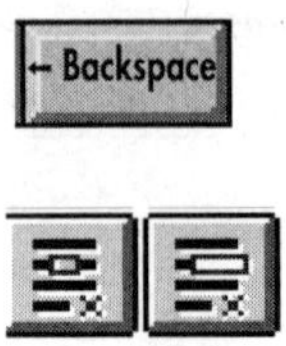

Deletion Shortcuts

To...	Do This...
Delete a word	Click inside the word and press Command+Delete or Backspace key (depending on your keyboard).
Delete every occurrence of a word	Select Find/Change from the Edit menu, or press Command+F. Type the word in the Find box and leave the Change box blank.
Delete a sentence	Press Command+Shift+U, or F6 (select the sentence) then press Delete.
Delete a paragraph	Press Command+Shift+Y (select the paragraph) then press Delete.
Delete and place on the Clipboard	Select Cut from the Edit menu or press Command+X.
Delete a character to the left	Press Backspace or Delete.
Delete a character to the right	Press Delete Right on the extended keyboard or the Decimal key with Number Lock off.
Delete to the end of a line	Press Command+right arrow or left arrow, or with Number Lock off, press Command+Number 1 on the numeric keypad.
Delete to the end of a page	Press Command+Page Down or Command+Number 3 on the numeric keypad with Number Lock off.
Delete a code	In the Codes Window, press Delete with the insertion point to the right of the code you want to delete.

Saving Your Work

Saving your work is probably the most important action you can perform. You need to "save" because when you type on WordPerfect's desktop, your work is placed in a nonpermanent area of memory. If your computer was accidently shut off, you would lose all of your work. WordPerfect provides a way to send your work from random access memory on to a location on your hard or floppy disk. This action is called *saving*. So, save early, save often.

The following tasks describe how to save a document, how to give a document a name for the first-time saving, and how to rename a document to save a copy without disturbing the original version.

To save a document:

Select Save from the File menu (**Figure 6**).

When you open a WordPerfect Document Editor window, WordPerfect gives the document the name "Untitled-1, 2, and so forth" (depending on how many new documents you open). The first time you save a document, WordPerfect displays the Save As dialog box so that you can select the location where you want to store your document and give it a name. Follow the procedures described in the Save As task below to save a document for the first time.

See Chapter 1: "Introduction" for a discussion of opening existing or new documents.

Shortcuts

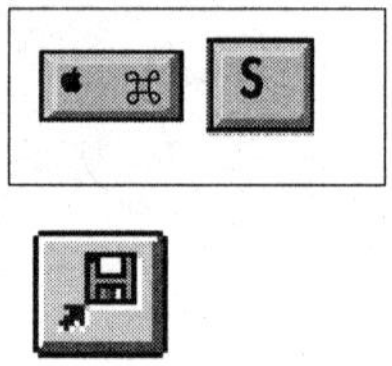

Figure 6: Select **Save** from the File menu.

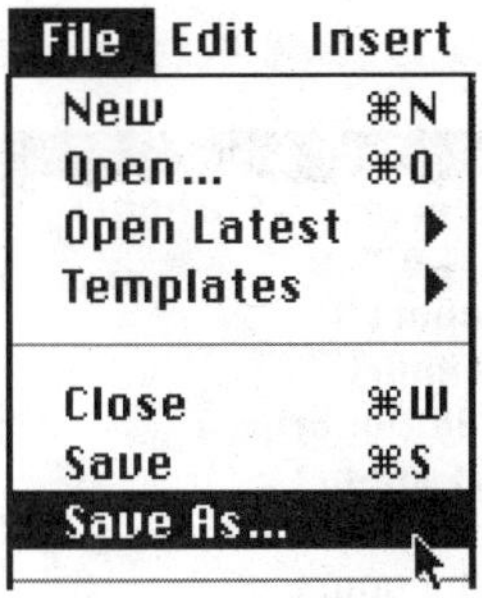

Figure 7: The **Save As** Command.

To save a document for the first time:

1. Select Save As from the File menu (**Figure** 7).
2. In the resulting Save As dialog box (**Figure** 8a), type a name for the document in the Save Document As text box.
3. *Optional:* if you do not want to save the document in the folder displayed in the Title bar, as shown in **Figure 8b**, use the Directory List box and Title bar pop-up menu to change the folder or volume.

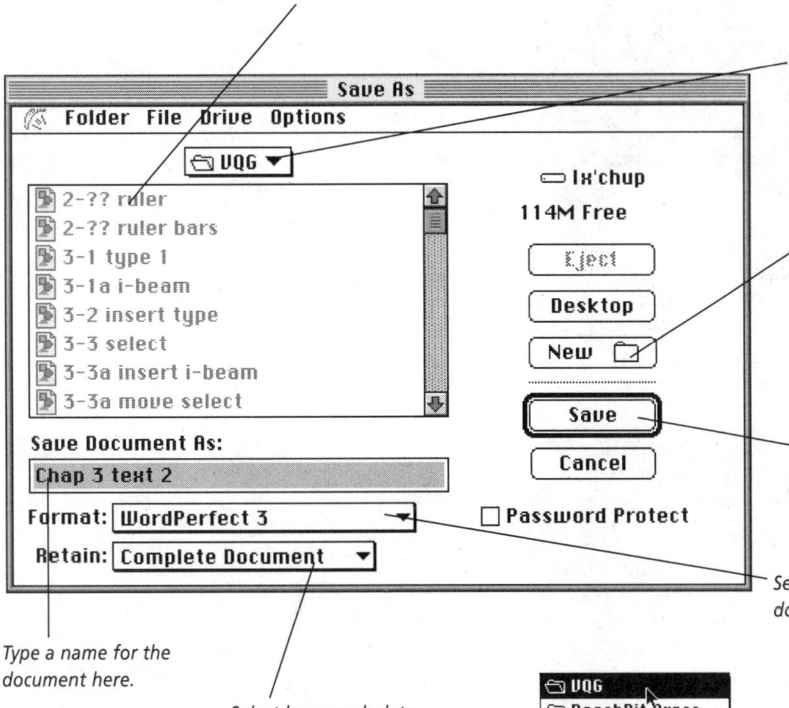

Figure 8a: The Save As dialog box.

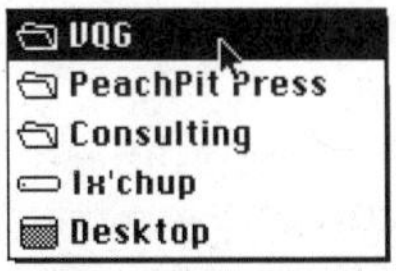

Figure 8b: Use the Title bar's pop-up menu to change the folder or disk where you save your document.

4. *Optional:* Change the file format by selecting an alternate from the Format pop-up menu (**Figure 8c**).
5. *Optional:* Change the amount of data saved with the document by selecting an alternative from the Retain pop-up menu (see **Figure 8a**).
6. Click Save.

The active document is saved and displayed with the new name in the Title bar.

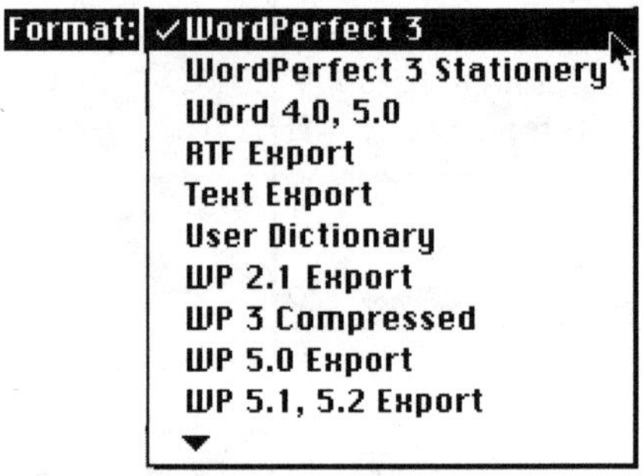

Figure 8c: Select a file format from the **Format** pop-up menu.

> **Tip**
>
> Here are some rules and hints to follow when saving a document.
>
> - If you want to save a document as a template to use to make multiple versions, select WordPerfect 3 Templates from the Format pop-up menu. The default format is WordPerfect 3, but you can also select WordPerfect 3 Compressed if you want to save space on your hard disk.
> - The Retain pop-up menu lets you choose how much of the document to save. If you are interested only in the style sheets of a document, retain only the Attributes or Formats. If you want to use the document in another application, you can opt to save only the text, or the text and attributes only, and so on.
> - As described in Chapter 1, to secure your document from unauthorized use, click the Password Protect check box before saving your document.
> - A document name can have up to 32 characters. You can use any alphanumeric or punctuation character except the colon (:).

To rename a document:

Select Save As to display the Save As dialog box (see **Figure 8a**). Type a different name in the Save Document As text box and click Save. The document is saved in the original location under a new name. You can also change the location by using the Directory list box and Title bar pop-up menu.

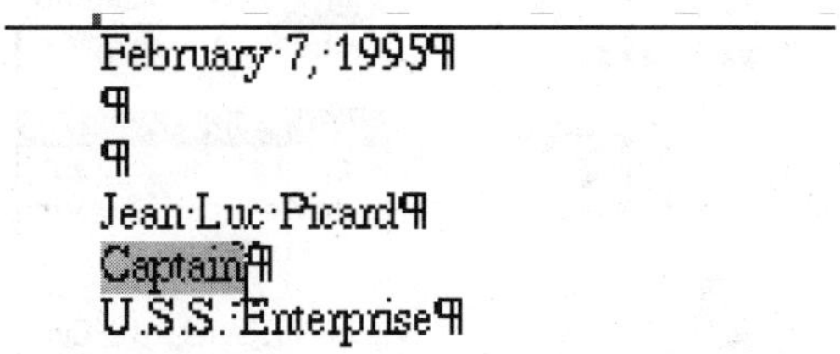

Figure 9: Select the text you want to copy or cut...

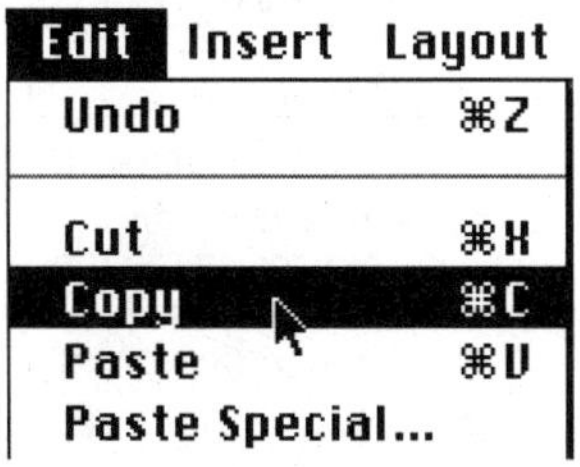

Figure 10: ...then choose the **Copy** command.

Copying or Moving Text

WordPerfect is a Macintosh program, and as such supports the basic Mac functions of Cut, Copy, and Paste. WordPerfect adds an enhancement to these features, with the capability of pasting text only or character formats only (via the Paste Special command). In addition, if you are running WordPerfect under System 7 or higher, you can forego the Cut, Copy, and Paste routine and select, drag, and drop text into place.

To copy an item:

1. Select the text you want to copy (**Figure 9**).
2. Pull down the Edit menu and highlight the Copy command (**Figure 10**).

To move an item:

1. Select the text you want to move.
2. Pull down the Edit menu and highlight the Cut command (Figure 11).

Figure 11: Select the **Cut** command from the Edit menu.

Figure 12a: Choose the **Show Clipboard** command to see the contents of the Clipboard.

Tip

To view the contents of the Clipboard, select **Show Clipboard** (**Figure 12a, b**) from the Edit menu.

To clear the Clipboard, copy a blank space on your screen. The blank replaces the previous contents of the Clipboard.

Figure 12b: The Clipboard contains the text you cut or copied.

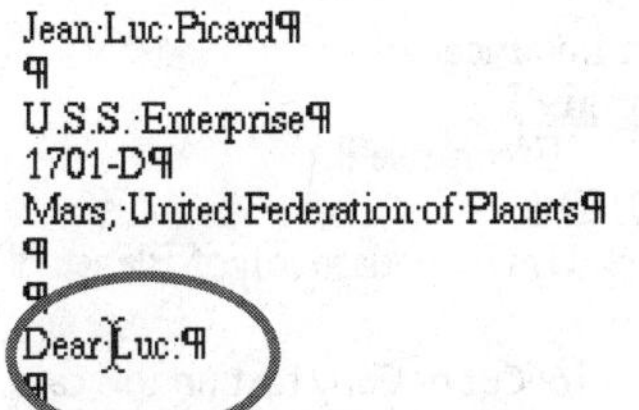

Figure 13: Place the cursor where you want to paste the item...

Shortcuts

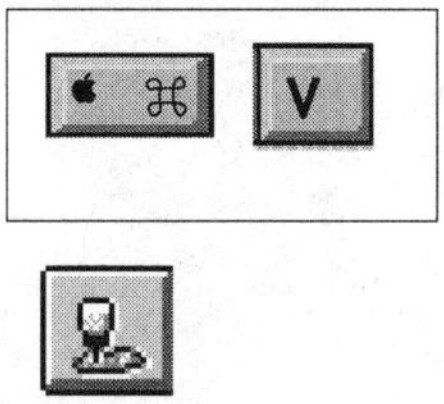

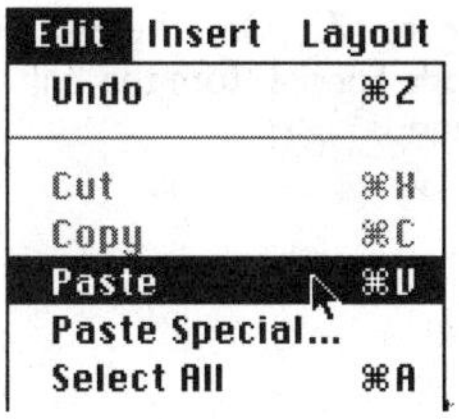

Figure 14: ...and choose the **Paste** command from the Edit menu.

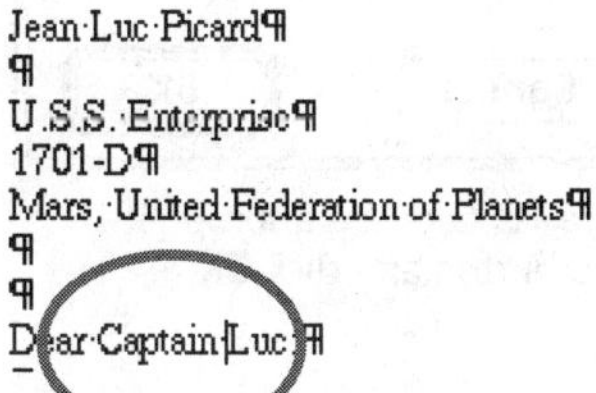

Figure 15: The item is placed at the insertion point.

To place an item into another location:

Assuming you have performed a copy or cut command, a copy of your selected text has been placed on the Clipboard.

1. Click the mouse to move the I-beam to where you want to place the text or graphic. The I-beam changes to a blinking cursor to indicate the insertion point (**Figure 13**). **Warning:** Be sure you do not select any text or it will be replaced with what you paste!
2. Pull down the Edit menu and select the **Paste** command (**Figure 14**).
3. The contents of the Clipboard is placed at the insertion point (**Figure 15**).

To paste only text or its attributes:

Assuming that you have cut or copied text on to the Clipboard, you can use the next task to paste only the text without formatting, or only the text's formatting without text on to another location.

This task is useful if you want to use special formatting over and over, say for bullets or emphasis in multiple paragraphs; or if you want to use text but not its formatting multiple times.

1. After copying or cutting text (**Figure 16**), place the insertion point where you want to paste the text or formatting. **Do not highlight text or it will be deleted.**
2. Pull down the Edit menu and select Paste Special (**Figure 17**).
3. In the resulting Paste Special dialog box, click the first radio button (Text Only) to paste text without formatting or the second radio button (Font, Size, & Style) to paste formatting without text (**Figure 18**).
4. Click OK.

> **Tip**
>
> You can undo a cut or paste by selecting **Undo** from the Edit menu or pressing the key combination Command+Z. You cannot undo a copy command, since copy only places an item on the Clipboard and makes no changes to the text in the Document Editor window.
>
> You can perform multiple pastes by selecting the **Paste** command or pressing Command+V repeatedly, since the item remains on the Clipboard until you perform another **Copy** or **Cut** command.

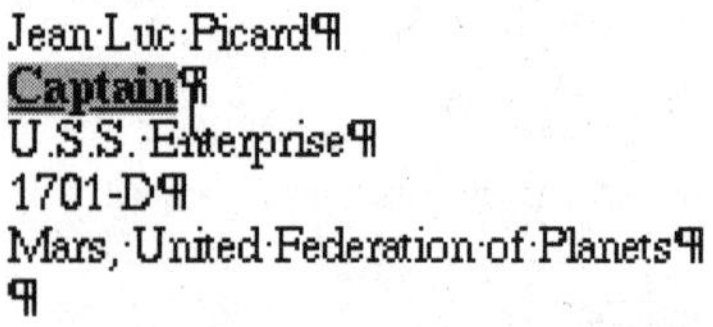

Figure 16: Cut or Copy text (in this case we are copying bold and underlined text formatting)...

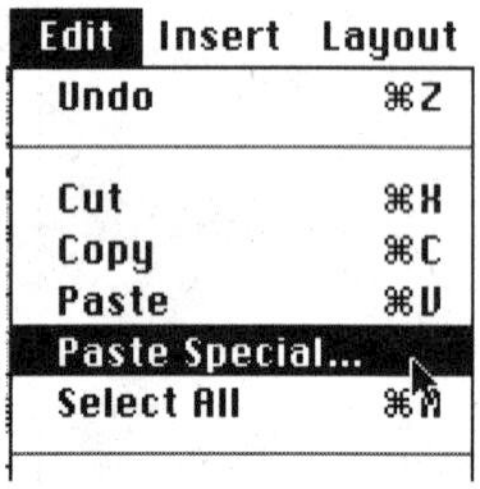

Figure 17: ...and choose **Paste Special** from the Edit menu.

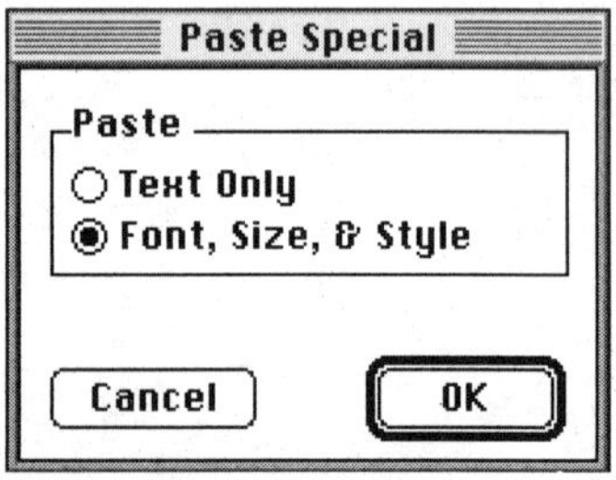

Figure 18: Click the appropriate radio button and click **OK**.

Shortcuts

⌘ F4 (text only)

Shift F4 (formatting only)

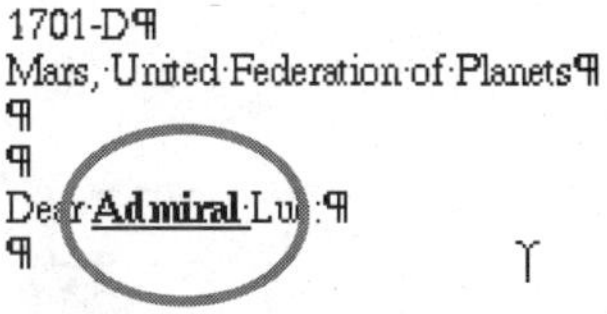

Figure 19: The next text you type will appear in the copied and pasted format (if you pasted formats only) or in the same format as the rest of the paragraph.

5. If you have pasted formatting only (as shown in **Figure 19**) the next text you type at that location will use the same formatting as the copied or cut text. If you pasted text, only it will appear with the formatting of the paragraph where it was inserted.

To copy or move an item without the Clipboard:

Note: Copying text using drag and drop can only be performed once, since no text is placed on the Clipboard. You can perform multiple moves by repeatedly selecting and dragging the text around your document.

1. Select the text you want to move (**Figure 20**).
2. With the item selected, move the cursor over your selection until it changes to a left-facing arrow.
3. Click and hold the mouse button and the selection changes to an outline marquee.
4. *Optional:* If you want to copy the item, press the Option key.
5. Drag the marquee to where you want to place the text; wait until a vertical line appears inside the marquee indicating the insertion point, and release the mouse button (**Figure 21**).
6. When you release the mouse, WordPerfect places the selection at the insertion point (**Figure 22**).

> **Tip**
>
> If you are running WordPerfect under System 7.5, you can drag and drop text between documents or on to the Mac's desktop. To drag a selection on to another document, open the document first and then follow the above task's steps dragging between documents.

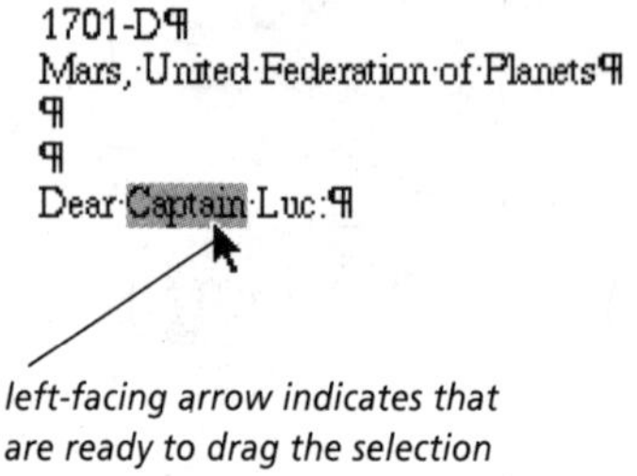

Figure 20: Select the text you want to move or copy...

Figure 21: ...and the selected text is displayed during the drag and drop process as a marquee or dotted-line box. Drag the box to where you want to place the text and release the mouse.

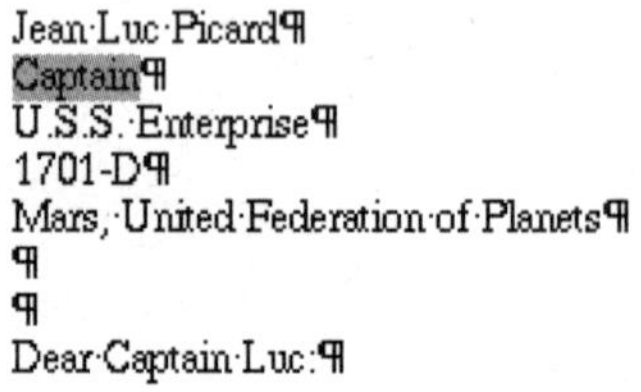

Figure 22: The selection is placed at the insertion point. Press Option-Drag if you want to copy text.

FORMATTING 4

WORDPERFECT LETS you change the appearance of text characters, paragraphs, pages, and documents. Each level of formatting has its own set of buttons, toolbars, and commands. This chapter describes how to change the appearance of characters, paragraphs, and pages using font styles, sizes, and types as well as paragraph indents, tabs, and page margins. **Note:** WordPerfect terminology can be confusing at times. When we speak of font *styles*, we mean the attributes of the font including whether the font has been changed to bold, italic, underline, and so forth. Later in the book we introduce the concept of **Style** sheets, or *Styles*. Styles with a capital "S" are conglomerations of font attributes and paragraph/page formatting that can be applied together by selecting a single name. Both styles and Styles rely on codes.

Those Funny Codes...

Every part of the appearance of your document is controlled by *codes*. Codes are powerful tools for controlling the minute behavior of your document. Codes can be as simple as turning boldfaced on or off or as complex as an index entry. As we said above, Style sheets are special codes that contain bundles of information used to format paragraphs of text. With these Style codes, you can build complex formatting structures to add specific text such as automatic table numbering, character spacing instructions, font styles, and so forth directly into a Style so that the click of your mouse rearranges large chunks of text.

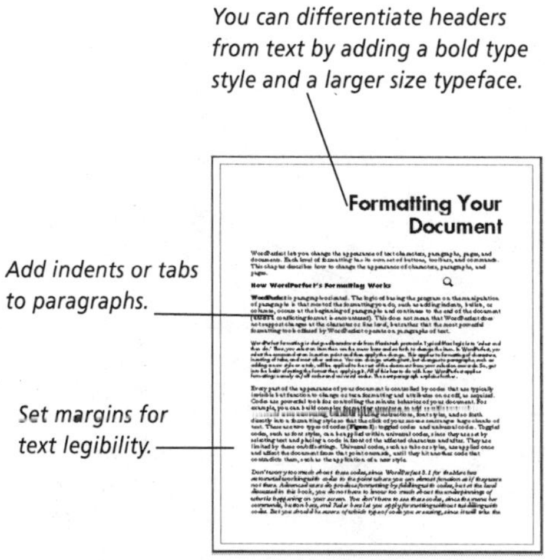

This chapter provides basic information about character, paragraph, and page formatting.

There are two types of codes (**Figure 1**): universal and toggled codes. Universal codes, such as tabs or Styles, are applied once and affect the document from that point onwards, until they hit another code that contradicts them, such as the application of a new Style. Toggled codes, such as bold, underline, or italic, and so forth, can be applied within universal codes, since they are set by selecting text and placing a code in front of the affected characters and after. They are limited by these on/off settings.

How WordPerfect's Formatting Works

WordPerfect operates by manipulating *these toggled states* of on and off codes (also called *tokens*). Therefore, to WordPerfect, all of your text is considered to be in some sort of state at all times, whether that state is "Normal" where no special font attributes have been applied, "Document" where no special Style sheet has been applied, or where text has a code for a particular font style or type, a tab setting, or a Style sheet attached. The benefit of operating at the textual level is that most of the formatting you do (such as adding indents, bullets, or columns) can be performed on as little text as a single character and these formatting options can be layered one on top of another ad infinitum. This flexible design can be confusing to the novice because any format you turn on in one paragraph is applied to all text to the end of the document (unless a conflicting state, such as another Style sheet, is encountered).

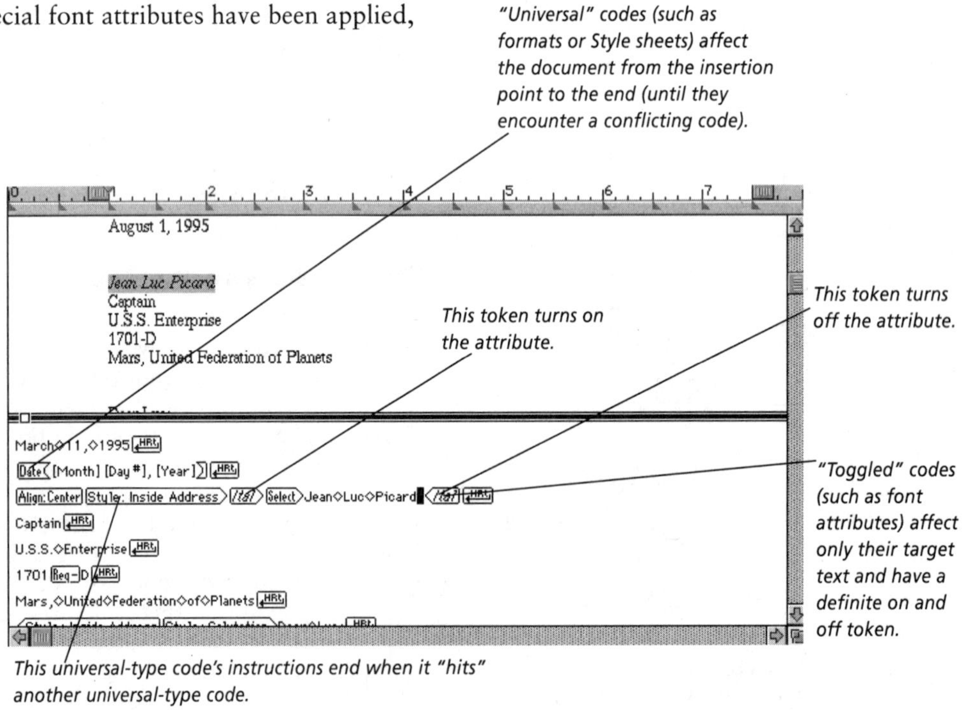

Figure 1: WordPerfect uses codes to apply attributes and formatting to a document.

A Word About Codes

Don't worry too much about the concept of codes, since WordPerfect 3.5 for the Mac has automated working with codes to the point where you can almost function as if they were not there. Advanced users do produce formatting by manipulating codes, but at the level discussed in this book, you do not have to know too much about the underpinnings of what is happening on your screen. You don't have to see these codes, since the Menu bar commands, Button bars, and Ruler bars let you apply formatting without twiddling with codes. But you should be aware of which type of code you are using, since it will take the mystery out of WordPerfect's performance. To see your codes, select Show Codes from the Edit menu. We'll see codes again in Chapter 6: "Styles," but will not discuss codes in any more detail because they are beyond the scope of this book.

WordPerfect's Formatting Tools Explained

WordPerfect provides four tools for manipulating the formatting and attributes of characters, paragraphs, and pages:

- **Button bars.** The buttons on the Button bar let you rapidly apply formats, such as indents, borders, and font sizes.
- **Ruler bars.** The Layout, Font, Ruler, and Styles Ruler bars let you access font styles, line spacing, paragraph spacing, and other formatting directly and let you access formatting dialog boxes for more detailed manipulation of your document's appearance.
- **Menus.** The commands on the Menu bar provide the most control over formatting.

  The Layout, Font, Size, and Style menus provide extensive character, paragraph, and page formatting dialog boxes.
- **Key Command Shortcuts.** You can set up keyboard shortcuts for any format command found on the Menu bar.

These methods of applying formats and attributes are described in this chapter. For convenience sake, the chapter is divided into three parts: character-based formatting, paragraph and line-based formatting, and page-based formatting.

Formatting at the Character Level

You can change a font's type, size, and style as well as manage the space between characters (called *kerning*) with commands located on the Layout, Font, Size, and Style menus.

There are literally thousands of type faces, also called fonts, available from Type Foundries such as Bit Stream, Agfa, Monotype, and Adobe. The Mac also comes with some fonts, as does WordPerfect. We are not going to discuss the differences between different font types, nor the difference between PostScript or Printer fonts and Screen or bit-mapped fonts. The only thing you need to know at this level of working with WordPerfect is that you can change which font type is used to display your text. WordPerfect lets you change the font type for existing text, new text, whole documents, or new documents.

To change the font of existing text:

1. Select the text you want to change (**Figure 2**).
2. Pull down the Font menu and select a new font (**Figure 3a**).

   or
3. Pull down the Font bar's Font pop-up menu and select a font (**Figure 3b**).

To change the font for new text:

1. Pull down the Font menu and select a font (**see Figure 3a**).
2. Type the new text (**Figure 4**).

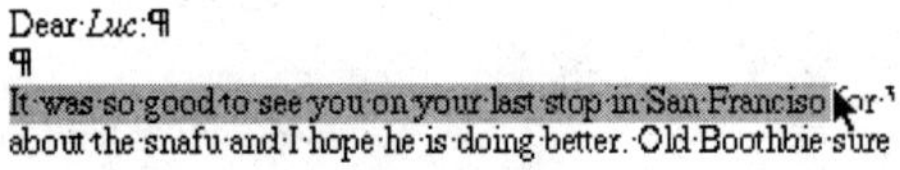

Figure 2: Select the text you want to change...

Fonts are listed in families when you have a System Extension installed that supports this feature.

Figure 3a: ...and select a new font from the Font menu.

Fonts are listed here in their "natural" state—by alphabetical order.

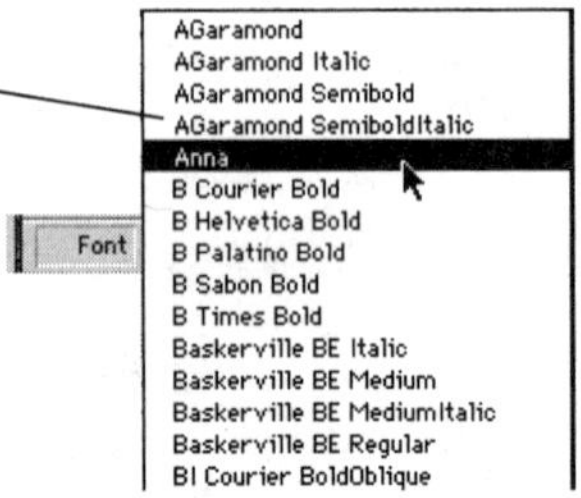

Figure 3b: As an alternative, you can select a font from the Font pop-up menu on the Font bar.

Figure 4: Type the new text after selecting a font and it automatically appears in your chosen font, in this case "Anna."

To change the font for the entire document:

1. Pull down the Edit menu and choose Select All (**Figure** 5).
2. Pull down the Font menu and select the font you want to use.

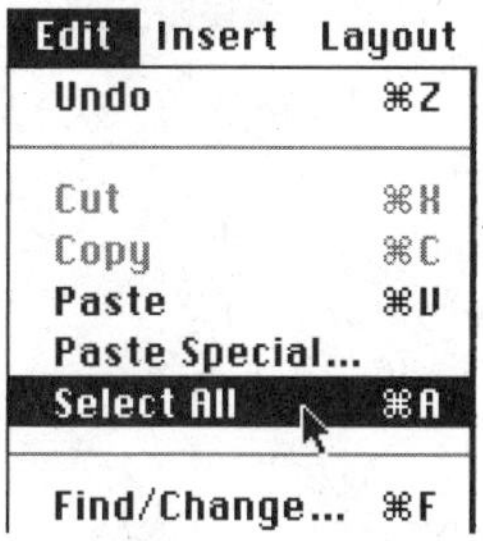

Figure 5: To change the font used in your total document, choose **Select All** from the Edit menu.

Shortcuts

Select a font from the Font list to change the font of new or selected text.

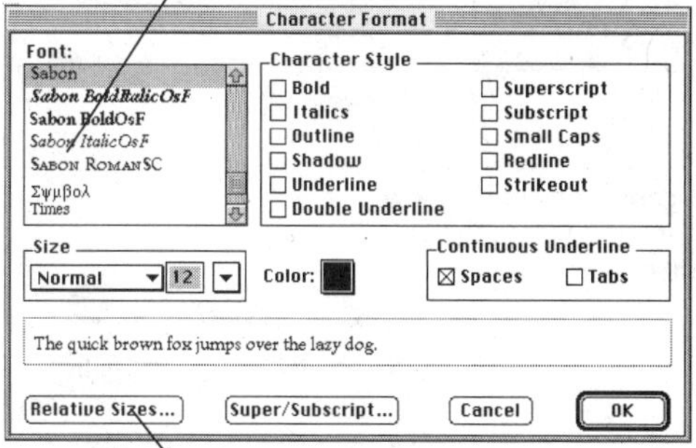

Click here to display the Relative Sizes dialog box (described in Figure 11).

Figure 6: The Character Format dialog box.

Tip

The default font in WordPerfect (meaning the font that appears when you open WordPerfect for the first time) is Geneva. This is a bit-mapped screen font that may be easy on the eyes on the screen, but does not print cleanly on PostScript printers. You can change the default font by either changing the Document style's font or by changing the font in the New Document Templates file. Note that if you change the Document style, all new and existing documents will change to the font you select. If you change the font in the New Document Templates, then only new documents will appear in the new font.

You can also change the type face and style of text using the Character Format dialog box accessed via the **Other** button on the Font Ruler bar (**Figure 6**). If you have a utility such as Now WYSIWYG Menus, the Font list will display the fonts as they actually appear on the screen. You can select a style, position, and size from the appropriate boxes and pop-up menus, as well as indicate how rules will appear.

Hint: Each time you add a new font or special character to your document, WordPerfect inserts a font code. These codes tell the program to download that font to the printer. If you do not delete these codes after changing a font, WordPerfect downloads the defunct font and then flushes it out of the printer, slowing down the printing process and using up precious memory. Delete the code by selecting **Show Codes** from the Edit menu and clicking after the code in the resulting Codes window. Then, press **Back-space** or **Delete** (depending on your keyboard) to delete the font codes you do not want to use.

See Chapter 6: "Styles," for a description of how to change a style sheet and Chapter 11: "Shortcuts," for a short description of the Templates documents and their uses.

To change the size of text:

1. Select the text having the size you want to change or place the cursor where you want to type the newly sized text.
2. Pull down the Size menu and select the new size from the list (**Figure 7**).

   or
3. You can also pull down the Size pop-up menu on the Font bar, and select a new size or type a size in the text box (**Figure 8**).

Shortcuts

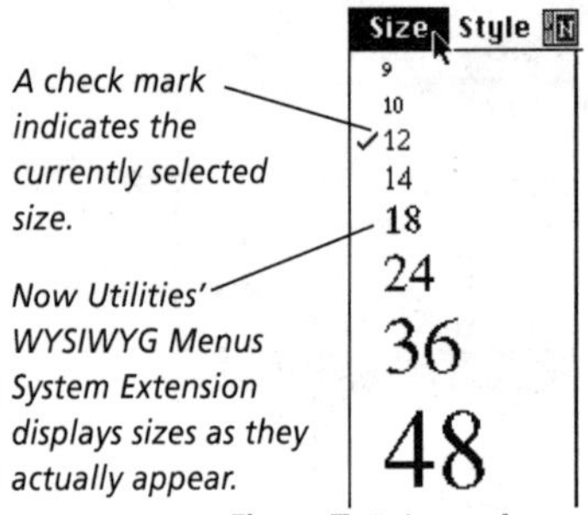

Figure 7: Select a font size from the Size menu.

Tip

There are several other methods to change the size of your text.

1. You can change the size of text to a nonstandard size by selecting **Other** from the Size menu (**Figure 9**). In the Other Font Size dialog box (**Figure 10**), type the font size in the text box and click **OK**.
2. The Character Format dialog box (displayed by selecting the **Other** button on the Font Ruler bar and shown in **Figure 6**) lets you specify font sizes by percentage by clicking the **Relative Sizes** button to open its dialog box **(Figure 11)**.
3. You can change a selected text's size by one-increment units (larger or smaller) by clicking the appropriate button on the Button bar (see the Shortcuts sidebar). You can perform the same function using the **Larger** or **Smaller** commands on the Size menu (see **Figure 9**).

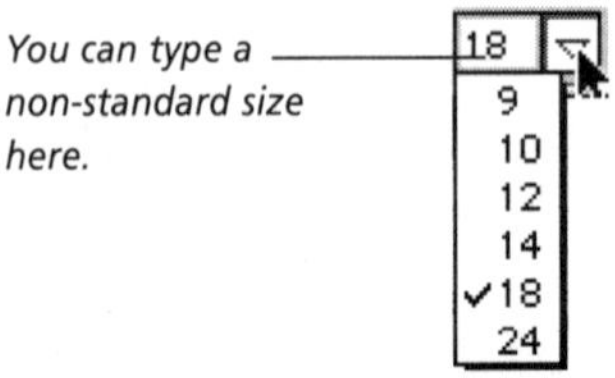

Figure 8: The Font bar's **Size** pop-up menu gives you another way to select a font size.

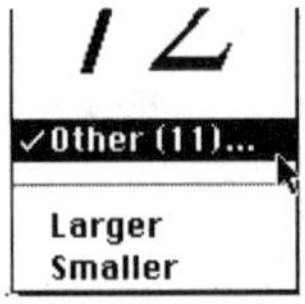

Figure 9: Select the **Other** command from the Size menu...

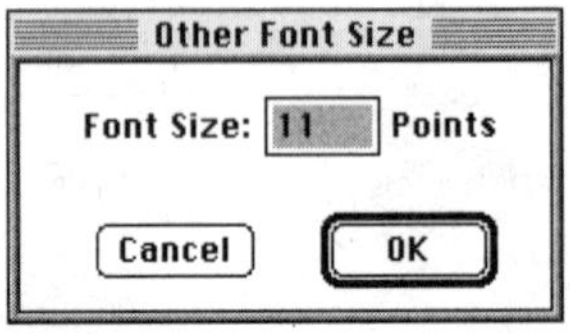

Figure 10: ...and type an integer in the **Font Size** text box.

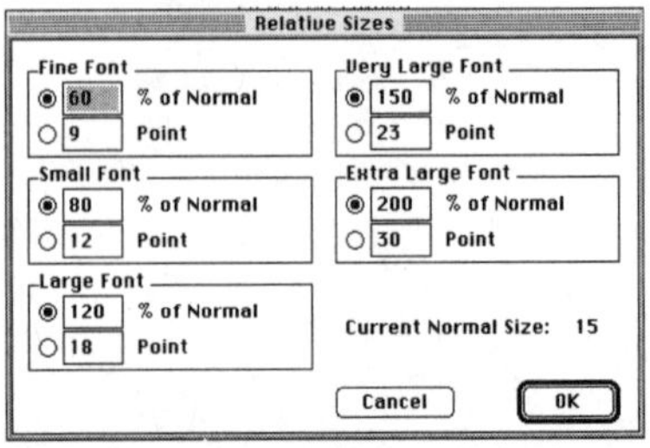

Figure 11: The Relative Sizes dialog box on the Character Format dialog box lets you set font sizes by percentages.

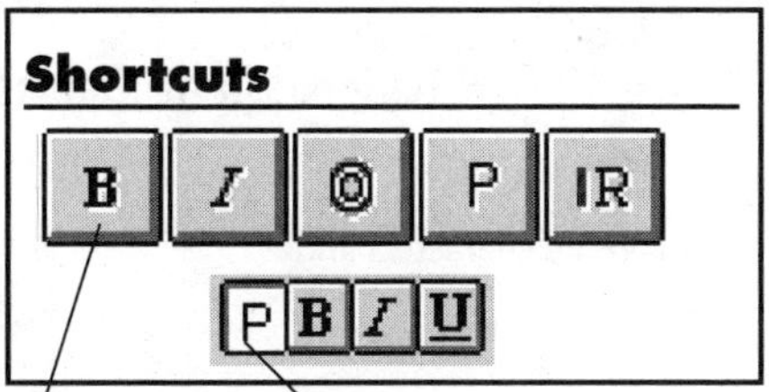

Button bar tools for selecting font styles.

Font bar buttons for selecting styles. The white button indicates the current style is Plain text.

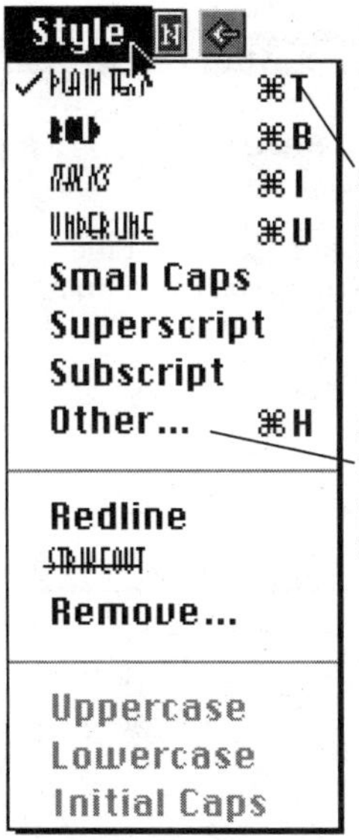

Keyboard shortcuts for individual styles are listed next to the style.

*Select **Other** to access the Character Format dialog box (see Figure 6) to select other styles.*

Figure 12 The Style menu.

Figure 13: Click the **Copy Font Attribute** button to copy a font format from one selection to another.

To change the style of text:

1. Select the text you want to change.

   or

2. Place the cursor where you want to type the new text.
3. Pull down the Style menu and select a new style from the list (**Figure 12**).

Tip

Try not to use the Mac's built-in font styles (such as bold and italic) if you are printing on a PostScript printer, since the styles are based on bit-mapped images and are not scaled as accurately by the printer as PostScript type faces can be. Always use an actual italic type face in the place of underline because the italic is more legible than underline. Redline and strikeout are available for use in editing documents. Redlines are lines that are placed in the margins of changed paragraphs and strikeout styles draw a line through text indicating that the text has been deleted.

You can copy the attributes (styles and size) of selected text to the Clipboard for further use by clicking the **Copy Font Attribute** button on the Font toolbar (**Figure 13**). Then you can paste the attribute on to another area of your document. *See Chapter 3: "Working," for a description of copying, cutting, and pasting.*

To adjust the spacing between characters in a word (known as kerning):

1. Place the insertion point between the characters you want to adjust (**Figure 14**).
2. Pull down the Layout menu and select Kerning (**Figure 15**).
3. In the Kerning dialog box (**Figure 16**), click the appropriate button to move the characters closer together (Move Together) or further apart (Move Apart).
4. Type the number of points you want to nudge the characters closer together or further apart in the Points text box. Note that there are 72 points to the inch.
5. The change is displayed in the dialog box.
6. Click the OK button.

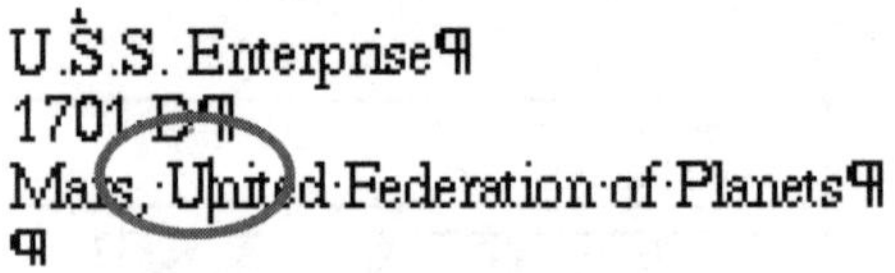

Figure 14: To kern two letters, place the cursor between the characters and...

Figure 15: ...select the **Kerning** command from the Layout menu.

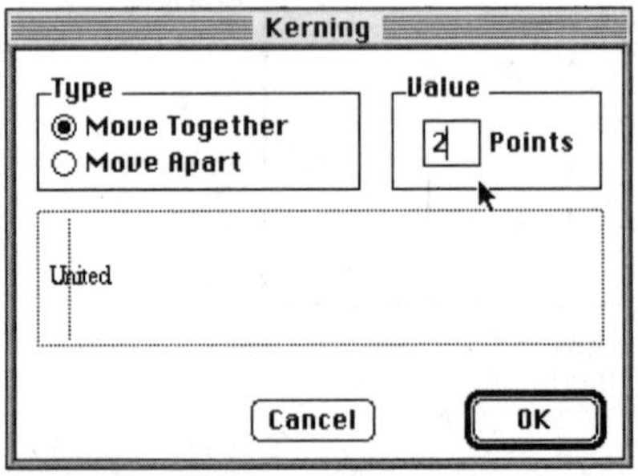

Figure 16: Change the distance between characters by typing a new integer in the **Points** text box.

Formatting at the Paragraph Level

Most of the work you will do in WordPerfect will entail changing how your paragraphs behave. The "power" of WordPerfect is how flexible these paragraph-based features can be and how easy it is to change paragraph-based formatting on the fly.

The effect of formatting on paragraphs

Adding indents and tabs, adjusting the spaces between lines and between paragraphs, and aligning the ends of paragraph lines (justification) is known as *formatting*. Formatting commands are "universal codes" as opposed to "toggled" codes such as those that change a text's attributes within paragraphs (and which were described in the previous paragraphs). Formatting affects your document from the paragraph point where you place your insertion point and affect the change to the end of the document (unless a conflicting command such as a token that turns off formatting is encountered).

The following paragraphs describe how to apply basic formatting to lines and paragraphs.

To set a left-hand tab using the Ruler bar:

1. Place your insertion point where you want to begin the tab. If you want the new tab to only affect specific text, select that text.
2. Drag the tab marker to where you want to set the tab (**Figure 17**).
3. Press the Tab key to insert a tab (**Figure 18**).

   or
4. *Optional:* Pull down the Insert menu and select Indent; then press Shift+Tab key to insert a hanging tab where the first line is not indented (see **Figure 18**).
5. *Optional:* Pull down the Insert menu and select Indent; then press Option+Tab to indent the entire paragraph (see **Figure 18**).

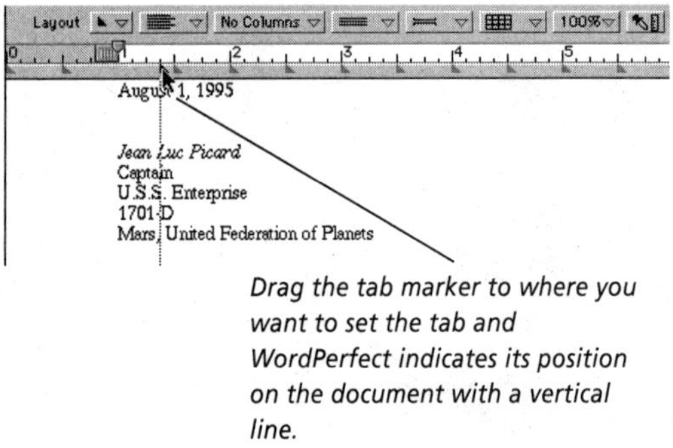

Figure 17: You can set a tab directly on the Ruler by dragging the tab marker.

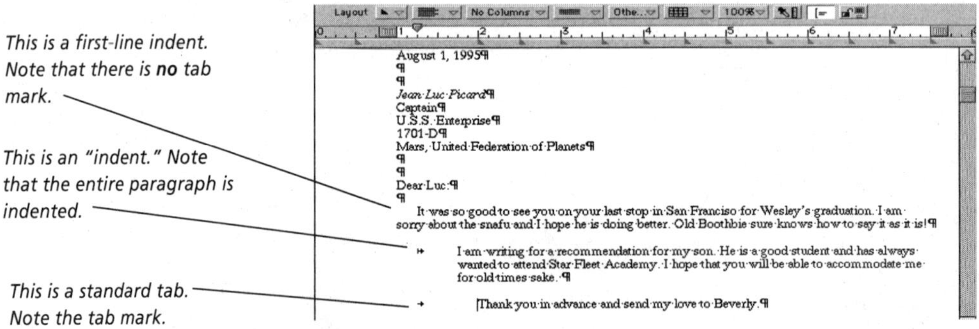

Figure 18: You can create different types of tabs by using the Indent command and various keystroke combinations.

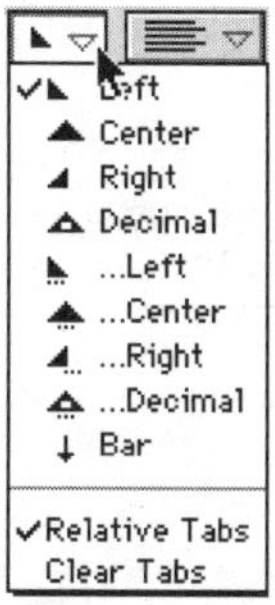

Figure 19: Change the tab type by selecting a new option from the Tabs pop-up menu on the Layout bar.

Figure 20: Select the **Tabs** command to display the Tabs dialog box.

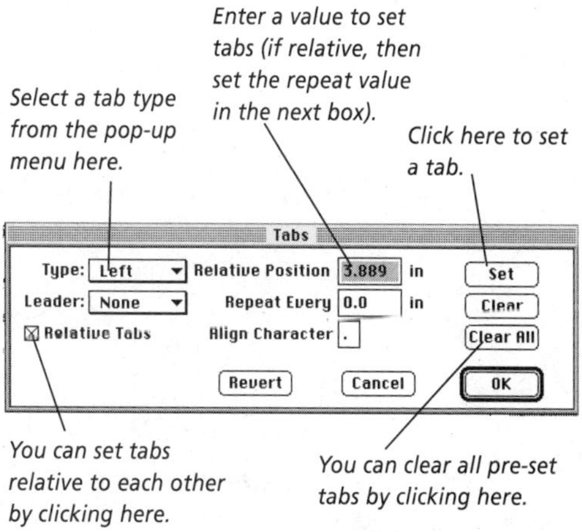

Figure 21: The Tabs dialog box provides enhanced precision when setting tabs.

> **Tip**
>
> Use the Tabs pop-up menu on the Layout Ruler bar (**Figure 19**) to select a different type tab, such as a right-hand, center, or decimal tab, or to add leading characters such as dotted lines to tabs. You can also clear all tabs on the Ruler. Pull down the Tab pop-up menu and select a tab then click the Ruler to add the new tab.

To set a tab using the Tabs dialog box:

1. Pull down the Layout menu and select Tabs (**Figure 20**).

   or
2. Double-click a tab on the Ruler bar.
3. In the resulting Tabs dialog box (**Figure 21**), make your changes. You can change the tab type, its leading characters, its relative position from other tabs (such as every two inches), which character is aligned with the tab (very handy if you are lining up numbered paragraphs or tabular materials), and the number of times the tab is placed on the ruler at a relative distance.
4. After entering a number in the Position text box, click Set. You can set multiple tabs by repeating steps 3 and 4.
5. When you are done, click the OK button.

> **Tip**
>
> You can copy your ruler settings to other parts of your document or to other documents by clicking the **Copy Ruler Settings** button (**Figure 22**) on the Layout bar. Clicking this button copies your tab settings on to the Clipboard so that they can be pasted elsewhere just as you would any other Clipboard item. *See Chapter 3: "Working" for a description of cutting, copying, and pasting.*

Figure 22: Click the **Copy Ruler Settings** button on the Layout bar to copy your tabs to the Clipboard for pasting in other parts of your document.

To remove a tab from the Ruler bar:

Click the tab with the mouse and drag it off of the Ruler bar (**Figure 23**). When you click a tab, WordPerfect displays a vertical line indicating the location of the tab on the page. The tab disappears when dragged off of the ruler.

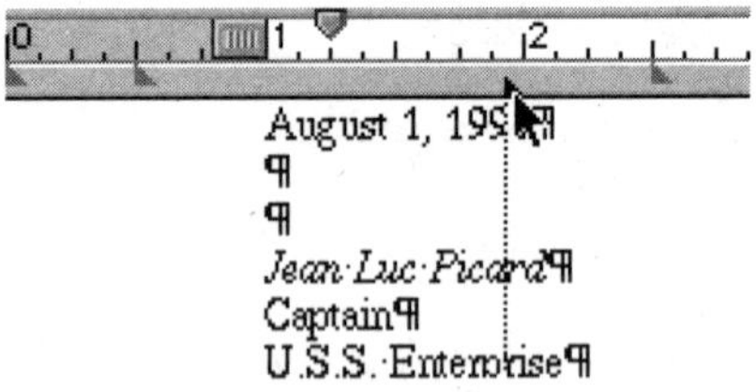

Figure 23: Drag the tab marker off of the Ruler bar to delete a tab or double-click the tab marker and then click Clear in the resulting Tabs dialog box.

To indent the first line of a single paragraph:

1. Place a tab marker on the Ruler bar at the spot you want to indent. (Typically this is five spaces in or 3/8-inch.)
2. Press the Tab key.

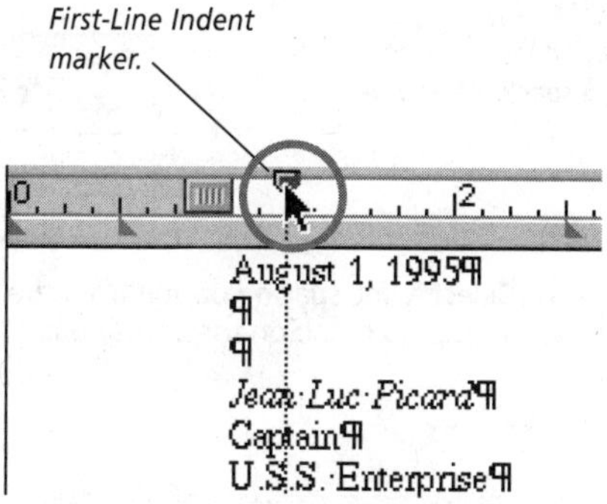

Figure 24: Drag the **First-Line Indent** marker to where you want to indent the first line of every paragraph in your document.

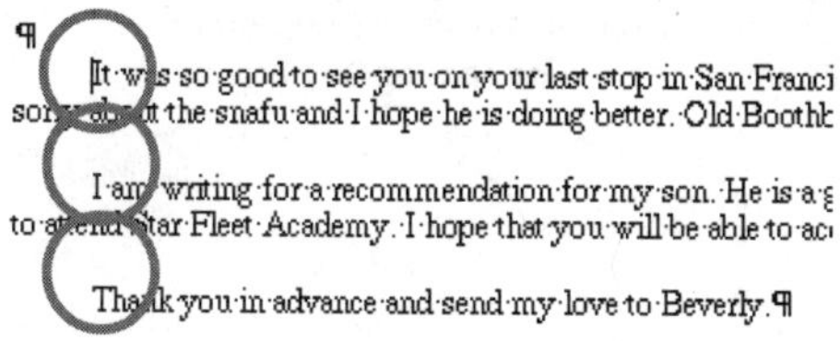

Figure 25: When you set the **First Line Indent** marker, every first line of each paragraph of your document is automatically indented the same.

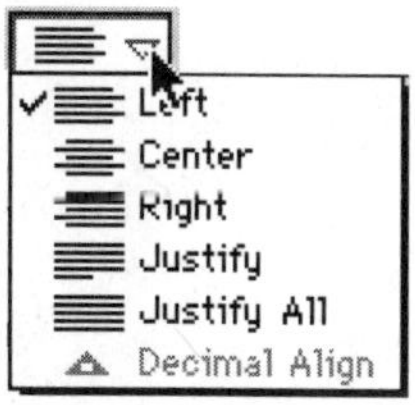

Figure 26: Select an alignment option from the **Alignment** pop-up menu on the Layout bar.

To indent the first line of every paragraph in a document:

1. Click on the first paragraph you want to indent.
2. Drag the First-Line Indent marker to the indent setting you want to use (**Figure 24**).
3. The first lines of each paragraph after your insertion point are indented (**Figure 25**).

To align text to margins:

1. Select the text you want to align or place the insertion point where you want to begin the alignment.
2. Pull down the Alignment pop-up menu on the Layout bar and select an alignment (**Figure 26**).

Tip

Try to avoid using the Justify All option on the Alignment pop-up menu **(Figure 26)** because WordPerfect cannot proportionally space words to fit lines in the manner of an advanced desktop publishing program. The end result is some pretty weird spacing problems. WordPerfect struggles to match alignments on both margins no matter if the words do or do not fit. As a rule of thumb, try to use left-alignment as your default because it is the most easy to read, especially if you are working in multiple columns.

To adjust line spacing:

1. Place your insertion point in the paragraph where you want to begin the change of line spacing; or select the text you want to change.
2. Pull down the Line Spacing pop-up menu (**Figure** 27) on the Layout bar and select a new line spacing option. You can choose between single, space-and-a-half, and double-spaced lines.
3. *Optional:* If you do not see a spacing option that suits your document, select the Other command from the Line Spacing pop-up menu (see **Figure** 27).
4. In the resulting Line Spacing dialog box (**Figure** 28a), type a spacing option in the Line Spacing text box or choose an option from 1 to 4 from the Line Spacing pop-up menu.
5. Click the OK button.

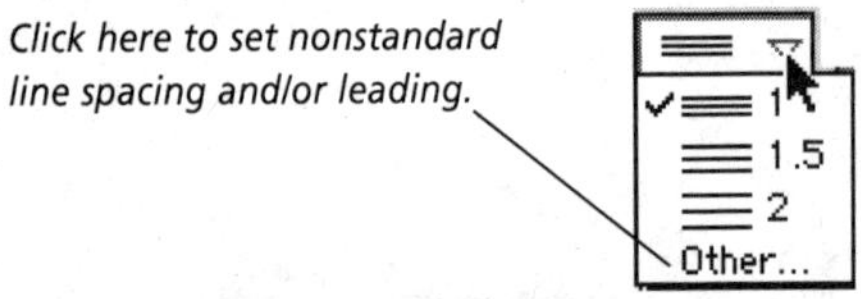

Figure 27: Select a line spacing option from the **Line Spacing** pop-up menu on the Layout bar.

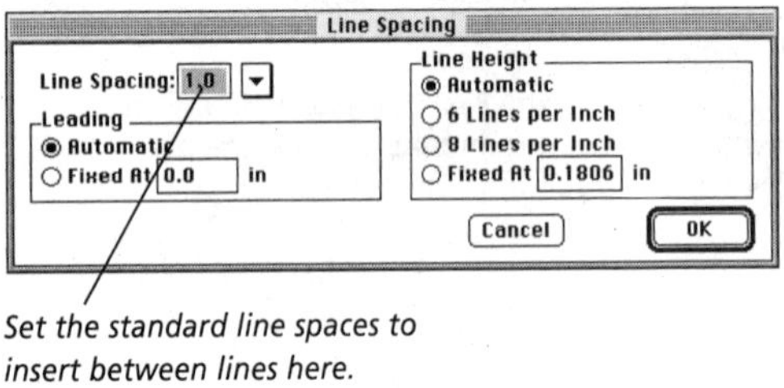

Figure 28a: Select a line spacing option from 1 to 4 in 1/2-point increments from the pop-up menu or type a number in the **Line Spacing** text box.

Set the leading, or distance in points between the top of a line and the ascending letter, here.

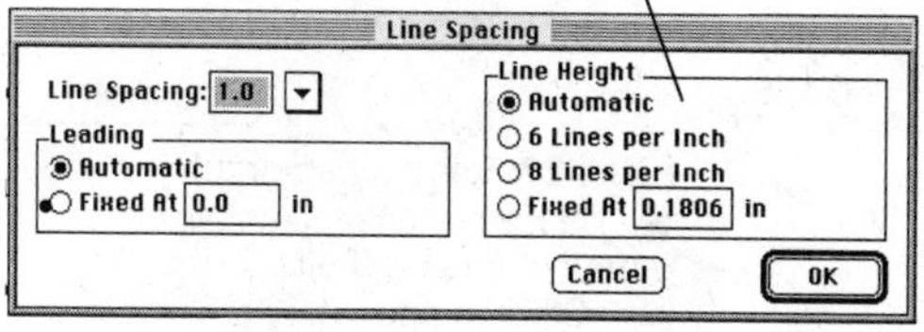

Figure 28b: Select the **Other** option on the **Line Spacing** pop-up menu to set the leading.

To adjust the distance between lines (known as leading):

1. Place your insertion point in the paragraph where you want to begin the change of line spacing; or select the text you want to change.
2. Select the Other command from the Line Spacing pop-up menu on the Layout bar (see **Figure 27**).
3. In the resulting Line Spacing dialog box (**Figure 28b**), click the Fixed At radio button to change the leading from automatic to manual.
4. Type a number in points in the Fixed At text box that you want to set the distance between lines. Use a negative number to move the lines closer or a positive number to move the lines further apart. Each point represents 1/72 inch.
5. Click the OK button.

To adjust the spacing between paragraphs:

1. Place the insertion point where you want to begin the paragraph spacing change or select the paragraph you want to change.
2. Pull down the Paragraph Spacing pop-up menu (**Figure 29**) from the Layout bar and select another spacing option.
3. *Optional:* If you do not see a spacing that meets your needs, select the Other command from the pop-up menu (see **Figure 29**).
4. In the resulting Paragraph Format dialog box (**Figure 30**), type a new distance in inches (or the unit you previously selected in the Edit menu's Preferences dialog box. *See Chapter 15: "Customizing" for a description of how to change measurement units*) in the Space Between Paragraphs text box.
5. Click the OK button.

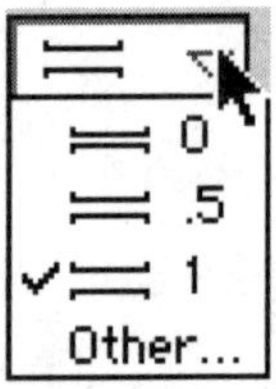

Figure 29: Select a paragraph spacing option from the **Paragraph Spacing** pop-up menu on the Layout bar or click **Other** to open the Paragraph Format dialog box (see Figure 30).

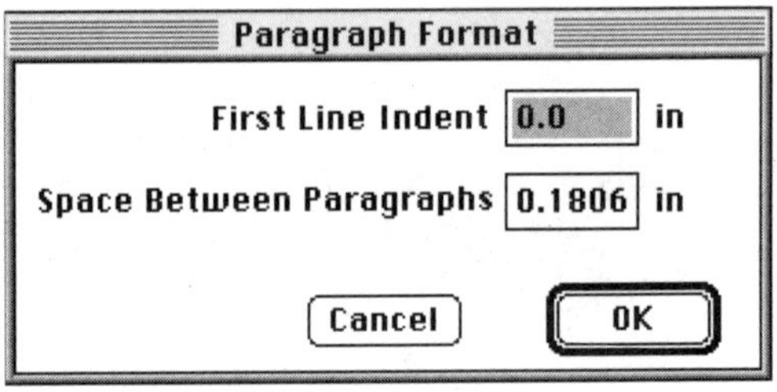

Figure 30: Type a number in the **Space Between Paragraphs** text box. You can change the units of measurement by changing your Preferences under the Edit menu.

Line and Paragraph Spacing

Formatting at the Page Level

WordPerfect provides several formatting tools that let you set how a page will appear. You can change the margins, alignment of text vertically, control widowed and orphaned lines of text by keeping lines together, where page breaks and column breaks will fall, and the size and orientation of the paper. This section describes how to set paper size, margins, and orientation, and how to apply manual page breaks. Later chapters will cover the management of widowed and orphaned lines, working with columns, and vertical alignment.

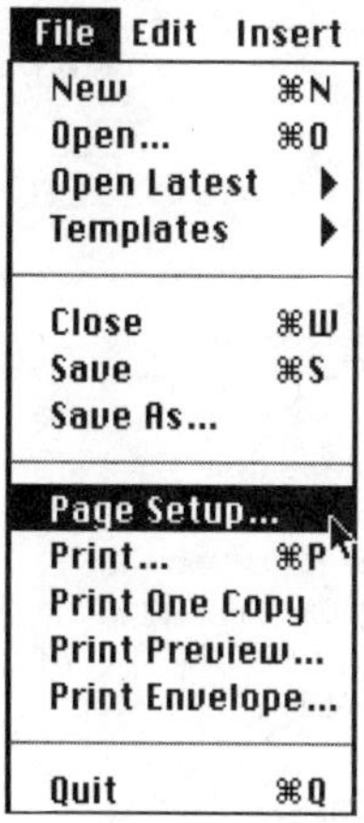

Figure 31: Select **Page Setup** from the File menu...

To set the size of your paper:

1. Pull down the File menu and select Page Setup (**Figure 31**).
2. In the resulting Page Setup dialog box (**Figure 32**), pull down the Paper pop-up menu and select a paper type from the list.
3. Click the OK button.

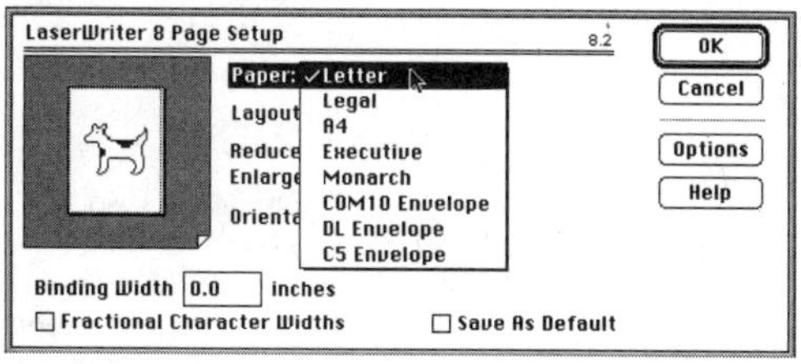

Figure 32: ...select a paper size option from the **Paper** pop-up menu. Set the paper size before setting your margins, since the size paper you use affects how much area you have available for writing.

> **Tip**
>
> The Page Setup dialog box's contents is governed by the type of printer you are using (and its printer driver). **Figure 31** displays the most current version (as of the printing of this book) of Apple's LaserWriter printer driver for PostScript printers. If you are printing on an inkjet printer, such as Apple's StyleWriter II or Hewlett-Packard's Deskjet, your Page Setup dialog box will not look exactly like **Figure 32**. *See Chapter 7: "Printing" for a short discussion of the differences in these drivers and their dialog boxes.*
>
> You can create custom paper sizes if you have installed QuickDraw GX under System 7.5. Use the Custom Page Setup dialog box to set up each page with a separate paper size (if you so desire). *See Chapter 7: "Printing" for a further description of the uses of QuickDraw GX.*

To change the orientation of your paper:

1. Pull down the File menu and select Page Setup (see **Figure 31**).
2. In the resulting Page Setup dialog box (**Figure 33**), click the page orientation that fits your needs. The Portrait option (the upright figure) prints your text vertically on the paper. The Landscape option (the sideways figure) prints your text horizontally on the page.
3. Click the OK button.

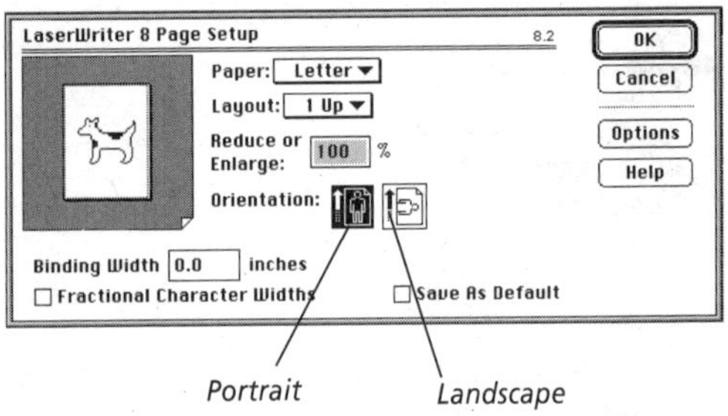

Figure 33: Click the picture of the little man that meets your page orientation needs. The upright picture is called "Portrait" and prints vertically; whereas the sideways picture is called "Landscape" and prints horizontally.

To change the margins of your document:

1. Pull down the Layout menu and select Margins (**Figure 34**).
2. In the resulting Margins dialog box (**Figure 35a**), enter the new margins in the appropriate text boxes. The current margins are displayed when you open the dialog box.
3. Click the OK button.

Shortcuts

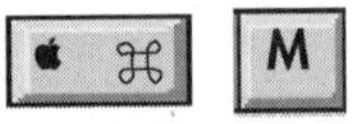

Figure 34: To display the Margins dialog box, select **Margins** from the Layout menu or double-click the Margins marker on the Ruler bar.

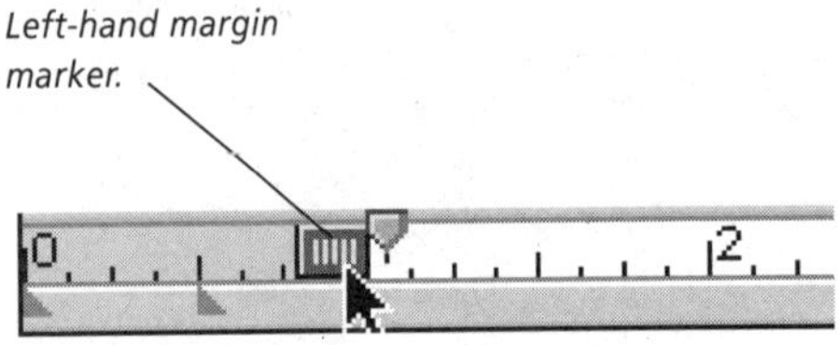

Figure 35b: Double-click on the **Margin** marker to open the Margins dialog box.

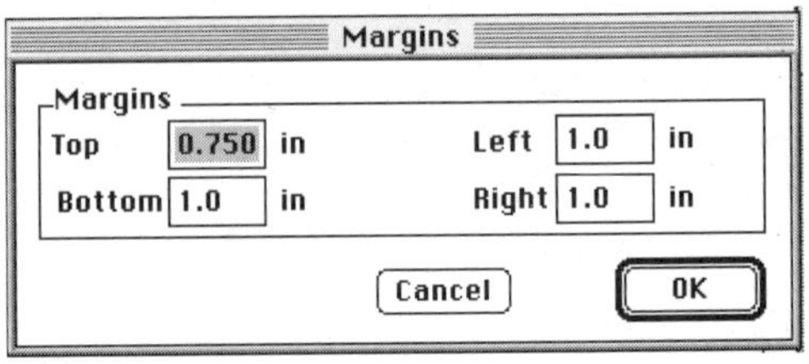

Figure 35a: Type your margin settings in the appropriate text boxes in the Margins dialog box.

Tip

You can access the Margins dialog box by double-clicking the margins marker on the Ruler bar (**Figure 35b**).

Figure 36: Select **Make It Fit** from the Layout menu.

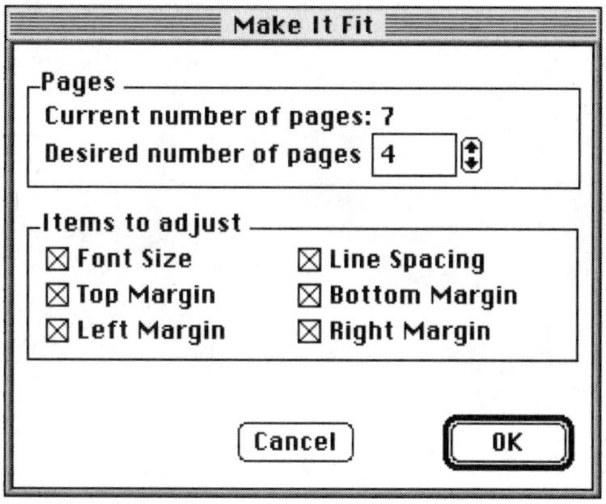

Figure 37: Select the options you want to use to resize the document.

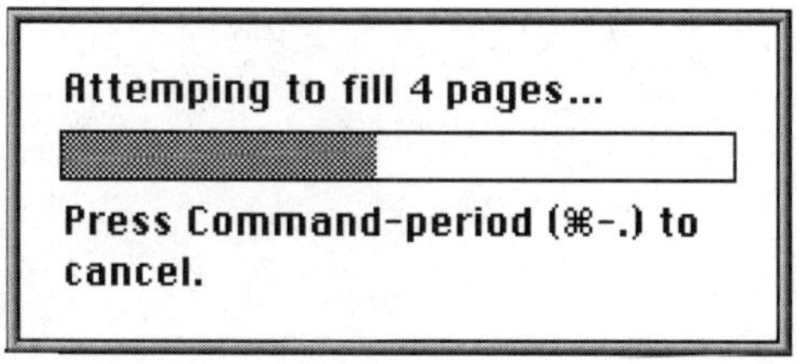

Figure 38: An alert box tells you the status of the resizing process.

Making Your Text Fit Your Page Requirements

If you are a journalist with limited and specific space to fill with text, such as a column in a newspaper, use the Make It Fit command to automatically convert documents from one page count to another. Make It Fit changes the margins, line spacing, and font sizes of your text to fit a specified page count. You can select which options to change to make the text fit so that any margin, font, or paragraph requirements are not inadvertantly changed during the space fitting process.

To make text fit on a specified number of pages:

1. Open a document whose sizing you want to change.
2. Pull down the Layout menu and select the Make It Fit command (**Figure 36**).
3. In the resulting Make It Fit dialog box (**Figure 37**), use the scrolling arrows to change the parameters in the Desired Number of Pages text box. You can also type in a target number.
4. Click the check boxes so that they are not selected for those formatting options you do not want to change in the Items To Adjust area.
5. Click OK.
6. WordPerfect displays an alert box that tells you that it is attempting to resize your document. Press Command+. (period) to end the process and return to the original sizing. You can also select the Undo command from the Edit menu (or press the keyboard combination Command+Z) to return to your original document size.

MORE FORMATTING 5

CHAPTER 4 DESCRIBED basic formatting options available to enhance your documents at the character, line, paragraph, and page levels. That chapter did not exhaust the opportunities for modification available in WordPerfect. This chapter continues the discussion through further descriptions of character, line, paragraph, and page-based formatting. The chapter describes the following layout enhancements possible with WordPerfect:

- Adding borders and fills at the line, paragraph, and page level.
- Using symbols and special text, such as automatic and hard-printed dates and times, to make your document more typographically professional.
- Inserting page-based document management features such as manual page breaks, page numbers, and headers and footers.
- Automatically numbering lines and paragraphs and using these paragraph numbers to build outlines.
- Using footnotes and endnotes.

When you complete this chapter you will have an extensive array of tools with which to manipulate your documents.

General Formatting

WordPerfect's versatile Borders command provides dialog boxes that adds borders and fills at all levels—be it characters, paragraphs, or pages.

To add a border:

1. Place your cursor in the line, paragraph, column, or page around which you want to place your border. You can also select text that you want bordered.
2. Pull down the Layout menu and select Character, Paragraph, Page, or Column from the Borders pop-up menu (**Figure 1** depicts a border for characters).
3. In the resulting Character Border Style dialog box (**Figure 2**), click the check boxes next to the areas you want a border to appear. You can also select the line type and color, as well as spacing between the border and your text.

   Note: Each type of border has its own type of dialog box.
4. Click OK.

> **Tip**
>
> Watch how you apply borders. If you add a 2-point border around a paragraph and a 1-point border to the top of the next line, the 1-point border will cancel out the 2-point border. To counteract this effect, add the 2-point border to three sides of the paragraph and then add the 1-point border to the bottom. Then, do not add the top 1-point border to the next paragraph.

Shortcuts

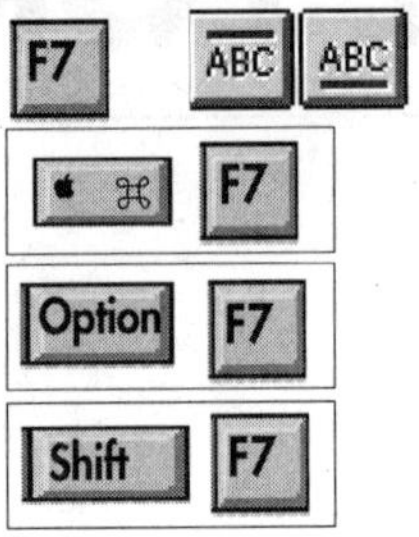

Figure 1: Select **Character** from the **Borders** pop-up menu to display the Character Border Style dialog box.

Select an option from the Border box for border position, line weights and color.

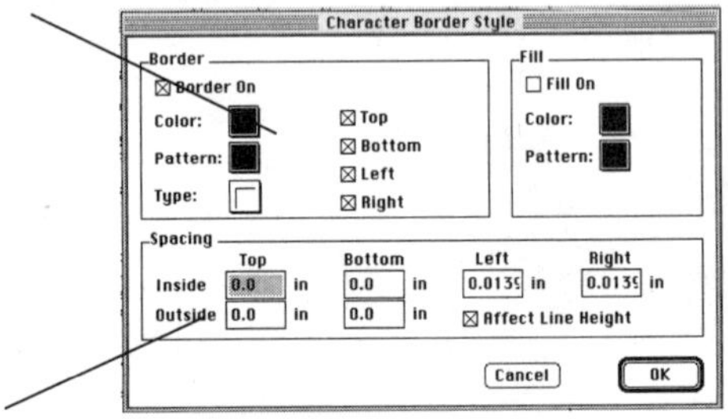

Enter the border distances from text in these text boxes.

Figure 2: The Character Border Style dialog box lets you control how borders around characters will appear.

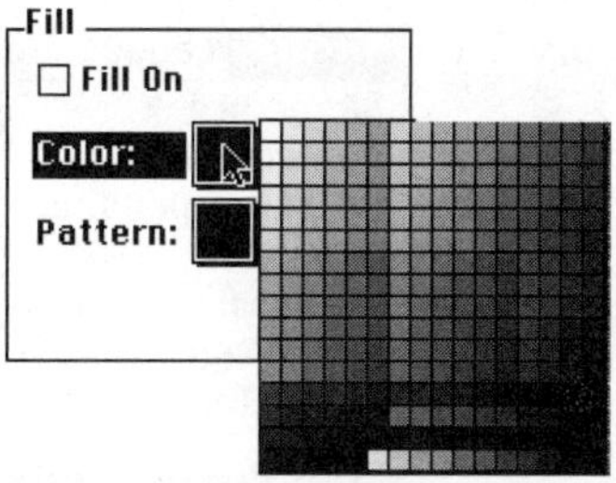

Figure 3a: Click the **Color** button to display the color palette. Drag the mouse over the palette and click on the color you want to use to fill a border.

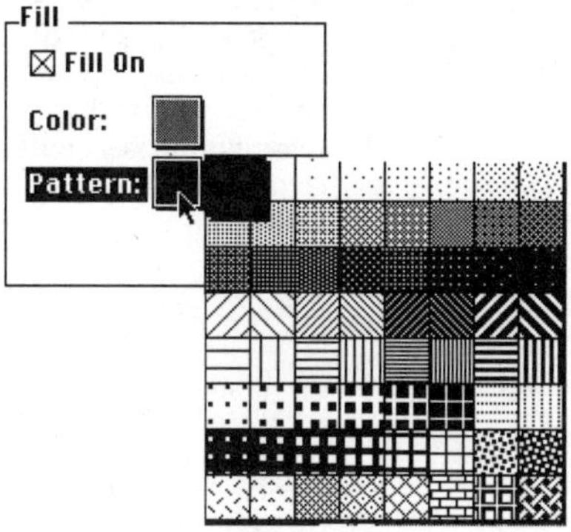

Figure 3b: Click the **Pattern** button to display patterns. Select a pattern to use in a fill from the pattern palette in the same manner as you did a color from the color palette.

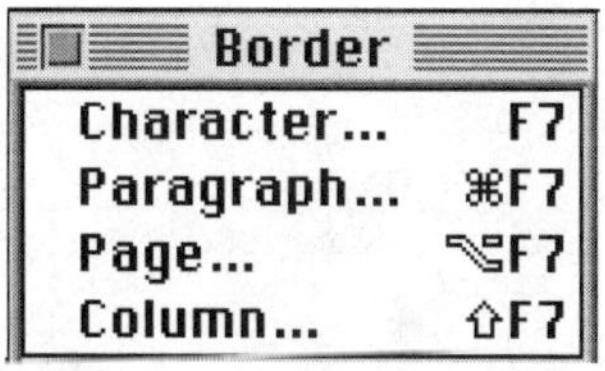

Figure 4: Selecting the **Borders** command on the Layout menu without selecting a sub-command displays the Border palette.

To add shading (also called fills):

1. Place your cursor in the line, paragraph, column, or page around which you want to add a fill. You can also select text that you want shaded.
2. Pull down the Layout menu and select Character, Paragraph, Page, or Column from the Borders pop-up menu (see **Figure 1**).
3. In the resulting dialog box (in this case the Character Border Style box (see **Figure 2**), select a color (**Figure 3a**) and/or a pattern (**Figure 3b**) from the pop-up menus by dragging your cursor across the color or pattern palettes.
4. Click OK.

Tip

If you want to add a border to more than one item, select Borders without choosing a sub-menu item. WordPerfect then displays the Borders options in its own floating palette (**Figure 4**). Note that different key combinations typed with the Function Key F7 opens the appropriate dialog box.

To insert a symbol:

1. Place the insertion point in your document where you want to insert the symbol.
2. Pull down the Insert menu and select Symbols (**Figure 5**).
3. In the resulting Symbol dialog box (**Figure 6**), select a symbol by clicking it.
4. Click the close box (see **Figure 6**) when you are done inserting symbols.

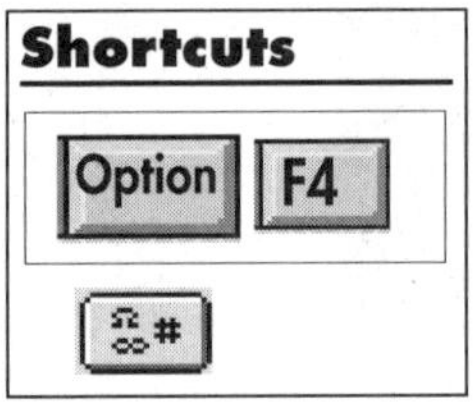

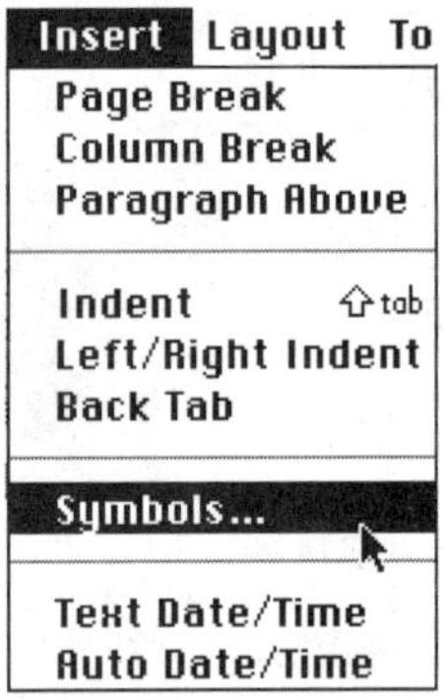

Figure 5: Select the **Symbols** command to directly insert a special character without selecting the **Key Caps** command (*see Tip below*).

Click the close box to return to your document..

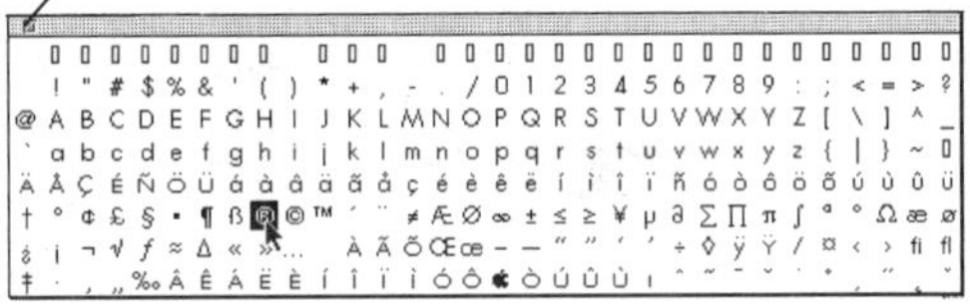

Figure 6: Click a symbol to insert it into your document.

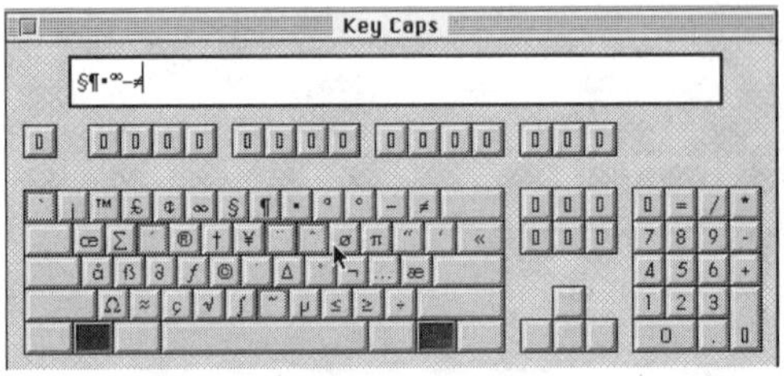

Figure 7: You can also insert a symbol from the **Key Caps** desk accessory accessed on the Apple menu.

Tip

The Symbol command displays the special character set for the currently selected font.

Each font has its own special character set. The symbols displayed on the Symbol dialog box represent the symbols available when you press the Option, Shift, or Option+Shift keys on your keyboard. If a symbol is not available in the font you choose, it is displayed as a white rectangle. To change fonts, choose another font, and the Symbol dialog box will reflect the change. The Symbol dialog box floats so you can move it around the screen to view your handiwork. You can also place your insertion point in different places to insert symbols in multiple spots while the box is open.

You can also select symbols by using Apple's KeyCaps command located on the Apple menu. With this desk accessory (shown in **Figure 7**), select a font from the KeyCaps menu and its symbols are displayed on its keyboard when you press different modifier keys. Click the keys on the dialog box with your cursor and the specified symbol is displayed on the preview box. Select the symbol and cut or copy it to the Clipboard. You can then paste the symbol into your document.

Shortcuts

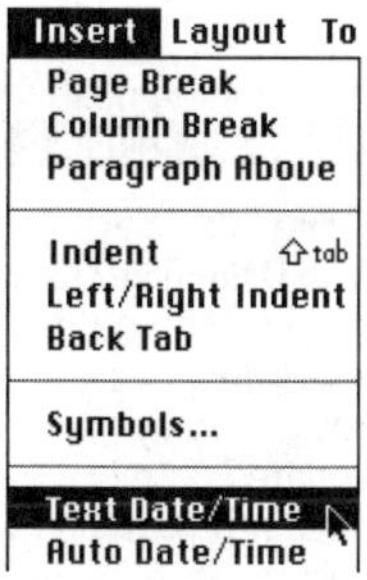

Figure 8a: Select **Text Date/Time** from the Insert menu.

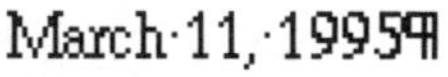

Figure 8b: WordPerfect inserts the current date or time as text into your document at the insertion point.

Pull down this menu to display the pop-up menu shown in Figure 10b.

If you do not like the preset formats on the Format menu, select independent formats for minutes, seconds, months, and so forth from these menus.

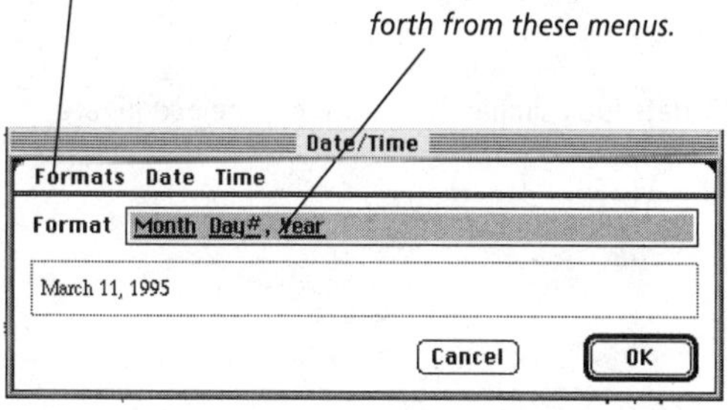

Figure 9a: Use the Date/Time dialog box on the **Preferences** command to configure how the date or time will appear.

To insert the current date or time as text:

1. Place your insertion point where you want to place the date or time.
2. Pull down the Insert menu and select Text Date/Time (**Figure 8a**).
3. As shown in **Figure 8b**, WordPerfect inserts either the Date, Time, or Date/Time combination (depending on how you configured the Date/Time option in the Edit menu's Date/Time Preferences dialog box).

Tip

To change the configuration of a date or time, pull down the Edit menu and select Preferences. Click the Date/Time button. In the resulting dialog box (**Figure 9a**), select text to change or click in the Format text box to add text and use the Format menu (**Figure 9b**) to alter the configuration. You can change how the Date or Time appears by using the Date and/or Time menus to change portions of the text. *Note:* the currently inserted date or time will not change when you change its format in Preferences. You need to delete the text and re-input the command.

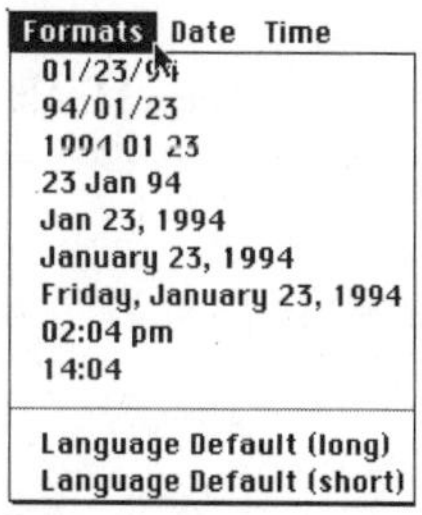

Figure 9b: Select a preset date or time format from the **Format** menu of the Date/Time dialog box.

To insert a date or timestamp that is automatically updated each time you open the document:

1. Place your insertion point where you want to place the date or time.
2. Pull down the Insert menu and select Auto Date/Time (**Figure 10**).
3. As shown in **Figure 11**, WordPerfect inserts a Date or Time that will be automatically updated each time you open the document.

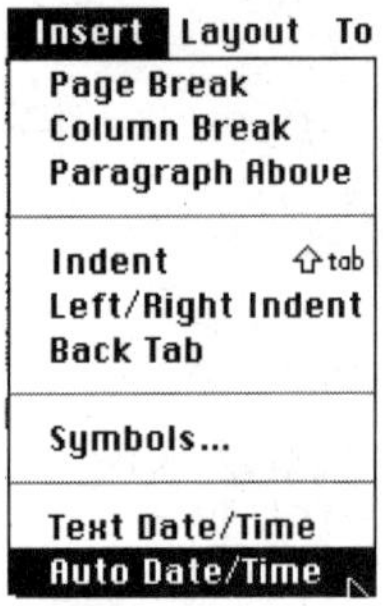

Figure 10: Select **Auto Date/Time** from the Insert menu to insert an automatically updated date or time into your document.

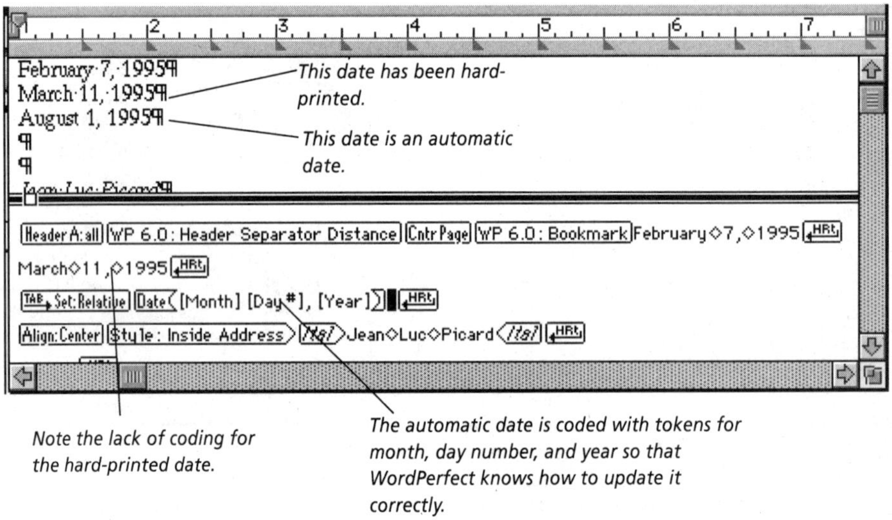

Figure 11: Although the text date and automatic date look similar on the screen, their codes are thoroughly different.

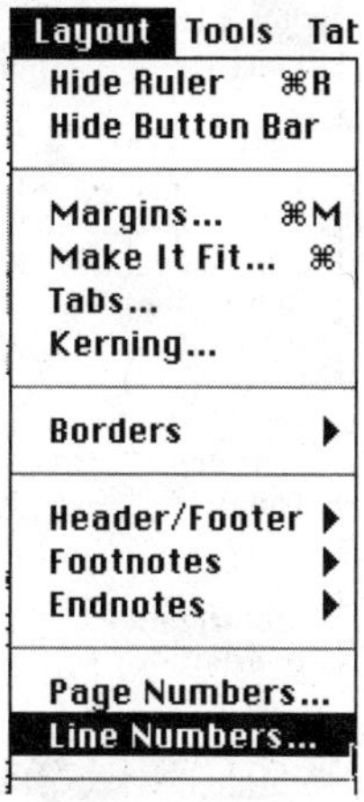

Figure 12: Select **Line Numbers** from the Layout menu to number individual lines.

Shortcuts

Shift F8

To number lines:

1. Select the text you want to number or place your insertion point in the line you want to number.
2. Pull down the Layout menu and select Line Numbers (**Figure 12**).
3. In the resulting Line Numbering dialog box (**Figure 13a**), choose the options you want to use. As shown in **Figure 13b**, you can number lines continuously through the document or restart on each page. You can also choose to skip (count the line but don't print the number), count and print the number, or ignore the line completely in counting and printing (**Figure 13c**).
4. Click OK.

Type a starting number here. The default is 1.

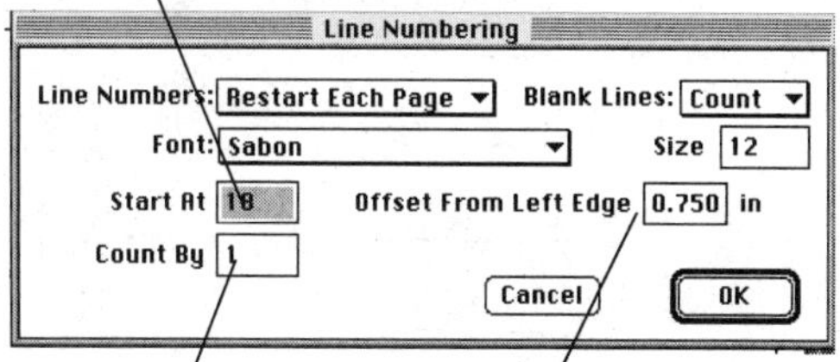

Type a counting increment here.

Type the amount of space to place between the paragraph and the number here.

Figure 13a: The **Line Numbering** dialog box.

Figure 13b: Select how you want the line numbers to function from the **Line Numbers** pop-up menu.

Figure 13c: Select a way to handle blank lines from the **Blank Lines** pop-up menu.

Select "Off" from the Line Numbers pop-up menu to turn off line numbering.

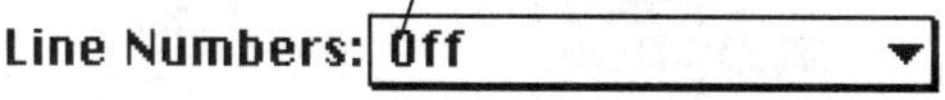

Figure 14: Use the Line Numbering pop-up menu to turn off numbering.

Tip

You can turn off the line numbering feature by re-selecting Line Numbers from the Layout menu and selecting the Off option from the Line Numbers pop-up menu (**Figure 14**).

To number every paragraph:

1. Place the insertion point on the line above the first paragraph you want to number. **Do not select any text.**
2. Pull down the Tools menu and select Outlining (**Figure 15**).
3. *Optional:* In the resulting Outlining dialog box (**Figure 16a**), select an outlining style from the Type pop-up menu (**Figure 16b**). The default style is Outline numbering.
4. *Optional:* Select a numbering style from the Style pop-up menu (see **Figure 16b**).
5. Make sure that the Outline On check box is selected and click the OK button.
6. Press the Return key (or Enter key on some keyboards). WordPerfect inserts the first outline number and moves the insertion point to the next line, placing a number to the left of the insertion point.

Shortcuts

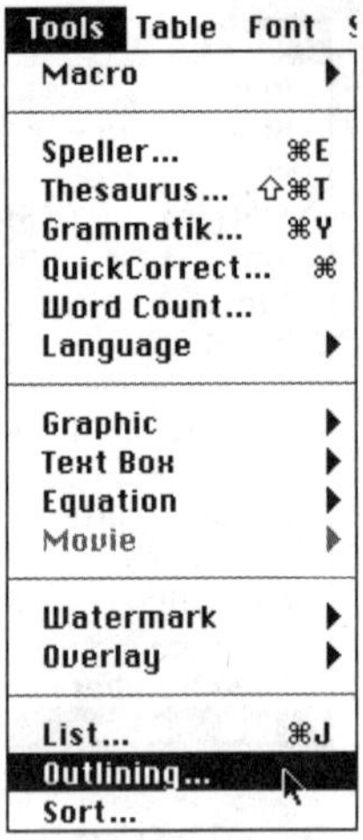

Figure 15: Select **Outlining** from the Tools menu.

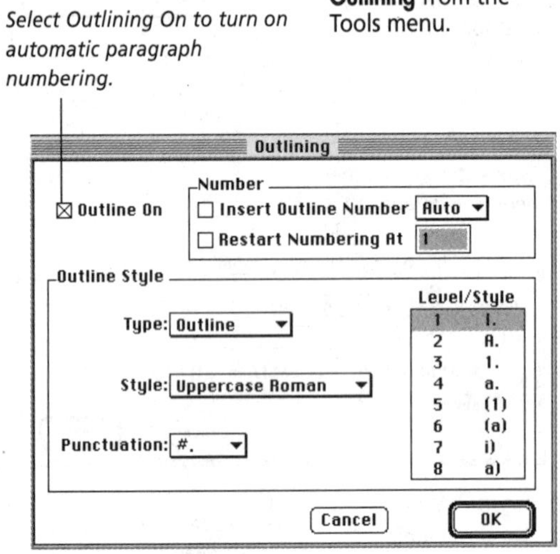

Figure 16a: The Outlining dialog box.

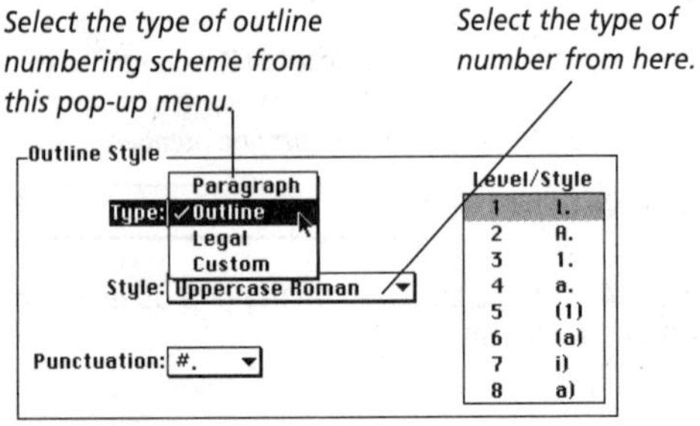

Figure 16b: Format paragraph numbers using the **Outline Style** area of the Outlining dialog box.

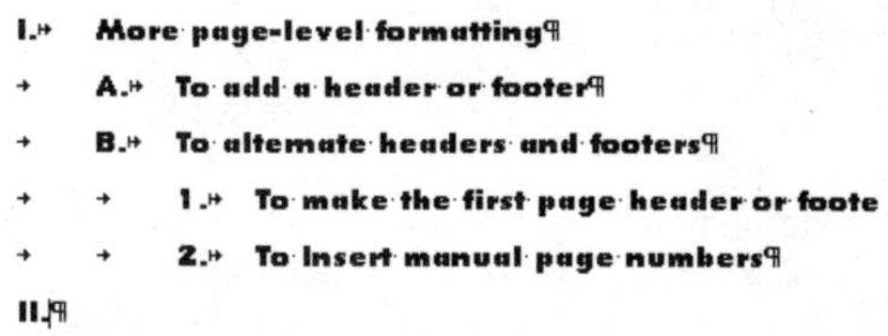
I. More page-level formatting¶
A. To add a header or footer¶
B. To alternate headers and footers¶
1. To make the first page header or foote
2. To Insert manual page numbers¶
II.¶

Figure 17: WordPerfect generates outline hierarchies of paragraph numbers whenever you press the Tab key.

To create an outline:

An outline is a hierarchical list of subordinated paragraphs. WordPerfect automatically creates subordinate numbers each time you press the Tab key with Outlining on. As shown in **Figure 17**, each paragraph has its own style of numbering based on what you selected in the Outlining dialog box.

Tip

The Outlining command actually generates an outline with numbered indented paragraphs in a hierarchy. The above task uses this ability to number paragraphs with first-level numbers. If you want to indent the entire paragraph after a number, select the Indent command from the Insert menu or press the key combinations Command+Shift+I or Option+Tab key. Every time that you press the Return or Enter key, WordPerfect inserts a number. Backspace to delete this number and WordPerfect remembers the number, thus not disturbing the automatic numbering scheme. To insert a blank line before a new paragraph, press the Return key twice.

Working with Outlines

To...	Do this...
To add items to an existing outline	Place your insertion point where you want to add the number, select **Outlining** (or press Command+Shift+O). Click **OK** and deselect **Outlining On**. Then, select **Insert Outline Number (see Figure 19a**) to add a number to an existing paragraph. WordPerfect adds the number and increases the subsequent paragraph numbers by one (or more depending on how many paragraphs you add to the outline).
To delete an item in an outline	Select the item and press either Backspace or Delete (depending upon your keyboard). WordPerfect renumbers all numbered paragraphs.
To restart numbering	Place your insertion point in the paragraph you want to renumber. Select **Outlining** (or press Command+Shift+O) and select the **Restart Numbering At** check box (see **Figure 19a**). Optionally, you can start numbering at any number by typing that number in the **Restart Numbering At** text box. Remember to use integers in this text box even if your numbering scheme uses some other numeric type (such as Roman numerals). All of the subsequent numbers are renumbered starting from the new number. This procedure is useful if you have a number of stepped tasks to write (such as are used in this book). You can keep Outlining selected and just restart each task at 1 and let WordPerfect insert the correct numbers automatically.
To start a new outline	Do the same procedure as you did to restart numbering only hit Return after typing OK to exit the dialog box. WordPerfect inserts the first outline number.

Figure 18: Select the **New** command from the **Footnotes** pop-up menu to create a new footnote.

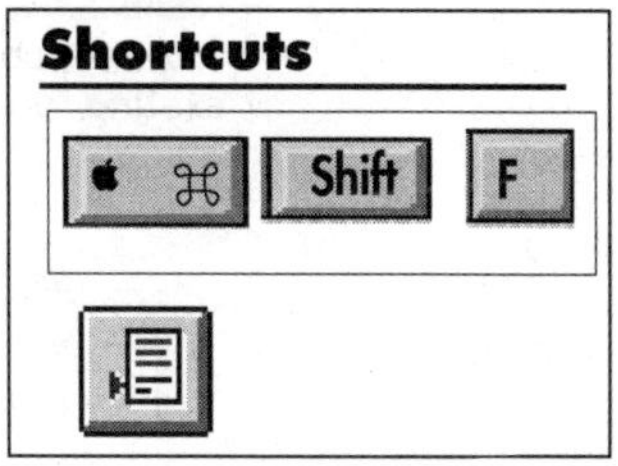

To insert a footnote:

1. Place your insertion point where you want to create a footnote.
2. Pull down the Layout menu and select Footnotes and the submenu called New (**Figure 18**).
3. In the resulting untitled Footnote window, type your footnote after the pre-entered number (**Figure 19**).
4. Click the Footnote window's close box.
5. WordPerfect adds a superscript footnote number at your insertion point and automatically renumbers later footnotes.

> **Tip**
>
> You can open more than one Footnote window at one time or use the arrows on the Footnote window's Footnote toolbar to scroll through your footnotes.

Scroll through your other footnotes by clicking these arrows.

If you accidentally delete the footnote number, click this icon to restore it.

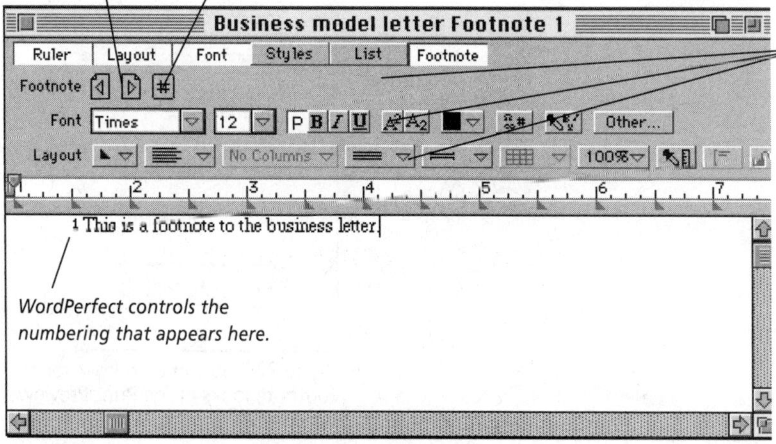

Use the toolbars or menus to change the font type, style, and layout of the footnote.

WordPerfect controls the numbering that appears here.

Figure 19: Type your footnote after the number and close the window.

To edit an existing footnote:

1. Pull down the Layout menu, select Edit from the Footnotes sub-menu (**Figure 20**).
2. In the resulting Edit Note dialog box (**Figure 21**), type the footnote number you want to edit in the Footnote Number text box.
3. WordPerfect opens that footnote's window (see **Figure 19**).
4. Edit the footnote using WordPerfect's menus and toolbars and click the close box when you are finished.

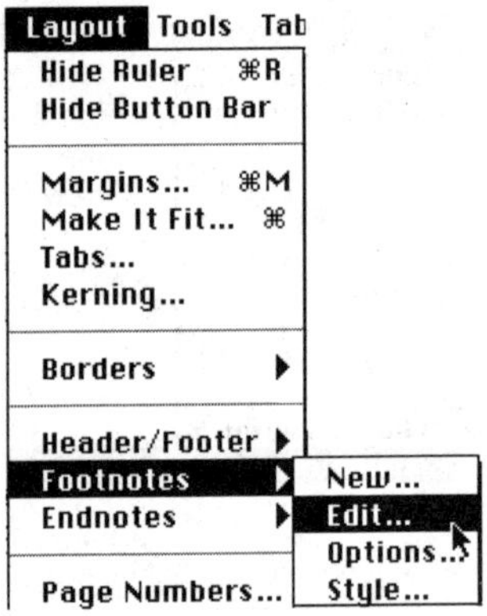

Figure 20: Select **Edit** from the **Footnote** pop-up menu to edit an existing footnote.

> **Tip**
>
> Be sure not to delete the footnote number in the Footnote window. If you accidentally do, click the number symbol (#) in the Footnote toolbar to restore the footnote number, select Undo from the Edit menu, or press Command+Z.
>
> You can use the Layout and Fonts toolbars and the associated Layout, Tools, Font, Size, and Style menus to edit your footnote in the Footnote window.
>
> To view how your footnote appears on the page, click the Print Preview button on the Button bar or select Print Preview from the File menu (**Figure 22**).

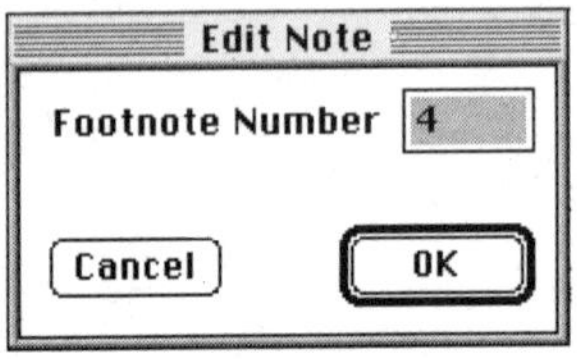

Figure 21: Type the number of the footnote you want to edit in the **Footnote Number** box. You can also double-click the footnote number itself if you do not remember its number.

Figure 22: You can view how your footnote looks in the Print Preview window.

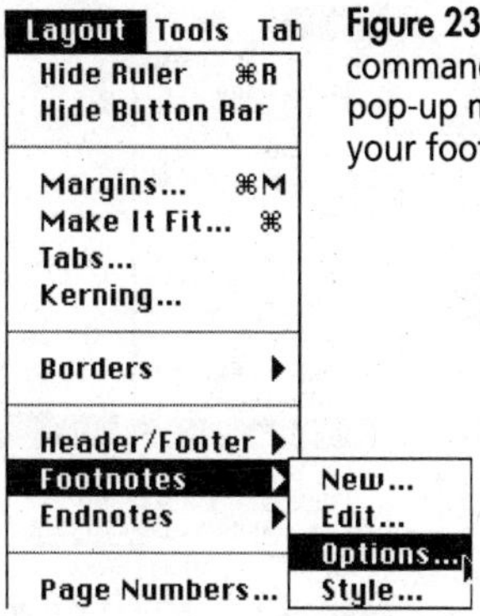

Figure 23: Select the **Options** command from the **Footnote** pop-up menu to change how your footnotes are displayed.

To change how a footnote operates:

You can change the footnote options that control numbering, spacing of lines (as well as how the footnotes will break should they be too long for a single page), position on the page, and how the separator line appears by using the Options command on the Footnotes sub-menu.

1. Place your insertion point where you want to begin the changes. Any changes affect the document from the insertion point to the end of the document, including all intervening footnotes.
2. Pull down the Layout menu and select the Options command from the Footnotes sub-menu (**Figure 23**).
3. In the resulting Footnote Options dialog box (**Figures 24a, b, c**), select the settings you want to change from the appropriate pop-up menus and text boxes.
4. Click the OK button.

Figure 24b: Select a footnote type from the **Type** pop-up menu. If you choose to use characters, type the character you are using in the **Note Characters** text box.

Figure 24c: Use the **Position** pop-up menu to place your footnotes at the end of chapters or at the bottom of the page on which they are referenced.

Select the footnote designator from this pop-up window. You can pick numbers, letters, or special characters.

Type the footnote number you want to use here. The default is to count from 1.

If you want to use a symbol for the footnote, select Characters from the Type menu and type a character here.

Type the amount of space you want to use between the last line of text and the footnote. You can also designate the amount of space to use between footnotes.

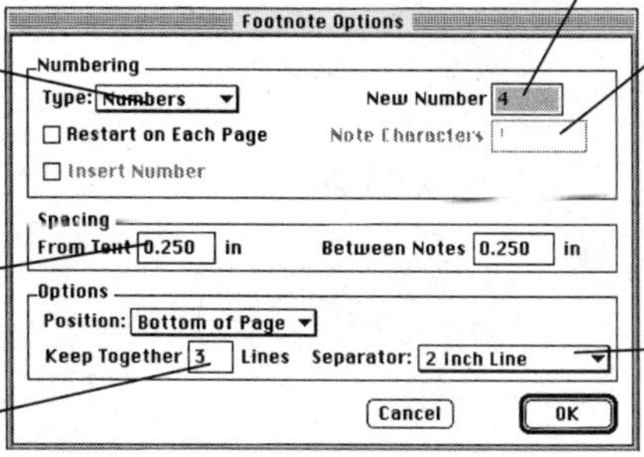

Use this pop-up menu to change the type of line used to separate the footnotes from your text.

Select where you want your footnotes to appear, how to break them across pages, and what type of separator to use from this box.

Figure 24a: The Footnote Options dialog box.

Working with endnotes:

Endnotes are references or notes that are placed at the end of books or chapters. WordPerfect uses the same type of dialog boxes to insert endnotes as are used to insert and edit footnotes. To insert an endnote, select New from the Endnotes sub-menu on the Layout menu (**Figure 25**). In the resulting Endnotes window (**Figure 26**), type your endnote. Close the Endnotes window by clicking its close box. WordPerfect inserts a subject number reflecting the note into your text. Use the Endnotes Edit command to edit your endnotes, as well as the Endnote Options command to set up the parameters for your endnotes.

Shortcuts

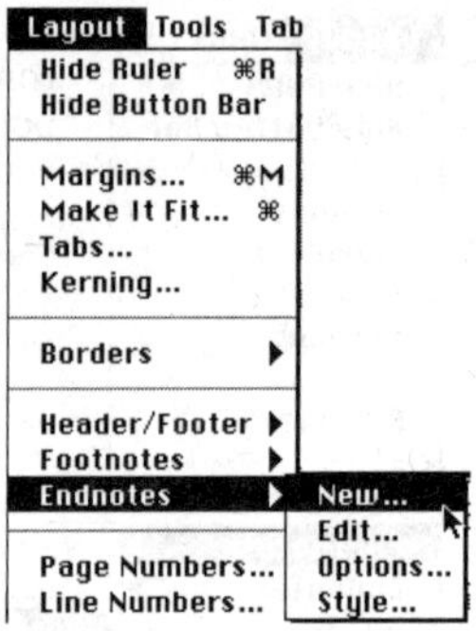

Figure 25: Select **New** from the **Endnotes** pop-up menu to create a new endnote.

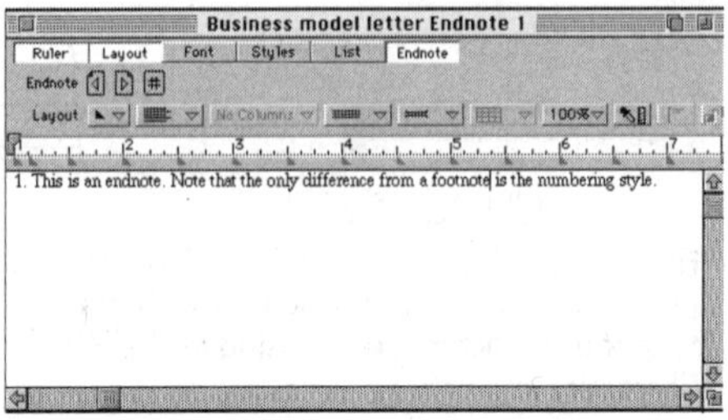

Figure 26: The Endnote window is used in exactly the same fashion as the Footnote window.

To delete a footnote or endnote:

1. Place your insertion point to the right of the footnote or endnote number you want to delete (**Figure 27**).
2. Press the Backspace or Delete key (depending on your keyboard).
3. WordPerfect deletes both the footnote or endnote number and text and renumbers the rest of the footnotes or endnotes (**Figure 28**).

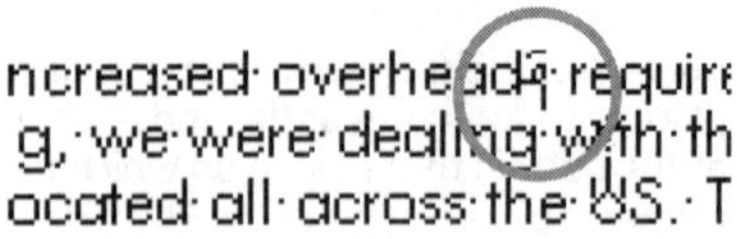

Figure 27: To delete a footnote, place your cursor behind the footnote designator (the superscript number in your text)...

WordPerfect deletes the selected footnote and automatically renumbers the rest.

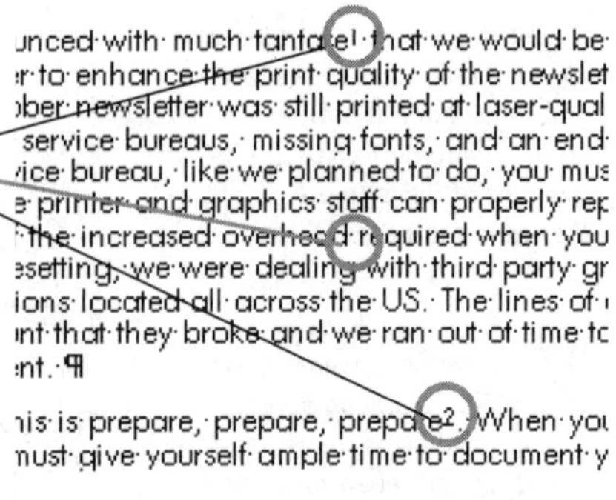

Figure 28: ...and WordPerfect deletes the total footnote/endnote and renumbers the remaining footnotes or endnotes.

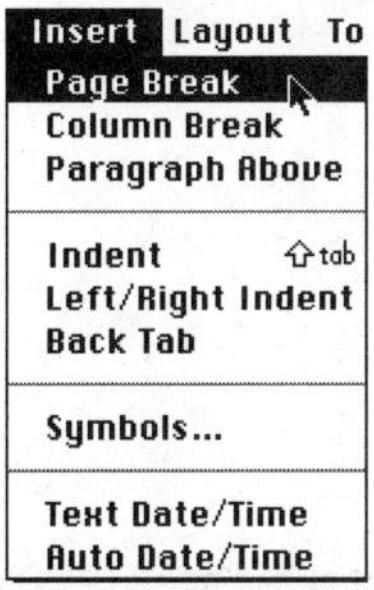

Figure 29: Select **Page Break** from the Insert menu to generate a manual page break.

To insert a manual page break:

1. Place your insertion point where you want to place the page break.
2. Pull down the Insert menu and select Page Break (Figure 29).
3. WordPerfect inserts a hard page break before your insertion point (Figure 30).

Tip

To delete a hard page break, click immediately after the page break and press the Backspace (Delete) key.

This is an automatic page break generated by WordPerfect based on your margin settings.

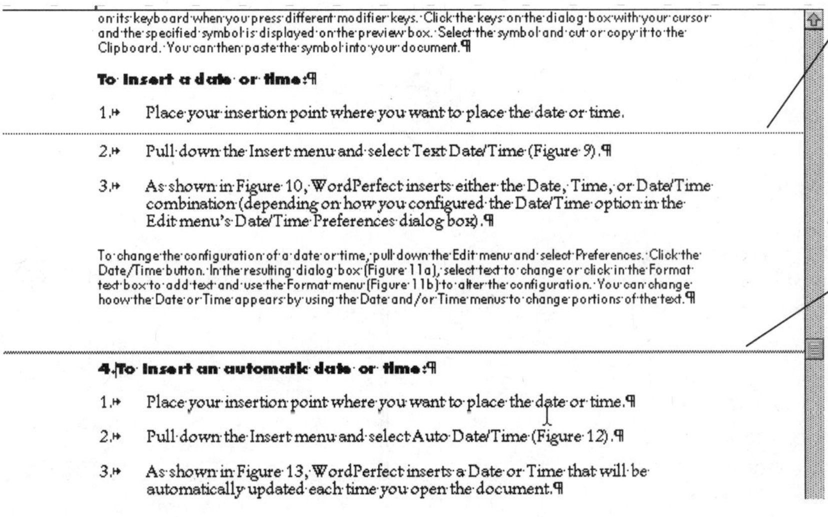

on its keyboard when you press different modifier keys. Click the keys on the dialog box with your cursor and the specified symbol is displayed on the preview box. Select the symbol and cut or copy it to the Clipboard. You can then paste the symbol into your document.¶

To insert a date or time:¶

1. Place your insertion point where you want to place the date or time.
2. Pull down the Insert menu and select Text Date/Time (Figure 9).¶
3. As shown in Figure 10, WordPerfect inserts either the Date, Time, or Date/Time combination (depending on how you configured the Date/Time option in the Edit menu's Date/Time Preferences dialog box).¶

To change the configuration of a date or time, pull down the Edit menu and select Preferences. Click the Date/Time button. In the resulting dialog box (Figure 11a), select text to change or click in the Format text box to add text and use the Format menu (Figure 11b) to alter the configuration. You can change hoow the Date or Time appears by using the Date and/or Time menus to change portions of the text.¶

4.To insert an automatic date or time:¶

1. Place your insertion point where you want to place the date or time.¶
2. Pull down the Insert menu and select Auto Date/Time (Figure 12).¶
3. As shown in Figure 13, WordPerfect inserts a Date or Time that will be automatically updated each time you open the document.¶

This is a hard page break you can insert by selecting Page Break or by pressing Command+Return.

Figure 30: There are two types of page breaks in WordPerfect: automatic and manual.

Working with headers and footers

Headers and Footers are text, dates, and/or page numbers that are placed on every page of your document. To WordPerfect, the inclusion of text that appears on every designated page is implemented by adding a headers and footers code that can be toggled on or off, as needed. Thus, headers and footers will be placed on the page where you typed them and on every following page until you discontinue the specific header or footer, or type another header or footer of the same specification.

This reliance on codes lets you manipulate how your headers or footers work on a page-by-page basis. You can also vary the headers separately from the footers. You can create as many as two headers or footers (called by WordPerfect "Header A or B" or "Footer A or B") for every page of your document. You can place different headers on facing pages or alternate the header and footer on every page. Thus, although this may be confusing, WordPerfect's method of inserting headers and footers is very flexible.

To add a header or footer:

1. Place your insertion point on the page where you want your header or footer to begin.
2. Pull down the Layout menu and select the New command from the Header/Footer sub-menu (**Figure 31**).
3. In the resulting New Header/Footer dialog box (**Figure 32**), select which header or footer you want to create (select either A or B).

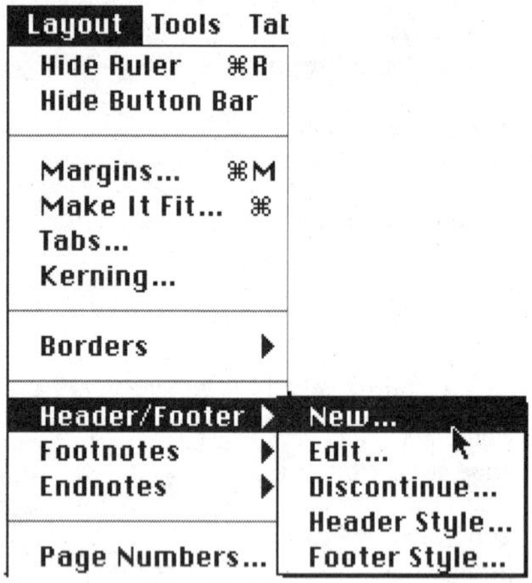

Figure 31: Select **New** from the **Header/Footer** sub-menu to create a new header or footer.

Shortcuts

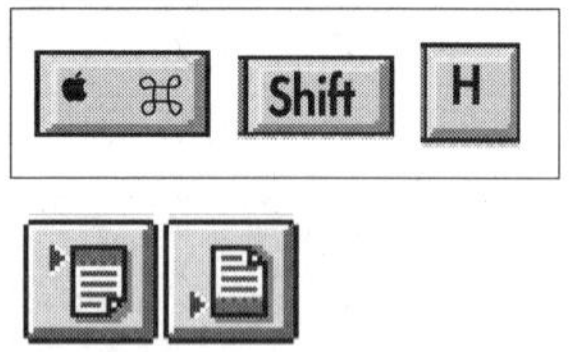

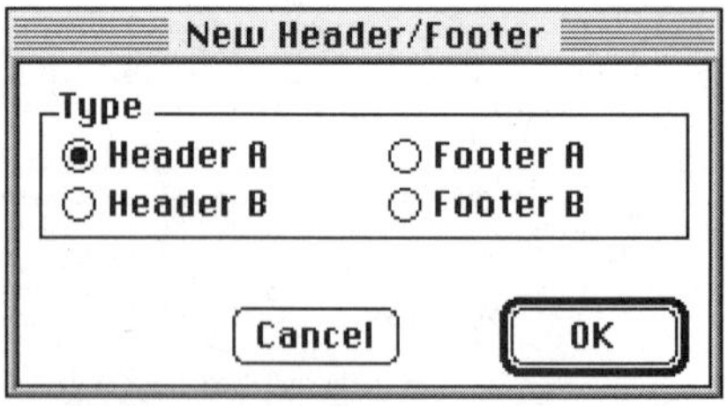

Figure 32: Every page in your document can have two headers and two footers, enabling you to create alternating header/footers and other enhancements. Use this dialog box to select which of the two headers or footers you want to create for the page.

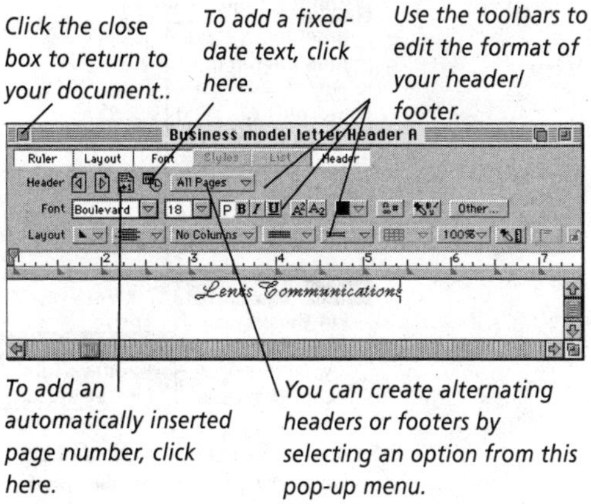

Figure 33a: Type and format your header or footer in the window.

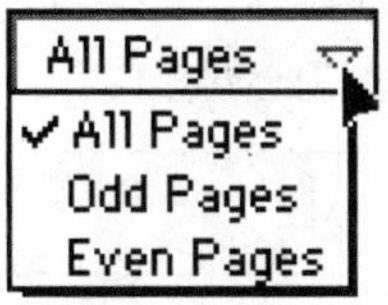

Figure 33b: Use the **All Pages** pop-up menu on the Header/Footer toolbar to create alternating headers or footers (footers that appear only on the even or odd pages of your document).

4. In the resulting untitled Header or Footer window (**Figure 33a**), type your text. You can use the formatting and font toolbars and menus to format your text.
5. Click the Header or Footer window's close box when you are finished.

To alternate headers and footers:

1. Open a header or footer window by following the previous task's steps.
2. In the Header or Footer window (see **Figure 33a**), type your text.
3. Select whether you want the header or footer to appear on all even pages or all odd pages, or on all pages by choosing the appropriate option from the All Pages pop-up menu (**Figure 33b**) on the Header or Footer toolbar. If you select an even page and your insertion point is on an odd page, your header or footer will not appear until the next page (and vice versa).
4. Click the close box when you are finished.

To discontinue headers or footers:

When you discontinue a header or footer, it is not displayed from the insertion point where you apply the Discontinue code to the end of the document. The headers and footers still exist and can be displayed again by reversing (deselecting) the appropriate Discontinue check box in the Header/Footer dialog box.

To permanently prevent headers or footers from displaying, you must delete them by selecting and pressing the Backspace or Delete keys (depending on your computer model).

1. Place the insertion point on the page where you want to discontinue the header or footer from.
2. Pull down the Layout menu and select Discontinue from the Header/Footer pop-up menu (**Figure 34**).
3. In the resulting Header/Footer dialog box (**Figure 35**), select the header or footer you want to discontinue (either A or B).
4. Click OK.

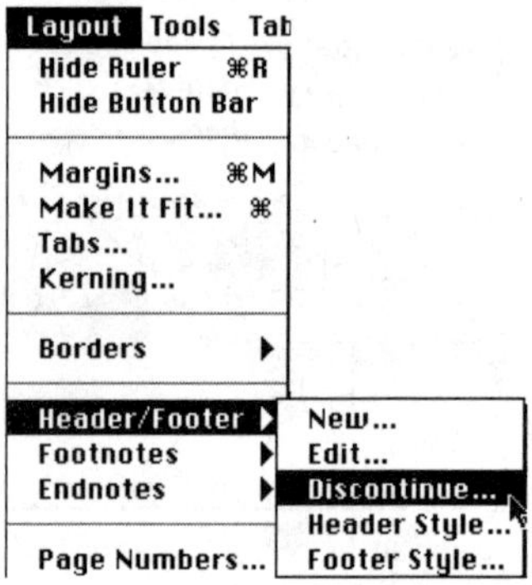

Figure 34: Select the **Discontinue** command from the **Header/Footer** pop-up menu to hide a header or footer.

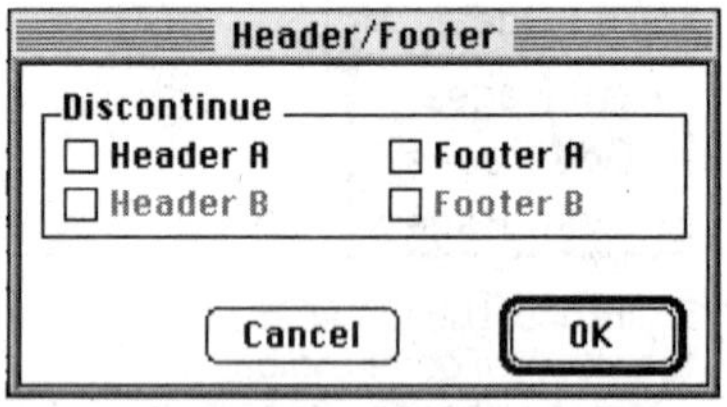

Figure 35: Since every page has up to two potential headers or footers, you must remember which one you want to hide and select it on the dialog box.

> **Tip**
>
> As discussed earlier, each page can have up to two different headers or footers, designated as A and B. If you discontinue Header A on page 7, but have another, different Header A, on page 10, only the Header As starting on page 7 and running to 10 will be discontinued since they are all the same. WordPerfect considers the page 10 Header A, a different header, and you need to separately discontinue it if you want it also to be hidden.

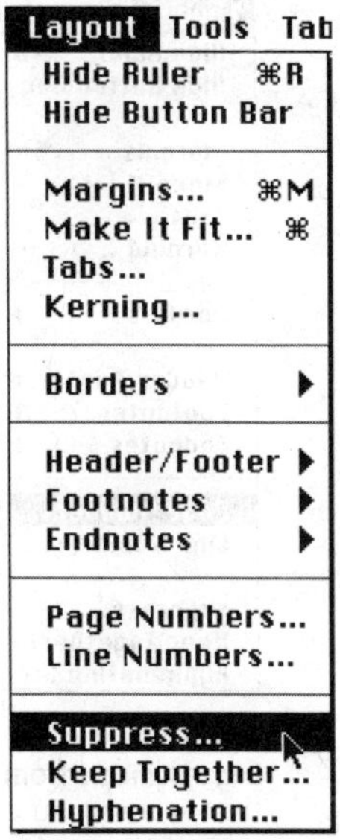

Figure 36: Select **Suppress** on the Layout menu to hide a single page's header and/or footer.

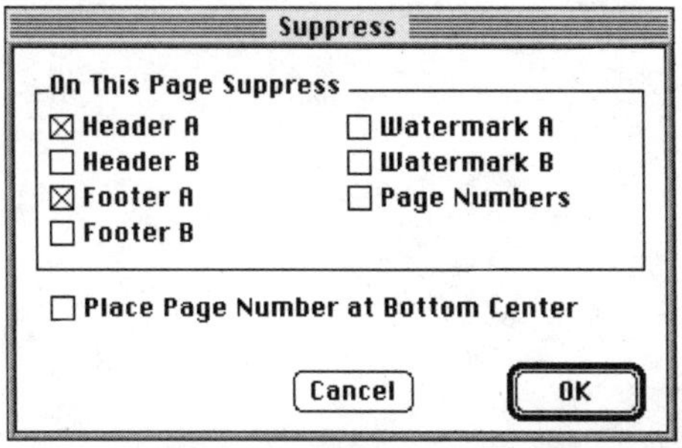

Figure 37: Select the Header or Footer letter (A or B) that represents the text on your first page. You can elect to only hide the Header and keep the Footer and vice versa by clicking the appropriate check box.

To create a blank first page header or footer:

1. Place your insertion point in the first page of your document.
2. Pull down the Layout menu and select Suppress (**Figure 36**).
3. In the resulting Suppress dialog box (**Figure 37**), select the check box of the header and footer letter (A or B) you used on the first page.
4. Click OK.

To add page numbers to documents:

WordPerfect can place page numbers directly on to your page at the top or bottom left, center, or right sides of the page. When you begin numbering pages, WordPerfect generates a page number from your insertion point to the end of the document. If you are using headers and footers that take up this space, then WordPerfect provides the option of placing the page number within the header or footer. WordPerfect controls the numbering of pages, adding blank pages when necessary, if you so choose, to keep the layout consistent. Once you turn on page numbering, it is automatic.

1. Place the insertion point where you want to begin numbering.
2. Pull down the Layout menu and select Page Numbers (**Figure 38**).

Shortcuts

Option F8

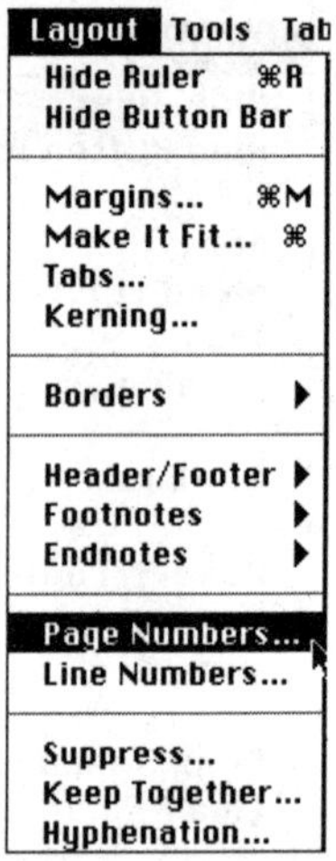

Figure 38: Select **Page Numbers** from the Layout menu to apply automatically paginated page numbers to your document.

Tip

To view page numbers as they will appear when printed, open the Print Preview window by either clicking the Print Preview button on the Button bar or by selecting Print Preview from the File menu.

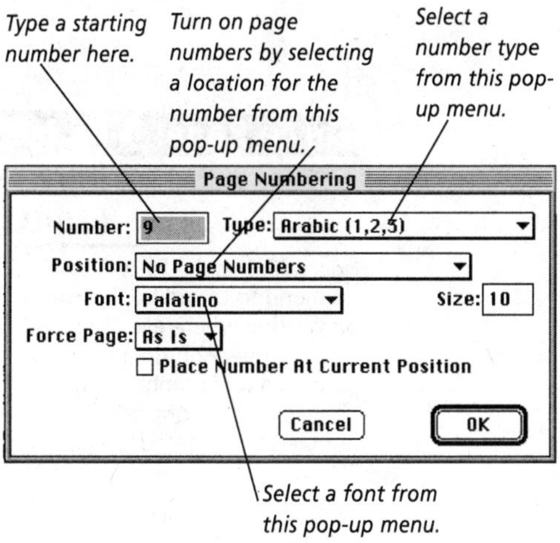

Figure 39a: Use the Page Numbering dialog box to place and edit your page numbers.

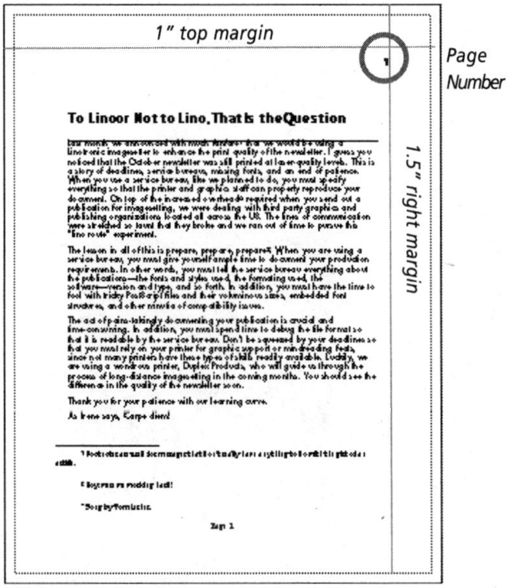

Figure 40: Reset your margins to move the location of a page number.

3. In the resulting Page Numbering dialog box (**Figure 39a**), pull down the Position pop-up menu and select a location for the page numbers (**Figure 39b**).

   Hint: If you are using headers or footers, you must turn on the page numbering within the header or footer for the page number to appear correctly on the document.

4. *Optional:* the page number will print in your default font unless you select a font type for your page numbers from the Font pop-up menu and type a size in the Size text box (see **Figure 38a**).

5. Click OK to begin page numbering.

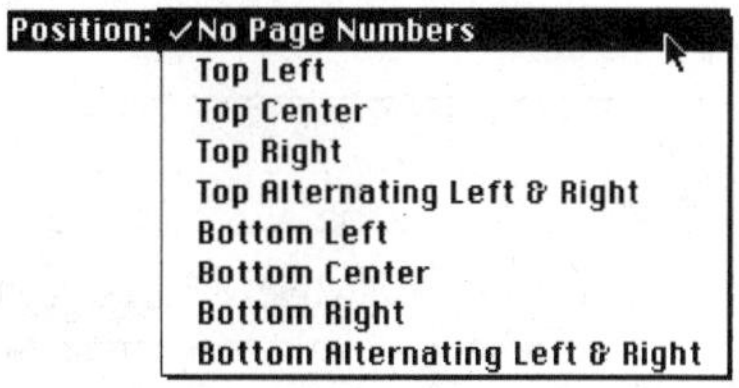

Figure 39b: Use the **Position** pop-up menu to place the page number in your document.

Tip

When you insert a page number into your document, it is placed exactly at your margins, whether you assign it to the top right, left, or center position or those at the bottom of your page. For example, as illustrated in **Figure 40**, if you have set your margins at 1 inch at the top and bottom and 1.5 inches on the right and left, then the page number positioned at the top right would be placed one inch down and 1.5 inches in from the edge of the page.

If you want to relocate where the page numbers will appear, reset your margins using the Margins command on the Layout menu. *See Chapter 4: "Formatting" for a description of how to set margins.*

To create even or odd page numbers (front and back book-type paginating):

1. Place the insertion point where you want to begin numbering.
2. Pull down the Layout menu and select Page Numbers (see **Figure 37**).
3. In the resulting Page Numbering dialog box (see **Figure 38a**), pull down the Force Page pop-up menu (**Figure 40**) and select either Front, to force even numbers to appear on the left side of a page, or Back to force odd numbers to appear on the right side of the page. Selecting this option tells WordPerfect to insert blank pages, if necessary, to force the page numbers to go to their correct locations.

Figure 40: Use the **Force Page** pop-up menu to create book-type pagination where even numbers always appear on the left-hand page and odd numbers always appear on the right-hand side of double-sided printed documents.

> **Tip**
>
> If you want to create book-type page numbers in headers or footers, be sure to create two different headers or footers, one for the odd page and one for the even page. Then open each separately and insert page numbers on the right or left side of the pages, as appropriate. See the above task describing the creation of even and odd headers and footers. Be sure that the **As Is** option in the Force Page pop-up menu is selected in the Page Numbering dialog box to allow WordPerfect to generate page numbers consistently.

To place a page number in a header or footer:

1. Open a header or footer window by following the task described on page 88.
2. In the Header or Footer window (**Figure 41**), place your insertion point where you want to place the page number or use a Layout tool to align the number on the page.
3. Click the Page Numbering button on the Header/Footer toolbar.
4. WordPerfect inserts a number at the insertion point.
5. Click the close box on the window.

Click the page number button here to insert a page number into a header or footer.

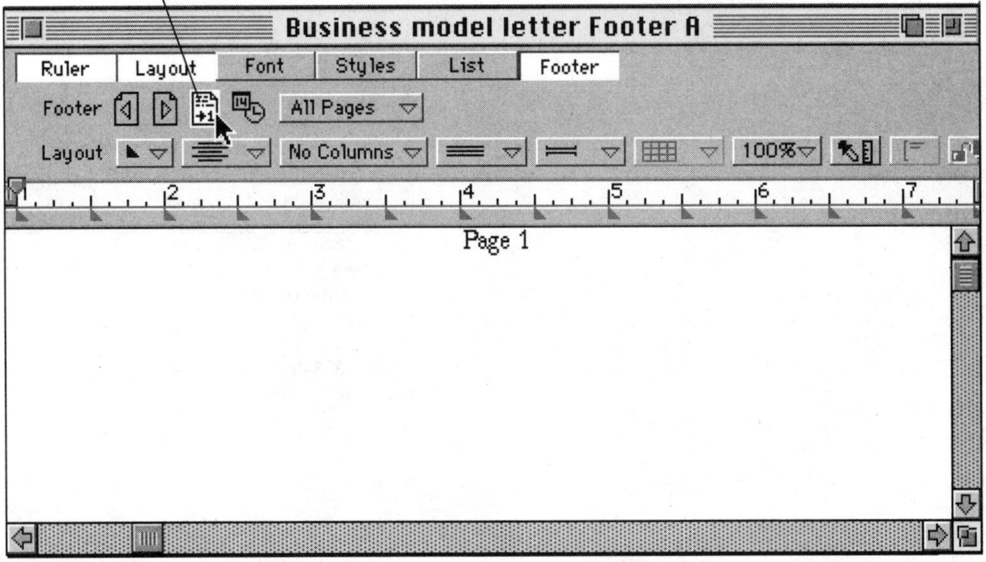

Figure 41: Place the page number in the header or footer if you are using headers and footers in your document and want to number your pages.

To suppress a page number on a page:

1. Place your insertion point in the page where you want to suppress the page numbering.
2. Pull down the Layout menu and select Suppress (**Figure 42**).
3. In the resulting Suppress dialog box (**Figure 43**), select the Page Numbers check box.

   or
4. *Optional:* You can also use this dialog box to move the page number to the bottom center of the page by checking the Place Page Number at Bottom Center check box rather than the Suppress check box.
5. Click OK.

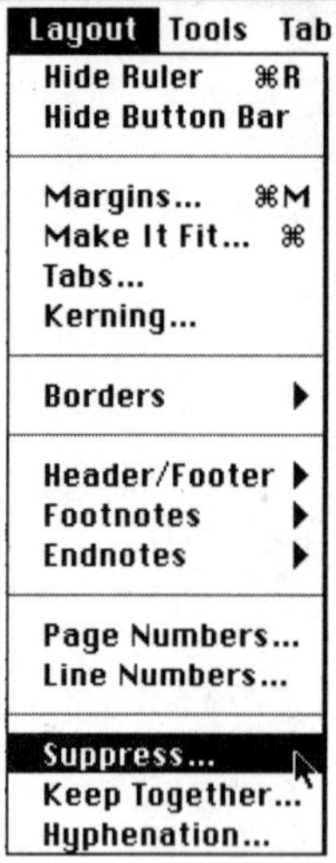

Figure 42: Select the **Suppress** command from the Layout menu to turn off a single page number in your document.

> **Tip**
>
> The **Suppress** command only suppresses one page at a time, so you need to use this command on every page where you want to suppress or move the number. This command will not turn off page numbering for the entire document. *See "To Turn Off Page Numbering" on page 100, for a description of how to permanently turn off numbering.*

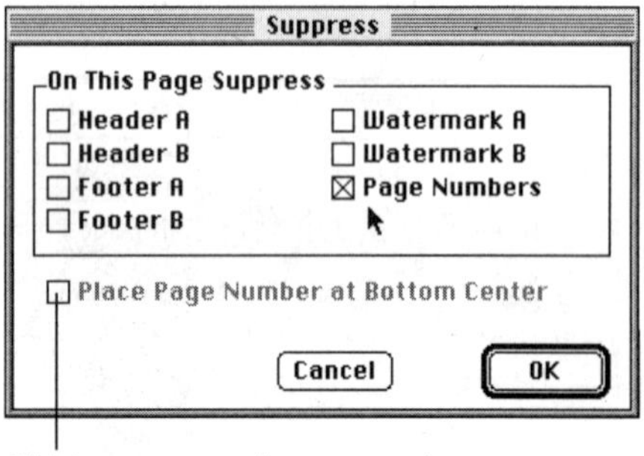

Click here to move the page number to the center of the bottom of your document.

Figure 43: Select **Page Numbers** to suppress the page number on a page.

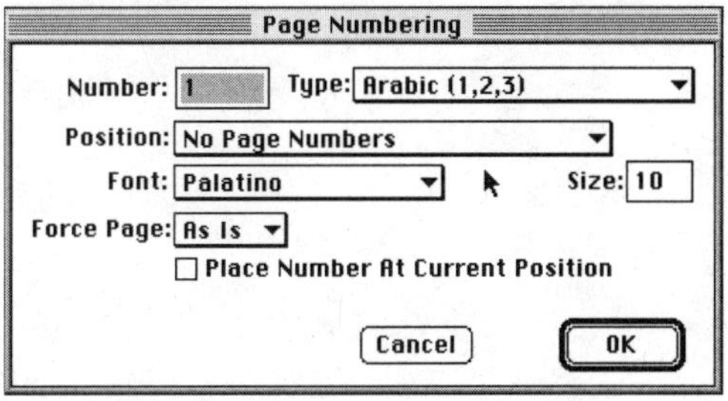

Figure 44: Select **No Page Numbers** from the Position pop-up menu to turn off page numbering from your insertion point to the end of the document.

To turn off page numbering:

1. Place your insertion point on the page where you want to end page numbering. (In other words, select the last page you want numbered, since every WordPerfect command affects everything forward of the insertion point.)
2. Pull down the Layout menu and select Page Numbers.
3. In the resulting Page Numbering dialog box (**Figure 44**), select No Page Numbers from the Position pop-up menu.
4. Click OK.

Tip

WordPerfect turns off page numbers for the rest of the document. You can restart page numbering by selecting a new position from the Position pop-up menu on the Page Numbering dialog box.

If you inserted page numbers into your headers or footers, in order to turn off page numbering you must discontinue the header or footer. See page 92 for a description of how to discontinue a header or footer.

STYLES 6

SO FAR in this book I have described how to manually change the look and behavior of text through the application of such things as tabs, indents, font types and sizes, page margins, numbers, and so forth. You may have noticed how tedious it can get to continually repeat the same operations over and over to create a consistent look for your document. In addition, you may even forget in the course of your work what you wanted a certain heading or paragraph to look like and apply formats, layouts, and fonts in error. Well, WordPerfect has a solution to this problem in the application of its *Styles*.

Style Sheets Explained

Styles are collections of layout and font details that can be applied to paragraphs. Styles work by letting you identify this collection of formats by a single name. Then, each time you want to apply the set of attributes and formatting that the name represents, you simply select the paragraph you want formatted, then select the name, and WordPerfect applies the underlying collection to the selected paragraph.

For example, in this book all subheads come in two flavors:

- **Subhead 1:** I gave the first level subhead the name "Subhead 1" and assigned a Futura Extra-Bold font in 12 point type, 12.5 point leading, 90 percent condensed with no tabs or indents to every selection of text to which the name was applied.

- **Subhead 2:** I gave the name "Subhead 2" to the second level headings (for instance the task names you see throughout the chapters). Subhead 2 applies a Style of Futura Extra Bold 11-point type with 12-point leading, normal tracking, and ten percent condensed kerning to text.

How easy it is now to select the text I want as a subhead and then select Subhead 1 or Subhead 2 from the Styles pop-up menu (or apply a keystroke shortcut assigned to that Style) rather than laboriously pulling down the Font, Style, and Size menus or clicking individual tools from the toolbars to create the same layout and format.

This is neat, but there is more.

You can assign the Style to paragraphs throughout a document or even a set of documents. Then, every time you edit the Style, the changes you make are applied consistently throughout. This way, by changing one thing, you affect every occurrence of the Style in the document without having to track and change each little detail. The ability to edit a document consistently is a great time saver as well as quality control device.

Wait, there is more.

You can tell WordPerfect to include certain Styles in the Table of Contents (up to five levels) or your Index by including the TOC, Index, or other list mark in the Style, and then WordPerfect will automatically build the Table of Contents based on the contents of the assigned paragraphs, each at its proper level.

Thus, with the application of Styles you get a shortcut to formatting as well as a way to ensure consistency throughout a document and even between documents (since your Styles can be stored in libraries for sharing with other documents and users).

More About Attributes and Formats

Earlier in the book we broke down the application of formatting into two groups: attributes and formats.

- Styles use the concept of attributes to define font-related items, such as font sizes, styles, and types. Think of attributes as anything having to do with the Font toolbar.
- Styles use the concept of formats to define layout-related items, such as the application of tabs, indents, margins, distance between paragraphs, line spacing, and so forth. Think of formats as anything that has to do with the Layout toolbar.

You will be asked to save either attributes, formats, or both attributes and formats as part of the task of creating Styles. If you want to apply the Style to characters, save its attributes only and if the Style is paragraph-based (as most are) you can save either both types of layouts (if your Style contains font information) or only formats.

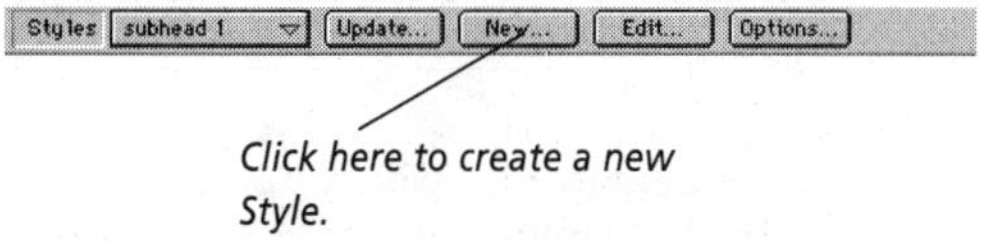

Figure 1: The Styles toolbar displays buttons to control the creation and manipulation of Styles.

Shortcuts

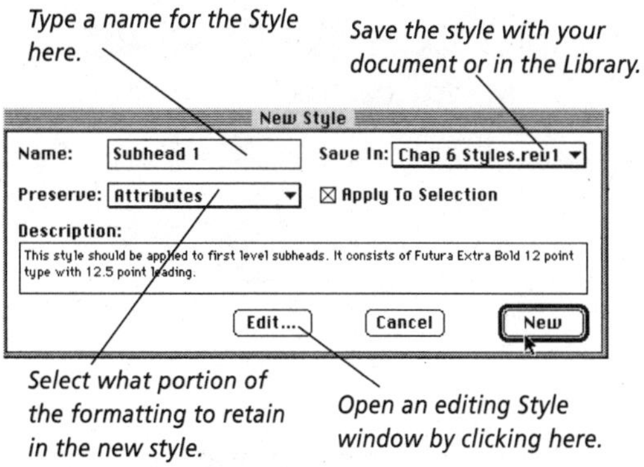

Figure 2a: Give your new Style a name and click **New** to create a new Style.

Working with Styles

WordPerfect provides all the tools you need to streamline the formatting of characters and paragraphs via the Styles toolbar. The following tasks describe how to use the New, Edit, and Update buttons to create and manage Styles.

To create a Style:

1. Apply font and layout tools to text you want to assign as a Style.
2. Select the text.
3. If the Styles bar is not displayed, click **Styles** in the Control bar. In the resulting Styles toolbar, click **New** (**Figure 1**).
4. In the resulting New Style dialog box (**Figure 2a**), type a name for the style in the **Name** text box. *Hint:* Give the style a descriptive name that helps you remember its purpose.
5. *Optional:* Type a short description of the contents of the style and its purpose in the **Description** box.
6. *Optional:* If you want to directly apply the new style to the selected text, make sure that the **Apply To Selection** check box is selected.

Creating a Style

Tip

When you apply a Style to a paragraph, WordPerfect applies the style from the paragraph where you place your insertion point to the end of the document.

7. Select a location where you want to save the style from the **Save In** pop-up menu (**Figure 2b**). You can save the Style with your document or in the universal Library(USA). Styles saved with documents are not available to other documents, but do override Library styles. Save the Style in Library if you want to share it with other documents. You can also create a new library with the **Library** button in the **Preferences** command. *See Chapter 15: "Customizing" for a description of how to use the Preferences command.*

8. Pull down the **Preserve** pop-up menu (**Figure 2c**) and select which parts of the text formatting you want to save. Here is where you must decide if you want to save **Attributes** only (those format items that are font-based) or **Formatting** (those format items that are layout-based), or both **Attributes and Formatting**.

9. *Optional:* You can use the formatting buttons located on the Font and Layout bars as well as the Ruler's margins, tabs, and indents to set up a Style directly. If you want to apply other formatting (such as hyphenation rules, kerning, and so forth) click **Edit** to open a Style window.

   (See the task on "Editing an Existing Style" on page 102, for a discussion of how to use the Style window.)

10. Click the **New** button.

Figure 2b: Save the Style with your document if you do not want to use it with any other document. If you want to share the Style, save it in the universal Library.

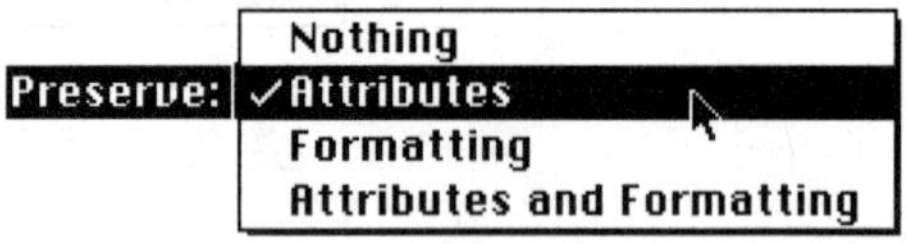

Figure 2c: Use the **Preserve** pop-up menu to save separate portions of your formatting with the Style: either only the font-related items, only the layout-related items, or all of the formatting.

> **Tip**
>
> If you save a new Style in Library(USA) and there is already another Style with the same name in the library, WordPerfect will overwrite the older Style with the contents of your new Style. Therefore, be very careful when you save Styles to the Library that they contain unique names or that you really want to replace original Styles with your new version.
>
> One way around this problem is to make a backup copy of the original Library(USA) file. Then, if you make an accidental change to the Library, restore the original.

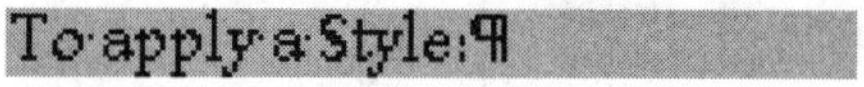

Figure 3: Select the text you want to format with a Style...

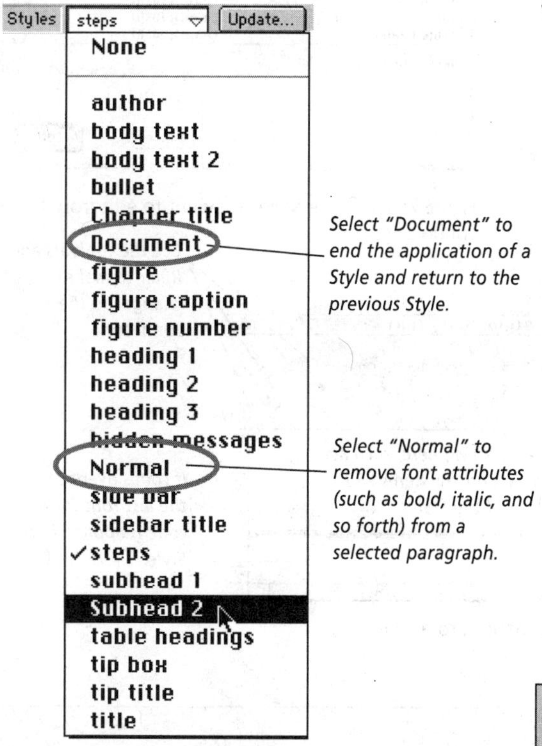

Figure 4...and select a Style from the **Styles** pop-up menu on the Styles toolbar.

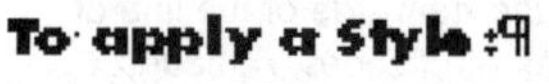

Figure 5: WordPerfect applies that Style to the selected text.

To apply a Style:

1. Place the insertion point in the paragraph where you want to begin the formatting (**Figure 3**), or select the text you want to format.
2. Pull down the **Styles** pop-up menu on the Styles toolbar and select the style you want to use (**Figure 4**).
3. As shown in **Figure 5**, WordPerfect applies the Style either to the selected text's paragraph or from the paragraph where you placed your insertion point until it meets another Style.

Tip

WordPerfect supplies the Document and Normal Styles in the Library(USA) so that they are available to all documents.

- Use the **Document** Style to end the application of a Style and return to the previous Style.
- Use the **Normal** Style to delete font attributes from selected text and return to Plain text.

To edit an existing Style:

1. Click the **Edit** button on the Styles toolbar (**Figure 6**).
2. In the resulting Edit Styles dialog box (**Figure 7**), select a Style name from the list box.
3. Click the **Edit** button.
4. WordPerfect opens a Style window for the selected Style (**Figure 8**).
5. Make your changes to the formatting of the Style using the Style window's Font and Layout toolbar buttons, and Ruler.
6. Click the close button to return to your document.

Shortcuts

Figure 6: Click the **Edit** button on the Styles toolbar to change the Style directly via a Style window.

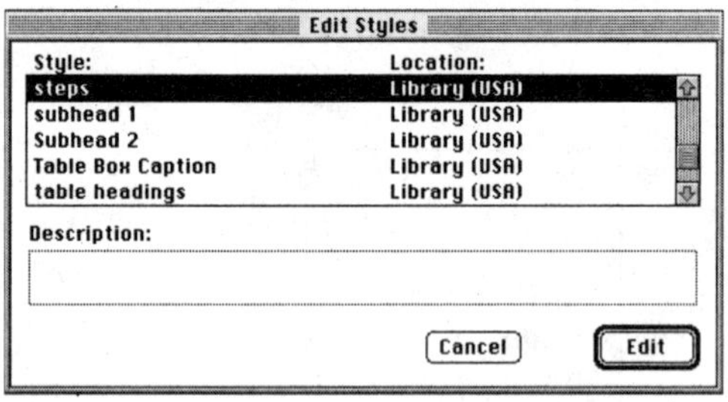

Figure 7: Select the Style you want to edit from the **List** box.

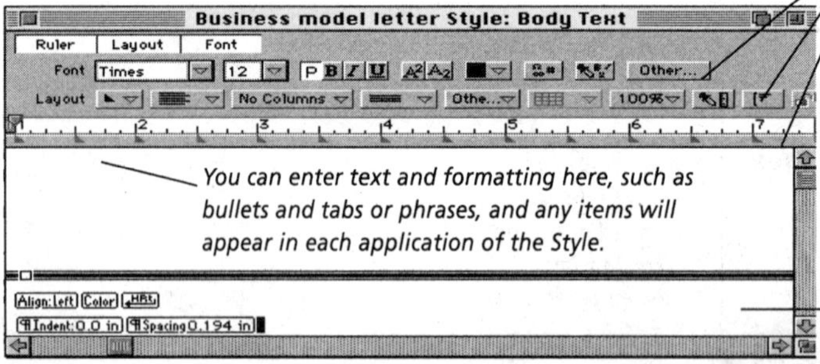

Figure 8: Use the Style window to make changes to a Style.

Tip

You can use the Font, Size, and Style menus on the Style window's Menu bar to make changes to your Style. You can also use the Character Format dialog box accessed using the **Other** button on the Font bar to make changes. (*See Chapter 4: "Formatting" for a description of how to use this dialog box.*) Remember to click the **Other** button of the Style window's Font bar and not the Other button on the Styles toolbar of the Document Editor window.

The Style window opens an auxiliary codes window showing the codes that make up the Style. When you change the Style the new codes are added to the right side of the line of codes, supplanting existing codes. Although WordPerfect does not delete older codes when you change a Style, only the newest code listed last in the window applies to the text of the selected paragraph and all other text that follows (until WordPerfect meets a new Style code set).

Shortcuts

Shift F10

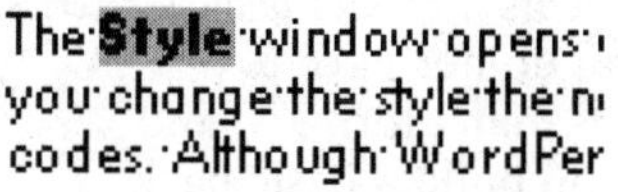

Figure 9: Use the toolbars, menus, and Ruler to change the format of selected text. In this case a Style called "Tip Box" has been altered to include bold-faced text.

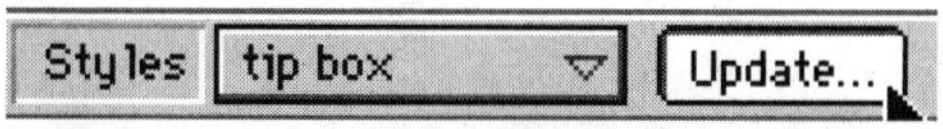

Figure 10: Click the **Update** button on the Styles toolbar. Update changes text and then lets the text become the contents of an existing Style.

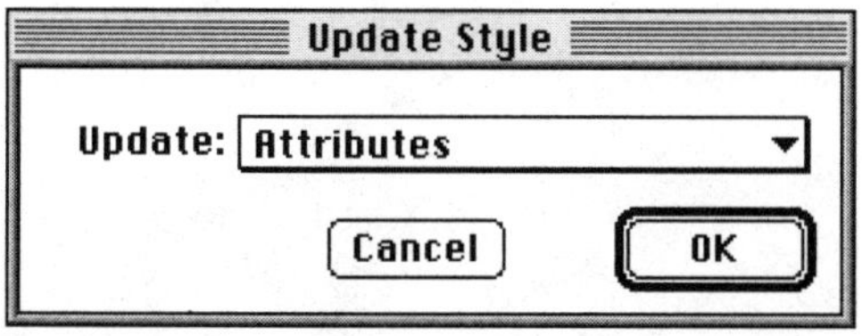

Figure 11: Select which formatting to retain with the updated Style from the **Update** pop-up menu.

To update an existing Style:

1. Select the text that uses the Style you want to edit, or place your insertion point in a paragraph containing the Style.
2. Edit the selected text using the Layout and Font toolbars, Ruler and/or appropriate menu commands (**Figure 9**).
3. Click the Update button on the Styles toolbar (**Figure 10**).
4. In the resulting Update Style dialog box, pull down the Update pop-up menu and select whether you want to preserve the attributes, formats, or both in the updated Style (**Figure 11**).
5. Click OK.

Tip

When you update a Style, any text formatted with that Style also changes to reflect your edit. If there is text you do not want updated, create a new Style for that text containing the older formatting options before performing the update on the original Style.

Making Styles More Efficient

WordPerfect provides two ways to increase the efficiency of your work with Styles: linking, and basing one Style on another.

- **Linking automatically moves from one Style to another.** WordPerfect applies Styles as open-ended changes of state. Thus, when you apply a Style, the whole rest of your document is changed to that Style's formatting (until it hits another Style). One way around this problem is to link Styles together so that one flows automatically to another with the pressing of your Enter key on the numeric keypad of an extended keyboard. Another benefit of this process is that you do not have to pull down menus to change styles if you regularly switch from one Style to another. For example, in this book the tasks are always headlined using a Subhead 2 Style and the steps themselves always use a Style called "Steps." The Styles are set up so that when I am in Subhead 2 Style and hit the Enter key, the next Style is automatically Steps.
- **Basing one Style on another provides a shortcut to Style design.** When one Style is only subtly different from another, then the easiest way to make a new style is to use the formatting options of the more complicated Style as its basis. This has two benefits: first, using another Style as a model is easier to do since you do not have to remember as many formats; and second, if you build a basic backbone Style for the document and base all other Styles on that base Style, if you decide to change the document you only have to change the base to change the rest of the Styles.

Figure 12: Click the Options button to display the Style Options dialog box...

Shortcuts

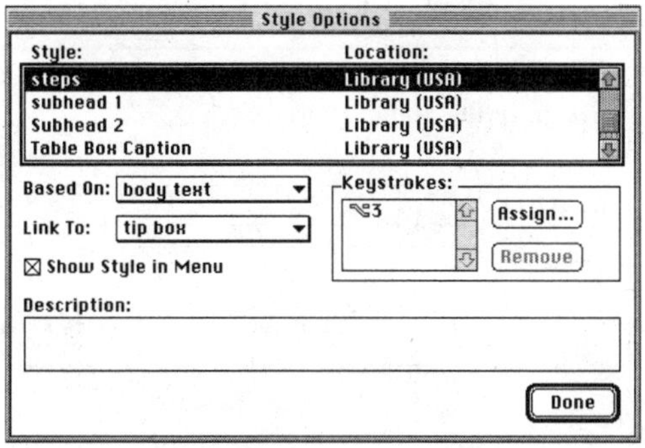

Figure 13: ...and select the first Style name you want to link to from the List box.

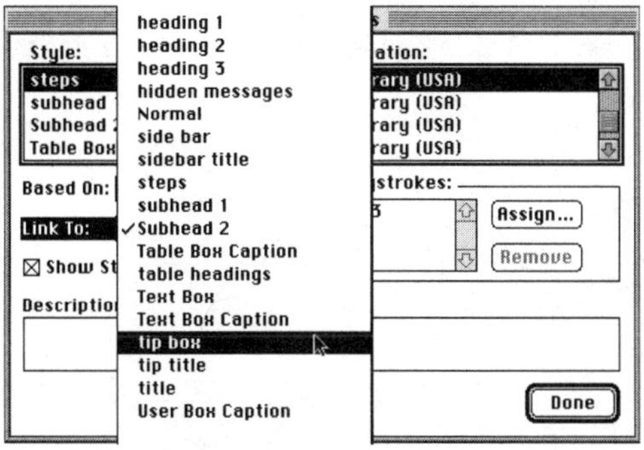

Figure 14: Select a Style to link to from the **Link To** pop-up menu.

To link together Styles:

1. Press the Options button on the Styles toolbar (**Figure 12**).
2. In the resulting Style Options dialog box (**Figure 13**), select the Style you want to apply first from the list box.
3. Pull down the Link To pop-up menu and select the Style you want to come next (**Figure 14**).
4. Click Done.

Tip

Remember to press the Enter key on the numeric keypad of an extended keyboard and not the Return key to go to the next Style. If you do not have an extended keyboard, use the Assign button on the Style dialog box to assign a keyboard shortcut and use that keystroke combination to go to the next Style. See the next task for a description of how to assign keyboard shortcuts.

To assign a keyboard shortcut to a Style:

1. Open the Style Options dialog box by clicking the **Options** button on the Styles toolbar.
2. In the Style Options dialog box (see **Figure 13**), click the **Assign** button.
3. In the resulting Assign Keystroke dialog box (**Figure 15**), keystrokes you type on the keyboard are displayed in the **Keystroke** text box.
4. *Warning:* If the keystroke is already assigned to another command in WordPerfect, that function is displayed in the Assigned text box. If you click the Assign button, your new assignment overrides the previous use of the keystroke combination.

   If you do not want to replace the assigned function, type another keystroke combination until you find one that is either not assigned or worth reassigning.
5. If you are satisfied with the shortcut, click **Assign**.

Tip

You can assign more than one keyboard shortcut to a command or Style. Each shortcut is displayed in the Assign list box on the Style Options dialog box. If you want to delete a shortcut, select it in the list box and click the Remove button.

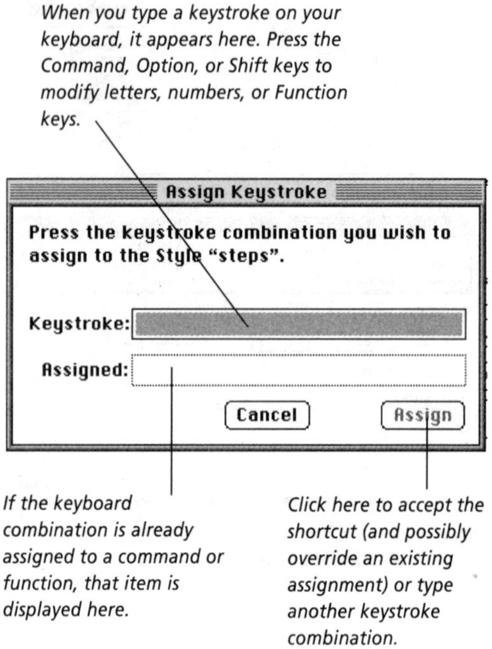

Figure 15: Type a keystroke combination to assign a shortcut to a Style.

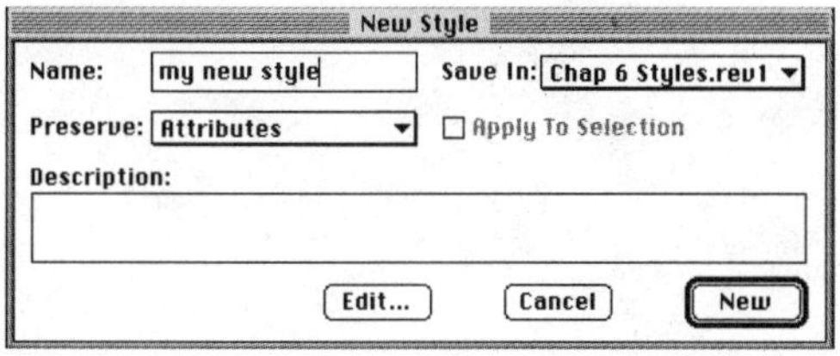

Figure 16: Create a new style using the New Style dialog box.

Figure 17: Select the new Style's name from the Style Option dialog box's list box.

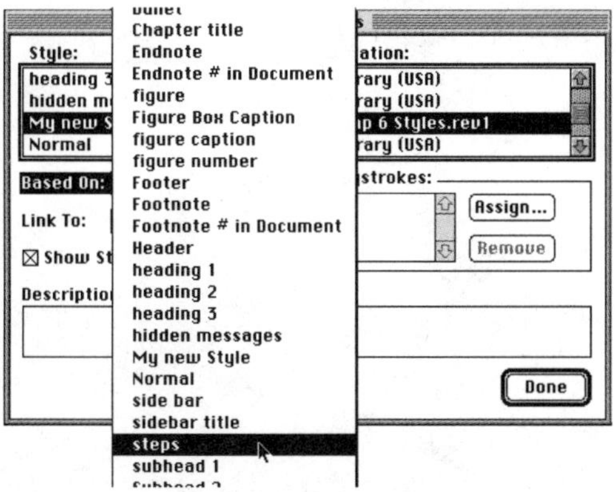

Figure 18: Select the Style you want to base the new Style upon from the **Based On** pop-up menu. You can then close the dialog box and edit the new Style using the editing tools available in the **Style** window.

To base one Style on another Style:

1. Create a new style following the procedures described above (**Figure 16**), but **do not** edit the Style.
2. Open the Style Options dialog box by clicking the **Options** button on the Styles toolbar.
3. In the resulting Style Options dialog box, select the new Style's name from the list box (**Figure 17**).
4. Select a style name upon which you want to base the formatting of the new style from the **Based On** pop-up menu (**Figure 18**).
5. Click **Done**.
6. Select the new style from the **Styles** pop-up menu.
7. Click the **Edit** button on the Styles toolbar to open a Styles window for that style.
8. Add any additional formatting to the style using the Style window's toolbars and Ruler.
9. When you are done, close the window by clicking its close box.

Tip

Any formats you add to the new style takes precedence over any conflicting format (for example a bold versus plain text) set up in the style you based the new style upon.

PRINTING 7

WORDPERFECT IS one of the few programs that support all of the new printing features of QuickDraw GX. With this System 7.5 enhancement installed, you can print different paper formats for each page of your document, print watermarks and other underlying graphics directly from your desktop, specify desktop printers, create customized page layouts, print envelopes from the desktop, and generally ease your printing efforts enormously.

Even without QuickDraw GX installed (and it does take up more than 6MB of hard disk room and 2MB of memory in addition to the 4 to 8MB your System needs), printing is very easy on the Mac.

There are three steps to printing using either standard QuickDraw or QuickDraw GX:

- Selecting a printer from the Chooser. (*Hint:* with QuickDraw GX installed, you only use the Chooser to create new desktop printers.)
- Setting up your document for printing using Page Setup.
- Printing using the Print command.

Each of these steps are described in the following pages.

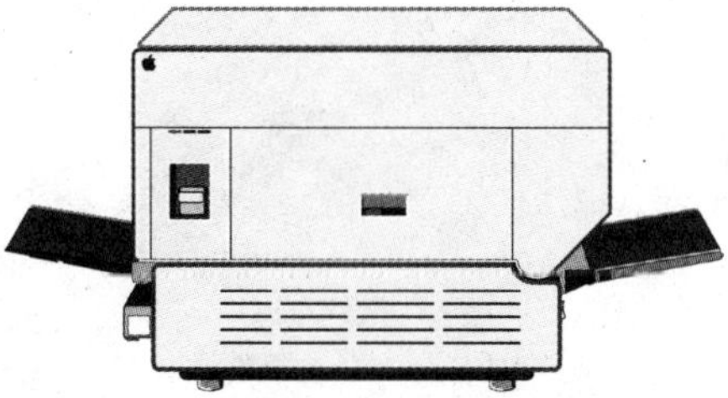

WordPerfect provides many printing options to enhance the quality of your output.

Standard Printing Processes Explained

The Mac makes printing easy by providing consistent printing dialog boxes across application programs. This standardization is accomplished by having each program call on centralized printer driver software for specifications on how documents from that application should behave during printing. Printer drivers are provided by the printer manufacturers and reside in the Extensions folder in the Systems folder.

WordPerfect, like all well-behaved programs, calls on the printer driver you selected from the Chooser to display dialog boxes for page setup and printing.

Most people print today on either a PostScript laser printer, a QuickDraw laser printer, or on an inkjet printer. Apple provides the LaserWriter 8.2 printer driver for PostScript laser printing with System 7.5, and Adobe provides PSPrint 8.2.1 for most other non-Apple Postscript printers. System 7.5 also supplies the LaserWriter Select 300 printer driver for QuickDraw laser printing, and the StyleWriter II 7.5 printer driver for inkjet printing. If you use another vendor's printer, the vendor should supply a driver along with the hardware, although Apple's drivers do support most third-party printers.

One more word about printing. System 7 introduced an additional complication to PostScript printing, the Printer Definition Document (PDD). Every PostScript printer driver is attached to a PDD that provides additional instructions on how the specified printer uses paper trays, idles, and other specific printer options. Luckily, Apple's LaserWriter 8.2 driver automatically find the correct PDDs when you select the LaserWriter 8 printer driver's icon in the Chooser. But if you have trouble printing, use the Create button on the Chooser to manually define a PDD for the selected driver.

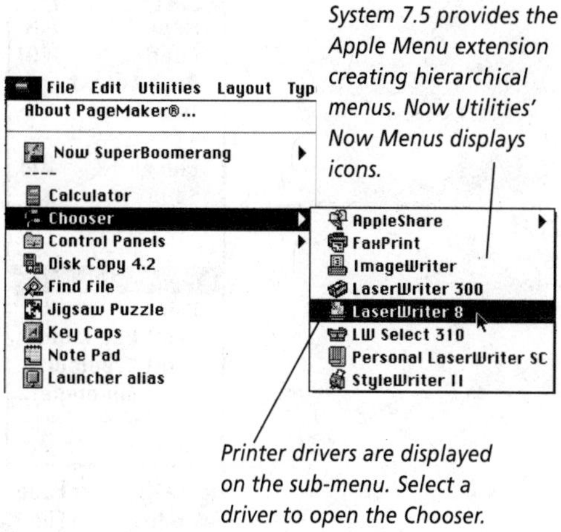

Figure 1: Pull down the Apple menu and select the **Chooser** (or a driver from its sub-menu, if available)...

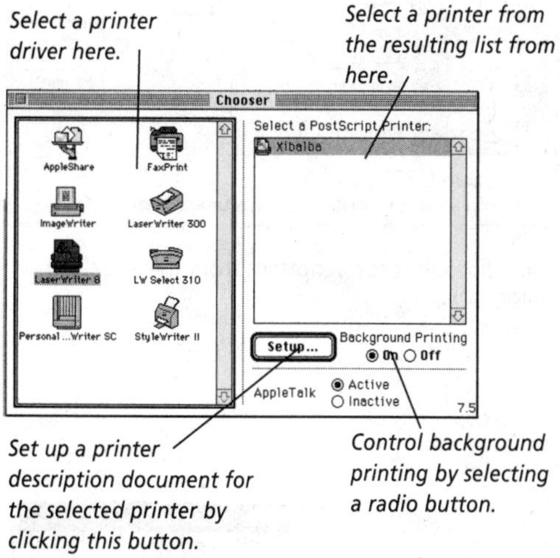

Figure 2: ...and select a printer driver and printer from the Chooser window.

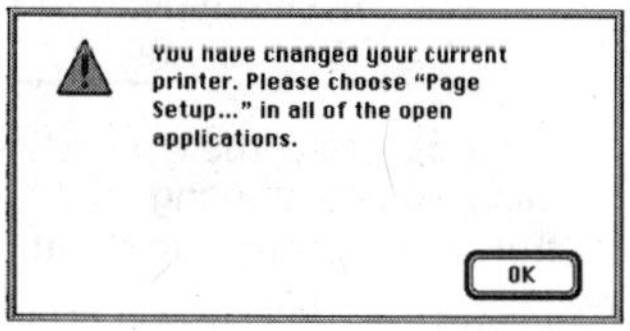

Figure 3: When you close the Chooser after selecting a new printer, the Mac displays this alert box.

To select a printer:

Hint: If you use one printer all of the time, you only have to set up the printer with the Chooser the first time you print after installing WordPerfect or when you change the System folder (by adding fonts, extensions, and so forth). In addition, the LaserWriter 8.2 printer driver is self-configuring and only has to be selected a single time.

1. Turn on your printer. Pull down the Apple menu and select the Chooser (**Figure 1**).
2. In the Chooser window (**Figure 2**), click a printer driver in the left-hand list box.
3. Click the name of the printer in the right-hand list box. Printer names are displayed only for their associated drivers. If no name appears, wait until your printer has initialized and try Steps 2 and 3 again.
4. *Optional:* If you are running WordPerfect on a multiple-zone network, you can select a printer from another AppleTalk zone by selecting the zone's name from the AppleTalk Zone list box.
5. Click the close box on the Chooser.
6. The Mac displays an alert box (**Figure 3**) with a reminder to use Page Setup after changing the printer driver. Click OK.

Tip

If you are running low on memory, turn off background printing by clicking the **Off** radio button in the Chooser. When printing in the foreground you cannot work until the print job is complete. Printing in the foreground does take less memory, since nothing is queued to the PrintMonitor.

Setting Up Your Document

The Page Setup command is used to select paper size, page orientation, the location and size of your print image (such as is used for magazine layouts and other bleeding-edge documents), and special effects (such as inverted or flipped images).

To set up your document for printing:

1. Pull down the File menu and select Page Setup (**Figure 4**).
2. In the resulting Page Setup dialog box (**Figure 5a**), select your paper type (**Figure 5b**), the number of images you want to print on the page, paper orientation, print scale, whether you want to include a binding width (*see Chapter 4: "Formatting," for a description of this option*), and whether you want to print with fractional character widths.

   Note: Selecting fractional character widths makes your text difficult to read on the screen because the monitor displays only 72 dots-per-inch which is not precise enough to display actual font proportions. However, the PostScript printer can determine the actual proportions of each character in fractions of a pixel and there for can accurately print fractional-width fonts.
3. Click OK.

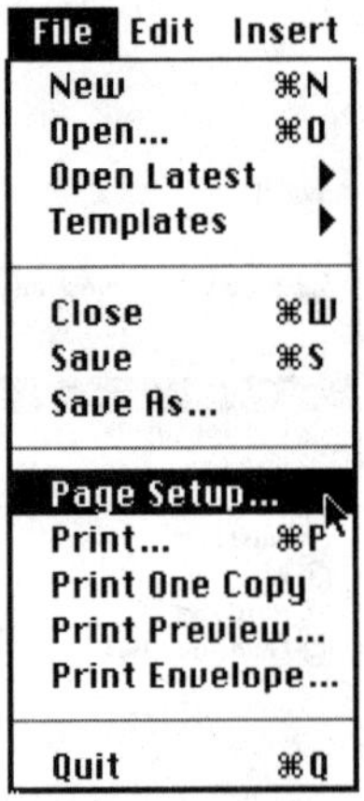

Figure 4: Select **Page Setup** from the File menu.

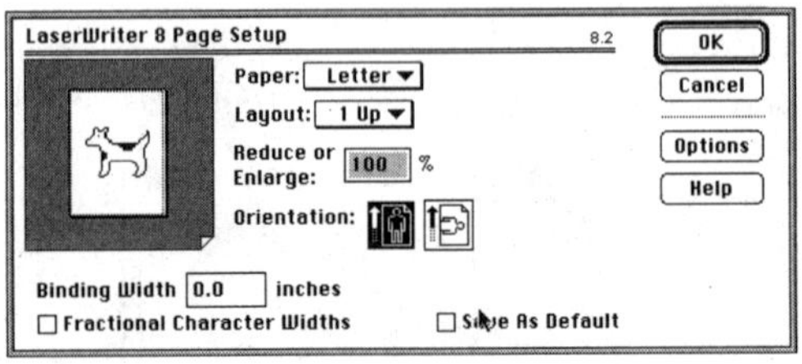

Figure 5a: Select setup options from the Page Setup dialog box.

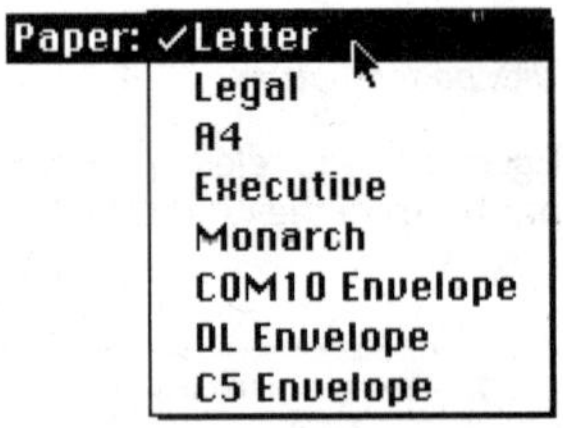

Figure 5b: Select the type of paper you are printing on from the **Paper** pop-up menu.

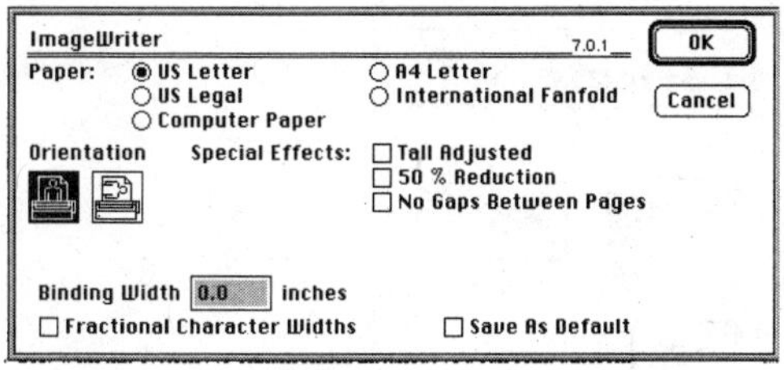

Figure 6: When you select the ImageWriter printer driver, you can set up printing for a dot-matrix printer.

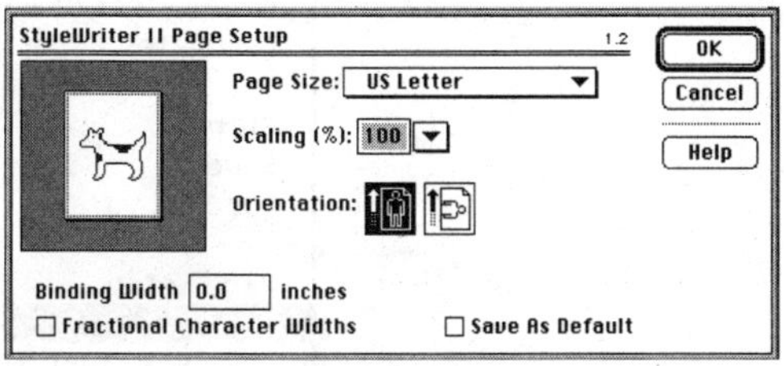

Figure 7: When you select the StyleWriter II printer driver, you can set up printing for an inkjet printer.

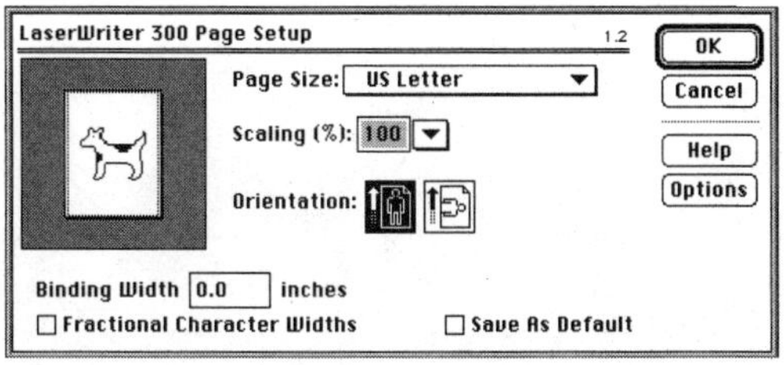

Figure 8: When you select the LaserWriter 300, printer driver you can set up printing for a QuickDraw laser printer.

Tip

If you select a different printer driver from the Chooser (see the first task for a description of how to select printers), your Page Setup dialog box will appear slightly different. Each driver provides its own Page Setup and Print dialog boxes containing those options supported by that printer. **Figure 6** displays the Page Setup dialog box for an ImageWriter dot-matrix printer. **Figure 7** displays the Page Setup dialog box for a StyleWriter II ink jet printer. **Figure 8** displays the Page Setup dialog box for a QuickDraw laser printer (the LaserWriter 300).

Printing Your Document

The Mac provides two methods to print documents:

- **From the Desktop:** Use the Print command from the File menu.
- **From within WordPerfect:** Print a single copy or use the print options from the Print dialog box. In addition, use the Open dialog box's File menu to print an unopened WordPerfect document.

Both of these printing methods are described in the following paragraphs.

To print a document with printing options:

1. Pull down the File menu and select Print (**Figure 9**).
2. In the resulting Printing dialog box (**Figure 10**), select the printing options you want to use from the radio buttons and check boxes.
3. Click Print.

Shortcuts

Figure 9: Select **Print** from the File menu.

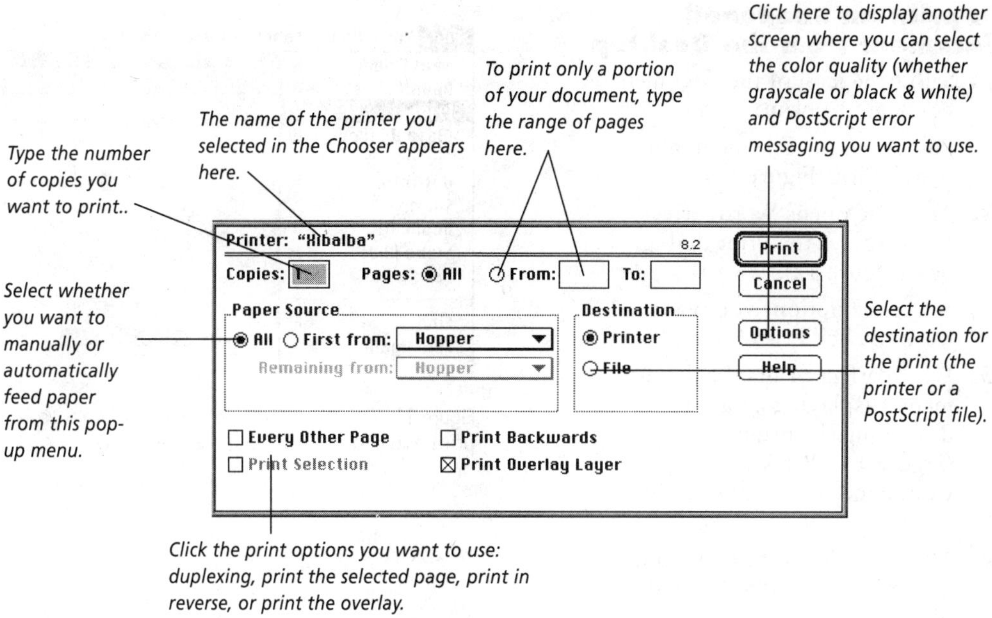

Figure 10: The LaserWriter 8 Print dialog box provides the same options as the QuickDraw GX Laser Writer version (see **Figures 21a – f**), only with less precision.

Using the Print Dialog Box

Select the check boxes, buttons, and radio buttons that meet your needs:

- Select the **From** and **To** radio buttons and type a range of pages to print.
- Select from the **Paper Source** area's options to pick the source of the paper.
- Click the **Options** button to choose whether you want a faster, less memory-intensive printing process using black and white, or a high-quality, but slower response time printing process, by using the color/grayscale options.
- Use WordPerfect's added options to print on both sides of the paper (called duplexing), print the order of the document from the last page to the first, or print only selected text.
- You can also select the destination of the print file (the file created by the PostScript processor). You can send the file to the printer or you can store it on your hard disk (this is called a PostScript file) for printing on a remote imagesetter or other type of printer.

To print an unopened document from the Desktop:

1. Select the icon of the document you want to print.
2. Pull down the File menu and select Print (**Figure 11**).
3. The Mac opens WordPerfect and displays the Print dialog box (**Figure 12**).
4. Select the options you want to use and click Print.
5. WordPerfect prints the document, displaying an alert box describing the print status (**Figure 13**). Press Command+.(period) to abort the print.
6. The Mac closes the program, and then returns to the Desktop.

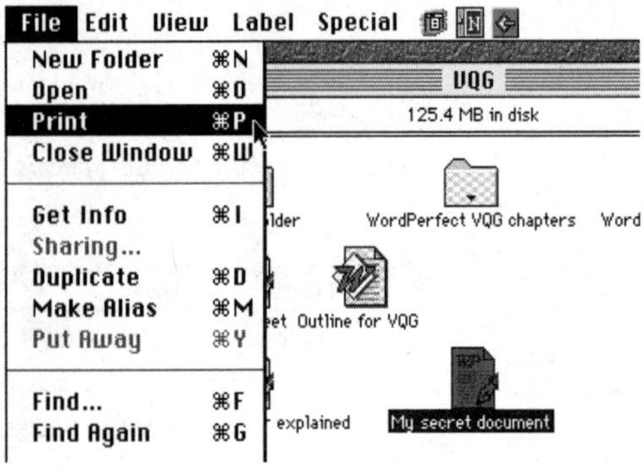

Figure 11: Select the document icon you want to print and choose **Print** from the File menu.

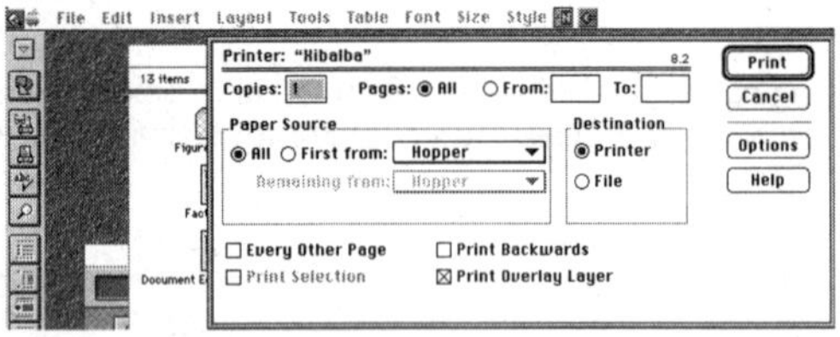

Figure 12: The Mac opens the document and displays the Print dialog box. Select the print options you want to use and click **Print**.

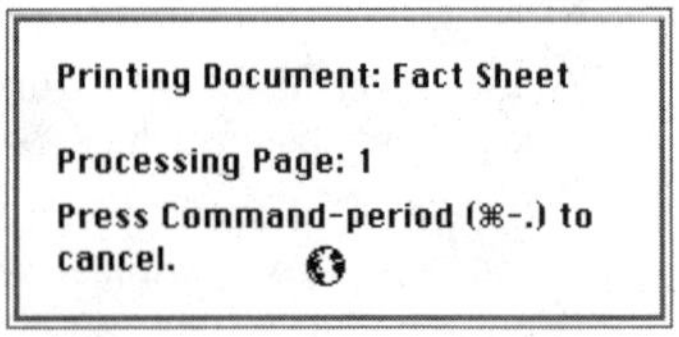

Figure 13: The Mac displays an alert box describing the status of your print job. Press Command+. to cancel.

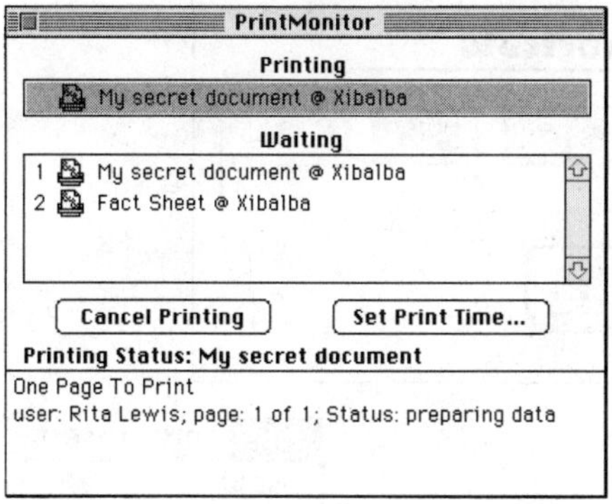

Figure 14: Use the PrintMonitor to control the priority of print jobs.

WordPerfect's menu bar provides shortcuts to commonly performed file management tasks.

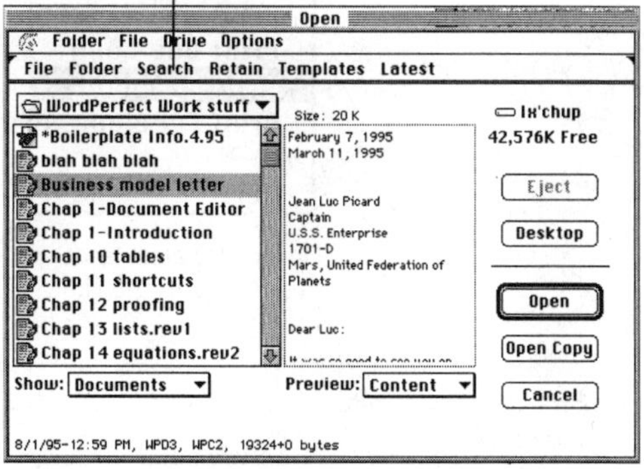

Figure 15a: Choose **Open** from the File menu to display the Open dialog box.

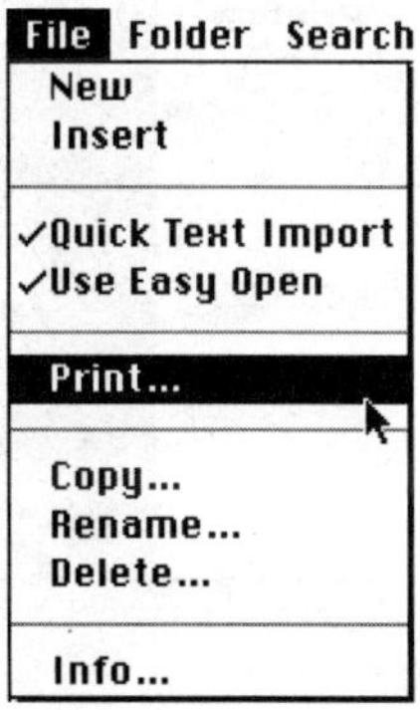

Figure 15b: Select a document from the Directory list box and choose **Print** from the Open dialog box's File menu.

> **Tip**
>
> To view the print queue and the status of your print job, pull down the Application menu and select **Print Monitor**. The PrintMonitor **(Figure 14)** manages print spooling when you have **Background Printing** selected in the Chooser. *See your System 7.5 manual for a discussion of how to use the PrintMonitor.*

To print an unopened document from within WordPerfect:

1. Pull down the File menu and select Open. *See Chapter 1: "Introduction" for a description of how to open an existing document from within WordPerfect.*
2. In the resulting Open dialog box (**Figure 15a**), select a document to print from the Directory list box and Title bar pop-up menu.
3. Pull down the Open dialog box's File menu and select Print (**Figure 15b**).
4. WordPerfect opens the document you selected and displays the Print dialog box (see **Figure 12**). Select the options you want to use.
5. Click Print.

Using the Print Preview Window

WordPerfect provides the Print Preview window (**Figure 17**) to let you see an exact version of what your document will look like when it is printed. You cannot edit the document in Print Preview mode. You can do four things in Print Preview:

- Scroll through your document one page at a time to ensure that the text is placed on the page exactly where you want it.
- View side-by-side pages to judge their aesthetics.
- Open the Page Setup dialog box to change the setup options for the document.
- Print the document.

To open the Print Preview window:

1. Pull down the File menu and select Print Preview (**Figure 16**).
2. WordPerfect displays the Print Preview window (**Figure 17**).
3. Click the close box to return to the Document Editor window.

Shortcuts

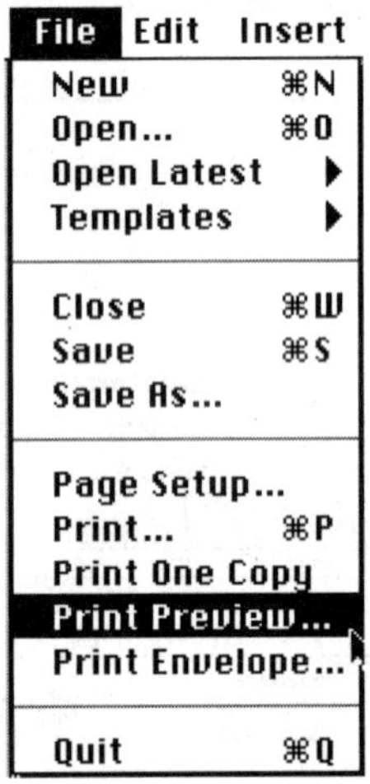

Figure 16: Select Print Preview from the File menu.

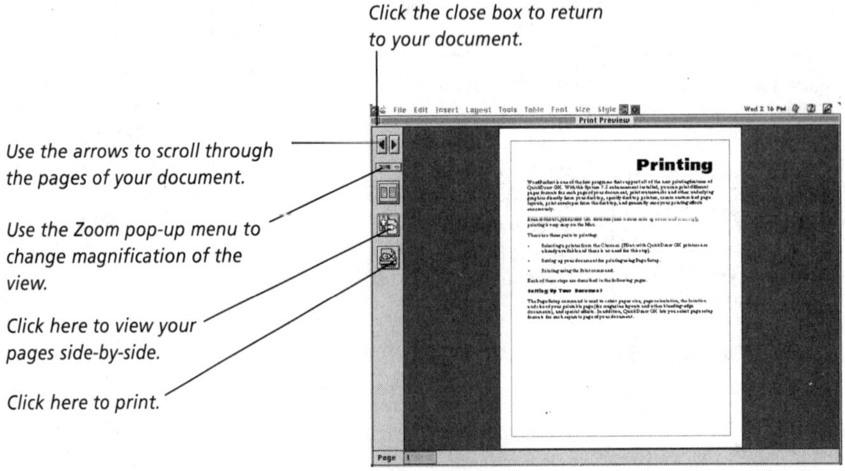

Figure 17: The Print Preview window.

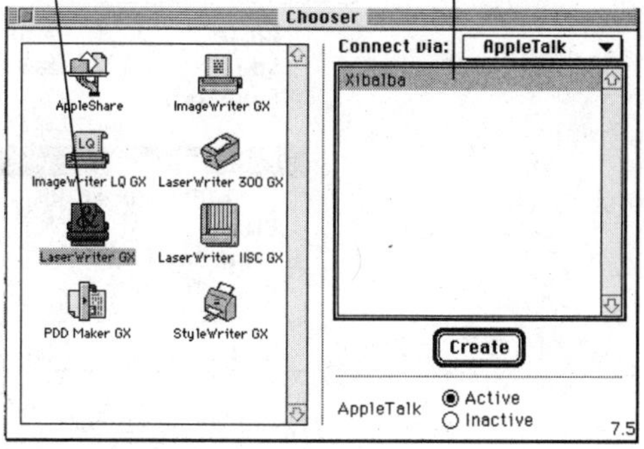

Figure 18: Create a desktop printer by selecting a driver and a printer, then clicking the **Create** button.

Figure 19: Use the Desktop Printer to print documents or set up a document for printing on multiple printers.

Using QuickDraw GX

System 7.5 introduced the advanced features of *QuickDraw GX*, an updated screen definition language. Among the many subtle enhancements of this upgrade to the Mac's desktop graphics program are new ways to set up pages and print documents. WordPerfect is one of the first programs that support QuickDraw GX.

The following pages describe setting up your document and printing under QuickDraw GX.

To create a desktop printer:

QuickDraw GX handles printer drivers slightly differently than the way you worked under standard QuickDraw. QuickDraw GX creates a desktop printer for every printer driver you select in the Chooser. You only have to create desktop printers the first time you print under QuickDraw GX, or if you install a new printer or require the use of an outside service bureau's printer.

1. Pull down the Apple menu and select the Chooser.
2. In the resulting Chooser window (**Figure 18**), select the printer driver for the printer you want to use from the left-hand list box.
3. Select the printer you want to use from the resulting printer list on the right side of the window.
4. Click Create.
5. The Mac generates a desktop printer for your selection (**Figure 19**).

Setting Up Your Document Under QuickDraw GX

Page setup under QuickDraw GX operates exactly like standard page setups, except that QuickDraw GX provides enhanced printing extensions. In addition, you can select page setup formats for each separate page of your document.

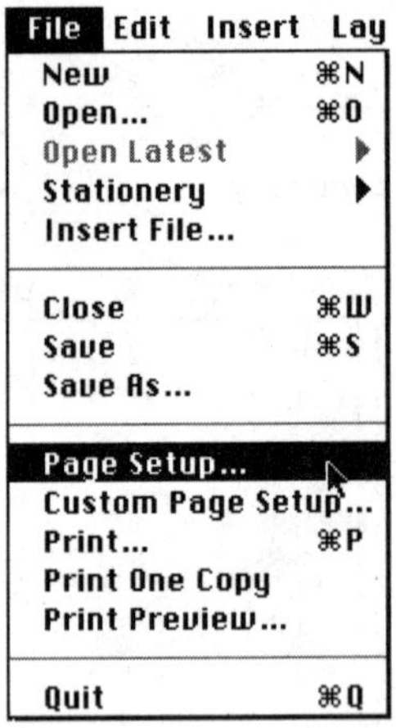

Figure 20: Select **Page Setup** from the File menu.

To set up your document for printing:

1. Pull down the File menu and select Page Setup (**Figure 20**).
2. In the resulting Page Setup dialog box (**Figure 21a**), select your paper type (**Figure 21b**), orientation, and scale.
3. Click Format.

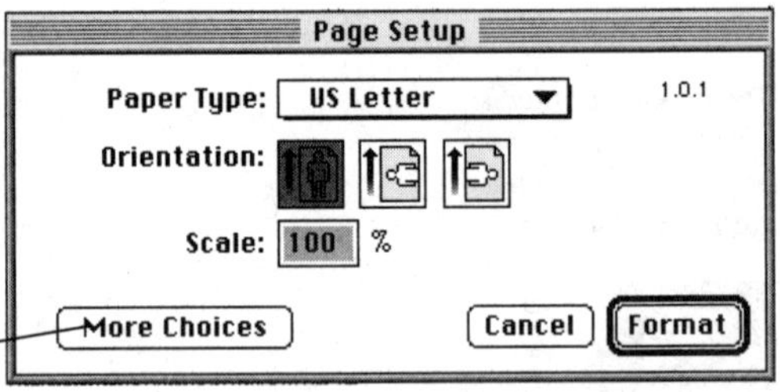

Click here to display the extended Page Setup dialog box's scrolling extensions list.

Figure 21a: Use the standard "Fewer Choices" Page Setup option to set page layout options for simple print jobs. Click More Choices to display the extended array of page setup options.

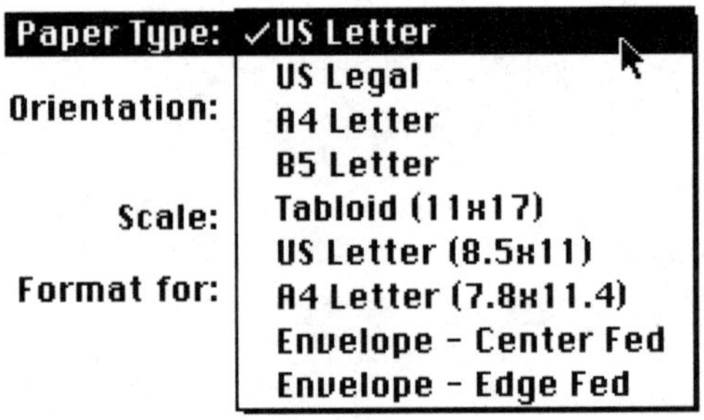

Figure 21b: Use the **Paper Type** pop-up menu to select the type of paper you are printing on.

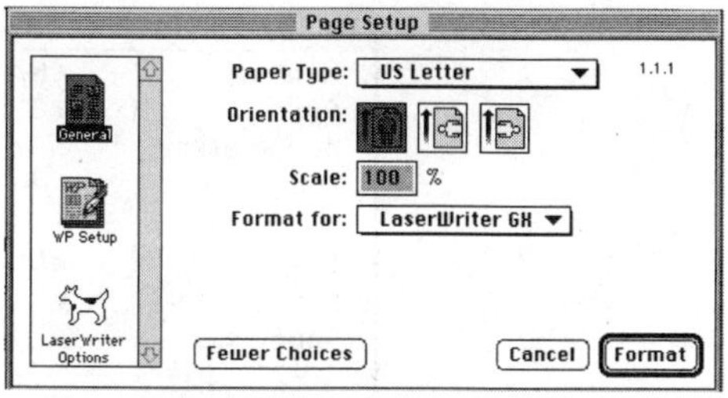

Figure 21c: The extended Page Setup General window lets you select multiple printers for a single document.

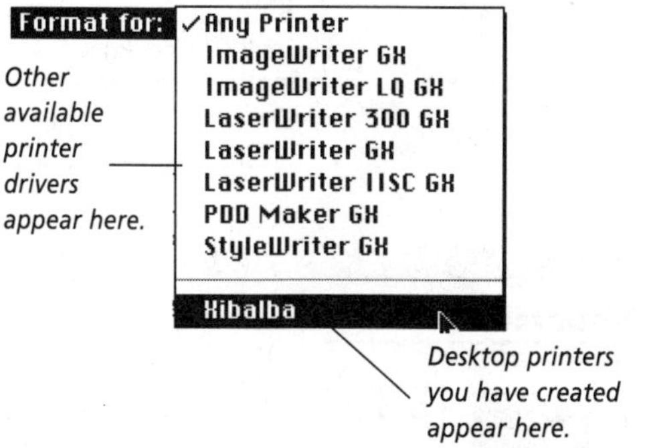

Figure 21d: Use the **Format For** pop-up menu on the extended General Page Setup window to select the printers you want to use to print. (For example, you can pick the StyleWriter as your proof printer, the ImageWriter as your draft printer, and the LaserWriter as your final printer by selecting Page Setup multiple times.)

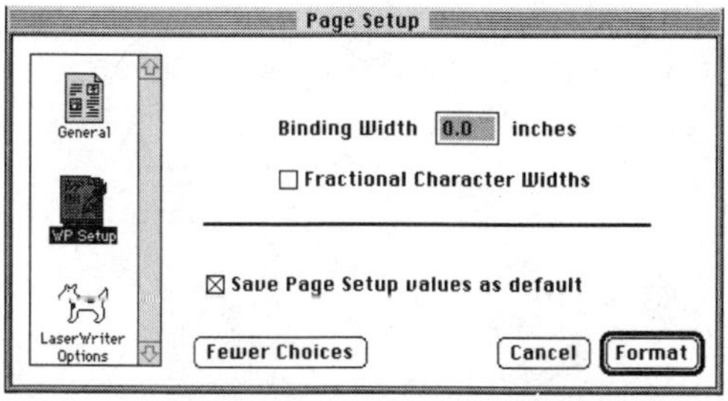

Figure 21e: Use the WordPerfect setup window to add specific printer effects to WordPerfect.

Tip

QuickDraw GX provides the ability to add printer extensions that enhance your printing environment. Apple includes a few extensions with the program, but third-party vendors are developing more, for example, the ability to add watermarks or custom backgrounds to printed materials, to do color separations, and so forth.

To access these extensions, click the **More Choices** button on the Page Setup dialog box. The resulting dialog box (**Figure 21c**) offers specific page setup options in a scrolling list, one for each extension.

The **General** extension adds the ability to choose a printer definition document under the **Format For** pop-up menu (**Figure 21d**). Change your printer description if you want to send a proof copy to one printer (such as a 300 dots per inch (dpi) PostScript laser printer) and a final version to another printer (such as a 2400 dpi Linotronic imagesetter). QuickDraw GX lets you select multiple printers for a single document and remembers which is which.

WordPerfect adds an extension (**Figure 21e**) that provides the options displayed directly on the LaserWriter 8's Page Setup dialog box, namely the ability to add a binding width (*see Chapter 5: "More Formatting" for a description of binding widths*) to your document's left margin, automatic fractional character printing, and the ability to save your settings as a default printing setup option.

Lastly, Apple provides a "dogcow" extension that offers the ability to create special effects such as inverting or flipping an image (**Figure 21f**).

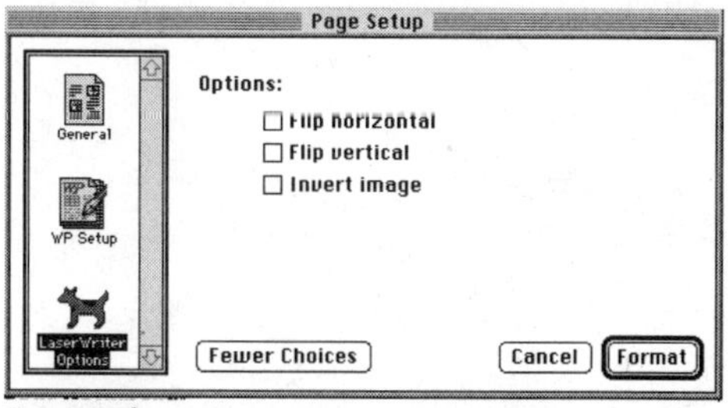

Figure 21f: Use the "dogcow" window to set up special printer effects.

Printing with QuickDraw GX

Printing with QuickDraw GX has been substantially simplified, since you no longer need to use the Chooser to select printers. There are two methods to print:

- **Drag and Drop.** Print a document on the Mac's desktop by dragging its icon on top of a desktop printer.
- **The Print command.** Use WordPerfect's Print command to select printing options.

You can also use the Print command to print from the Desktop and print a single copy of your document from within WordPerfect without going through the Print dialog box. The following paragraphs describe these various printing procedures.

Figure 22: Select **Print** from the File menu.

Shortcuts

To print a document with printing options:

1. Pull down the File menu and select Print (**Figure 22**).
2. In the resulting Print dialog box (**Figure 23**), select a printer from the Print to pop-up menu.
3. *Optional:* Click the From radio button and type a range of pages to print in the text boxes.
4. *Optional:* Type the number of copies to print in the Copies text box. The default number is one copy.
5. Click Print.

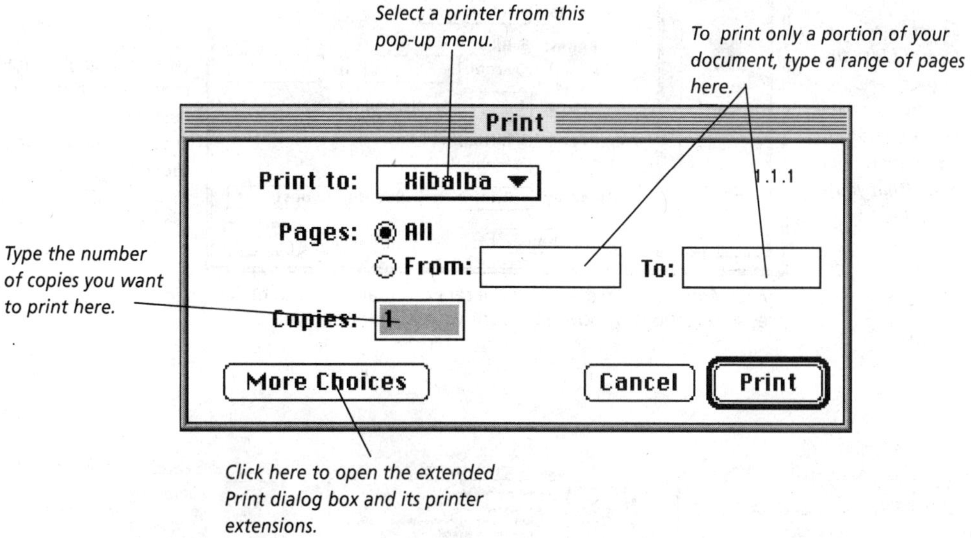

Figure 23: Select the options you want to use to print from the Print dialog box. Use the Easy Print dialog box to print simple documents.

Tip

If you want to further enhance your printed copy, click **More Choices** to display the extended version of the General screen as well as a scrolling list of Printing Extensions. In the extended General screen (**Figure 24a**), you can select what type of paper feed to use (manual or a tray type that is dependent on the printer driver you selected in the Chooser), whether you want to print to the printer or to a PostScript file for external printing at a service bureau (*see the Using a Service Bureau task later in this chapter for a discussion of PDD files*), and whether you want to print a draft or final version (this option is dependent on what levels of print quality your printer supports).

Click the **Print Options** icon in the scrolling list to display additional printing options (**Figure 24b**). Select the appropriate check box to create duplex output (printing every other page for two-sided copies), print only the selected text, print the document in reverse order with the last page first, or deselect the Print Overlay Layer check box to ensure that any graphic overlays you added to your document do not print.

You can set the printing times as well as its priority in a printing queue by clicking the **Print Time** icon (**Figure 24c**).

Select the **N-Up Print** icon (**Figure 24d**) to print thumbnail images of your document or multiple images on a single sheet.

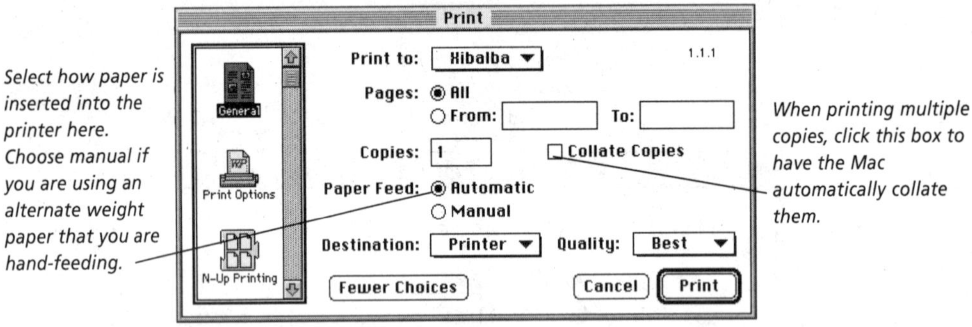

Figure 24a: Use the extended General Print dialog box to make precise selections of how you want your document printed.

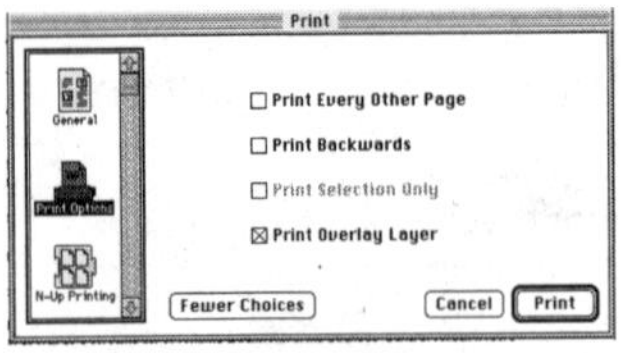

Figure 24b Use the Print Options window to select specialized print quantity options.

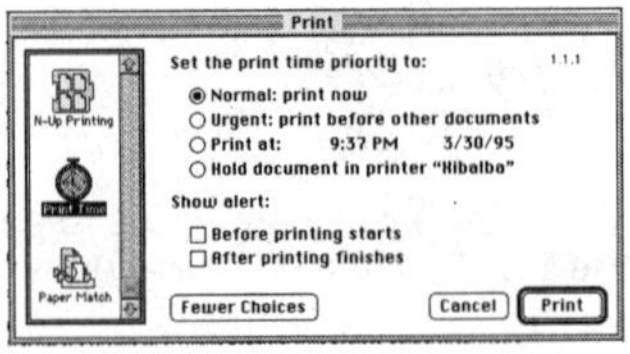

Figure 24c: Use the Print Time window to set printer queuing priorities.

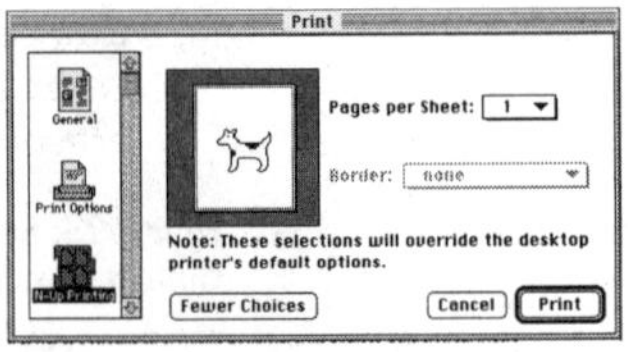

Figure 24d: Use the N-Up window to set how many images you want produced per page.

Figure 25: The LaserWriter desktop printer that I created for "Xibalba."

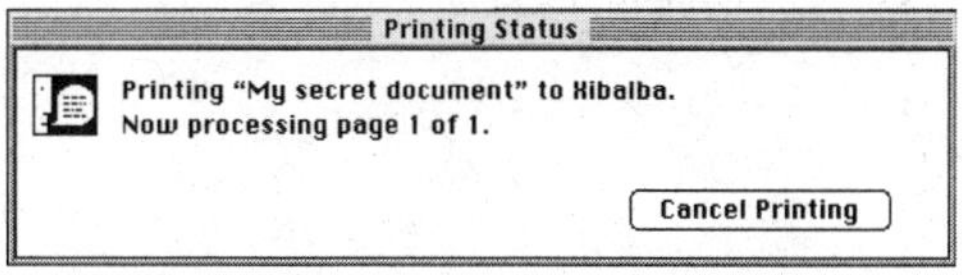

Figure 26: Drag your document's icon on top of the desktop printer's icon, and the Mac displays an alert box informing you about the status of your print job. Click **Cancel Printing** to abort the process.

Figure 27: When the desktop printer completes the preparation portion of the print job, it displays a "document" on its front. Double-click the icon to display the PrinterShare window.

To print an unopened document from the desktop using the GX-generated desktop printer:

Drag the unopened document's icon on top of the desktop printer (**Figure 25**). WordPerfect displays an alert box informing you of the status of your print job (**Figure 26**). When the document is finished processing, the desktop printer's icon changes to indicate that the job is printing (**Figure 27**). You can double-click the desktop printer icon to display the printer status window (**Figure 28**) for that printer.

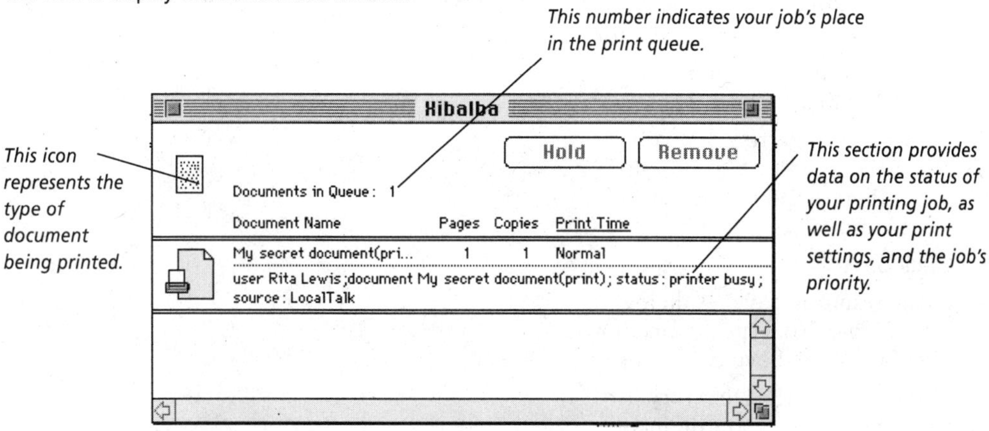

Figure 28: The PrinterShare window displays the status of the print job. Use the window's Print menu to halt, resume, and prioritize your printing jobs.

Working with a Service Bureau

WordPerfect, running under QuickDraw GX, supports the ability to create portable digital documents, versions of your documents that can be read by other people who may not own the WordPerfect program. To read a portable digital document you need a viewer, such as Apple's Simple Text, that supports PDDs. There are several such viewers available. Adobe Acrobat offers a free viewer with newer versions of their Type on Call CD and Common Ground Software (formerly No Hands Software) offers a PDD viewer called Common Ground. PDDs are also useful if you need to print a document off-site and do not want to download numerous fonts, since you can embed the fonts directly in the PDD (although doing this takes up enormous hard disk room making the files unwieldy to transport by disk).

To create a portable digital document:

1. Open the Chooser and create a PDDMaker desktop printer. *(See page 117 for a description of how to create a desktop printer.)*
2. Pull down the File menu and select Print (see **Figure 22**).
3. In the resulting Print dialog box, pull down the Print to pop-up menu (**Figure 29**) in the General screen and select PDD Maker GX.
4. Click Save.
5. In the resulting Save As dialog box (**Figure 30**), type a name for the PDD in the Save as text box.
6. *Optional:* Use the Directory list box and Title bar pop-up menu to change the folder where you want to save the PDD.
7. Click Save.

Figure 29: Select **PDD Maker GX** from the **Print To** pop-up menu on the extended General Print dialog box.

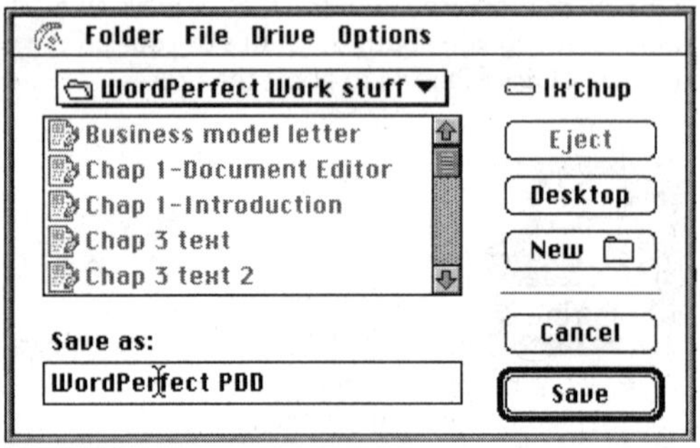

Figure 30: Save the PDD file on your hard disk.

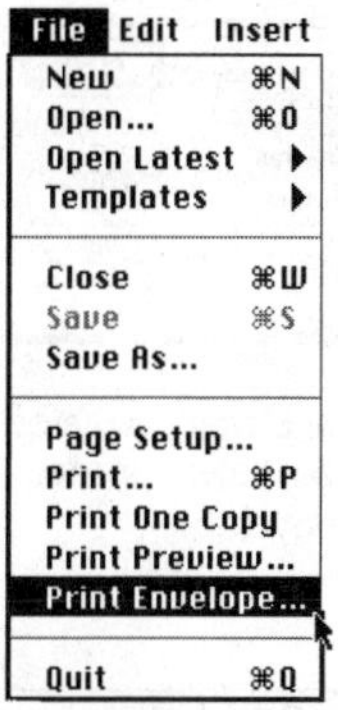

Figure 31: Select the **Print Envelope** command from the File menu.

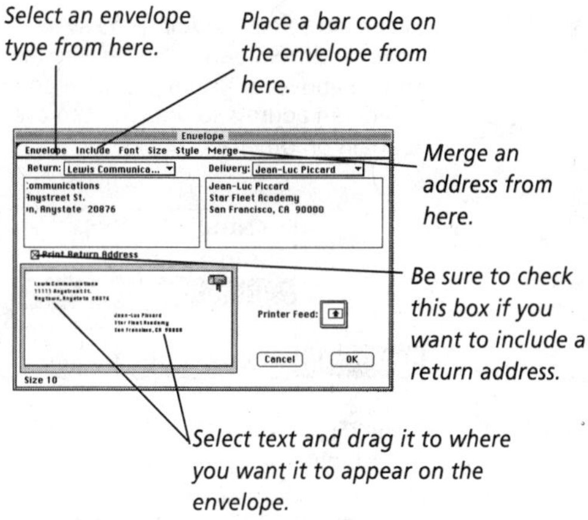

Figure 32a: The Envelope dialog box is used to set up the format and contents of an envelope before printing.

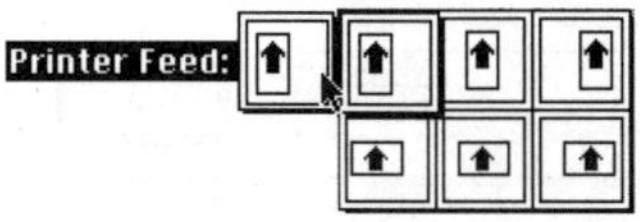

Figure 32b: Select a physical envelope position correlation between the printer and WordPerfect from the **Printer Feed** pop-up menu.

Printing an Envelope

WordPerfect 3.5 introduces the ability to print envelopes directly from your word processor. You can use the Envelope dialog box to select from many standard size envelopes or create your own customized format. You can also use the Print Envelope command to merge data from address data bases, print return addresses, and format both return and delivery addresses to appear as you require.

To print an envelope:

1. Select the Print Envelope command from the File menu (**Figure 31**).
2. In the resulting Envelope dialog box (**Figure 32a**), type a return address in the Return Address area. You can also select an existing address from the Return pop-up menu

   Note: Be sure to click the Print Return Address check box if you want the return address to appear on the envelope.
3. Type a delivery address in the Delivery area or select a delivery address from the Delivery pop-up menu.
4. Everything you place in the Return and Delivery areas is displayed in the Envelope Preview area. Drag the text boxes around the area to place them where you want them to appear.
5. Review the Printer Feed box to ensure that the envelope's position in your printer is reflected in the Envelope dialog box. If you need to select another position, click the Printer Feed box to display its options in a pop-up menu (**Figure 32b**).
6. Click OK.

7. In the resulting Print dialog box (**Figure 33**), select your options as described in the task "To print a document with printing options" on page 115.
8. Click Print.

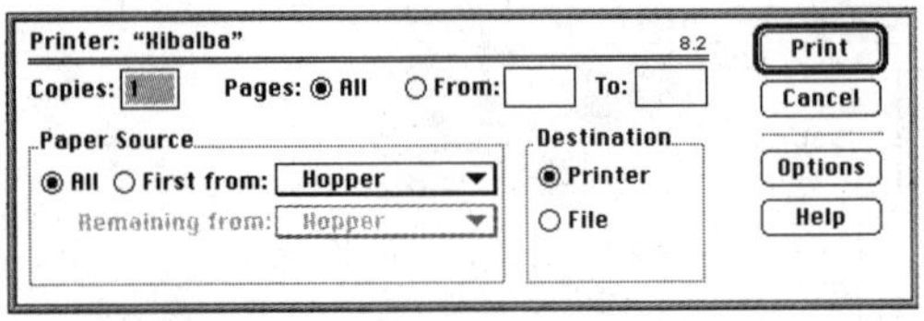

Figure 33: When you click OK on the Envelope dialog box, the Print dialog box is displayed. Select printer options and click **Print** to print the envelope.

To add an address to the Return or Delivery areas of the envelope:

1. Select the Print Envelope command from the File menu (see **Figure 31**).
2. In the resulting Envelope dialog box (see **Figure 32a**), type the address in the Return or Delivery boxes.
3. Pull down the Return or Delivery pop-up menu and select Add To Menu (**Figure 34**). The address' name is added to the bottom of the pop-up menu.

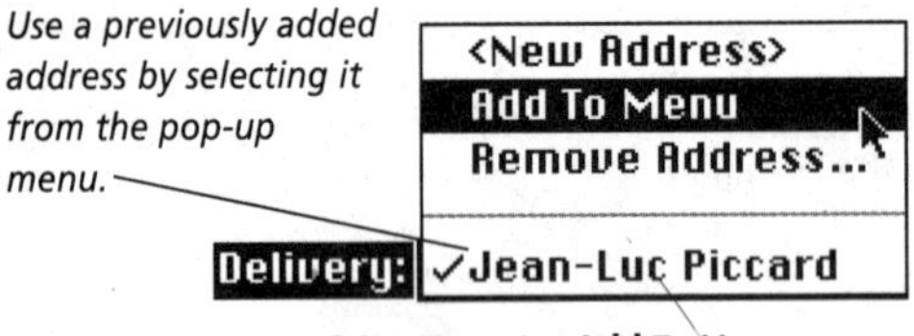

Figure 34: Select the **Add To Menu** command from either the **Delivery** (as shown above) or **Return** pop-up menus to add an address so that you can use it again on other envelopes.

To delete an address from a menu:

1. In the Envelope dialog box (see Figure 32a), select an address from the bottom of the Return or Delivery pop-up menu (see Figure 34).
2. When the address appears in the box, select Remove Address from the pop-up menu (**Figure 35**).
3. In the resulting Remove Address dialog box (**Figure 36**), select the address you want to delete and click Remove. Click the Remove All button to delete all of the previously saved addresses.

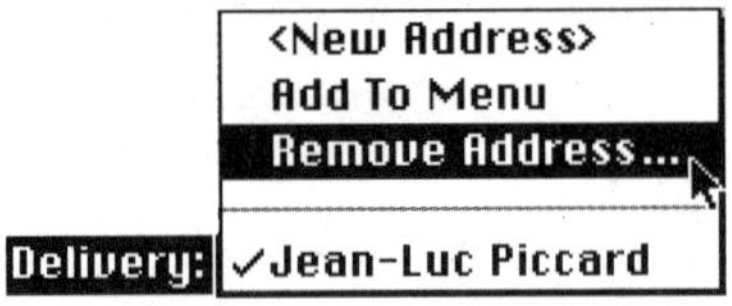

Figure 35: After entering an address by either typing or selecting it from the pop-up menu, you can delete it from the menu by selecting the **Remove Address** command.

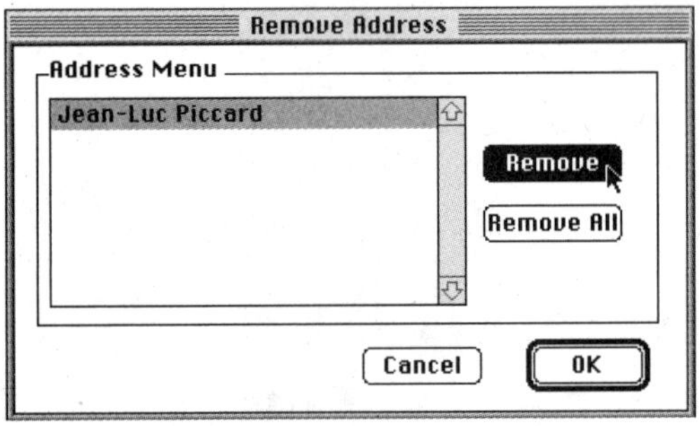

Figure 36: In the resulting Remove Address dialog box, select the address you want to delete, and click **Remove**.

GRAPHICS 8

IN CHAPTER 1: "Introduction," I introduced the three editor windows available in WordPerfect. In this chapter, I discuss how to work in the Graphics Editor window.

Graphics come in several flavors and each can enhance the readability and aesthetics of your documents. WordPerfect lets you draw vector-based graphics like those that are created in other drawing programs, such as Claris' ClarisDraw or Deneba's Canvas. These pictures are based on mathematical algorithms, such as straight lines, squares, rectangles, circles, and polygons. WordPerfect imports painting-type drawings from such applications as MacPaint, Dabbler, SuperPaint, and so forth. You cannot edit such bit-mapped images from within WordPerfect. In addition, you can import PostScript-based art from such programs as Adobe's Illustrator and Macromedia's FreeHand. Although you cannot see them on your screen, they will print on your PostScript printer.

Mini-Glossary

Drawing Object — The graphic components of a drawing. Objects can be manipulated or grouped together to form graphics.

Text Object — Boxes containing text that can be manipulated like a graphic object. For example, you can resize, rotate, and move the box along with its text or edit its textual contents. *See Chapter 9: "Layout" for more information about text boxes.*

Grouped Objects — One or more drawing or text objects that have been locked together so that they can be manipulated as a single unit.

Encapsulated PostScript — Graphics created using the PostScript page description language. *EPS graphics* are actually generated at your PostScript laser printer, and thus cannot be displayed on the screen by WordPerfect, although they can be imported into the program and printed on the laser printer.

How WordPerfect's Graphics Work

Every WordPerfect document is divided into three layers: the document layer, an overlay on top of the text layer, and a watermark underneath the text layer. WordPerfect lets you place your graphics into these three layers with the following effects.

- **Document layer.** Graphics are placed in-line, meaning that they interact directly with text, either anchoring to paragraphs so that the graphics move with their associated text, or anchored on a page where they do not move. Document graphics cause text to wrap around their edges. Use the Graphics command on the Tools menu to work on this layer. The Graphics Editor's document layer is described in this chapter.
- **Overlay layer.** Graphics can be placed on top of the text, much as a transparency is placed on a piece of paper. The graphic does not interact with the text but resides on an independent layer. Use the Overlay command on the Tools menu to work on this layer. *See Chapter 9: "Layout" for information about creating overlays.*
- **Watermark layer.** Graphics can be placed behind your text as a watermark, where it will appear on every page of your document, every other page, or only on specified pages. Use the Watermark command on the Tools menu to work on this layer. *See Chapter 9: "Layout" for information about creating watermarks.*

The Graphics Editor

Figure 1 presents an illustration of the Graphics Editor window. You can open the Graphics Editor by clicking its button on the Button bar, by double-clicking an existing graphic, or by choosing the New Graphic command from the Tools menu.

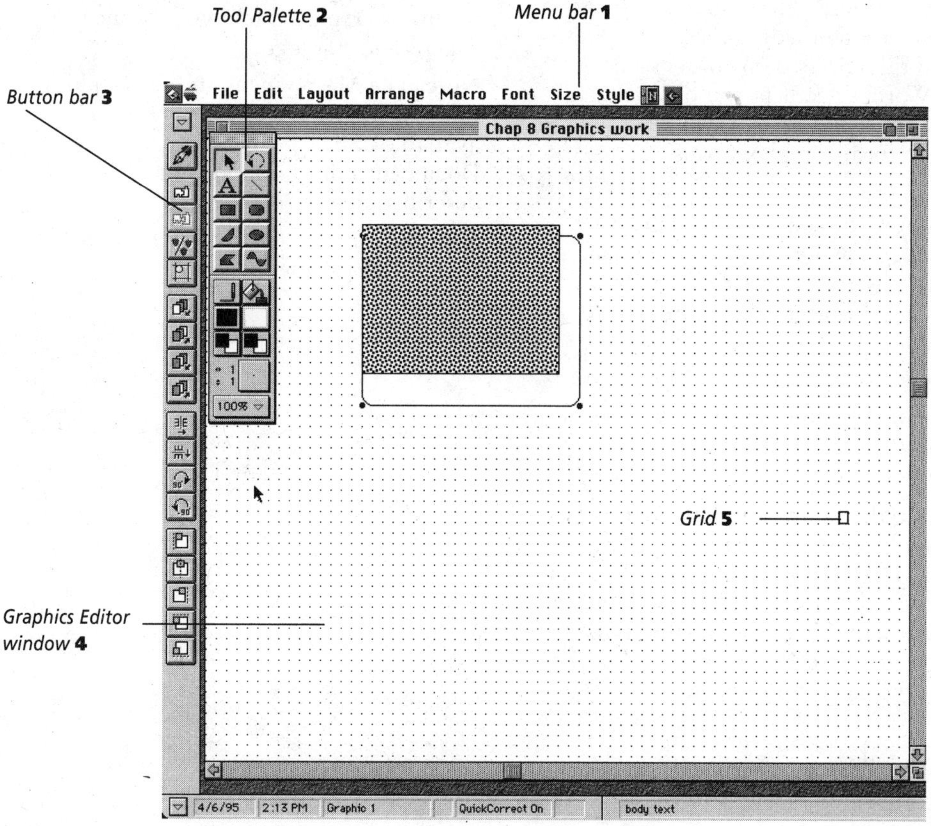

Figure 1: Navigating around the Graphics Editor window.

The Graphics Editor Explained

1 *Menu bar*
The Menu bar contains commands pertaining to the production of graphics in eight menus.

2 *Tool palette*
A vertical toolbar for producing and manipulating graphic objects. The toolbar contains graphic objects such as polygons, squares, rectangles, and lines, as well as tools to fill objects with colors or patterns. WordPerfect lets you draw bézier curves, arc segments that can be easily edited to form complex forms.

3 *Button bar*
The Button bar contains shortcuts to graphics commands such as alignment, bring to the front or move to the back, rotate or flip objects, duplicate, group/ungroup objects, and so forth.

4 *Graphics Editor window*
Use the area within the window to work on your drawings.

5 *Grid*
The Graphics Editor window contains a grid that lets you automatically align objects via a "snap-to" function. You can change the dimensions of the grid and choose whether it automatically snaps by invoking the Grid Snap command in the Layout menu.

Graphics Editor Menus Explained

When you open the Graphics Editor window, WordPerfect replaces the contents of the Document Editor's menus with graphics commands. The following pages describe these menus: the File, Edit, and Layout menus. The Size menu is not altered, the Font and Style menu are slightly changed, and the Tools and Table menus are replaced by two new menus: Macro and Arrange.

Note: The Macro menu in the Graphics Editor window is a pop-up menu also available under the Tools menu in the Document Editor window, and so is not described here.

See Chapter 11: "Shortcuts" for a description of how to use this menu.

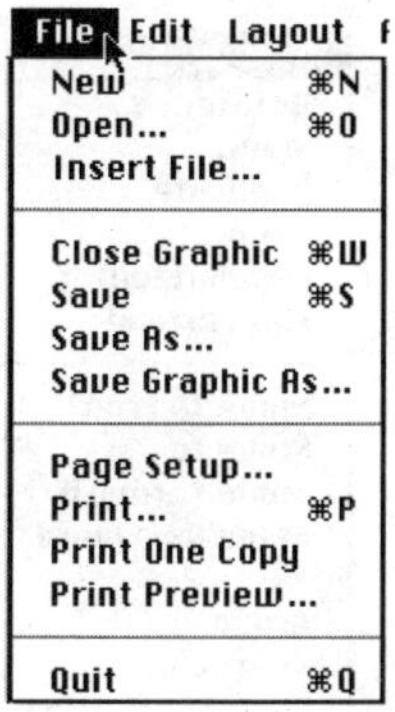

Figure 2: The File menu.

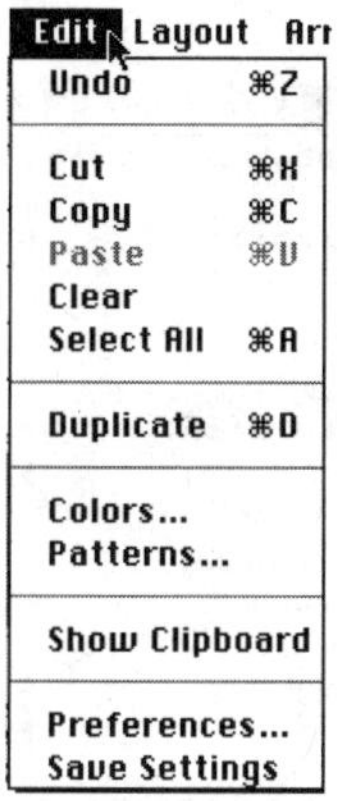

Figure 3: The Edit menu.

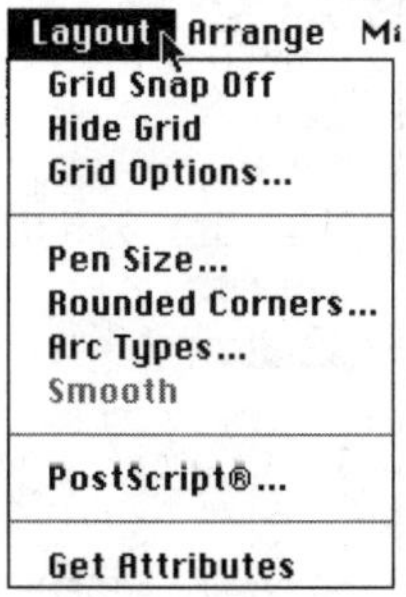

Figure 4: The Layout menu.

The File menu

The File menu (**Figure 2**) adds two new commands that let you close the current graphic and return to the Document Editor window as well as save a copy of the current graphic as a new document.

The Edit menu

The Edit menu (**Figure 3**) adds five commands to assist your graphics work. The Clear command deletes selected objects. The Duplicate command copies a selection and places the copy on the desktop, bypassing the Clipboard. You can change the colors available by editing a color palette with the Color command. The Patterns command lets you change the patterns available for use on objects and lines. You can save the settings you made in a graphics window by using the Save Settings command.

The Layout menu

The Layout menu (**Figure 4**) offers tools for editing. These commands are also available on the Button bar and Graphics Palette. Layout tools include commands that define how grids work, provide ways to change your pen size, define how rounded corners behave, and also define how arcs will be rendered. In addition, you can smooth straight angles into curves and enter PostScript scripts by using the appropriate commands located on this menu.

The Arrange menu

The Arrange menu (**Figure 5**) is a new menu for manipulating objects on the Graphics Editor window. You can rotate, resize, replicate objects (with specifications for location, size, angle, and appearance) numerous times, align objects, flip, rearrange from front to back and vice-versa, group and ungroup, and lock and unlock objects.

The Font menu

The Font menu (**Figure 6**) adds a Symbols command that lets you insert special characters into text boxes. *See Chapter 9: "Layout" for a discussion of text boxes.*

The Style menu

The Style menu (**Figure 7**) gives you the tools to change the color of your text as well as the text's alignment. *These commands are described in Chapter 9: "Layout."*

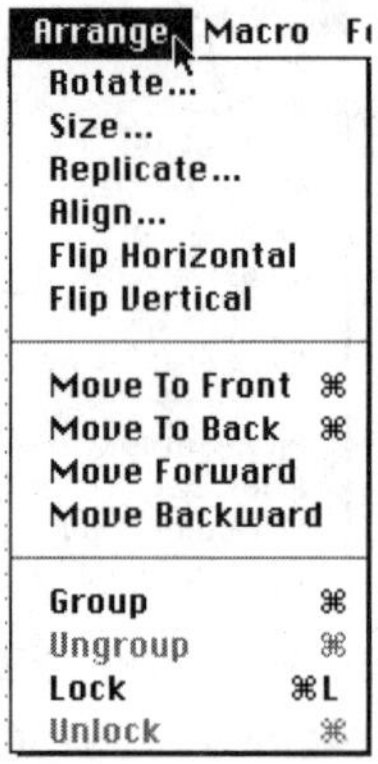

Figure 5: The Arrange menu.

Figure 6: The Font menu.

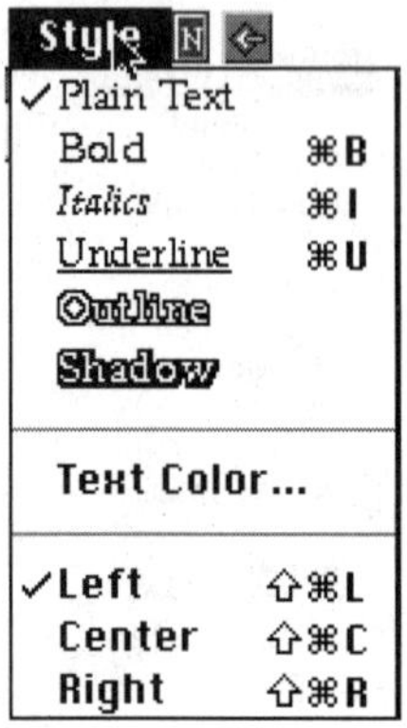

Figure 7: The Style menu.

The Graphics Button Bar Explained

The Graphics Editor replaces the standard Button bar with a specialized bar containing shortcuts to graphics commands located on the Arrange and Layout menus. **Figure 8** displays the Button bar.

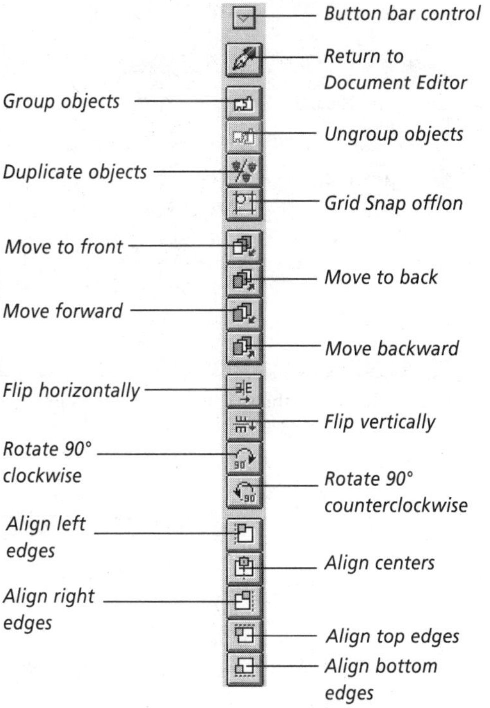

Figure 8: The Button bar.

The Graphics Tool Palette

The Graphics Editor does not use a series of toolbars such as those that are indispensable in the Document Editor, rather it relies on a floating tool palette containing the drawing tools. **Figures 9a through f** illustrate the tool palette's components.

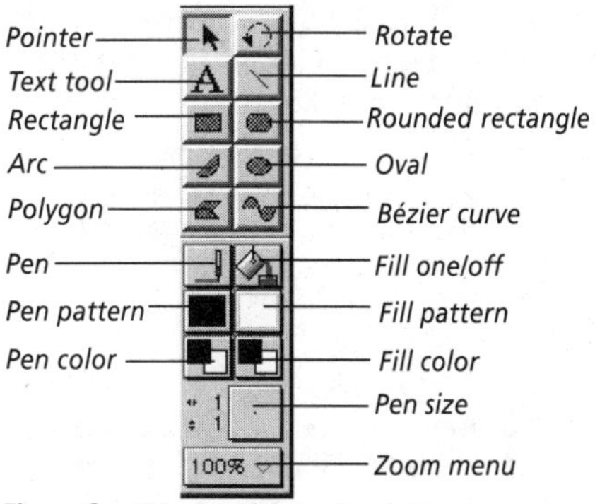

Figure 9a: The Graphic tool palette.

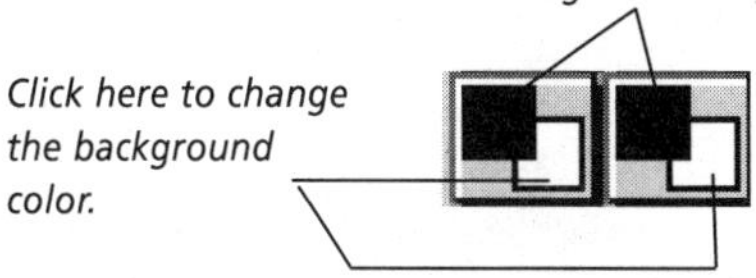

Figure 9b: The Pen and Fill Color tools let you change both the foreground and background colors.

Figure 9c: You can change the pattern of fills and pens with the Fill and Pen Pattern palettes.

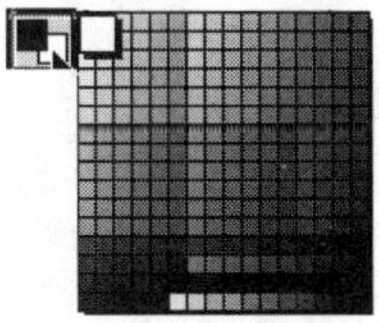

Figure 9d: Use the Fill and Pen Color palettes to change the foreground and background colors.

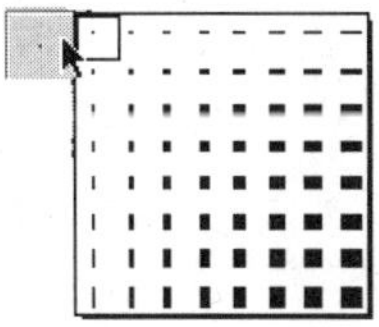

Figure 9e: Use the Pen Width palette to change the pen size.

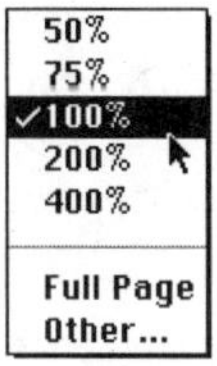

Figure 9f: Change the magnification using the Zoom menu.

To insert an existing graphic into WordPerfect:

1. *Optional:* If you want to anchor the graphic to a paragraph, place your insertion point in that paragraph.
2. Pull down the File menu and select Insert File (**Figure 10**).
3. In the resulting Insert dialog box (**Figure 11a**), select a graphic to insert. Use the Show pop-up menu (**Figure 11b**) to identify the formats you want to use.

   Note: PICT- and Paint-based graphics can be previewed in the Preview window, whereas EPS-based graphics are not displayed.
4. Click Insert.
5. The graphic is placed into the window (**Figure 12**). WordPerfect 3.5 comes with over 50 clipart images in PICT format for your use. Use the same Insert File command for these graphics as you would for other images.

Figure 10: Select **Insert File** from the File menu.

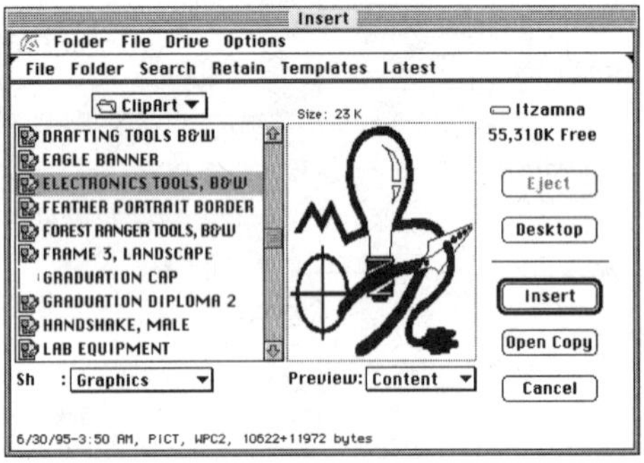

Figure 11a: Select the graphic you want to insert from the Directory list box.

Figure 11b: To add visible files, pull down the **Show** pop-up menu and select a different file format.

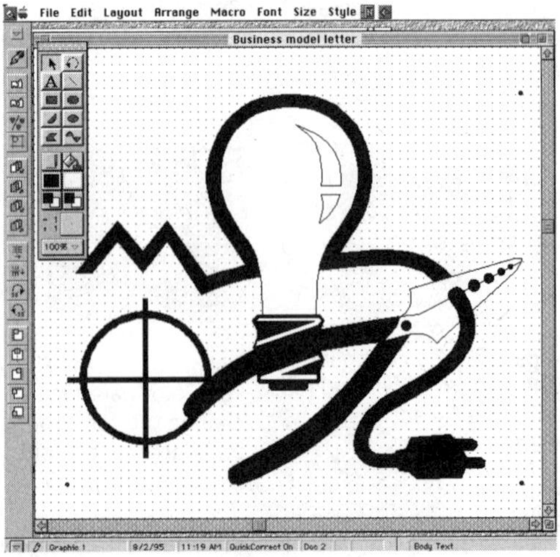

Figure 12: When the insertion process is complete, WordPerfect places the PICT, Paint, or EPS document into your window. Note that EPS files are not displayed, but will print on a PostScript laser printer.

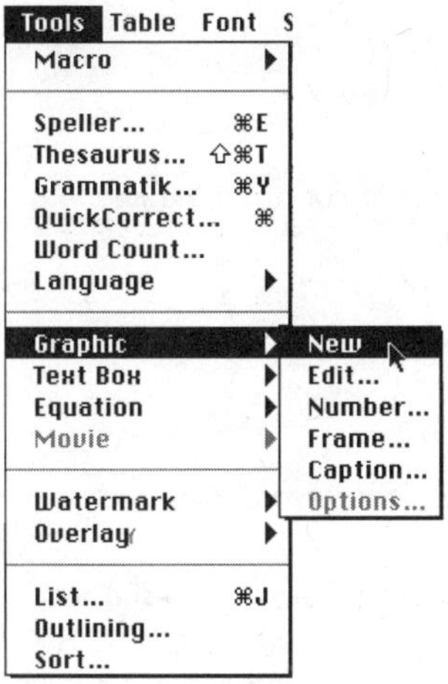

Figure 13: One way to open the Graphics Editor window is to select **New** from the **Graphic** pop-up menu on the Tools menu.

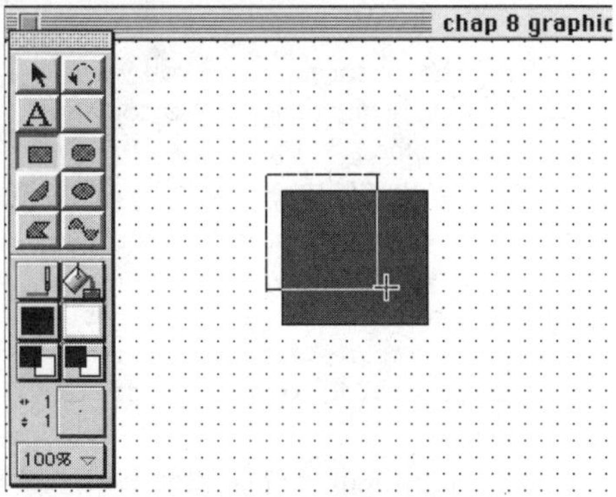

Figure 14: The Tool palette provides several geometric shapes you can use to draw objects. Select a shape, in this case a rectangle, and drag the mouse to draw it to your desired size.

To draw an object:

1. *Optional:* If you want to anchor the graphic to a paragraph, place your insertion point in that paragraph.
2. Pull down the Tools menu and select New from the Graphic pop-up menu (**Figure 13**).
3. In the resulting Graphics Editor window, select a drawing tool.
4. Click on the window and drag the cross cursor to where you want to end the object (**Figure 14**).

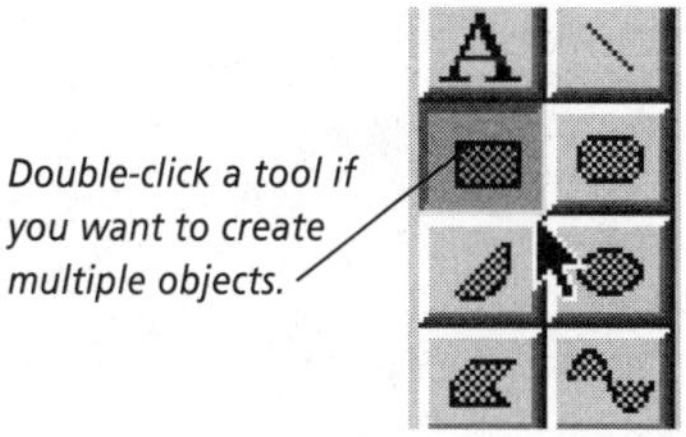

Figure 15a: Click once on a tool to draw a single object and click twice to use the tool more than once.

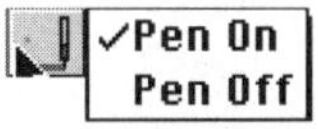

Figure 15b: Turn off the pen to create a graphic without a border.

Figure 15c: Turn off the fill to create a transparent graphic.

Tip

As shown in **Figure 15a**, double-click a graphic tool to use the tool multiple times. Every object is outlined with a border unless you select the **Pen Off** command from the Pen tool palette (**Figure 15b**). Every object is also filled with a color (the default is white) unless you select Fill Off from the Fill palette (**Figure 15c**) which causes the object to be transparent.

Using the Drawing Tools

To Draw...	Use This Tool...	Which does this...
Straight Line		Press Shift while dragging the cursor to constrain the line to a 45 degree angle.
Rectangle		Click the rectangle tool and drag the cursor to create a rectangle of the size you desire.
Square		Press Shift while dragging the cursor to constrain the rectangle to a square.
Polygon		Click to begin the object and then drag the cursor to shape each side. Click the mouse to create each angle. Double-click to create an open polygon or click on the starting point to close the shape.
Oval		Ovals are drawn with vertical and horizontal axes. Use the Rotate tool to change an oval's orientation.
Circle		Press Shift while dragging the cursor to constrain the oval into a circle.
Arc		An arc is $^1/_4$ of an oval. Drag the cursor to where you want the arc to end. Press the Shift key while dragging to constrain the arc into a quarter circle. Use the Arc Type command on the Layout menu to change how an arc appears.
Bézier curve		Click the mouse to anchor the curve, then drag the mouse to create two control points outside of the curve. Continue clicking for anchor points and dragging for control points until you draw the shape you want. Press Command while dragging to join the last control point to the last anchor point. Click again to end the figure.
Freehand curves		Press Command while click and dragging the cursor. Press Control to temporarily turn off Snap To Grid while drawing a freehand shape.

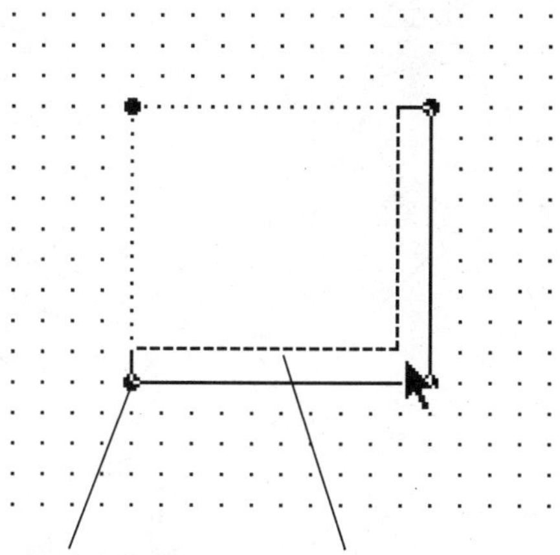

Figure 16: Grasp a resizing handle and drag the shape towards its middle to reduce its size or away from the center to enlarge its size. Hold down the Shift key while dragging to constrain the shape.

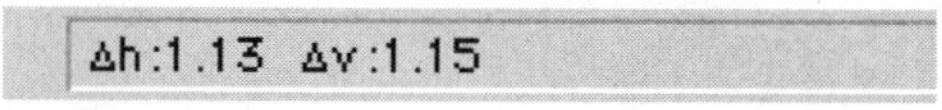

Figure 17: Use the information displayed in the Status bar to guide you in dragging the object's size to exactly where you want it.

To reshape an object:

1. Double-click a graphic to open its Graphic Editor window.
2. Select the object or objects you want to reshape.
3. Click a handle and drag it in or out to reduce or enlarge the object (**Figure 16**).

> **Tip**
>
> The Status bar displays the height and width of any object when you select the object (**Figure 17**). This information changes as you drag the resizing handles of the object. You can use the Status bar's dimensional data to increase the precision of your drawings because you can draw to scale.
>
> Constraining the object with the Shift key while you reshape the object causes the height and width to remain proportional during the resizing process. You can see this fact by looking at the Status bar while you perform the resizing task.

To change the shape of a bézier curve:

1. Double-click on the bézier curve to display its anchor points (**Figure 18a**).
2. Click an anchor point to display its control points (**Figure 18b**).
3. Select a control point and drag it. The bézier object is reshaped (**Figure 18c**). The opposite control point moves linearly to the selected point. Click the following modifier keys to control how you reshape the bézier curve.
   - If you want the opposite point to remain fixed, press the **Command** key while dragging.
   - If you want the opposite point to move the same distance as the point you are dragging, press the **Option** key while dragging.
   - If you want to constrain the reshaping to 45 degree angles, vertical or horizontal movements, press **Shift** while dragging.

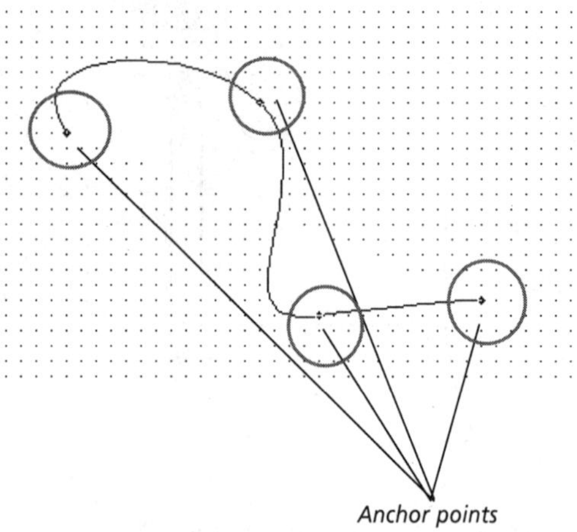

Figure 18a: Anchor points define the curve segments of a bézier curve. Click the object to display its anchor points.

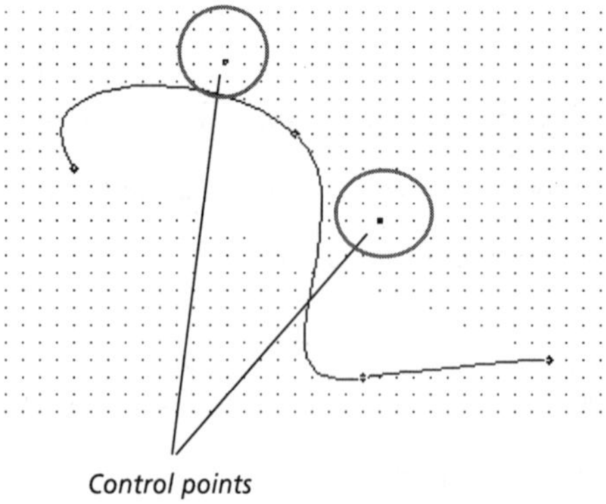

Figure 18b: Control points define how each curve will bend. Click an anchor point to display its control points.

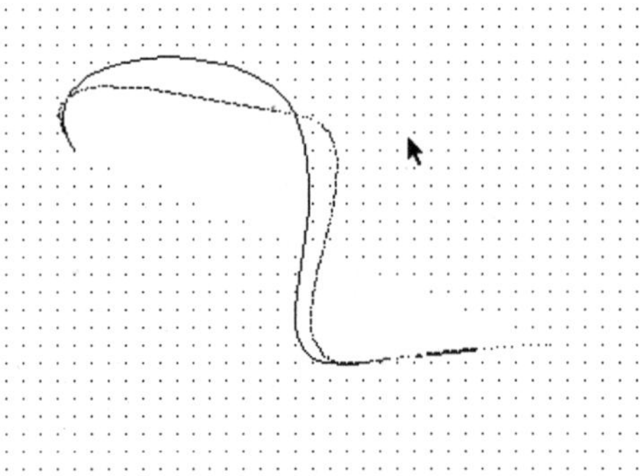

Figure 18c: Drag a Control point up or down to reshape a curve.

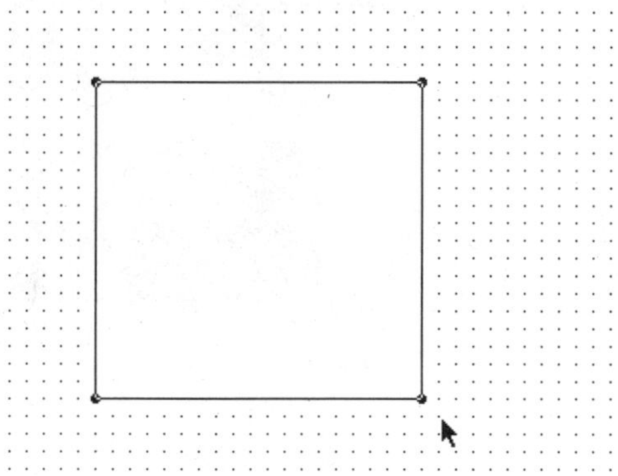

Figure 19: Select the object...

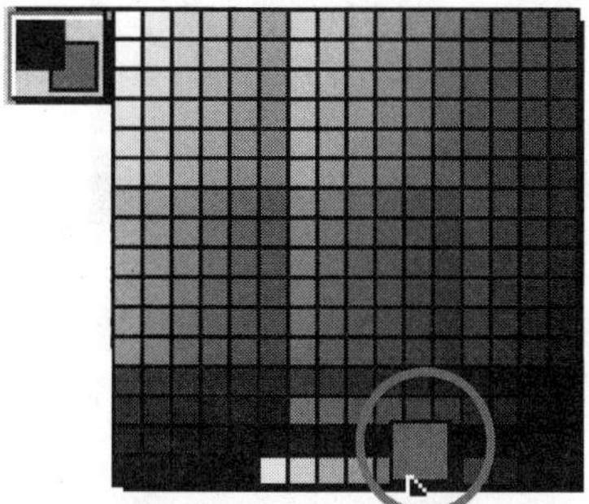

Figure 20a: ...and select a pen color from the palette by clicking the **Pen Color** tool and dragging the cursor over to a color.

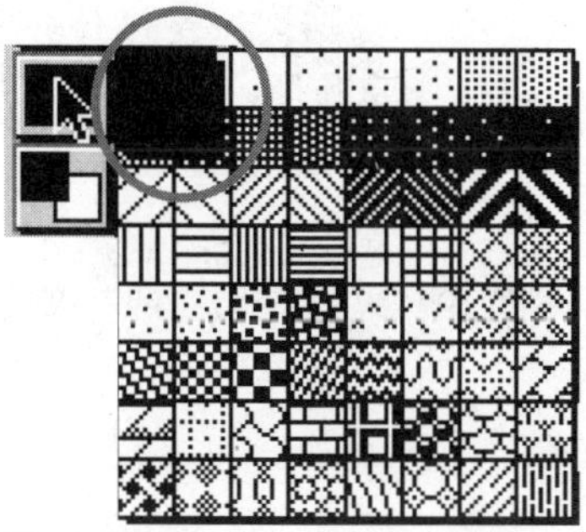

Figure 20b: You can change the pen's pattern by clicking the **Pen Pattern** tool and dragging the cursor over another pattern.

To change the color or pattern of a line:

1. Select the object you want to change (**Figure 19**).
2. Click the Pen Color tool and select a color from the open palette (**Figure 20a**).
3. *Optional:* You can change the pen pattern by clicking the Pen Pattern tool and selecting a new pattern from its palette (**Figure 20b**).
4. The object is changed to reflect your selections (**Figure 21**).

Figure 21: When you release the mouse, the object changes to reflect your pen choices. In this case, we selected gray (see Figure 24a).

To change the color or pattern of a fill:

1. Select the object you want to change.
2. Click the Fill Color tool to open its palette, and select a color (**Figure 22**).
3. *Optional:* You can change the fill pattern by clicking the Pen Pattern tool and selecting a new pattern from its palette.
4. The object is filled with your selected patterns and/or colors (**Figure 23a**).

   Note: You can change the foreground and background colors of fills by selecting the front or back squares of the fill color tool in the same fashion as you did with the pen tools (**Figure 23b**).

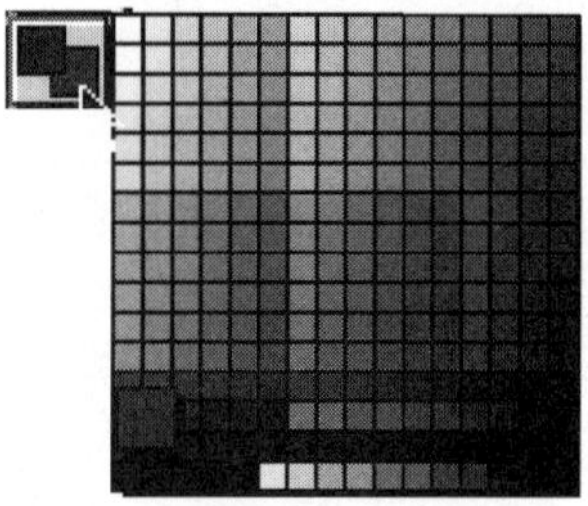

Figure 22: Select a color from the **Fill Color** palette.

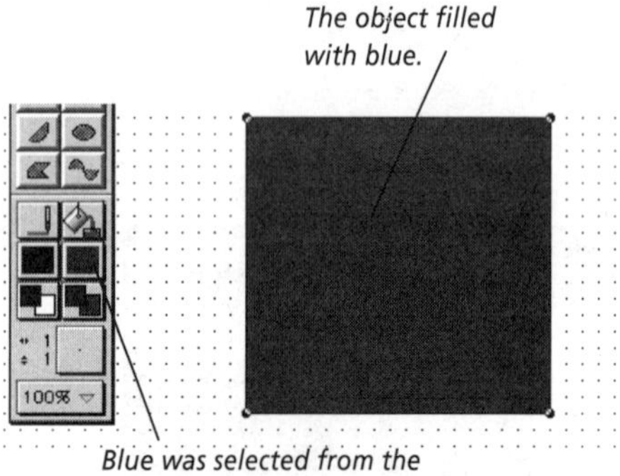

Figure 23a: When you release the mouse, the object is filled with your selected colors.

> **Tip**
>
> You can create interesting effects by varying the background and foreground colors of a pattern. Click the front square (foreground) **Fill or Pen Color** tool and select a color from the palette. Then click the back square (background) of the color tool and select a color from its palette. To see the effect of your foreground and background color selections, choose a new pattern from the pen pattern tool (**Figure 23c**).
>
> To draw the figure in a different color or pattern, select colors and patterns before drawing a new object.

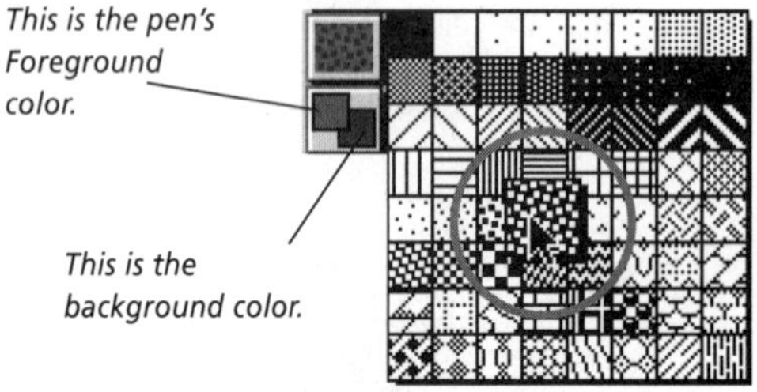

Figure 23b: By varying the background and foreground colors, you can change the pattern's appearance.

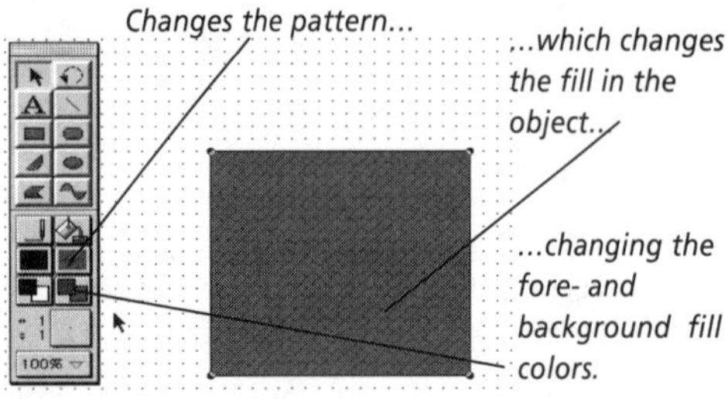

Figure 23c: Manipulating the Fill colors and patterns lets you create interesting fill effects.

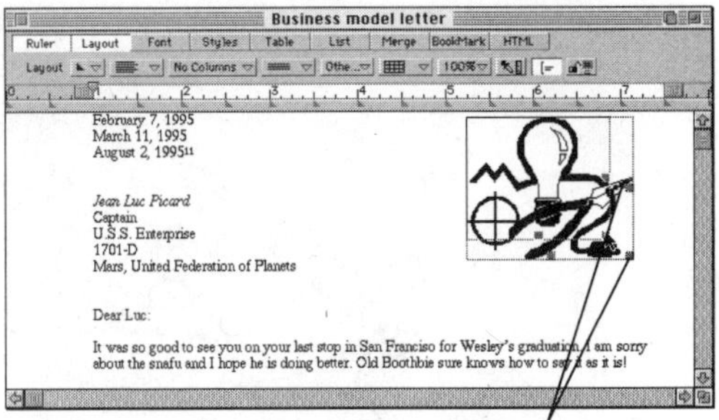

Resize handles.

Figure 24: Select a resizing handle and drag towards the center of the object to reduce its size, or away from the center to enlarge the graphic. Hold down the Shift key to ensure that the graphic is resized proportionally.

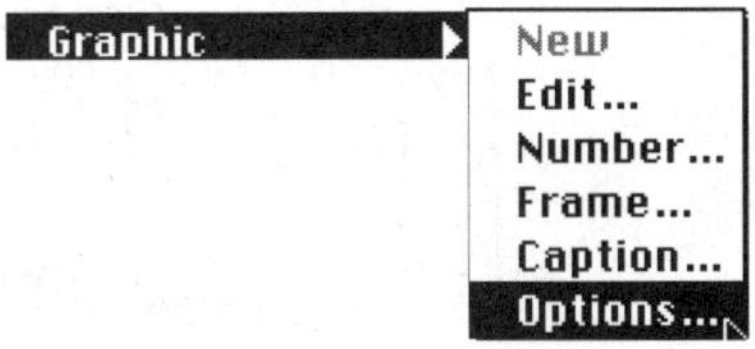

Figure 25: Select **Options** from the **Graphic** pop-up menu on the Tools menu...

Type new percentages in these boxes.

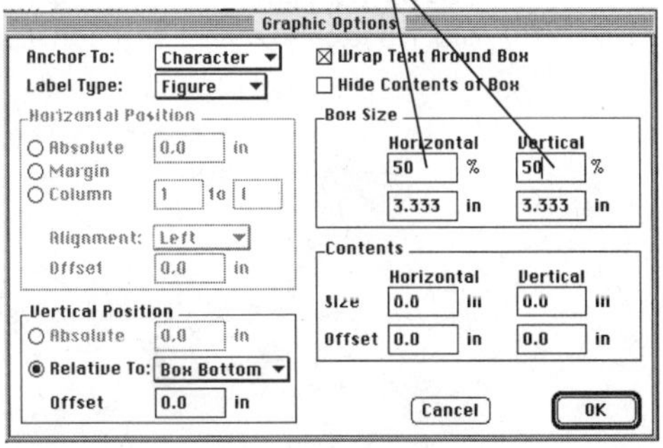

Figure 26:...and type the dimensions or percentages in the Box Size area text boxes.

Editing a Graphic

Sometimes your graphic will not fit into a document at its current size. You can scale a graphic in two places: the Document Editor and the Graphics Editor. Use the Document Editor to scale or select only a portion of the graphic (called cropping) and use the Graphics Editor to scale one or more objects in a graphic.

To scale a graphic in the Document Editor window:

1. In the Document Editor, select the graphic you want to resize.
2. Drag the resulting resizing handle to decrease or increase the size of the drawing (**Figure 24**). Use the Status bar's dimension information to track your progress. Hold down the Shift key while dragging to proportionally scale the graphic.
3. Click outside of the graphic to turn off the handles.

> **Tip**
>
> You can also resize a graphic by selecting the graphic box and choosing **Options** from the **Graphic** pop-up menu on the Tools menu (**Figure 25**). In the resulting Graphic Options dialog box (**Figure 26**), type the percentages you want to reduce or increase the graphic box in the **Horizontal** and **Vertical** text boxes in the Box Size area or type actual dimension in the appropriate text boxes and click **OK**.

To scale an object in the Graphics Editor window using a dialog box:

1. Select the object(s) you want to scale (**Figure 27**).
2. Pull down the Arrange menu and select Size (**Figure 28**).
3. In the resulting Size Object dialog box (**Figure 29**), either select a Horizontal and Vertical percentage from their pop-up menus, or type percentages in their text boxes.
4. Click the radio button of the anchor point to indicate the direction you want to size.
5. Click OK.
6. The items are scaled as you specified (**Figure 30**).

> **Tip**
>
> To proportionally scale an item, make sure that you select identical vertical and horizontal size percentages. To enlarge an item, select a percentage larger than 100 percent: to reduce an item, select a size less than 100 percent. A good rule of thumb is reduce or enlarge an item from 100 percent, starting over each time you want to make a change. Otherwise, scaling can become very confusing.

Figure 27: Select an object to scale...

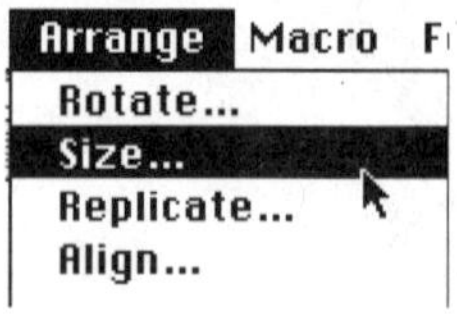

Figure 28:...and select **Size** from the Arrange menu.

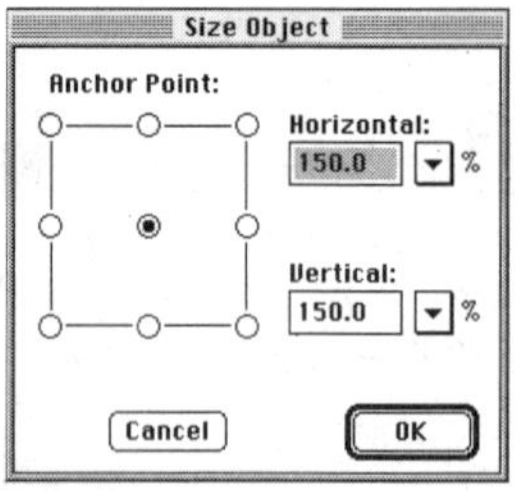

Figure 29: Pull down the **Horizontal** and **Vertical Size** pop-up menus and select a new percentage scale; then click a button to change the anchor...

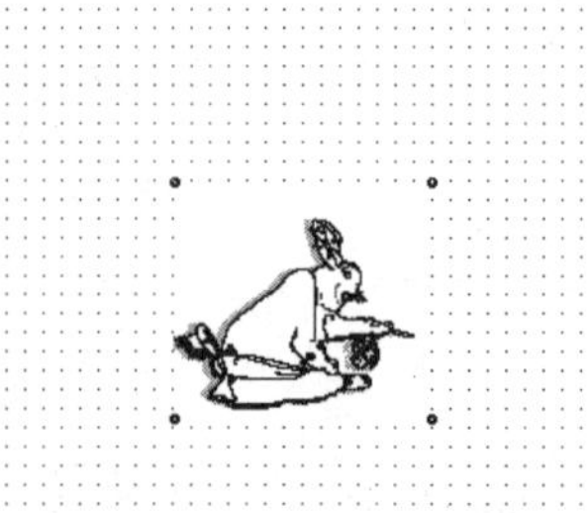

Figure 30 :...and the item is scaled. Select identical percentages in the **Horizontal** and **Vertical** pop-up menus to ensure proportional scaling.

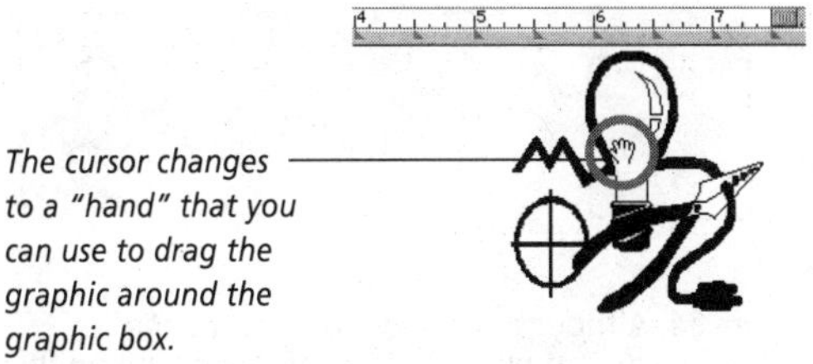

Figure 31a: Drag the graphic around the graphic box to position it so that only the part you want visible is displayed.

Figure 31b: The resulting cropped image hides a portion of the graphic from view (although it is still available for display).

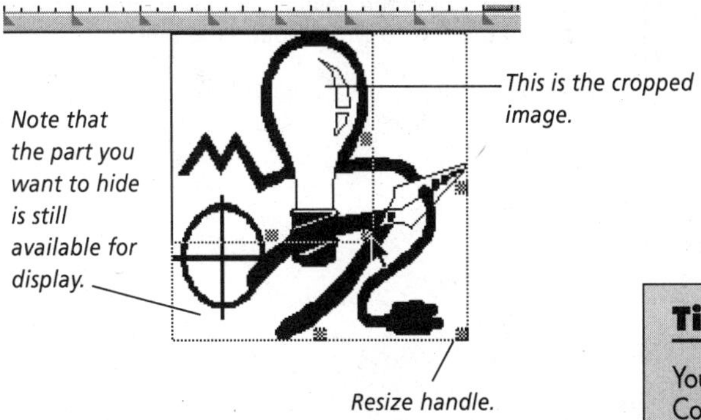

Figure 32: Press Command and drag the Resize handle to change the box size, thus cropping the graphic.

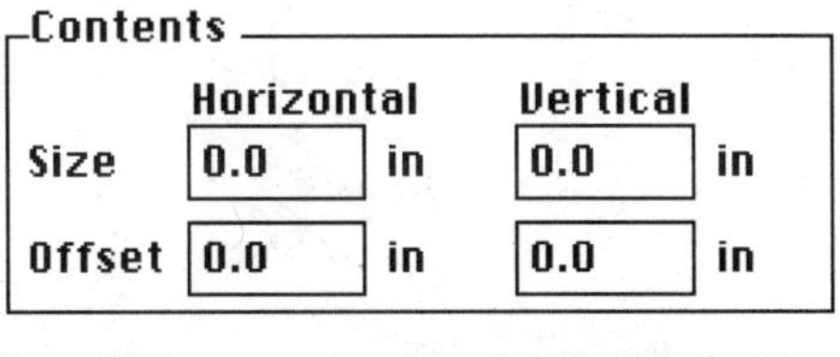

Figure 33: You can also open the Graphic Options dialog box and type dimensions for the graphic box's contents in the appropriate text boxes.

To crop a graphic in the Document Editor window:

1. Select the graphic you want to edit.
2. Place your insertion point inside the graphic box and press the Command key while clicking the graphic. The cursor changes to a tiny hand (**Figure 31a**) and the marquee disappears.
3. Drag the graphic by the hand cursor to a new location in the box (**Figure 31b**).

Tip

You can also crop a graphic by pressing Command while dragging the resize handle (**Figure 32**).

Use the Graphic Options dialog box's **Box Contents** area to crop a graphic with more precision (**Figure 33**).

Caution: When you crop a graphic, the entire graphic is still in existence even if a portion is hidden. Graphics tend to take up a lot of hard disk and memory space. If you are short on storage or memory, use a graphics program to delete that part of the graphic you do not need and then import only the necessary parts of the graphic.

To move a graphic in the Document Editor:

1. Select the graphic in the Document Editor that you want to move.
2. Click the pointer anywhere inside the graphic box and drag the graphic to another location (**Figure 34**).

   Caution: Do not select a handle or double-click the graphic.
3. The graphic is anchored to another location and the text at that place wraps around the graphic (**Figure 35**).

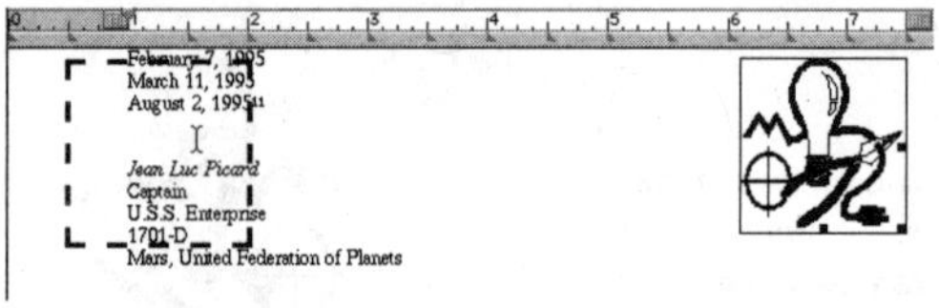

Figure 34: Although the codes do not change location, you can place the graphic anywhere on the page by dragging its box. WordPerfect indicates its location by displaying a marquee. Release the mouse...

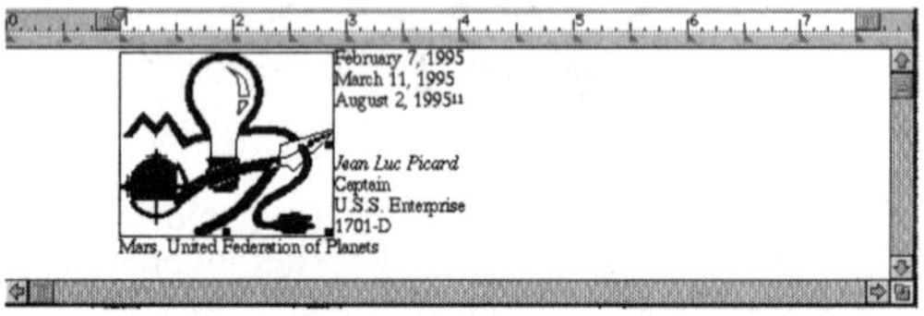

Figure 35: ... and the object falls into its new location causing the text to wrap around the graphic.

> **Tip**
>
> To duplicate a graphic in another part of the page, press the Shift or Option key while dragging the image (**Figure 36**).
>
> If you are running WordPerfect under System 7.5, you can drag the graphic to another document on the desktop or from one page to another.

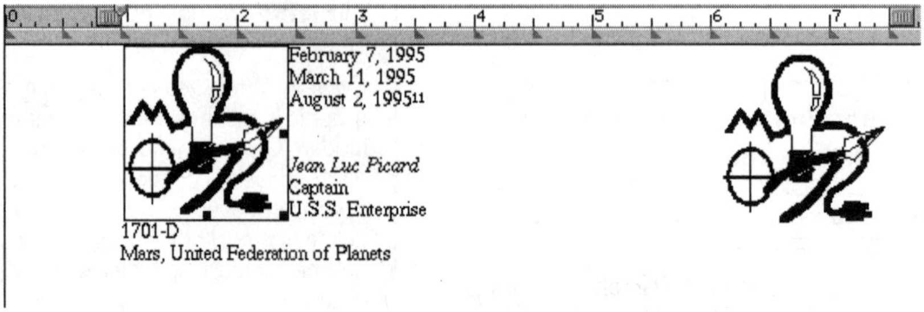

Figure 36: Shift-dragging or Option-dragging a graphic duplicates it in another portion of your page.

LAYOUT 9

ONE OF THE innovations provided by Macintosh technology was to bring professional publishing standards to the desktop. WordPerfect offers many features that support desktop publishing, including the following:

- **Easy production of multi-column layouts.** The Columns pop-up menu on the Layout toolbar lets you switch effortlessly from single to multiple column formats.
- **Easy manipulation of graphics with text.** WordPerfect supports text wrapping around framed graphics or text boxes. Just drag and drop frames into your documents and the surrounding text will wrap appropriately.
- **Automatic captioning of figures.** WordPerfect lets you create figure or table captions and tracks them for inclusion in your Table of Figures or Contents.
- **Numerous special effects.** WordPerfect's layers approach lets you create graphic overlays and underlays, as well as embed anchored graphics or text boxes in your document. Create watermarks, banners, and drop caps easily using this feature.

This chapter introduces WordPerfect's desktop publishing tools.

WordPerfect provides an extensive array of advanced desktop publishing tools.

Working with Columns

WordPerfect provides extensive precision in its column-management features. You can create from two to 24 columns on a page. You have extensive control over the spacing between columns and how columns interact with each other.

WordPerfect lets you create two types of columns: newspaper-type columns and side-by-side columns.

- **Newspaper-type columns** (**Figure 1**) are used when you want text to flow from one column to another. For example, in newsletters you place columns of text that flow from the top of one column to the bottom of that column and then down the next column. You can also discontinue the text flow and start it on another page. You can wrap the text around a graphic or text box and the text will continue to flow down the page and around the box until you direct it to the next column.
- **Parallel columns** (**Figure 2**) are used when you want to lay paragraphs next to each other, such as you see in resumes, scripts, and lists. This type of column is also called a *side-by-side column*. Parallel columns are groups of columns across a page. Because the row acts as a single unit, when the contents of one cell hits a page break, the entire row will flow to the next page. Rows of columns adjust for the contents of the largest cell in the row. A special version of the parallel column is the *extended column*, where the contents of a column are allowed to flow to the next page without taking the total row of text with one column.

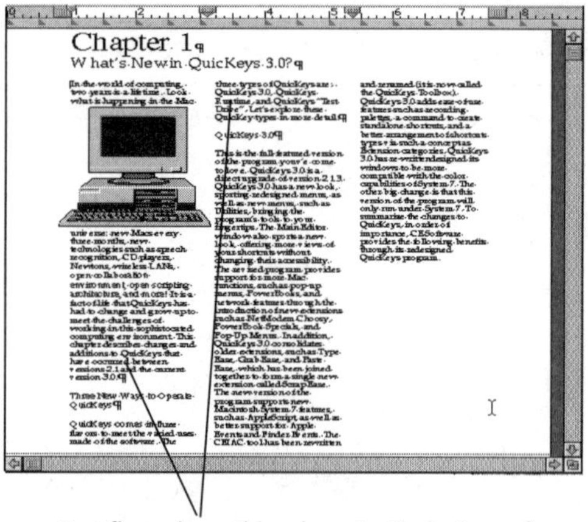

Text flows down this column to the bottom of the page, then continues down the next column.

Figure 1: Newspaper columns flow down the page and up a column continuously.

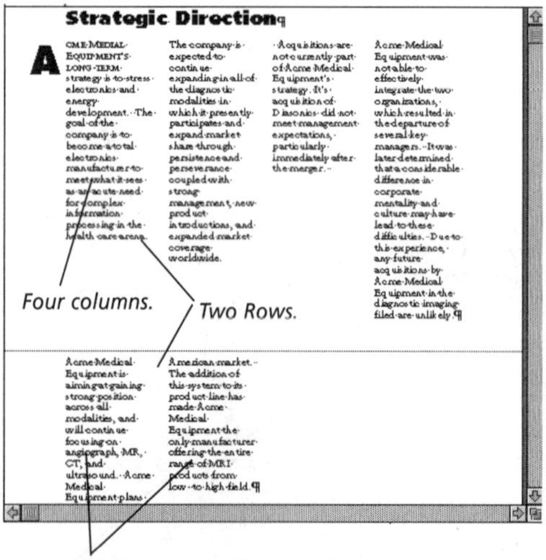

Text flows across the page from column to column and row to row.

Figure 2: Parallel columns run horizontally across a page with text flowing across rows of columns.

Mini-Glossary

Gutter This is the space between the right margin of a column and the left margin of the next column (**Figure 3**). You can change this white space by adjusting the margins of your columns by either dragging the Ruler margin markers or using the Column Format dialog box. The default spacing for evenly-spaced margins is 0.25-inch gutters.

Set When you use the Columns pop-up menu to change the number of columns, you create a "set" (see **Figure 3**). Sets exist from the first appearance of new column type on a page to a hard column break that signals the insertion of a new column format. Everything you do to format your columns is done to the column set.

Row Parallel columns are broken into rows, consisting of the column at the left margin and working across the page to the last column on the right margin (see **Figure 2**). A set of columns can have a single row or multiple rows.

To set up multiple newspaper-style columns:

1. Place your insertion point where you want to begin typing in columns. You can also type your text and then select it to place existing text into columns. Another alternative is to place the insertion point inside a paragraph you want to place in a column. In this latter case, the column will begin at the beginning of the paragraph where you placed the cursor.
2. Pull down the Columns pop-up menu from the Layout toolbar and select the number of columns you want to insert (**Figure 4**). (In this case no columns were selected.)

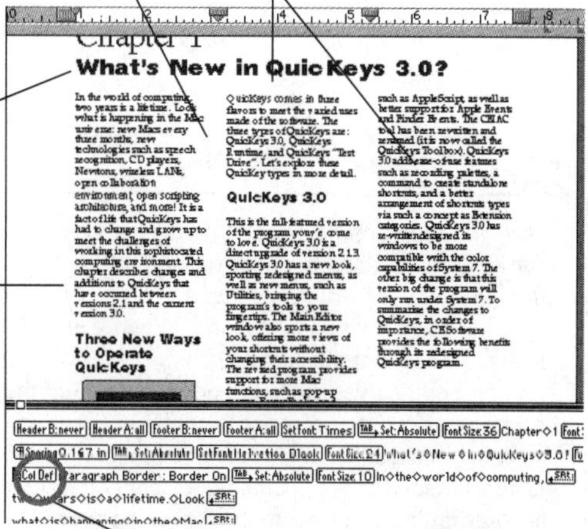

Figure 3: Columns are defined by Column codes (Set and Break) into rows of columns.

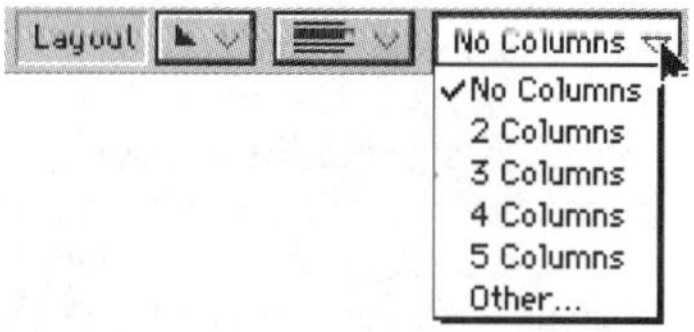

Figure 4: You can use the **Columns** pop-up menu on the Layout menu to create newspaper-type columns.

To set up multiple parallel columns:

1. Place the insertion point in the paragraph you want to insert into columns, or place the insertion point where you want the columns to begin.
2. Pull down the Columns pop-up menu from the Layout toolbar and select Other (**Figure 5**).
3. In the resulting Column Format dialog box (**Figure 6**), click the Parallel or Extended radio button in the Type section.
4. Type a number in the Number Of Columns text box.
5. Click OK.

Shortcuts

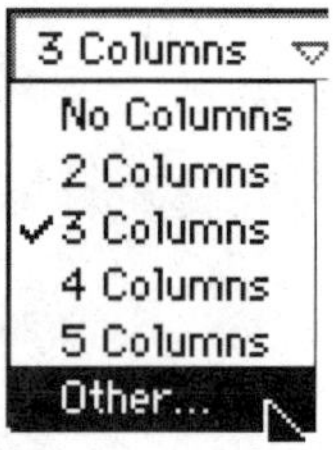

Figure 5: Select **Other** from the **Columns** pop-up menu on the Layout menu.

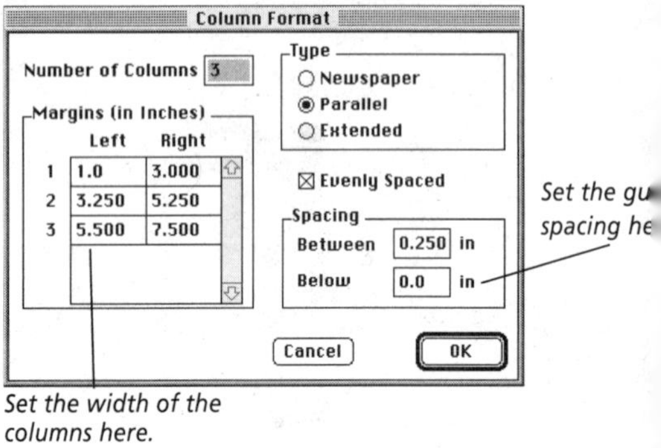

Figure 6: Select either **Parallel** or **Extended** columns from the **Type** section and type the number of columns.

Tip

When you type in newspaper-type columns and your text reaches the bottom of a page, the insertion point and your next text is placed at the top of the page in the next column. When you reach the bottom of the second column, the insertion point moves to the left-hand column on the next page. If you do not want to continue typing in a column, choose the Column Break command from the Insert menu (or press Command+Shift+Return). The insertion point moves to the top of the next column. The key to this type of column is that each column is independent of another with text flowing down and then up.

When you type text in parallel-type columns, the text is inserted across the page in rows, like the cells of a spreadsheet. Each column can be a page in length. If you want to create longer columns, use the Extended column option in the Column Format dialog box. When you want to place text into the next column, use the Column Break command in the Insert menu. The insertion point moves to the top of the next column to the right of your text's column. Text is inserted to the right until you run out of columns. Columns move as rows to another page unless you use the Extended column option. The key to this type of column is that columns are bound together in groups, called "rows" that move together. Text in columns flows horizontally across the page and **not** up and down.

Figure 7: Select **Column** from the Borders pop-up menu...

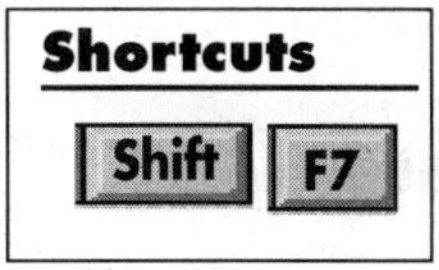

To add a border and fill to a set of columns:

1. Place the insertion point in the column set you want to border.
2. Pull down the Layout menu and select Column from the Borders pop-up menu (**Figure** 7).
3. In the resulting Column Border Style dialog box (**Figure** 8), select your border and fill options.
4. Click OK.
5. As illustrated in **Figure** 9, WordPerfect generates your selected border and fill options for the entire column set.

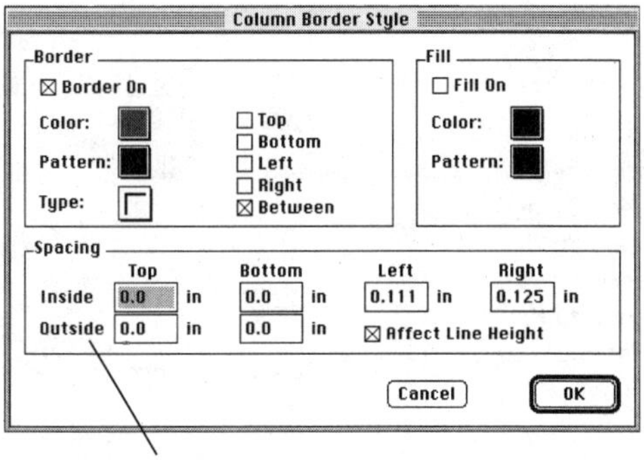

Use this section to define how to offset the border from your text.

Figure 8: ...and use the Border and Fill areas of the Column Border Style dialog box to apply borders to your columns.

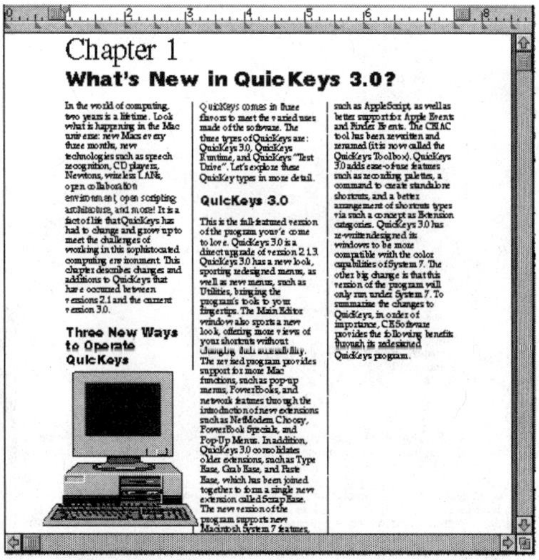

Figure 9: WordPerfect draws borders and fills based on your specifications.

To discontinue the column set:

1. Place the insertion point at the end of the text you want to include in columns.
2. Pull down the Insert menu and select Column Break (**Figure 10**).
3. The text moves right across the columns with each use of the command. Keep selecting Column Break until the text and insertion point moves to beneath the last row of text in the first column (**Figure 11**).
4. Pull down the Columns pop-up menu on the Layout toolbar and select No Columns (**Figure 12**).
5. As shown in **Figure 13**, all of the text after the insertion point is changed to "no columns."

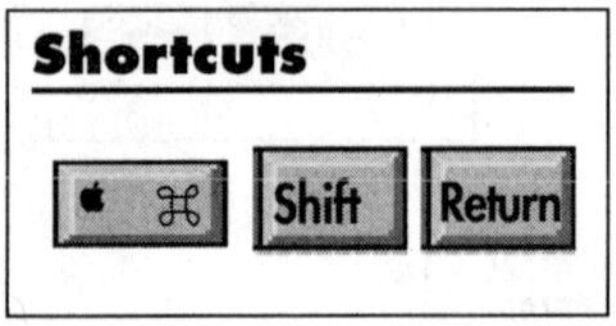

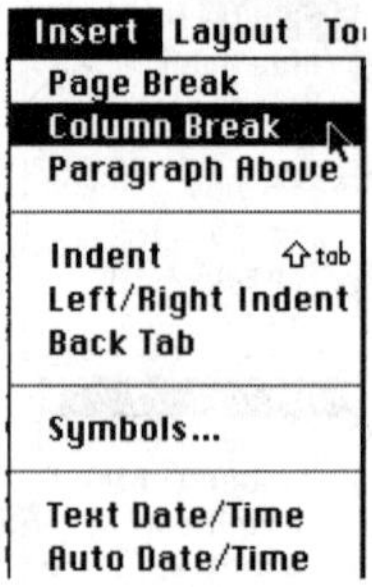

Figure 10: Select **Column Break** to move the selected paragraphs to below the first column.

Each time you select Column Break, the selected text is moved to the right one column.

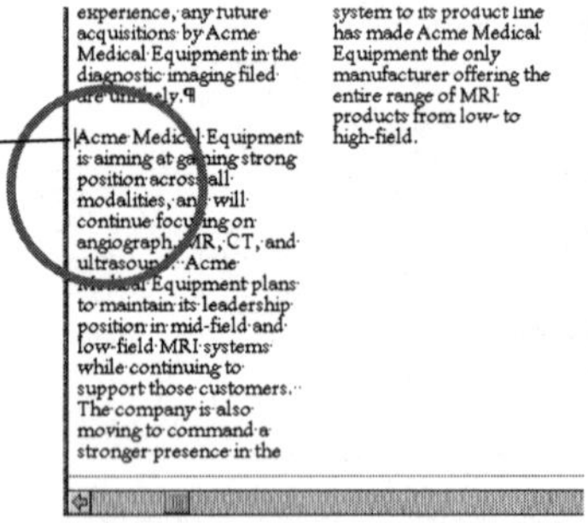

Figure 11: Use this command until the text is beneath the first paragraph...

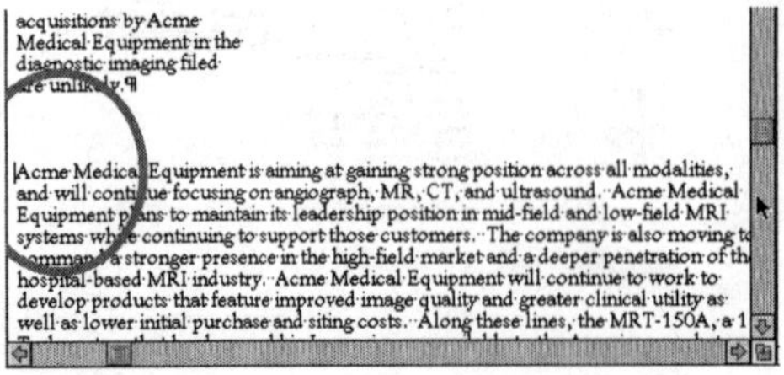

Figure 13: The text is positioned without columns.

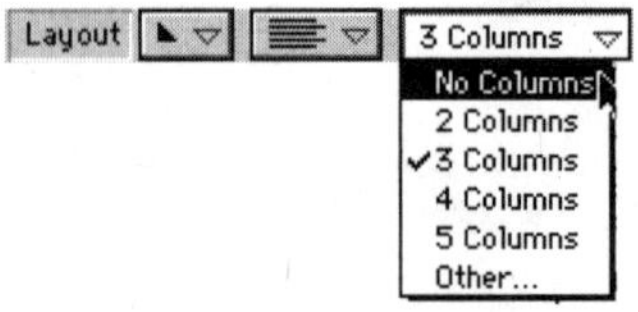

Figure 12: ...then select **No Columns** from the **Columns** pop-up menu.

Discontinuing a Column Set

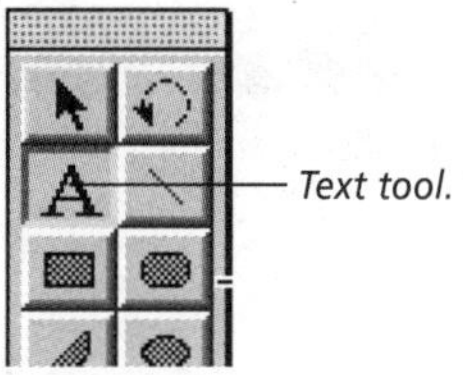

Figure 14: Select the Text tool on the Graphics tool palette. Double-click if you want to draw more than one text box.

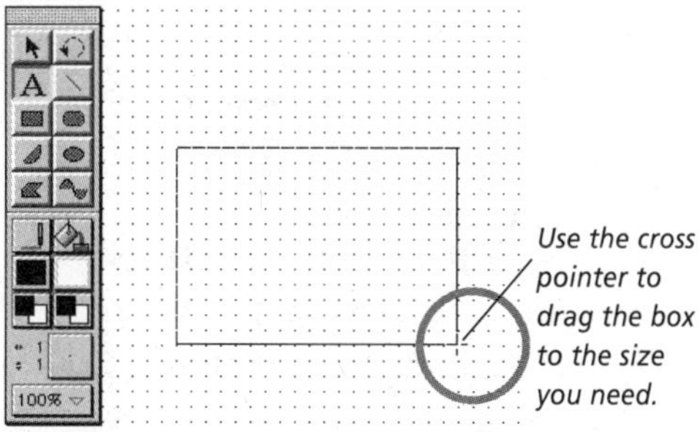

Figure 15: Drag the Text Box pointer to create the text box.

Figure 16: Then, type the text at the insertion point. You can manipulate the text object like any other graphic object, coloring, rotating, and grouping it.

> **Tip**
>
> You can insert a file into a text box by pulling down the File menu in the Graphics Editor window and selecting **Insert File**. Select a document from the Insert dialog box's directory list box and click **Insert**. WordPerfect inserts the document into a text box.

Text Boxes Examined

WordPerfect lets you create *text objects* in *text boxes*. Text objects are boxes filled with text and are treated like graphics that you can manipulate in the Graphics Editor window. You can also create and work with text boxes (movable windows containing text) within the Document Editor window. Both windows let you manipulate the text.

Use the Graphics Editor to rotate, resize, flip, duplicate, fill, and/or color the text, just as you would any other object.

Use the Document Editor to frame, move, scale, and edit the style of the text in the text box.

Use text boxes for creating drop caps, such as the one shown in **Figure 1**, sidebars, or placement of text in non-standard areas of your document. The text in your document will wrap around a text box as it does in any graphic.

To create a text box in the Graphics Editor window:

1. If you are not in the Graphics Editor window, click the Graphics Editor button on the Button bar.
2. Click the **Text** tool on the Graphics tool palette (**Figure 14**).
3. Drag the resulting pointer across the Graphics Editor window and release the mouse when the resulting marquee reaches the size you want for your text box (**Figure 15**).
4. At the blinking cursor inside the text box, type the text you want to insert into the text box (**Figure 16**).

Shortcuts

To create a text box in the Document Editor window:

1. Place your insertion point where you want to place the text box.
2. Pull down the Tools menu and select New from the Text Box pop-up menu (**Figure 17**).
3. WordPerfect displays a box outline (**Figure 18**). Type your text in the box. The text box will expand as you type. Use the Font and Layout toolbars, as well as the Layout and Insert menus, to format the text.
4. Click outside the text box to return to your document.

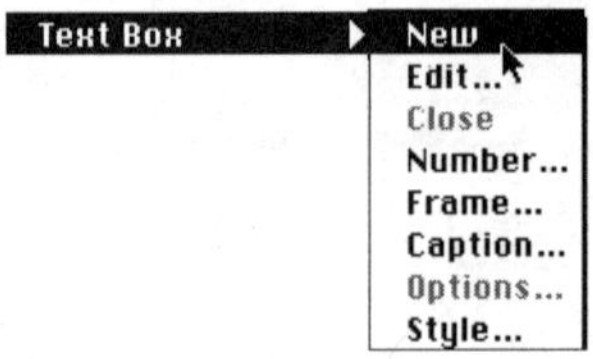

Figure 17: Select **New** from the **Text Box** pop-up menu on the Tools menu.

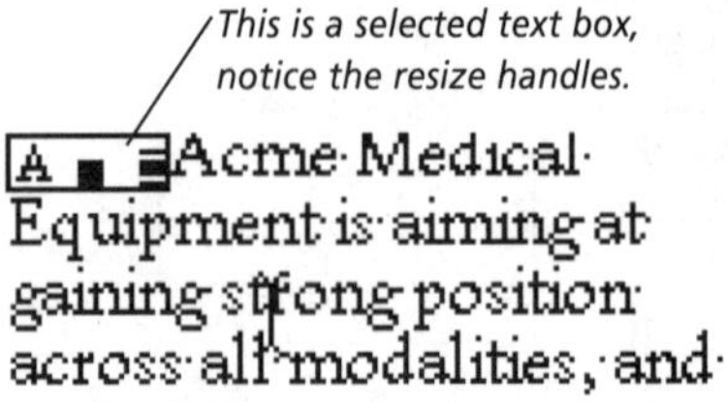

Figure 18: Type your text at the blinking cursor. When you click outside the box, WordPerfect selects the box.

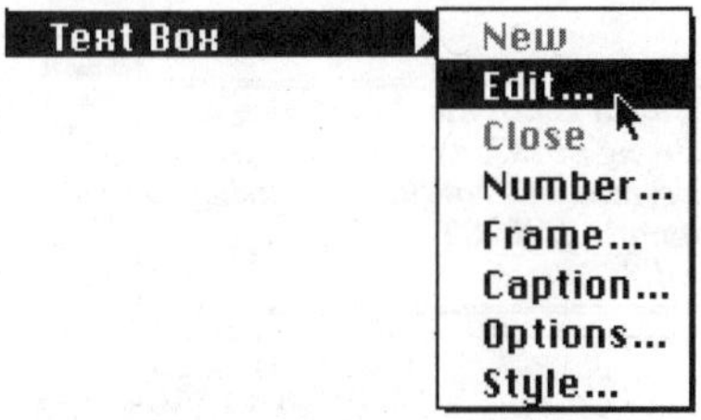

Figure 19: Select **Edit** from the **Text Box** pop-up menu on the Tools menu.

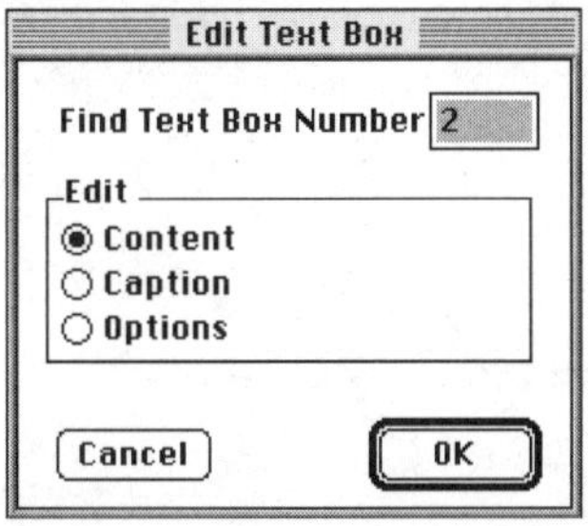

Figure 20: Select **Content** to edit the text in the box.

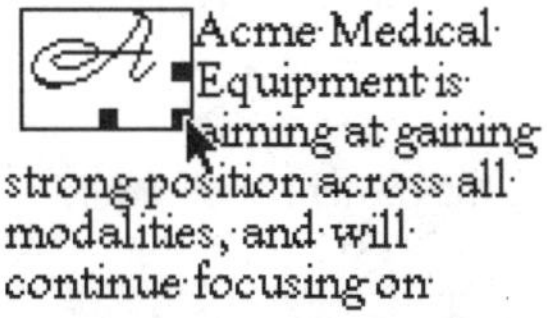

Figure 21: Compare **Figure 18** to this figure of an edited text box. Use the Font, Size, and Style menus, as well as the Layout toolbar to reformat your text. Then click outside the box. The text box is resized to fit the new text.

To edit a text box in the Document Editor window:

1. Double-click the text box to display the insertion point.

   or

2. Select the text box and pull down the Tools menu and select Edit from the Text Box pop-up menu (**Figure 19**).
3. In the resulting Edit Text Box dialog box (**Figure 20**), make sure that the Content radio button is selected.
4. Click OK.
5. Make the changes to the text in the text box.
6. Click outside the box to return to your document.
7. As shown in **Figure 21**, the text is reformatted to fit your selections and the box resizes itself to fit the changes.

To resize a text box:

1. Select the text box. WordPerfect displays the box's resize handles (**Figure 22**).
2. Click a resize handle and drag it away from the text to enlarge the box or towards the text to reduce the size of the box. Hold down the Shift key while dragging to ensure that the box is resized proportionally (**Figure 23**).

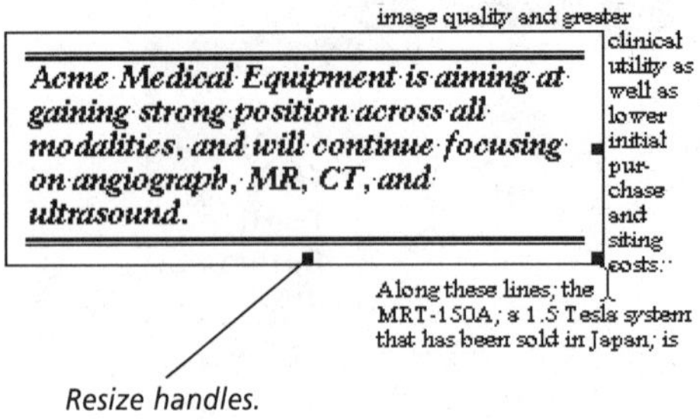

Figure 22 Click once on the text box to display its resize handles. Be sure not to double-click as this displays the insertion point.

> **Tip**
>
> Use the dimensional data displayed in the Status bar (see **Figure 23**) to guide you during the resizing task. Notice that the text size does not change when you resize the box, causing the text to wrap around the newly sized box.
>
> You can resize text boxes in the following ways.
>
> - You can resize text in the Document Editor, with the Size menu or by pressing Command+Shift+> to enlarge the text one point size or Command+Shift+< to reduce the text size one point.
> - You can open the Graphics Editor window to group and resize the text with the box.
> - You can crop the text box without affecting the size of text by moving your cursor inside the box and then pressing Command while dragging the text around the inside of the box, just as you did to crop a graphic. *See Chapter 8: "Using Graphics" for a description of how to crop.*

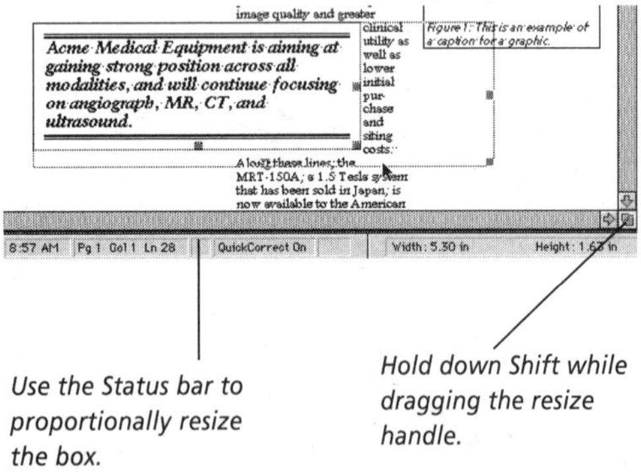

Figure 23: Click and drag the corner handle while holding down the Shift key to proportionally resize the text box.

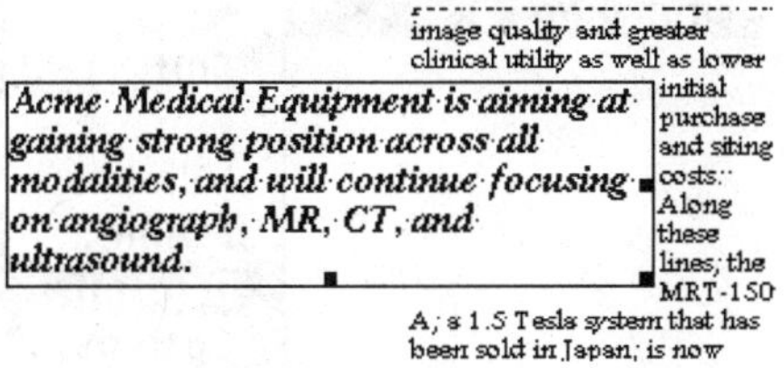

Figure 24: Select the text box by clicking once...

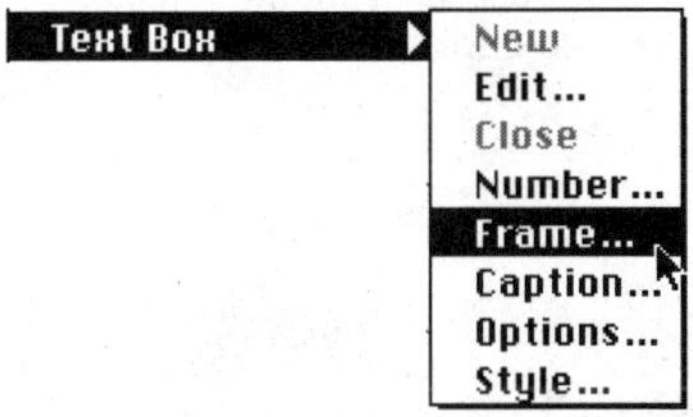

Figure 25: ...then pull down the **Text Box** pop-up menu and select **Frame**.

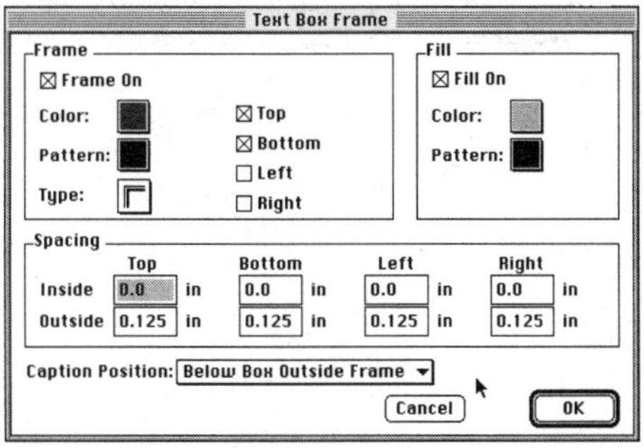

Figure 26: Select frame and fill options from the **Frame** and **Fill** sections. You can also edit the distance of the frame from the text in the **Spacing** area.

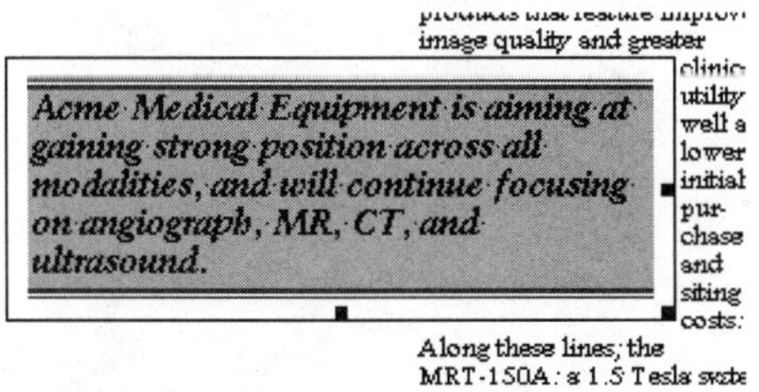

Figure 27: The text box is framed based on your specifications.

Working with Frames

Frames are borders for text boxes. Use frames to set text boxes off from body text. For example, when you want to use a pull quote to reiterate a salient point from your document, you can copy the text for the quote into a text box and create a bottom and top frame for the box. Then, when you position the box, the frames delineate the pull quote from the rest of the text. Frames can also be used to fill text boxes with screened tints. Use this option to separate a side bar from the rest of your text. Frames can be edited to create varying borders by changing their frame type, line weight, color, and pattern.

To create a frame around a text box:

1. Click the text box (**Figure 24**).
2. Pull down the Tools menu and select Frame from the Text Box pop-up menu (**Figure 25**).
3. In the resulting Text Box Frame dialog box (**Figure 26**), select frame options from the Frame area. Use the Top, Bottom, Left, and/or Right check boxes to draw lines in those areas of the frame. Select all of the check boxes to surround the text box with a frame.
4. *Optional:* Select a color or pattern from the Fill area.
5. *Optional:* Type new specifications in the Spacing area's text boxes to change the distance from the frame to the text box.
6. Click OK.
7. A frame fitting your specifications is placed around the text box (**Figure 27**).

Working with Captions

WordPerfect will automatically manage figure numbers and coordinate figure captions with its Table of Contents. You can add captions with automatically updated numbers to text boxes and graphic boxes.

To add a caption to a text box:

1. Select the text box you want to caption.
2. Pull down the Tools menu and select Caption from the Text Box pop-up menu (Figure 28).
3. Type your caption after the number (**Figure** 29).
4. Click outside the text box to return to your document.

> **Tip**
>
> Captions can be as long as a single page or 32 kilobytes of data. You can change the location of the text box by changing the location option in the Text Box Frame dialog box (see **Figure 28**).

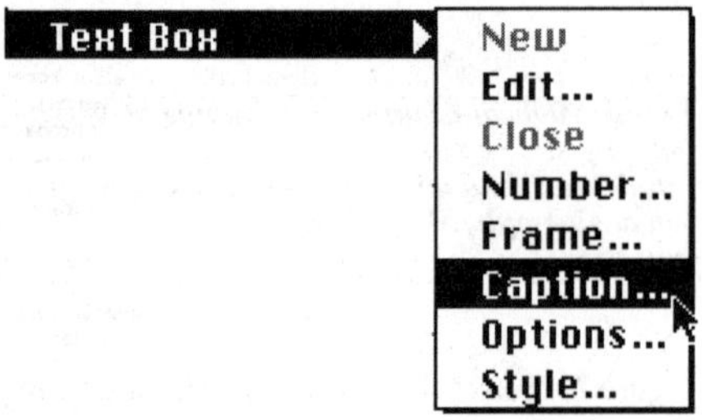

Figure 28: Select **Caption** from the **Text Box** pop-up menu to display a caption box and number.

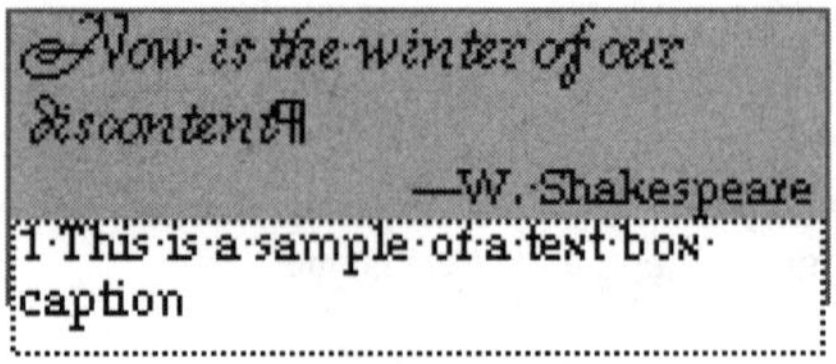

Figure 29: Type your caption text after the WordPerfect-assigned number in the caption box.

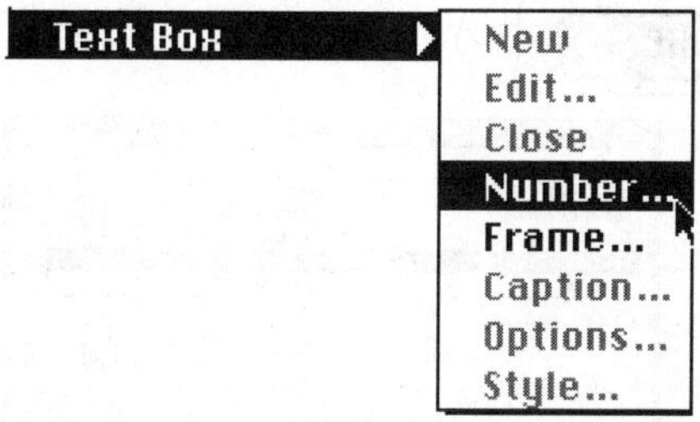

Figure 30: Select **Number** from the **Text Box** pop-up menu to reset caption numbers.

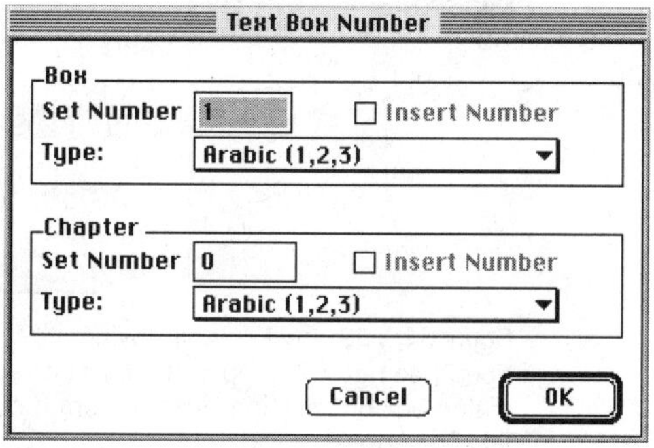

Figure 31: Type a new number in the **Set Number** text box.

Figure 32: Use the **Type** pop-up menu to change the type of number displayed.

To renumber a text box:

Every time you create a text box, WordPerfect assigns it a number. (This is the number you see in the Edit Text Box dialog box's Find Text Box Number text box. [see **Figure 21**]) Whether or not you choose to display this number, it is available for use in generating cross-references or lists (*see Chapter 13: "Lists" for a description of how to use the reference number in lists*). You can change the type of number used by renumbering the text box's caption.

1. Select the text box.
2. Pull down the Tools menu and select Number from the Text Box pop-up menu (**Figure 30**).
3. In the resulting Text Box Number dialog box (**Figure 31**), type a new number in the Set Number text box.
4. *Optional:* You can change the type of number displayed (such as alphabetic, Roman numerals, and so forth) by selecting a new option from the Type pop-up menu (**Figure 32**).
5. Click OK.

To add a chapter number to the caption:

1. Select the Edit button on the Styles toolbar.
2. In the Edit Styles dialog box (**Figure 33**), select the Text Box Caption style.
3. Click Edit.
4. With the resulting Edit Style window open, place your cursor in front of the Text Box number, pull down the Tools menu and select Number from the Text Box pop-up menu (**Figure 34**).

   See Chapter 6: "Using Styles" for a description of how to use the Edit Styles window.
5. In the resulting Text Box Number dialog box's Chapter section (**Figure 35**), click the Insert Number check box.
6. A chapter number is inserted at the insertion point (**Figure 36**). As shown in the figure, you can add punctuation between the two numbers.
7. Close the Style Edit window by clicking its close box.

Shortcuts

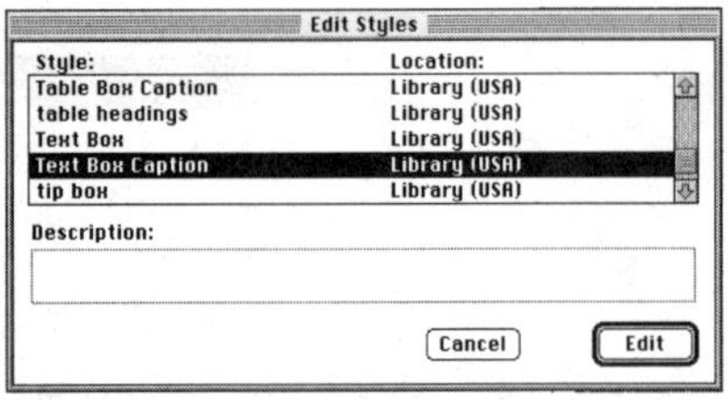

Figure 33: Select the **Text Box Caption** style from the Edit Styles dialog box.

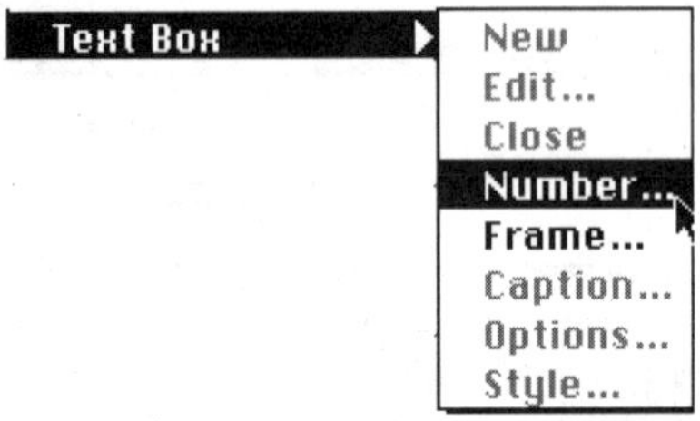

Figure 34: With the Edit Styles window open (see **Figure 37**), open the Number dialog box by selecting **Number** from the **Text Box** pop-up menu.

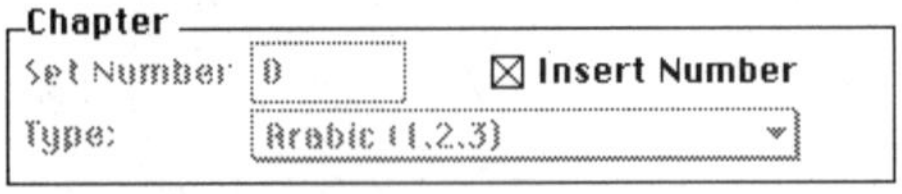

Figure 35: Click the **Insert Number** text box to insert a chapter number in front of the text box number.

You can type a caption descriptor, such as "Figure" or "Table," before the chapter number. This will appear on every caption.

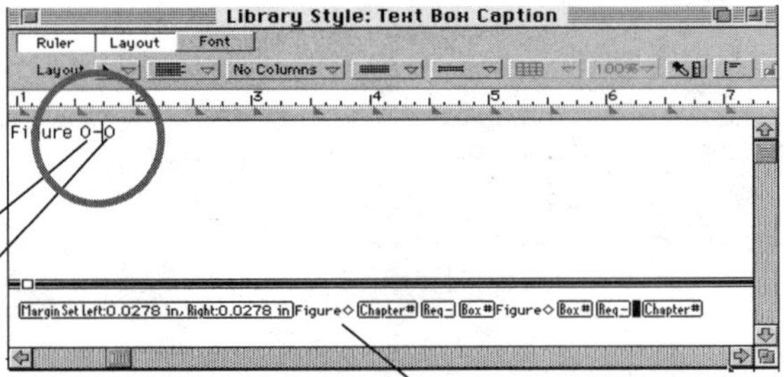

Chapter number.

Caption number.

The Number dialog box's Insert Number command places a Chapter Number code in the document.

Figure 36: A space holder for the chapter number is placed to the left of the text box number.

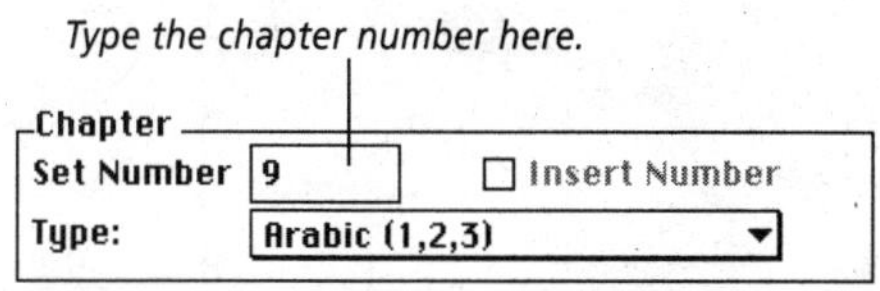

Figure 37: Type a chapter number in the **Set Number** text box of the **Chapter** section of the Text Box Number dialog box.

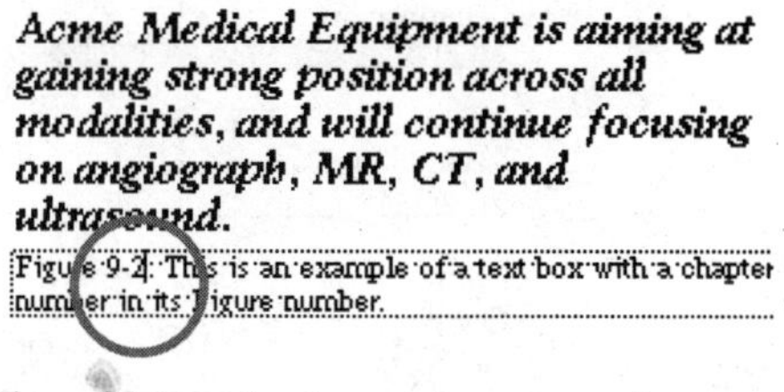

Figure 38: The chapter number appears in every caption.

8. You can change the chapter number by selecting a text box in the document and opening the Text Box Number dialog box again (**Figure 37**).
9. Type a chapter number in the Set Number text box and click OK.
10. As shown in **Figure 38**, the caption will reflect your setting.

Working with Layers to Create Special Effects

You can overlay and underlay graphics and text in documents to create interesting effects, such as banners and watermarks. Use overlays to add edit marks to documents that are easily removable without harming the actual text of the document. Use underlays to identify the priority or status of a document by printing watermarks or logos behind your text on every page.

To create an overlay:

1. Pull down the Tools menu and select Draw from the Overlay pop-up menu (**Figure 39**).
2. WordPerfect displays a transparent drawing window on the current page of your document.
3. Use the Graphic tools palette and Button bar to design your graphic overlay in this drawing window (**Figure 40**).
4. Click the Document Editor button to return to your Document and display the overlay.

> **Tip**
>
> You can open the overlay drawing layer by holding down the Option key while clicking the Graphics Editor button on the Button bar. Return to the Document Editor from the overlay graphic layer by clicking the overlay window's close box. You can also use the **Insert File** command on the File menu to import a graphic into the overlay layer.

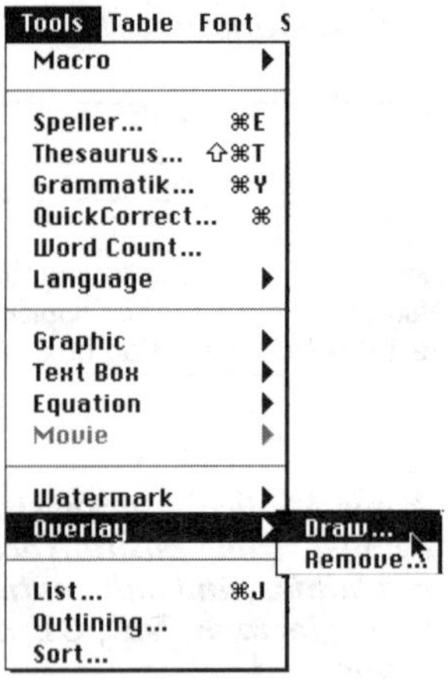

Figure 39: Select **Draw** from the **Overlay** pop-up menu.

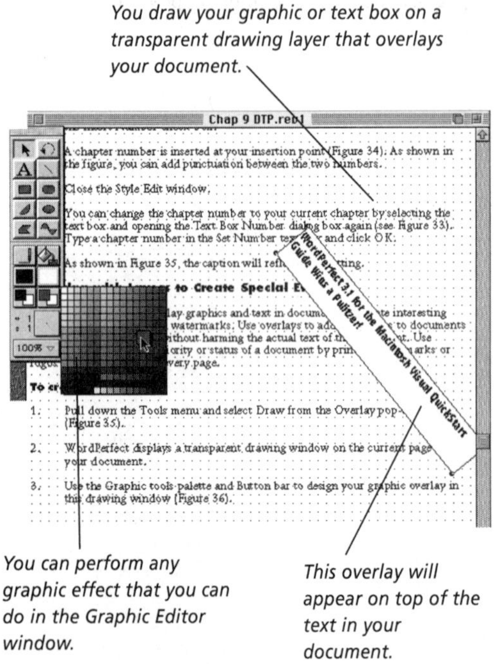

Figure 40: Use the transparent overlay layer to draw banners or headlines and they will appear as if floating on top of your text in the document.

Figure 41: Select **Remove** from the **Overlay** pop-up menu on the Tools menu.

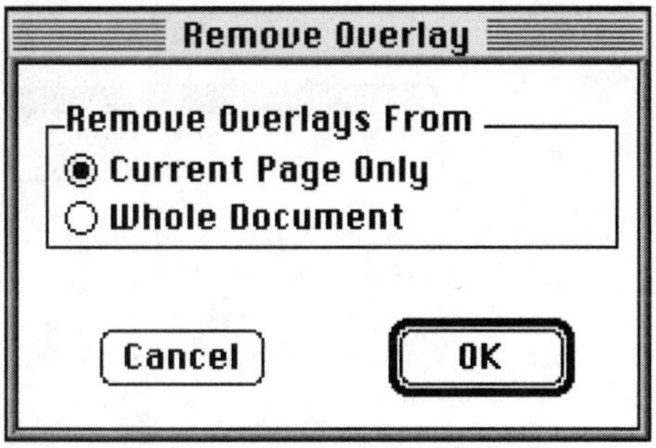

Figure 42: Select which overlays you want to remove by clicking the appropriate radio button.

To remove an overlay:

1. Move your insertion point to the page that contains the overlay you want to remove.
2. Pull down the Tools menu and select Remove from the Overlay pop-up menu (**Figure 41**).
3. In the resulting Remove Overlay dialog box (**Figure 42**), select the Current Page Only radio button if you want to remove only one overlay or the Whole Document radio button if you want to remove all of the overlays in your document.
4. Click OK.

To create a watermark:

1. Place the insertion point on the page where you want the watermark to begin.
2. Pull down the Tools menu and select New from the Watermark pop-up menu (**Figure 43**).
3. In the resulting New Watermark dialog box (**Figure 44**), select a watermark radio button. You can create up to two watermarks per page (A and B), giving you the ability to create alternating page watermarks.
4. Click OK.
5. WordPerfect displays the Graphics Editor window. Use its tool palette and buttons to create the watermark (**Figure 45**).
6. Click the Document Editor button on the Button bar or the Graphics Editor window's close box.
7. The watermark is placed on each page until a new watermark is detected.

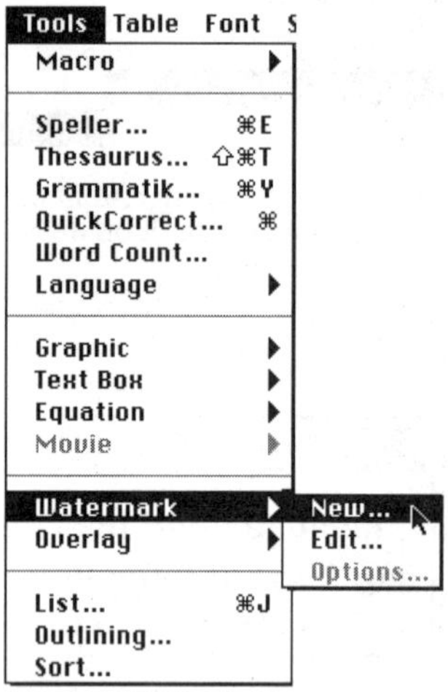

Figure 43: Select **New** from the **Watermark** pop-up menu on the Tools menu.

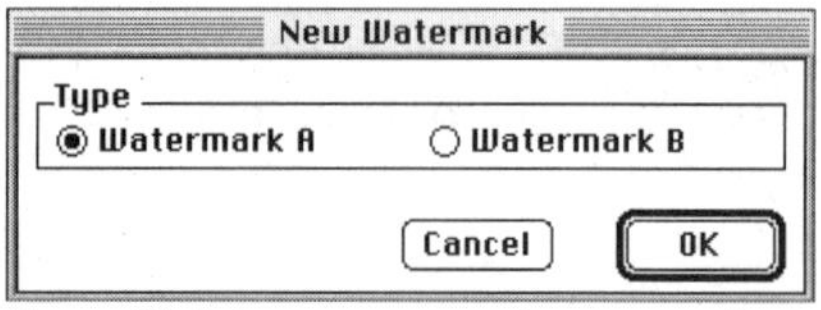

Figure 44: Select a watermark to create from the two options. You can create up to two watermarks per page (giving you the ability to alternate underlays).

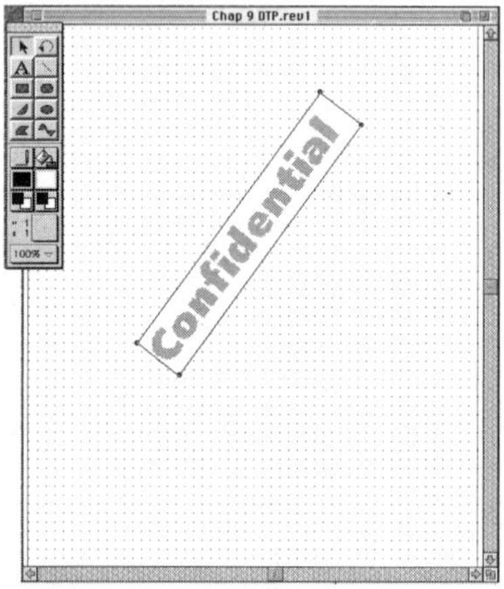

Figure 45: The underlying graphics window lets you create a watermark.

Tip

Use the **Edit** command from the **Watermark** pop-up menu to change the watermark you create. Use the **Options** command to display the Watermark Options dialog box where you can set how watermarks behave.

You cannot see the watermark directly in the Document Editor window. Select **Print Preview** from the File menu (or click the Print Preview button on the Button bar) to open the Print Preview window and view the watermark.

TABLES 10

WHEN YOU WANT to create a list of items in a matrix you can use the Tab key on the keyboard and the Ruler bar to align the various components. This method of building a matrix works if you only have single lines of text in each cell of the array. If you want to word-wrap text, tabs just don't work. For this work you need to use WordPerfect's Table toolbar tools to build tables.

Tables offer several benefits over conventional tabbed matrices, as follows:

- You can reformat text using all of your formatting tools and cause the text to re-wrap around a cell without fooling with additional tabs to align the text.
- You can add rows and/or columns without using additional tabs.
- You can perform math with components of the table.
- You can move the table around in a text box as a single item.
- You can create a caption for a table and include the table in a List of Figures. WordPerfect automatically tracks table numbers.

Mini-Glossary

Cell The space that contains a unit of data within a table. Cells can hold numbers, text, graphics, and endnotes, or equations.

Active Cell The cell that contains the insertion point. The active cell is also indicated by a gray veritical line in the Ruler bar.

Row The horizontal arrangement of cells in a table.

Column The vertical arrangement of cells in a table.

To create a table:

1. Place the insertion point where you want to place the table.
2. Pull down the Table menu and select New (**Figure 1**).
3. In the resulting New Table dialog box (**Figure 2**), type the number of columns you want to use in the Columns text box and the number or rows you want to use in the Rows text box.
4. Click OK.
5. In the resulting blank table (**Figure 3**), type your data into the cells of your new table, pressing a Tab or Right arrow after each item to move the cursor to the next cell.
6. *Optional:* Press the Tab key at the end of a row to create a new blank row.
7. Click outside the table when you are done (**Figure 4**).
8. *Optional:* You can create a new table by pulling down the Table pop-up menu on the Layout menu and dragging your mouse over the cells down and across to build the table (**Figure 5**).

Tip

When you select **Other** on the **Table** tool, the New Table dialog box (**see Figure 5**) is displayed.

When you create a new table, WordPerfect automatically opens the Table toolbar. Use its tools to format your table (*see pages 165 – 170, for information on editing a table*).

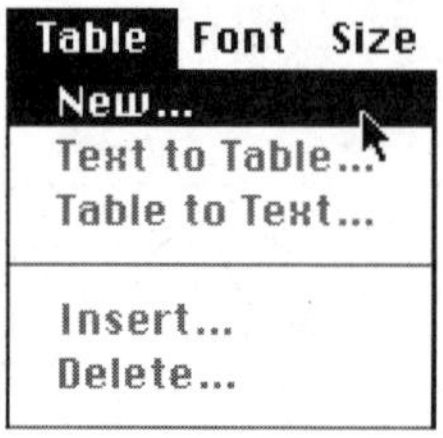

Figure 1: Select **New** from the Table menu.

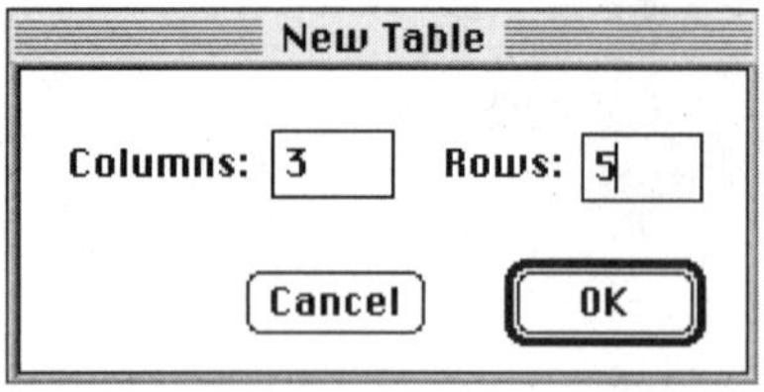

Figure 2: Type the number of columns and rows you want to use in the table in the appropriate text box.

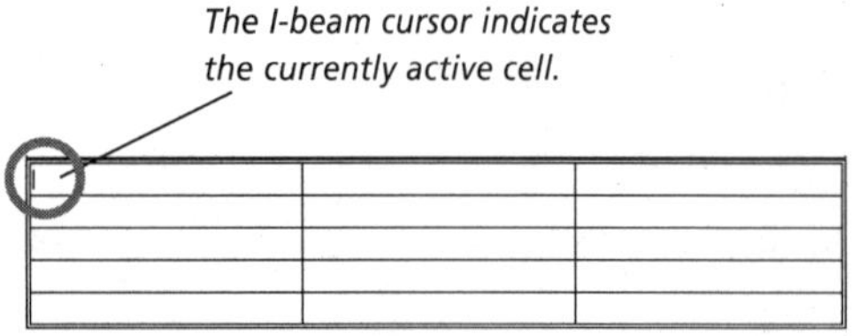

Figure 3: Type your data, pressing Tab to move to the next cell.

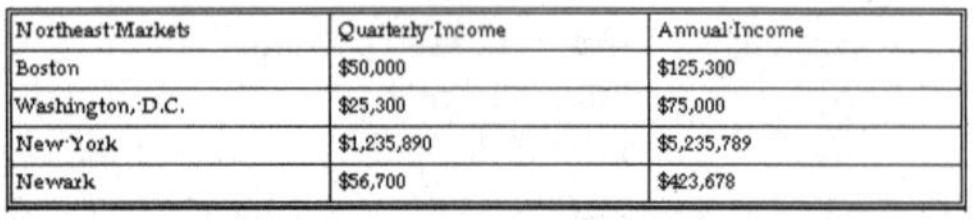

Northeast Markets	Quarterly Income	Annual Income
Boston	$50,000	$125,300
Washington, D.C.	$25,300	$75,000
New York	$1,235,890	$5,235,789
Newark	$56,700	$423,678

Figure 4: When you have entered your data, click outside the table to return to your document.

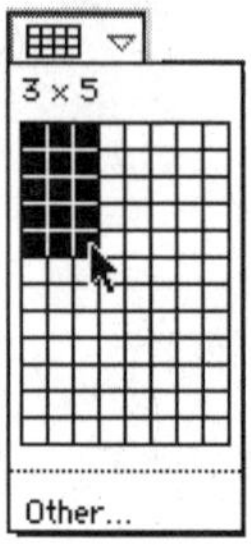

Figure 5: As an alternative to using the **New Table** command, use the **Table** pop-up menu on the Layout toolbar to create your table.

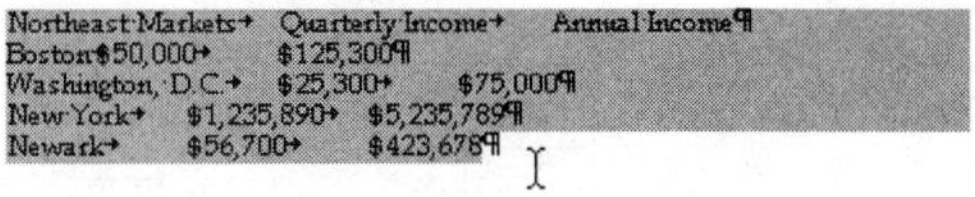

Figure 6: Select the text you want to place in the table...

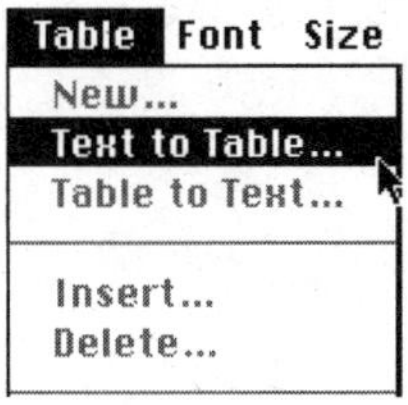

Figure 7: ...and select **Text to Table** from the Table menu.

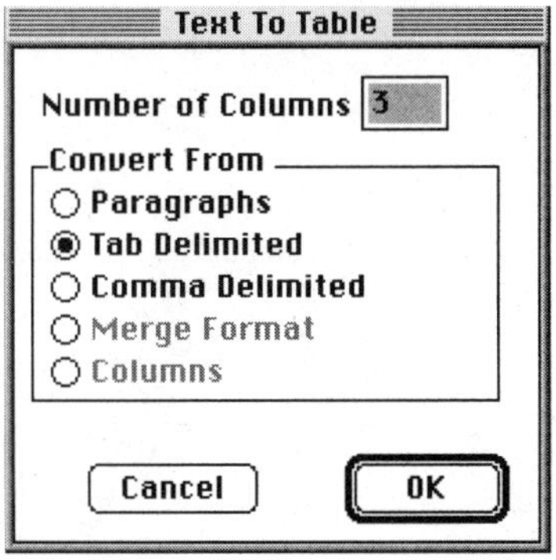

Figure 8: Edit the resulting Text To Table dialog box to fit your needs.

Northeast Markets	Quarterly Income	Annual Income
Boston	$50,000	$125,300
Washington, D.C.	$25,300	$75,000
New York	$1,235,890	$5,235,789
Newark	$56,700	$423,678

Figure 9: When you click **OK**, the selected data is placed in the correct cells of the table.

To create a table from existing text:

1. Select the text you want to include in the table (**Figure 6**). It is a good idea to use tabs to separate the data into columns and the Return key to indicate a new row when typing text you want to include in a table. You do not have to set up tabs on the Ruler bar.
2. Pull down the Table menu and select Text to Table (**Figure 7**).
3. In the resulting Text to Table dialog box (**Figure 8**), make sure that the proper cell delineator is selected (in this case the Tab Delimited radio button).
4. *Optional:* If you want to add additional blank columns to the end of the table, type a different number in the Number of Columns text box. The new column(s) are added on the right.
5. Click OK.
6. The table is created and selected so as to be ready for formatting (**Figure 9**).

Tip

You can convert an existing table to text by selecting the table and choosing **Table to Text** from the Table menu. In the resulting dialog box, click the radio button for the column delimiter you want to use. WordPerfect translates the table into text. This trick is useful if you want to export the data into a program that does not accept WordPerfect's tables, such as Adobe PageMaker.

To select items in a table:

When you position the pointer cursor over the outer edge of the table, the cursor changes to the outline of an arrow (depending on which edge is being pointed at). Clicking the mouse selects the entire column and/or row (depending on where you are pointing). To select an individual cell (see **Figure 10c**) you must double-click outside the text in the "white area" of the cell. **Figures 10a, b, and c** illustrate the different selection areas.

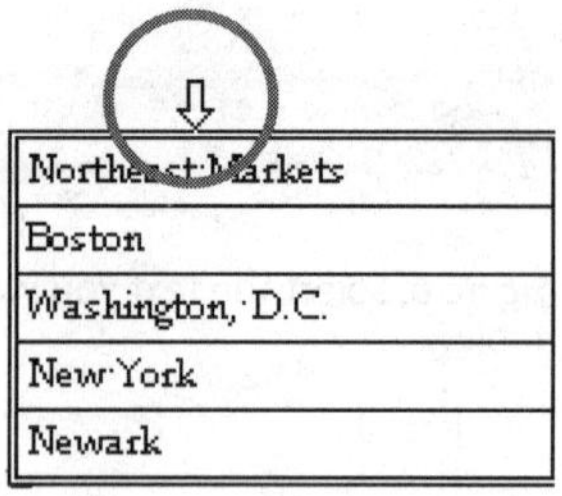

Figure 10a: Click once to select a column.

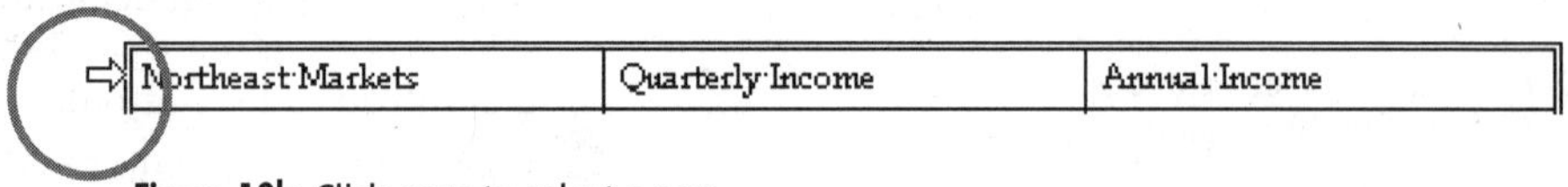

Figure 10b: Click once to select a row.

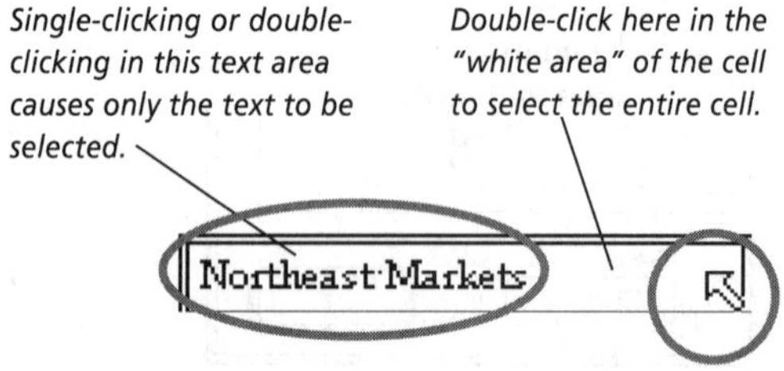

Figure 10c: Select a cell by double-clicking in the "white space" following the last text in the cell.

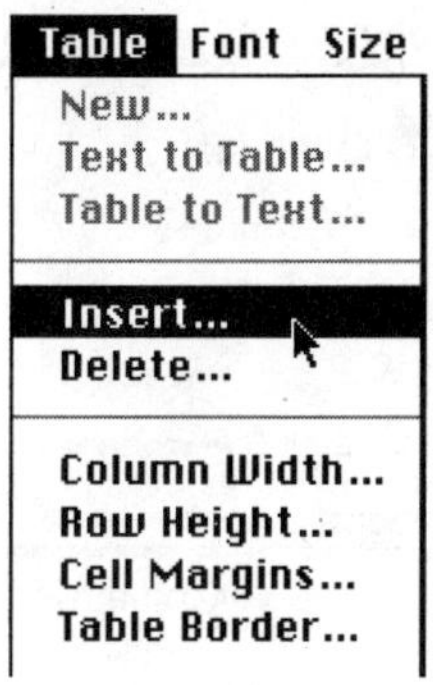

Figure 11: Select **Insert** from the Table menu.

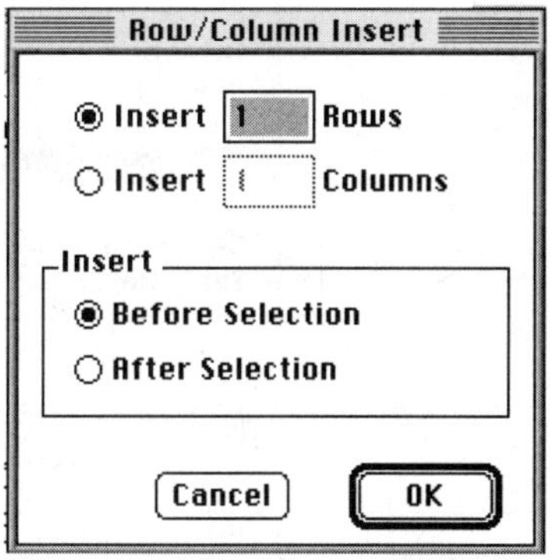

Figure 12: Select Row or Column options from the **Insert** area and radio buttons.

Editing Tables

You can join together cells to center text over more than one column, insert columns or rows into tables (or split merged cells apart again), delete rows or columns, manipulate the height of rows or width of columns, and add borders and fills to cells. You can also format the contents of tables with the standard formatting tools you have used on text, such as the Font and Format toolbar's tool sets.

To insert a column or row into a table:

1. To insert a new column, place the insertion point in the column to the right of where you want the new column to appear. To insert a row, place the insertion point in the row beneath where you want the row to appear.
2. Pull down the Table menu and select Insert (**Figure 11**).
3. In the resulting Row/Column Insert dialog box (**Figure 12**), type the number of rows or columns you want to add in the appropriate text box.
4. *Optional:* You can also specify if you want the row or column to appear above or below the row, or to the right or left of the column where you have your insertion point.
5. Click OK.

Tip

You can also use the **Insert Row** or **Insert Column** tools on the Table toolbar to perform an insert.

To delete a column or row:

Use the Delete Row/Column tool on the Table toolbar to delete a selected cell, row, or column in your table.

You can also pull down the Table menu and select Delete to display the Row/Column Delete dialog box (**Figure 13**) to delete more than one row or column at a time and gain precision about which row or column is deleted.

Warning: Be sure that you want to delete the entire table before clicking Delete Entire Table, because once the table is deleted you cannot get it back.

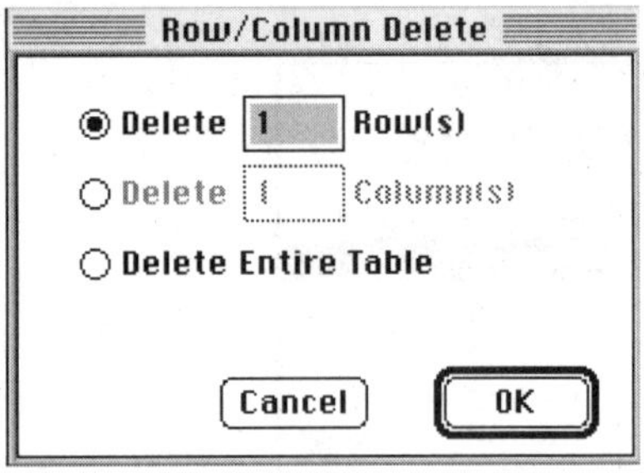

Figure 13: Type the number of rows or columns to delete in the text boxes.

To adjust the width of a column:

1. Select the column whose width you want to change.
2. Pull down the Table menu and select Column Width (**Figure 14**).
3. In the resulting Column Width dialog box, type the new width in the Column Width text box (**Figure 15**).
4. Click OK.

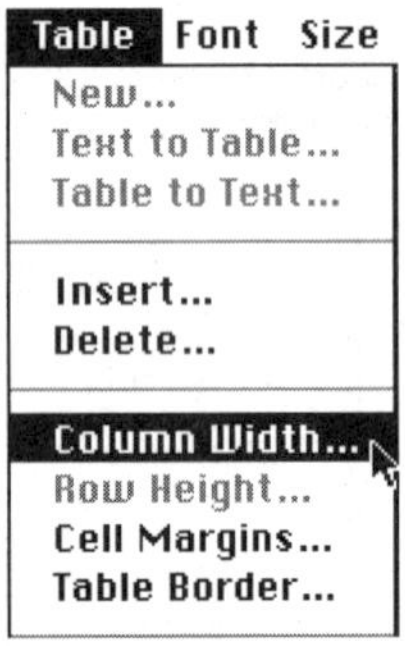

Figure 14: Select **Column Width** from the Table menu.

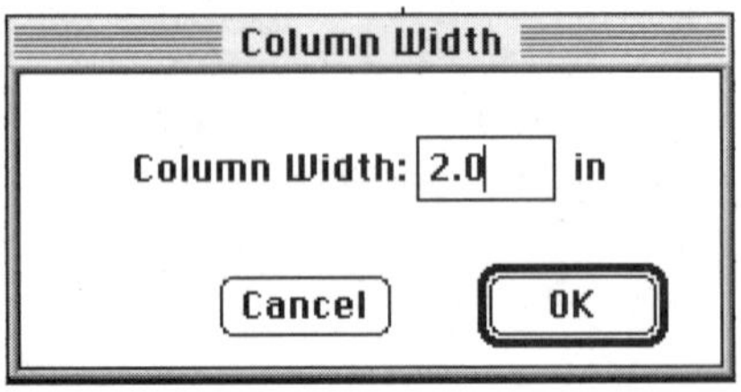

Figure 15: Type the width you want to set for the selected column in the **Column Width** text box. Click the "in" units to display other measurement units.

> **Tip**
>
> You can also adjust the width of a column on the screen by moving the cursor to the edge of a column. When the cursor changes to a margin cursor (**Figure 16**), drag the column to the required width. When you release the mouse, the column's contents adjusts to the new width.
>
> Ordinarily, when you resize a column, the table's margins change accordingly. You can move a single column's border without resizing the rest of the table's margins by pressing Option while dragging the mouse.

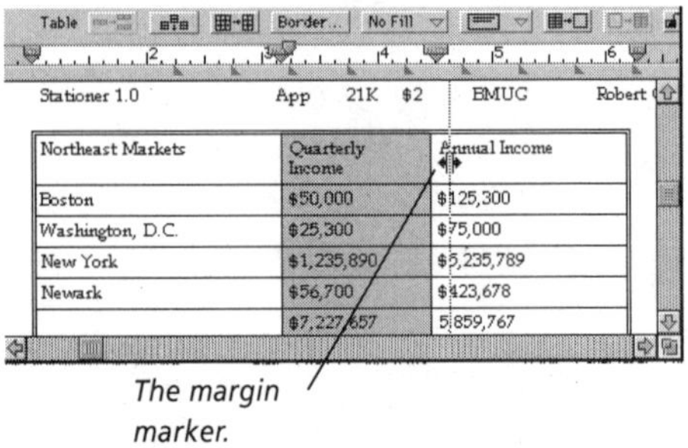

Figure 16: Drag the margin marker to the new width. Use the Ruler bar to add precision to your choice.

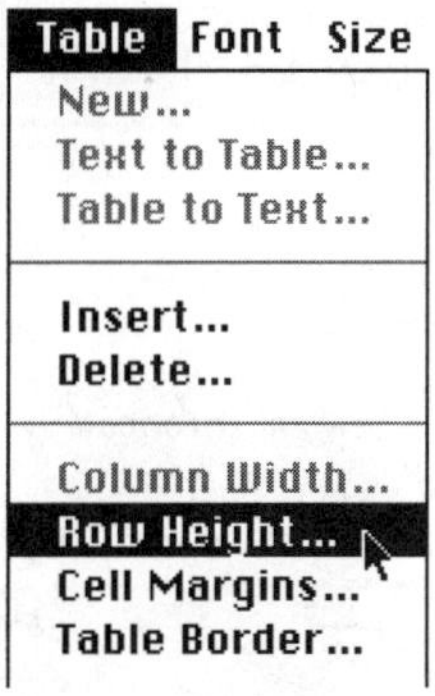

Figure 17: Select **Row Height** from the Table menu.

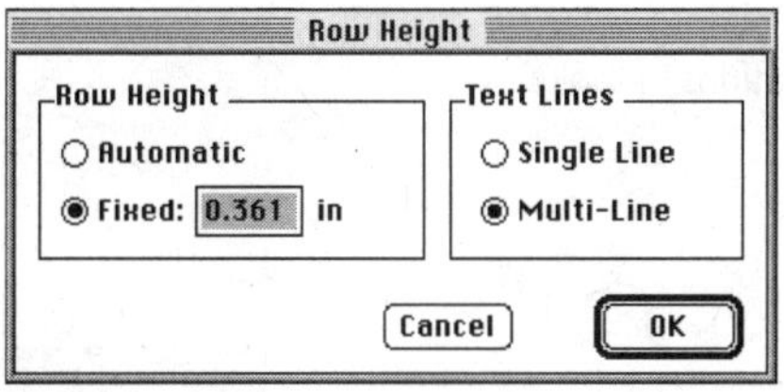

Figure 18: Select **Automatic** to let WordPerfect adjust the heights of rows to fit your text; or **Fixed** to manually assign a row height.

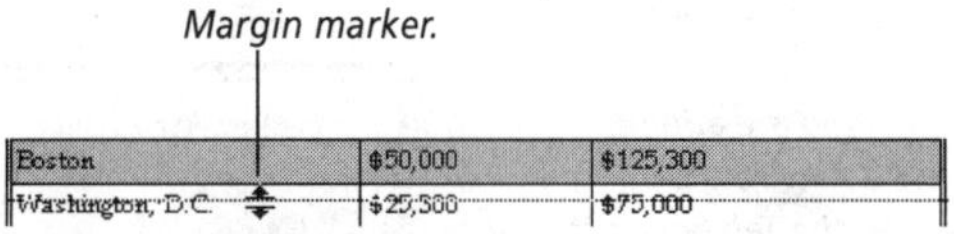

Figure 19: Drag the margin marker down or up to adjust the row height.

To adjust the height of a row:

1. Select the row whose height you want to change.
2. Pull down the Table menu and select Row Height (**Figure 17**).
3. In the resulting Row Height dialog box (**Figure 18**), click the Fixed Row radio button and type the new height in its text box.
4. *Optional:* You can also specify if you want the text to wrap in a cell by clicking the Single Line (no wrapping) or Multi-Line (text wrapping) radio buttons.
5. Click OK.

Tip

Like with the on-screen adjustment of columns, you can drag the edge of a row to adjust its height. Pass the cursor over a row's edge until it turns into a margin cursor. Drag the cursor (**Figure 19**) to resize the row.

To add a column of numbers:

1. *Optional:* If there is no blank cell beneath the column, or to the right of the row you are adding, press Tab at the last cell of the table to add another row to the table.
2. Place the insertion point in the cell directly beneath the column you are adding.
3. Click the Math button on the Table toolbar (**Figure 20**).
4. In the resulting Extended Table toolbar (**Figure 21**), pull down the arrow button on the Function text box and select a function (either Sum or Average). In this case, select Sum (**Figure 22**).
5. The function for adding an array of numbers is placed in the Function text box.
6. Drag the cursor down the column to include the first and last cell that you want to add in the column (**Figure 23**).
7. The cell axes (for example B5 designating column B, row 5) are placed in the function (**Figure 24**). (A colon between the cell axes indicates an array of numbers was selected.)

Figure 20: Click the **Math** button on the Table bar to display the Extended Table bar.

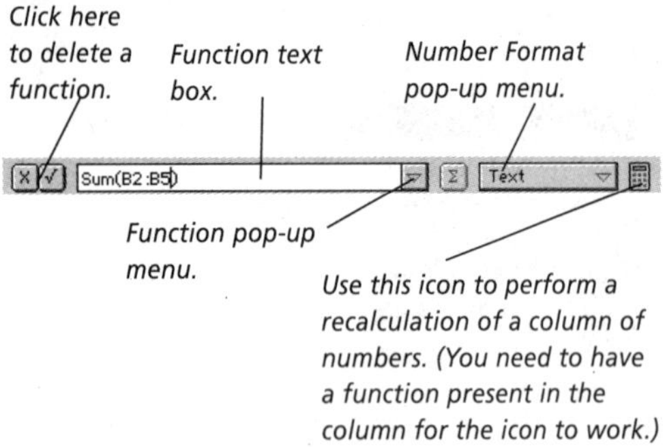

Figure 21: Use the Extened Table bar to perform calculations in tables.

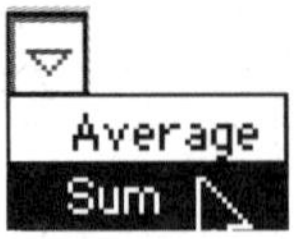

Figure 22: Select a pre-set function from the **Function** pop-up menu, or type your own.

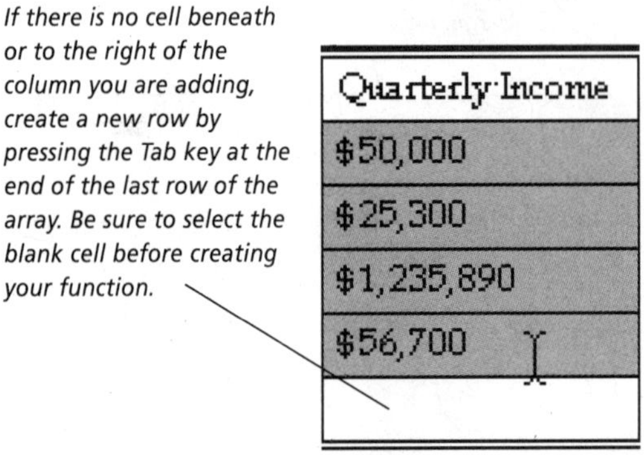

Figure 23: Select a function and then drag the mouse through your array to place their cell identifications in the function.

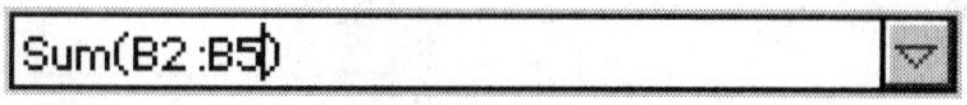

Figure 24: WordPerfect uses standard spreadsheet notation in the functions on the Extended Table bar.

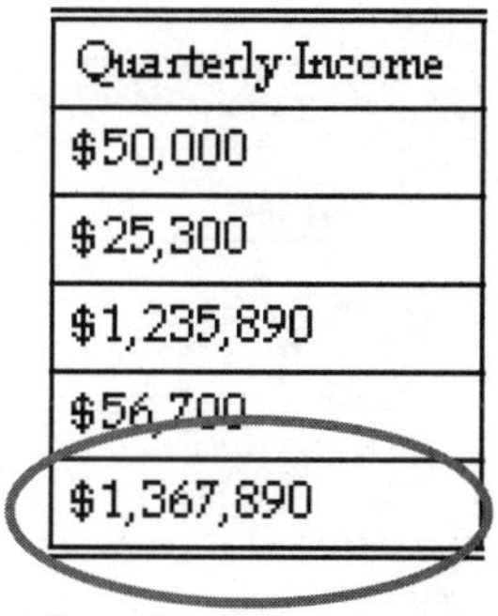

Figure 25: The result of the calculation is placed in the cell beneath the array.

8. Click the check mark tool in the Function text box to accept the formula. You can also press the Enter key on the numeric keypad of an extended keyboard. You can delete the formula by clicking the X tool.
9. The result is placed in the cell where your insertion point is located (**Figure 25**).

> **Tip**
>
> You can also type or import a spreadsheet formula into the Function text box and click on appropriate cells to include them in your customized function. You can also type numbers and operators directly into the Function text box. Use +, -, *, and / to indicate addition, subtraction, multiplication, and division, respectively.
>
> You can perform a quick sum by clicking the **Sigma** (Σ) tool on the Extended Math toolbar.

To format numbers in a table:

1. Select the number(s) you want to change.
2. Pull down the **Number Format** tool from the Extended Table toolbar (**Figure 26**) and select a pre-set format or **Other** to create a customized format.
3. If you selected **Other**, the Number Format dialog box is displayed (**Figure 27**). Select a format from the list box and select appropriate format check boxes to customize the selection.
4. Click **OK**.

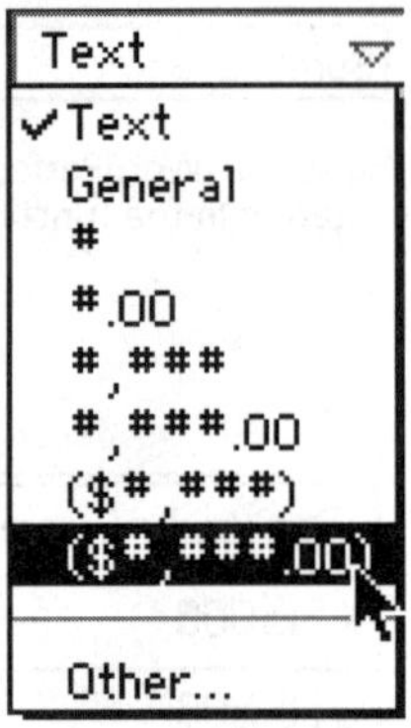

Figure 26: Use a pre-set format from the **Number Format** pop-up menu on the Extended Table bar (see Figure 21) to format table numbers.

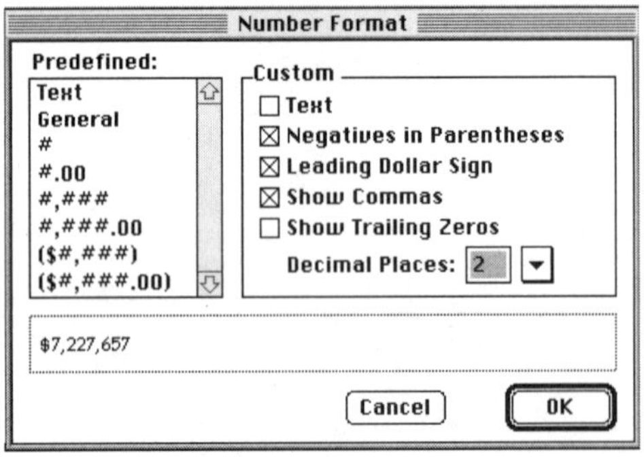

Figure 27: Select and edit the pre-set formats to meet your requirements.

Tip

WordPerfect displays numbers up to seven decimal places. You can enter larger decimals, but WordPerfect automatically rounds them off to the nearest seventh place.

SHORTCUTS 11

NOW THAT YOU have become proficient at performing some of WordPerfect's myriad commands and procedures, you can take pride that you know the long way to do many things. Thank goodness WordPerfect recognizes that the hard way is not always the best way to accomplish goals, and provides shortcuts that make performing common processes much shorter and easier. Some of these shortcuts are built into the program, some are customizable, and some are simply tools you use to build your own shortcuts. This chapter describes how to use the following shortcuts:

- **Templates.** WordPerfect Templates files are pre-constructed documents that contain formatting, graphics, macros, and layout that assist you in performing business and personal work. WordPerfect 3.5 provides over 80 templates. These documents are contained in their own Templates folder in the WordPerfect 3.5 folder.
- **QuickCorrect.** QuickCorrect is a small program within WordPerfect that runs behind the scenes to correct your spelling and spell out acronyms. QuickCorrect can learn your typing foibles and correct them on-the-fly.
- **Macros.** WordPerfect contains a powerful, yet easy to use, macro language that you can use to create your own scripts to perform repetitive processes.

Using Templates

WordPerfect provides template files to assist your productivity. You open a template the same way you open any other document in WordPerfect. The difference is that WordPerfect does not open the original file, but makes a copy for your use and opens the copy.

Templates are stored in the Templates folder in the WordPerfect 3.5 folder.

There are three ways to open templates:

- Select Open from the Templates pop-up menu on the File menu and then select a template from the resulting Open dialog box.
- You can also open template files from the Open dialog box by pulling down the Templates menu and selecting a title.
- Create a document and save it as a template using the Save As command.

The following pages describe how to use Templates files to produce documents.

To open an existing template:

1. Open WordPerfect.
2. Pull down the File menu and select Open from the Templates pop-up menu (**Figure 1a**).
3. In the resulting Open Templates dialog box (**Figure 1b**), select a template from the list box or open the More Templates folder to display additional selections.
4. Click Open.

Figure 1a: Select **Open** from the **Templates** pop-up menu.

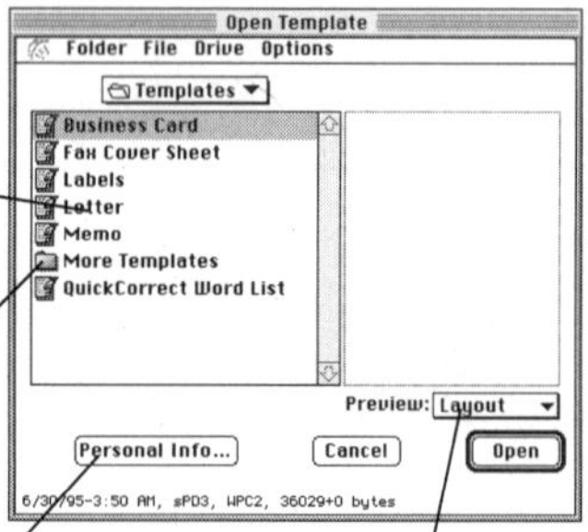

Figure 1b: Select a template from the Open Templates dialog box or open the More Templates folder to select from alternate template folders.

> **Tip**
>
> WordPerfect provides over 80 templates, plus areas to enter personal information for use in the other templates via macros, as well as the capability to create a new template, and the ability to update your QuickCorrect file.

Templates are opened as an untitled document.

WordPerfect provides a pre-built macro (see page 182 for information about macros) that lets you complete the memo's addresses from WordPerfect's address list.

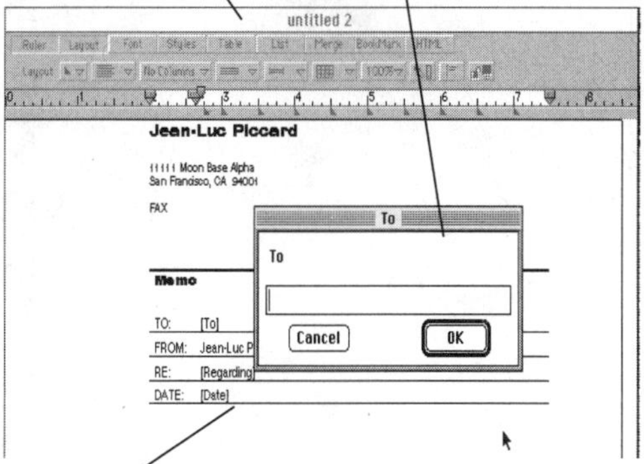

Templates are documents with areas describing how to input your text within WordPerfect.

Figure 2a: The Memo template, along with the Letter and Fax file, as well as many other templates, supplies macros that assist you in completing your job.

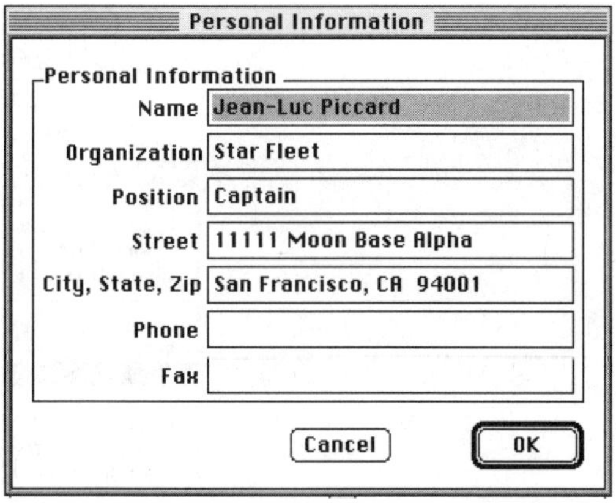

Figure 2b: The information you enter into this dialog box is used to complete many of the templates.

5. WordPerfect opens a template file as an untitled document (**Figure 2a**).
6. Fill in the template and create your document.
7. Save the document as you would any other file by selecting **Save As** from the File menu.

   See Chapter 1: "Introduction" for a discussion of how to save your documents for the first time.

Tip

In Figure 2a, notice that WordPerfect has built a macro that assists you in completing the sections of the document, such as name of recipient and so forth. If you do not want to answer these questions, click Cancel and then respond to the query about future responses to the macro. WordPerfect automatically turns on the macro when you open the Letter and Memo Templates.

The first time you open a macro-based template, such as the business card, memo, letter, or fax template, WordPerfect displays the Personal Information dialog box (**Figure 2b**). Complete the form so that WordPerfect can automatically fill in the pertinent data in the template. You can also select the Personal Data option from the Open Templates dialog box should you wish to change the information at a later date.

See page 178 for a description of how to create your own Templates.

To create new templates:

1. Create the document you want to save as a template (**Figure 3**).
2. Pull down the File menu and select Save As (**Figure 4**).
3. In the resulting Save As dialog box (**Figure 5**), select WordPerfect 3 Templates from the Format pop-up menu.
4. Give the document a name by typing a name in the Save Document As text box.
5. *Optional:* If you want to be able to access the new template from the File menu and a dialog box's Templates menu, save the document in the Templates folder in the WordPerfect 3.5 folder.

   See Chapter 3: "Working," for a description of how to open new folders using the Title bar and how to save a file in another location Directory list box.
6. Click Save.

Figure 3: You can create your own template files containing information you use regularly.

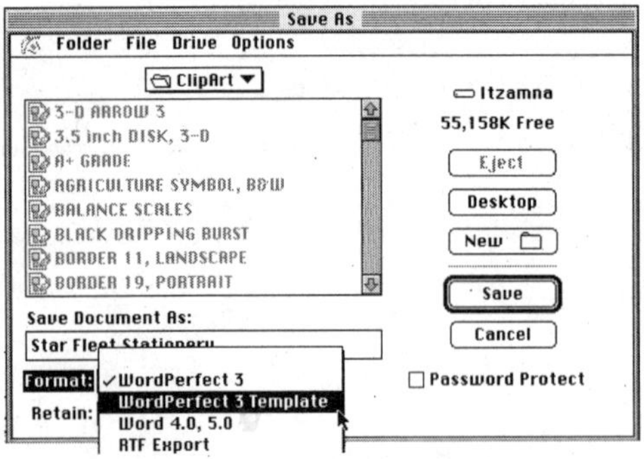

Figure 5: Type a name for the template file and save it in the Templates folder to access it from the File menu.

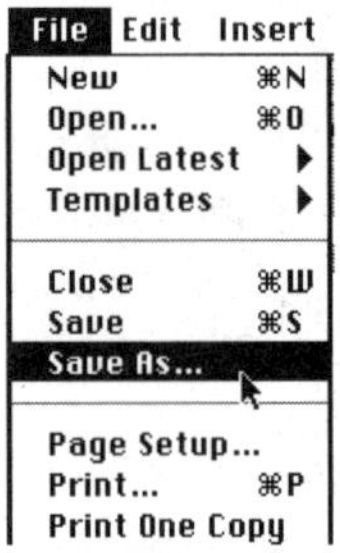

Figure 4: Select **Save As** from the File menu.

Using QuickCorrect

QuickCorrect is three tools in one:

- An automatic spelling checker
- An automatic simple grammar checker
- A tool to speed up your data entry.

The first two uses for QuickCorrect are covered in the next chapter, Chapter 12: "Proofing."

This chapter discusses using QuickCorrect to spell out acronyms and abbreviations on-the-fly. Abbreviations are converted as soon as you press the Spacebar or type the next punctuation after typing the abbreviation.

To turn on QuickCorrect:

1. Pull down the Edit menu and select Preferences (Figure 6).
2. In the resulting Preferences window, click QuickCorrect (Figure 7).
3. In the resulting QuickCorrect dialog box (Figure 8), make sure that the Enable QuickCorrect check box is selected.
4. Click OK.

> **Tip**
>
> You can also double-click the QuickCorrect area of the Status bar (**Figure 9**) to access the QuickCorrect dialog box. If QuickCorrect is not displayed, select its option from the Status Bar pop-up menu. *See Chapter 2: "Basics," for a description of how to add items to the Status bar.*

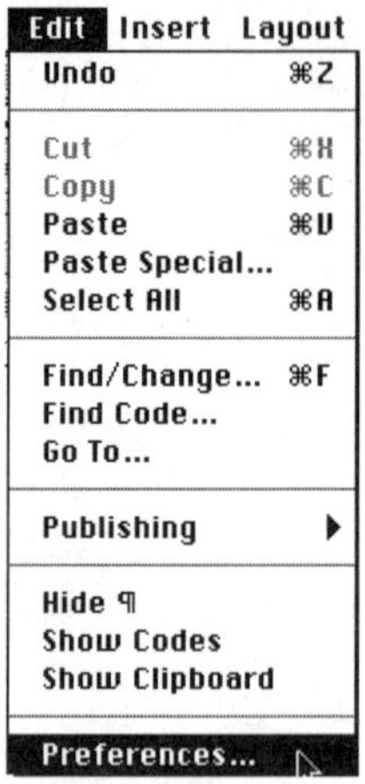

Figure 6: Select **Preferences** from the Edit menu to turn on QuickCorrect.

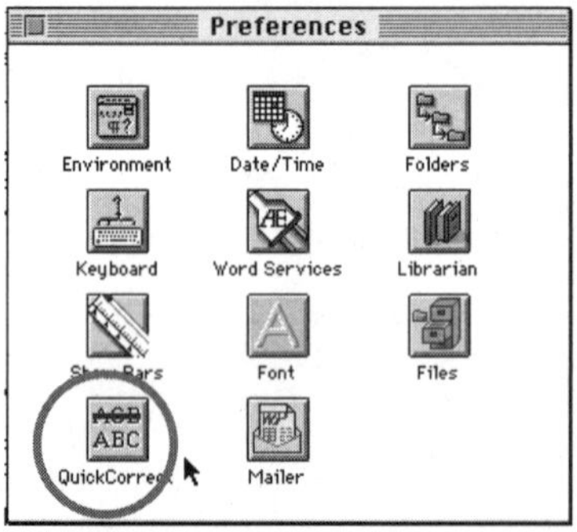

Figure 7: Click the **QuickCorrect** button.

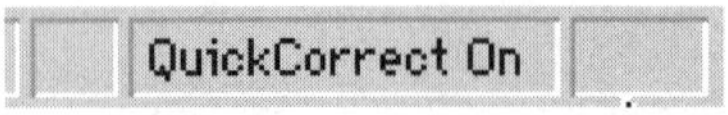

Figure 9: Select **QuickCorrect** from the Status bar pop-up menu to display the QuickCorrect status on the Status bar. Double-click the QuickCorrect status button on the Status bar to display its dialog box, shown in Figure 8.

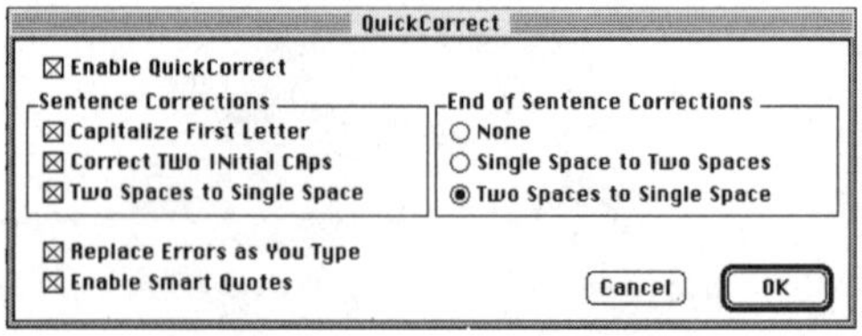

Figure 8: WordPerfect enables QuickCorrect as a default, but if you have inadvertently turned it off, click **Enable QuickCorrect** to turn it back on.

Figure 10: Select QuickCorrect from the Tools menu.

To add terms to QuickCorrect:

1. Pull down the Tools menu and select QuickCorrect (**Figure 10**).
2. In the resulting Edit QuickCorrect List dialog box (**Figure 11**), type the abbreviation or acronym you want identified and spelled out in the Replace text box.
3. Type the full spelling of the word(s) in the With text box.
4. Click Add. WordPerfect places the full spelling into the QuickCorrect list in alphabetical order.
5. Repeat steps 2 through 4 for each acronym or abbreviation you want spelled.
6. Click OK.

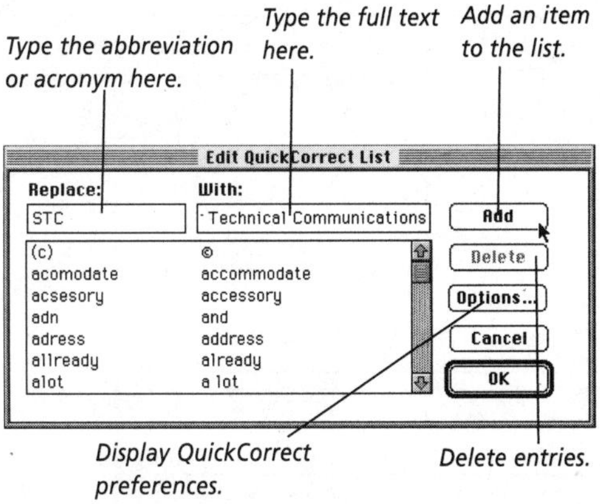

Figure 11: When you click **Add**, WordPerfect places your acronym or abbreviation and its full text into the alphabetical list.

When you next type the term, WordPerfect replaces it with the full spelling as soon as you type punctuation or press the Space bar.

Tip

You can delete terms from the QuickCorrect list by selecting the term from the list and clicking **Delete.** You can change the QuickCorrect preferences by clicking the **Options** button to display the QuickCorrect dialog box.

Using Macros

Macros are scripts that you can write to automate repetitious actions within application programs. WordPerfect supports a strong macro language for writing such scripts. These little collections of actions can be as simple as opening a document and saving it under a new name or as complex as asking you questions to complete a form letter.

If you are a novice at writing programs, you can let WordPerfect copy your mouse clicks and cursor movements to generate a macro. **Figure 12** presents an illustration of the Envelope macro that comes with WordPerfect. This is a very complicated script that accomplishes several goals: formating and printing envelopes, and maintaining mailing lists. The result is shown in **Figure 13**, the Envelope Data window.

This section covers how to record, playback, and edit macros. See WordPerfect's online Macro help on the Help menu (*see Chapter 1: "Introduction" for information on the Help menu*) to learn more about writing your own scripts.

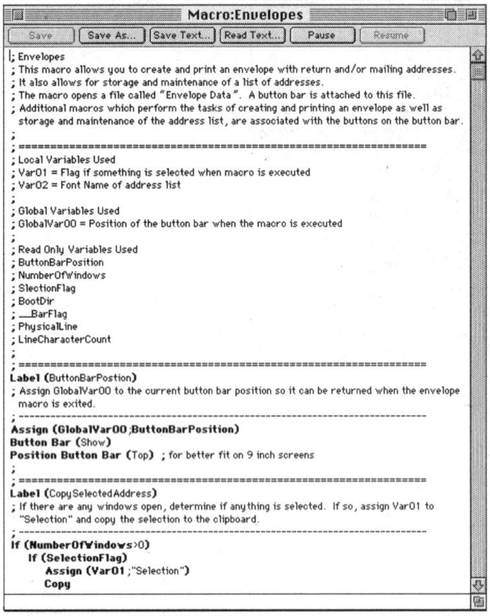

Figure 12: The Envelope macro is a sophisticated script that not only prints envelopes, but manages an address list as well.

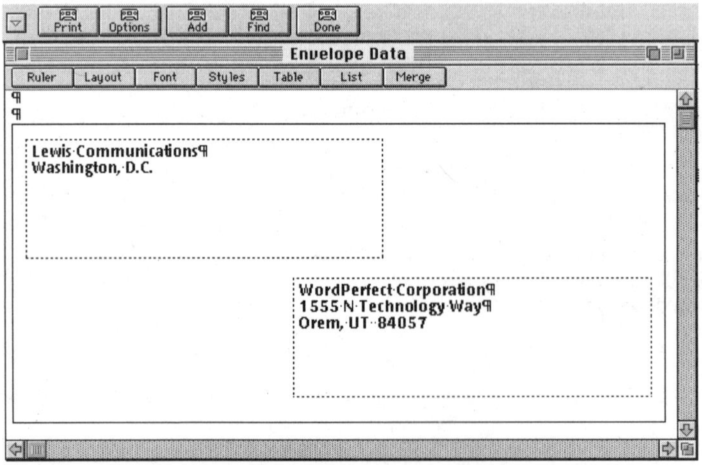

Figure 13: When you run the Envelope macro, WordPerfect invokes a self-contained program produced by the script shown in Figure 12.

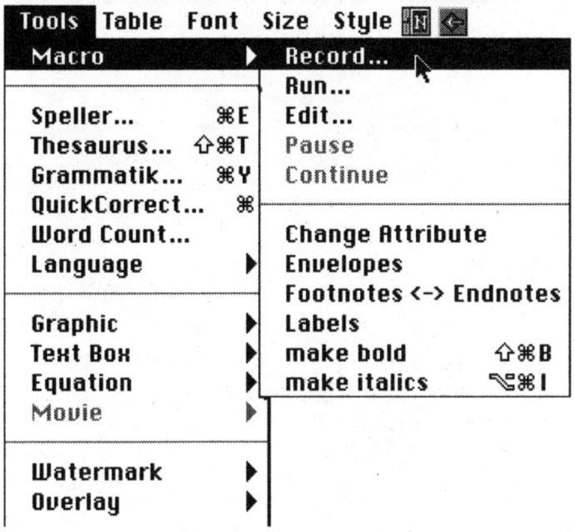

Figure 14: Select **Record** from the **Macro** pop-up menu.

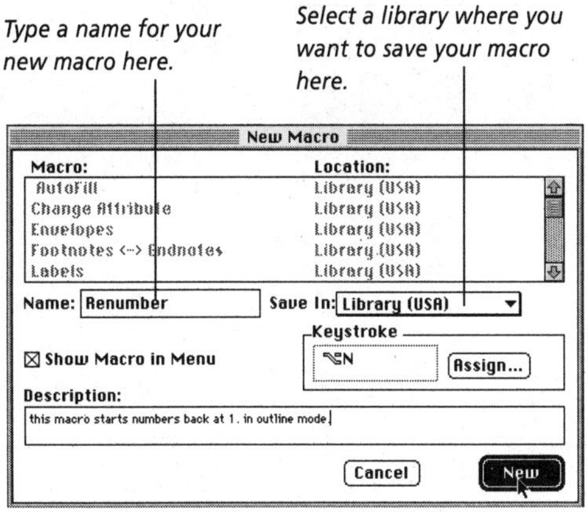

Figure 15a: Use the New Macro dialog box to set up your macro, then press **New** to start recording.

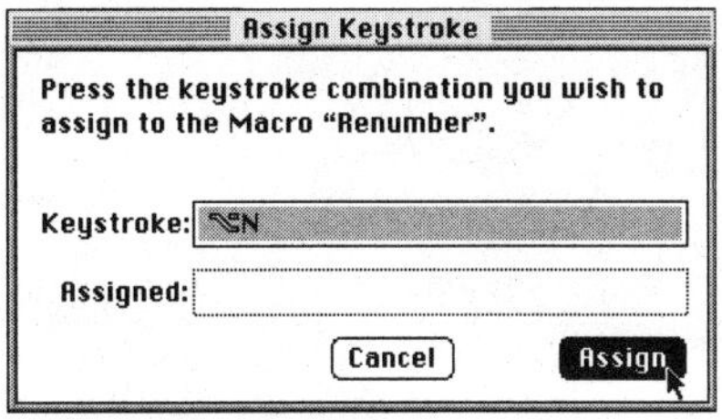

Figure 15b: Use the Assign Keystroke dialog box to provide a shortcut for your macro.

To record a macro:

1. Pull down the Tools menu and select **Record** from the **Macro** pop-up menu (**Figure 14**).

   Note: You do not have to be in an open document to record a macro, although if you want to record a macro in a document, place your insertion point in the document before selecting **Record**.

2. In the resulting New Macro dialog box (**Figure 15a**), type a name for your new macro in the **Name** text box.
3. *Optional:* If you want to run the macro solely with the currently active document, select its name from the **Save In** pop-up menu. The default is to save the macro in the **Library(USA)** library so that the macro is accessible to all of your documents.
4. *Optional:* If you are planning to use the macro often, assign a keystroke combination to it by clicking **Assign**. Type the keystroke and click **Assign** to register it (**Figure 15b**).
5. *Optional:* Type a description for the macro in the **Description** text box. This is a good idea if your macro does something cryptic that only you understand from its title.
6. Click **New**. WordPerfect closes the New Macro dialog box and displays the Macro Editor window. If you are recording a macro in a document the Macro Editor window is displayed behind the currently active document's window.

7. Perform the keystrokes, mouse movements, command selections, and text typing that you want included in the macro. In this case, I am creating a macro that invokes the Outline command automatically to start numbering back at number 1 in a list or paragraph series.
8. *Optional:* If you want to temporarily stop recording, Select the Pause command from the Macro pop-up menu on the Tools menu. When you want to begin recording again, select the Resume command from the Macro pop-up menu (see **Figure 14**).
9. When you finish recording the macro, select Stop Recording from the Macro pop-up menu on the Tools menu **(Figure 16)**.

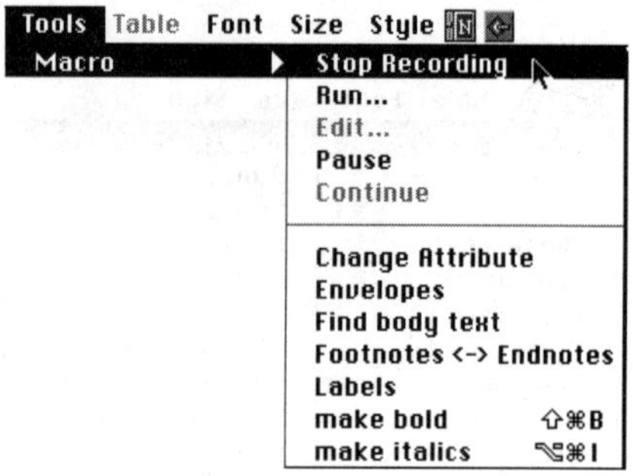

Figure 16: When you have finished creating the macro, select **Stop Recording** from the Macro pop-up menu.

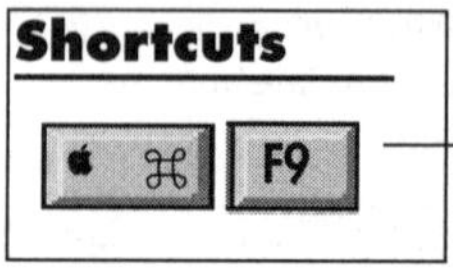

Use this keystroke combination to invoke the New Macro dialog box.

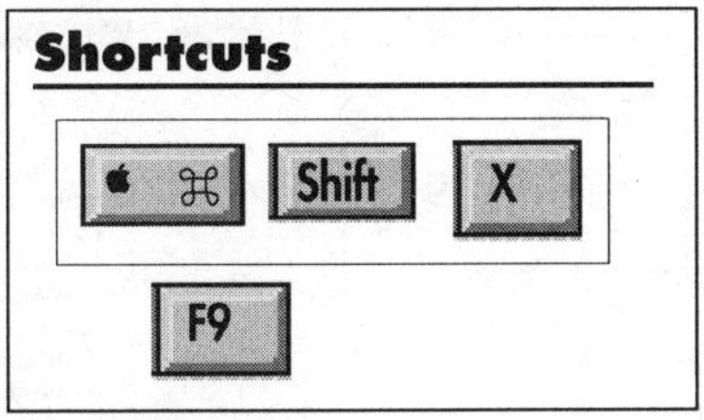

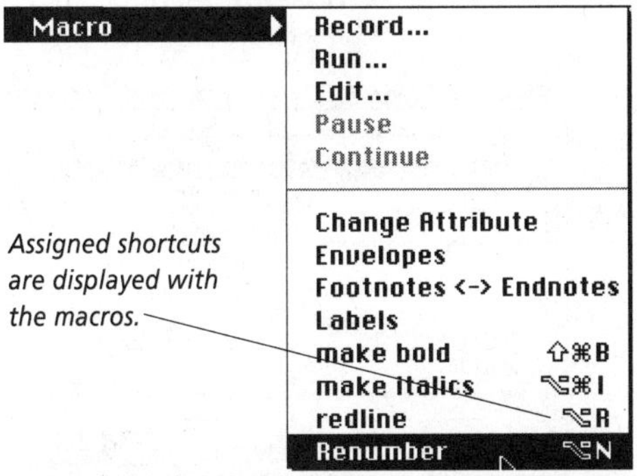

Figure 17: Select the name of the macro from the **Macro** pop-up menu or press its keystroke combination.

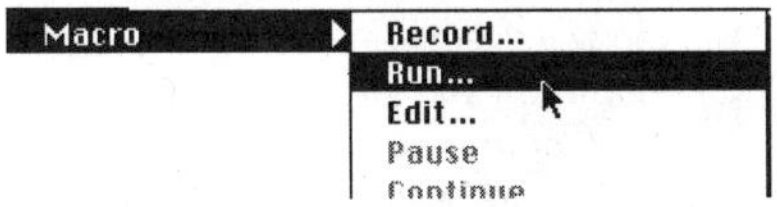

Figure 18: You can also use the **Run** command on the **Macro** pop-up menu if you do not know exactly which macro you want to use.

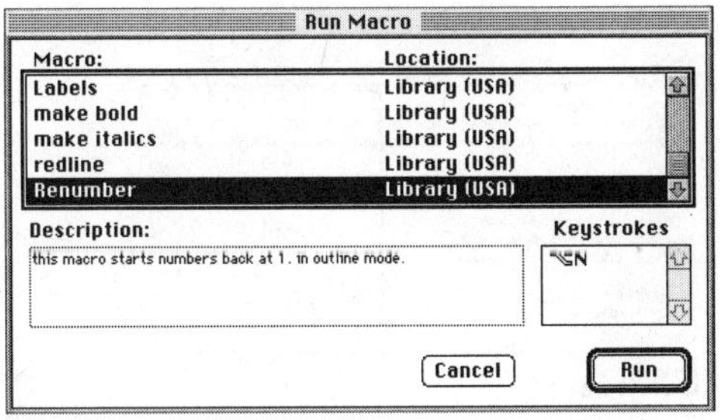

Figure 19: Select the macro's name from the **Macro** list box and click **Run**.

To play back a macro:

1. Open the document that contains the macro you want to run. If you have saved the specified macro in the Library(USA) library, you can run it in any document.
2. Pull down the Tools menu and select the macro's name from the Macro pop-up menu (**Figure 17**). Note that if you assigned a keystroke combination to the macro, you can press the keystroke combination to invoke the macro.

   or
3. Pull down the Tools menu and select Run from the Macro pop-up menu (**Figure 18**).
4. In the resulting Run Macro dialog box (**Figure 19**), select the macro's name from the Macro list box.
5. Click Run.

To edit a macro:

1. Pull down the Tools menu and select **Edit** from the Macro pop-up menu (**Figure 20**).
2. In the resulting Edit Macro dialog box (**Figure 21**), select the macro's name that you want to edit from the **Macro** list box.
3. Click **Edit Content**.
4. Make your changes in the Macro Editor window (**Figure 22**) using the six buttons on the Macro Editor toolbar:
   - **Save** (saves the new edited version of the macro under the old name)
   - **Save As** (saves the edited version of the macro under a new name)
   - **Save Text** (saves a macro as text)
   - **Read Text** (converts macros saved as text back to macros)
   - **Pause**, and **Resume**. Pause temporarily stops the recording or playback and Resume starts it again.

   You can use the **Record, Stop Recording**, and **Pause/Resume** commands while the Macro Editor is open to make changes to the macro. Switch between the document and Editor to use these commands.
5. Click **Save** on the Macro Editor toolbar and then the Macro Editor's close box to exit the Macro Editor and return to your document.

Shortcuts

Shift F9

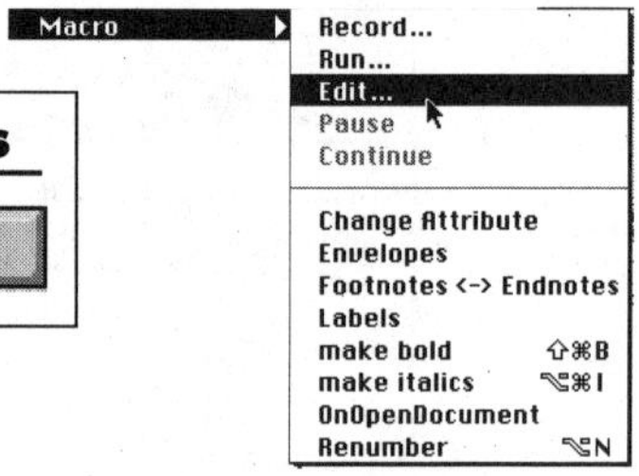

Figure 20: Select **Edit** from the **Macro** pop-up menu.

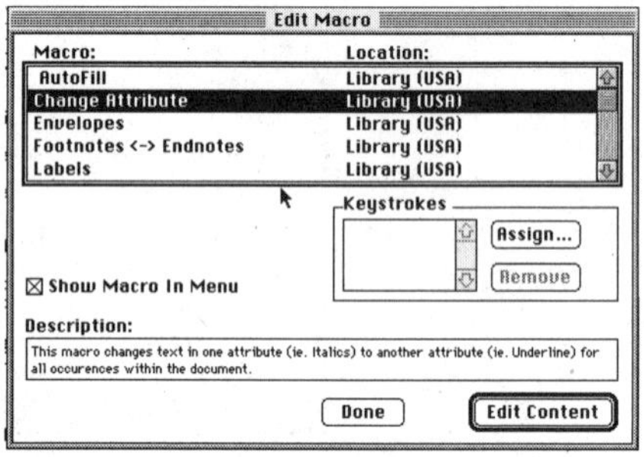

Figure 21: Select the macro's name from the **Macro** list box and click **Edit Content**.

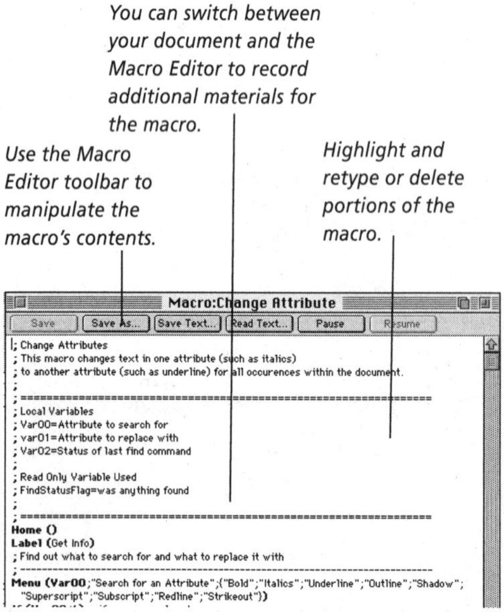

Figure 22: Use the Macro Editor window to edit the macro's contents. *See Macro Help on the Help menu for more information on how to write scripts and edit them.*

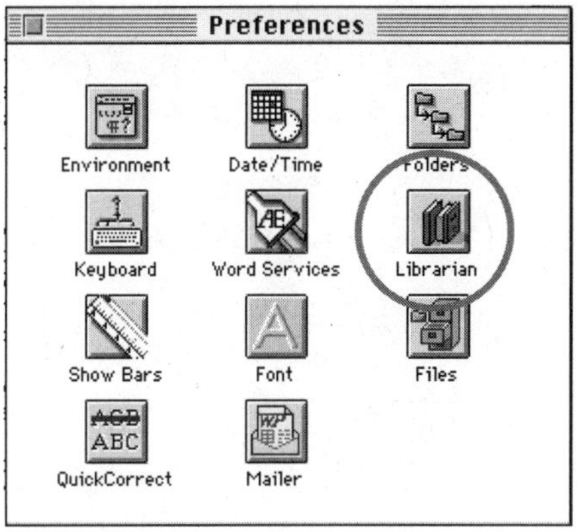

Figure 23: Select the **Librarian** button on the Preferences window.

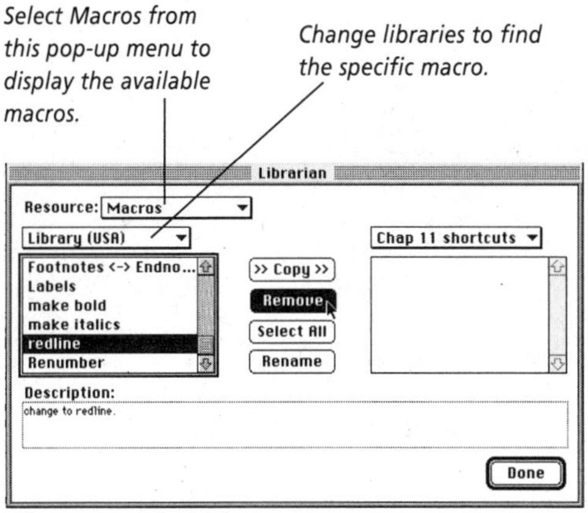

Figure 24: Select the macro you want to delete and click **Remove.**

To delete a macro from WordPerfect:

1. Pull down the Edit menu and select Preferences.
2. In the Preferences window, click the Librarian button (**Figure 23**).
3. In the resulting Librarian dialog box (**Figure 24**), if the Macros list box is not displayed, select Macros from the Resources pop-up menu.
4. Select the macro you want to delete and click Remove.
5. Click Done.

Tip

As shown in **Figure 24**, if your macro has been saved in a library, the macro can be located using the left-hand list box and pop-up menu. If your macro has been saved with the document, look in the right-hand list box for your macro's name. The **Remove** button works in either direction, as do the **Copy** and **Rename** buttons.

PROOFING 12

EVEN THE BEST writers and most proficient grammarians need help in making their documents letter-perfect. WordPerfect provides several tools that help you in this endeavor:

- **A Spelling Checker.** WordPerfect provides an extensive spelling checker with the program. WordPerfect's Speller not only checks for misspellings, but also capitalization errors and repeated words. The program also has connections to QuickCorrect to teach WordPerfect about your common errors. QuickCorrect uses these additions to catch and correct the errors as you type.
- **A Thesaurus.** Have you ever searched for the perfect word, only to be stymied by a faulty memory? WordPerfect includes a large collection of homonyms, synonyms, and antonyms in a thesaurus that you can use to find the perfect word.
- **A Grammar Checker.** WordPerfect includes the third-party grammar checker called Grammatik as part of its package. You use Grammatik to check common grammar problems based on your selected style of writing (for example, formal, informal, report, and so forth).

- **QuickCorrect.** QuickCorrect is an adjunct program to the Speller and Grammatik. QuickCorrect (described in the previous chapter) corrects your common spelling and punctuation errors on-the-fly. Use the Edit QuickCorrect List dialog box, accessed via the QuickCorrect command on the Tools menu, to add words beyond those you add during your Speller sessions.
- **Word Count.** Most writers who write on assignment are given a page limit or word limit for their goals. WordPerfect provides a fast word counting feature that helps you stay on track.
- **Find and Change.** Even if you use the spelling checker, thesaurus, and grammar checker, there still will be times when you want to locate text, codes, or attributes and formats and replace them with an alternative. This pair of tools lets you search your document and performs this function quickly and easily.
- **Sorting.** Alphabetizing lists is easy when you use the sorting function built into the program.

The following pages describe how to use these tools to proofread and correct your documents.

Using the Spelling Checker

WordPerfect provides a large dictionary that you can use to check the spelling of text in your document. In addition, you can build custom dictionaries that contain specialized words not found in the standard dictionary.

To check the spelling of your document:

1. Place the insertion point where you want to start checking the spelling. You can also move to the top of your document and check the entire document or select text to check only that text.
2. Pull down the Tools menu and select Speller (**Figure 1**).
3. In the resulting Speller dialog box (**Figure 2**), click Start.
4. Speller runs through your document and when it finds a questionable word, highlights it and displays alternatives in the list box (**Figure 3a**).
5. Click the appropriate button to add the unknown word to the dictionary, look up phonetic alternatives from those displayed on the list, or select a word from the list. When you have made your selection or edits, click Replace to correct the spelling of the word.

Figure 1: Select **Speller** from the Tools menu.

Shortcuts

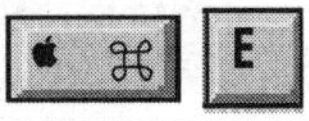

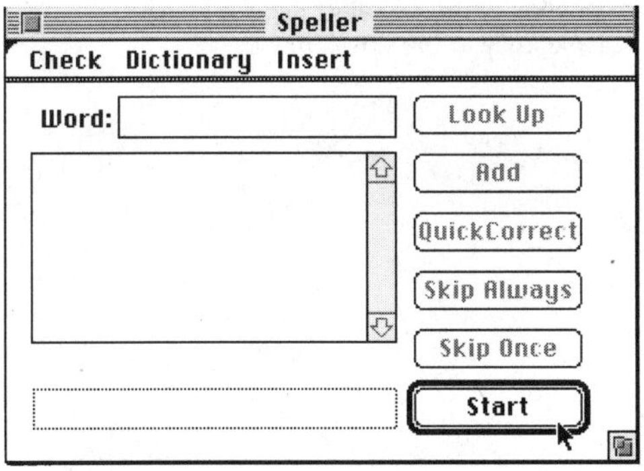

Figure 2: Click **Start** to begin the spell check.

The misspelled word is listed here. You can click and edit its spelling in the text box.

Click here to add the word to the dictionary.

The Speller makes a best-guess of the correct spelling here.

The Speller generates a list of phonetic alternatives here.

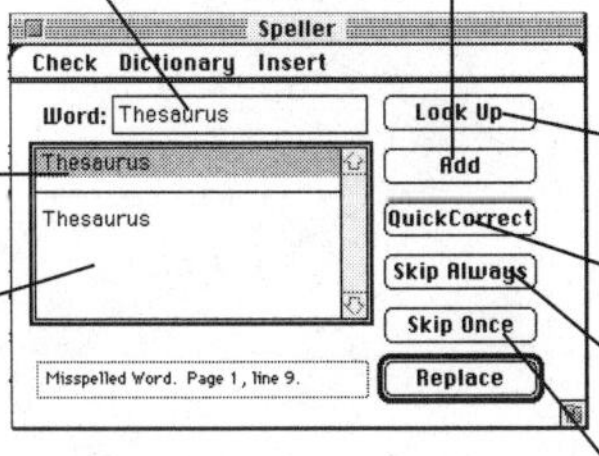

Use the dictionary to look up the spelling of a word by clicking here.

Add the word to QuickCorrect by clicking here.

Click here to always skip the displayed spelling.

Click here to skip the displayed word.

Figure 3a: Select the spelling you want to replace the misspelled word with from the list box and click **Replace.**

6. *Optional*: If you want to leave the word as it is spelled (for example, if it is a common name) you can click Skip Once or Skip Always and WordPerfect will either not ask you about that word again (Skip Always), or will ask each time it comes upon that word (Skip Once).
7. *Optional*: If the misspelled word is a mistake you commonly make, click QuickCorrect to add the word to your QuickCorrect list. *See Chapter 11: "Shortcuts" for a description of how to use the Edit QuickCorrect List dialog box.*
8. Click the close box when you are finished spell checking or the program states that it has completed a round of checking.

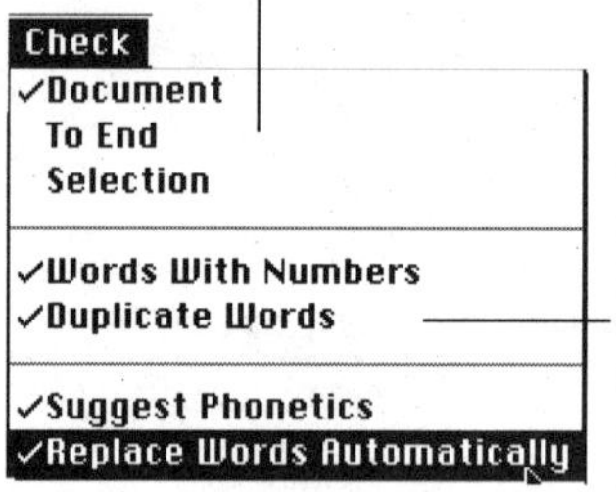

Figure 3b: If you do not want WordPerfect's Speller to automatically correct later occurrences of a misspelled word, de-select **Replace Words Automatically** in the Check menu.

Tip

It is a good idea to save your document prior to spell checking in case you make an error and correct a correctly spelled word. If you save prior to spell checking you can revert to the saved version of the document to correct an inadvertent correction.

Save your document after spell checking so that you do not lose any of the corrections should your system crash. This way, you will not have to repeat the often tedious task of spell checking the document.

You can edit the misspelled word in the Word text box and click **Replace** to correct the word's spelling in your document.

Each time you make a correction, the Speller will correct each additional occurrence of the misspelling automatically. To stop the automatic correction of already corrected words, turn off **Replace Words Automatically** in the Check menu of the Speller (**Figure 3b**).

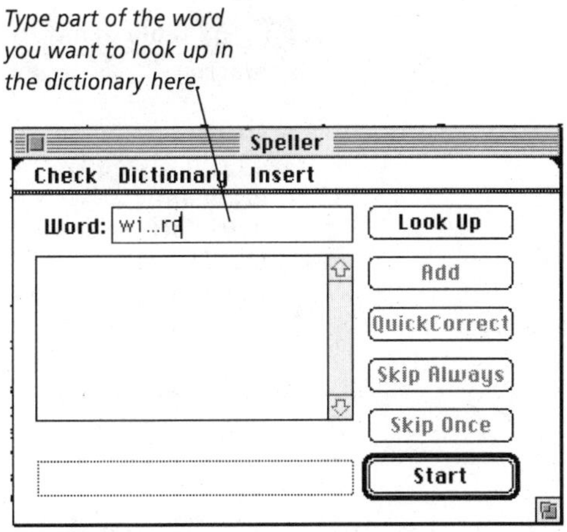

Figure 4a: Use the Speller as a dictionary by typing the word (including any wild cards from the **Insert** menu) in the **Word** text box and click **Look Up**.

Figure 4b: Use the Insert menu to insert "wild card" characters into the word you want to look up.

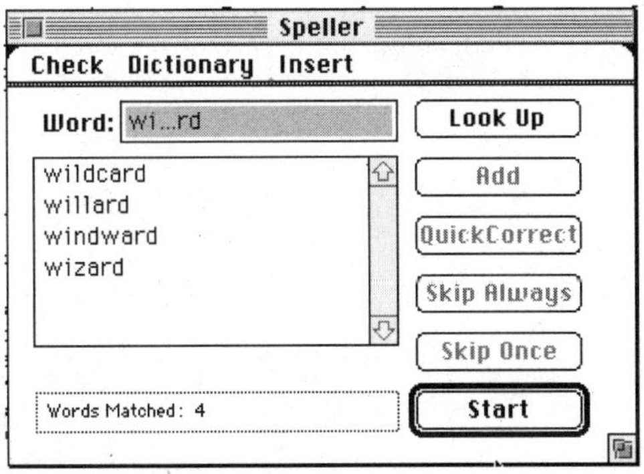

Figure 5: When you click **Look Up**, the Speller searches for phonetic relatives of your word.

To use the Look Up feature of the Speller:

1. If Speller is not open, pull down the Tools menu and select Speller.
2. In the resulting Speller dialog box, type the word you want to find in the Word text box (**Figure 4a**).
3. *Optional*: Insert a "wild card" character for any letter you are not sure of. To insert a single-letter wild card, pull down the Insert menu on the Speller dialog box and select Match One Character (**Figure 4b**) or you can type a question mark. To insert a "wild card" that represents from zero to multiple characters, select Match Multiple Characters from the Insert menu. WordPerfect inserts an ellipse that represents the wild cards. You can also type an asterisk to represent the missing characters.
4. Click Look Up.
5. Possible spellings of the word are displayed in the Look Up list box (**Figure 5**).
6. When the spelling checker reaches the end of the document or selection, it beeps.

Using the Thesaurus

If you're searching for just the right word to use in a document, you can call up WordPerfect's thesaurus. A thesaurus is a collection of words with similar meanings (synonyms) and opposite meanings (antonyms). WordPerfect contains a large thesaurus that is easy to use.

To find a word in the thesaurus:

1. If you want to look up synonyms or antonyms for a word in your document, place the insertion point in that word.
2. *Optional:* If you want to simply look up words, place the insertion point anywhere in the document.
3. Pull down the Tools menu and select Thesaurus (**Figure** 6).
4. In the resulting Thesaurus dialog box (**Figure** 7), select a word in the list box. Or, if you did not identify a word, type a word in the Word text box.
5. After selecting or typing a word, click Look Up. If the word is not in the thesaurus, it beeps. Select an alternate word and click Look Up again.
6. The Thesaurus displays a list of words that are either synonymous or opposites of your typed word. The target word is placed at the top of the list in bold. Words with more listings (called *headwords*) are preceded with bullets. Double-click a bulleted word to view its synonyms and antonyms.

Figure 6: Select **Thesaurus** from the Tools menu.

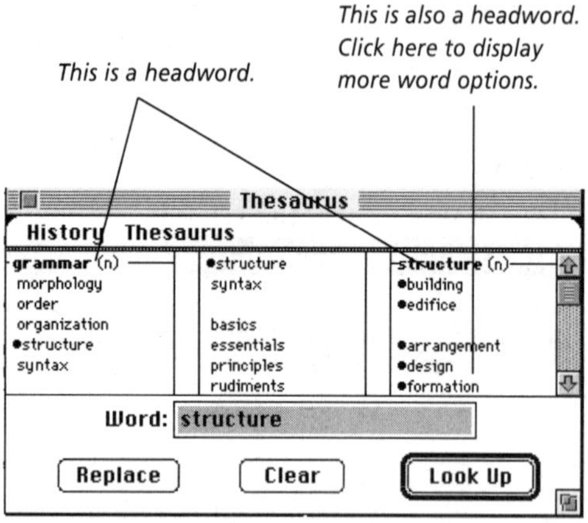

Figure 7: The Thesaurus displays a series of synonyms and antonyms based on which headword you select. Any word preceded by a bullet is a headword containing further word options. Selected words appear in the **Word** text box and at the top (bolded) of their associated list of terms.

Mini-Glossary

Synonym	A word that has a similar meaning to another word.
Antonym	A word that means the opposite of another word.
Homonym	A word that sounds the same as another word but has another meaning.

7. *Optional*: If you have selected a word in your document, it appears in the **Word** text box and as a target word in the list box. Select an alternative and click **Replace** to replace the targeted word with the new word.
8. *Optional:* If you want to look up another word, click **Clear** to clear the active list box (the one with the highlighted scroll bar) (see **Figure** 7).
9. Click the close box to close the Thesaurus and return to your document.

Using Grammatik

Grammar checkers are historically not very sophisticated tools for checking grammatical errors in your writing. The problem is the complexity of grammar, the thousands of interacting rules that underlie how we speak and write. Computers are literal-minded, and it is difficult to teach a computer program the vagaries of good writing.

So, use the grammar checker sparingly. Grammar checkers should be used to check for common errors such as subject/verb agreement, correct use of possessive forms and articles (an, a, and so forth), and pronoun agreement—things that follow actual rules of behavior. Don't expect any grammar checker, even the very good one included in WordPerfect, to be able to correctly identify when it is correct grammar to write in the passive voice (almost never), or when it is ok to include informal language or partial sentences.

A good rule of thumb is not to solely rely on the grammar checker for your grammar because, it is only as good as the programmer who created it, and thus no match for your editor's wits.

To check your document's grammar:

1. Place the insertion point in the document where you want to begin checking the grammar, or select the text you want to check.
2. Pull down the Tools menu and select Grammatik (**Figure 8**).
3. In the resulting Grammatik dialog box (**Figure 9a**), select a writing style by pulling down the Style menu and selecting a style (**Figure 9b**).

Shortcuts

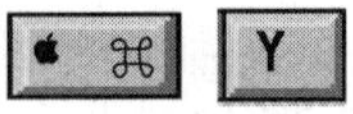

Figure 8: Select **Grammatik** from the Tools menu to invoke the grammar checker.

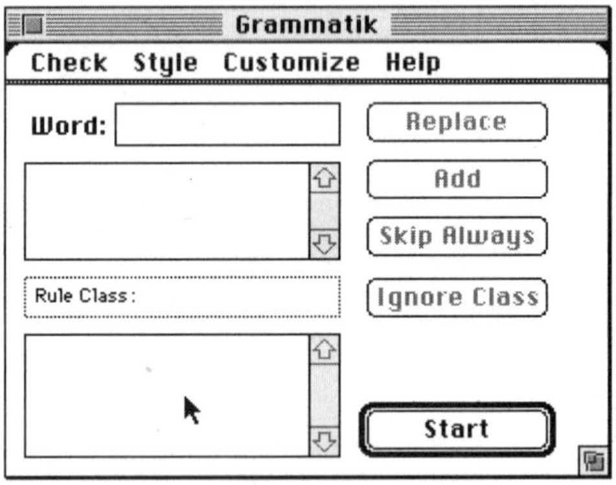

Figure 9a: Click **Start** to begin grammar checking.

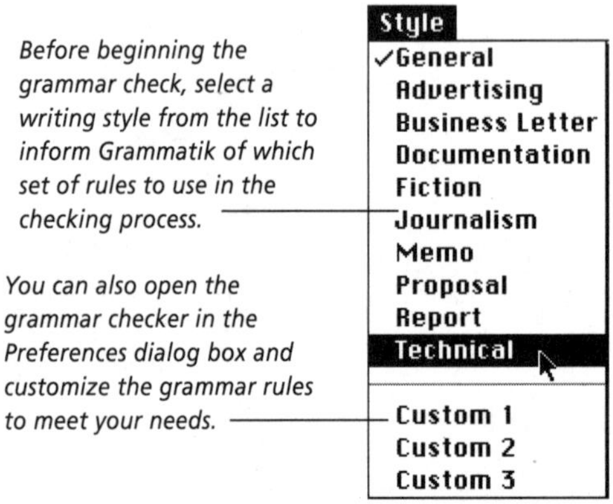

Figure 9b: Select a writing style from the Style menu before clicking **Start**.

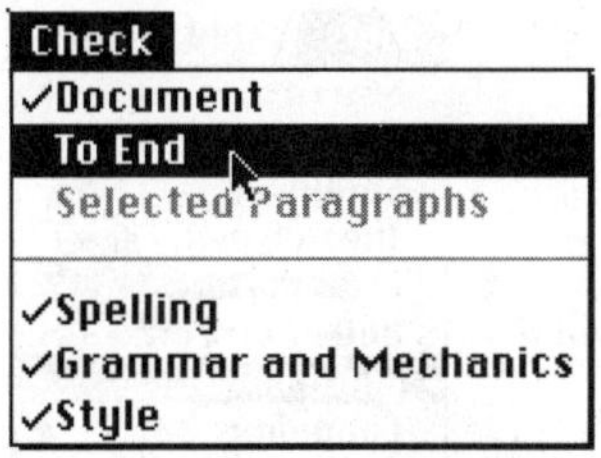

Figure 9c: You can limit the grammar checker's scope by deselecting options on the **Check** menu.

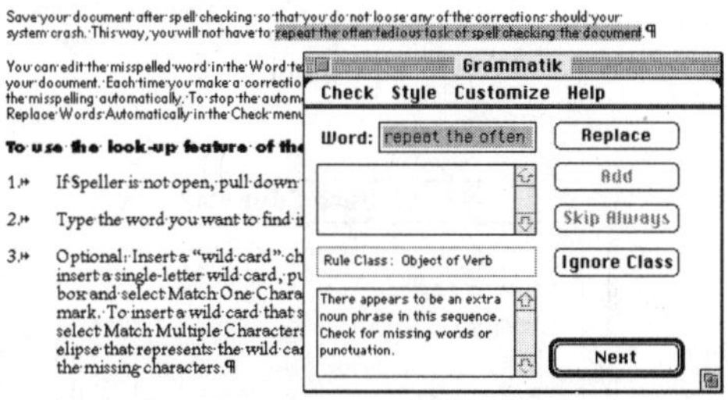

Figure 10: When Grammatik finds an error, it highlights it and displays an error message. You can correct the error in the **Word** text box and click **Replace** to update your document.

4. *Optional*: If you want to check only part of the document, pull down the Check menu on the dialog box and select another option (**Figure 9c**).
5. Click Start.
6. Grammatik checks your document and highlights the questionable words. The questionable word(s) are displayed in the dialog box, along with advice on how to correct the alleged error (**Figure 10**).
7. If you agree with Grammatik's assessment of the error, correct the text in the Word text box and click Replace.
8. Click the Next button to continue the grammar check while skipping the current selection. If you do not want Grammatik to stop each time it hits the selected phrase or sentence, click Skip Always. If you do not want Grammatik to check a class of grammar, click Ignore Class. (*Classes* are grammatical rules that apply to a type of word usage, such as passive voice or verb/adverb agreement, and so forth.) You can turn on the ignored class by re-selecting the writing style from the Style menu on the dialog box (see **Figure 9b**).
9. When the grammar checker reaches the end of the document or selection, it beeps.
10. Click the close box to return to your document.

Counting words

Many writers operate within stringent limits. The limitations may pertain not only to the time allotted for the writing, but the size of the document. WordPerfect provides a way to track the size and structure of your document through its Word Count feature. The Word Count command provides a report on your document that lists the number of characters and words in the document, the number of lines and sentences, the number of paragraphs and pages, the average length of your words, and the average length of your sentences.

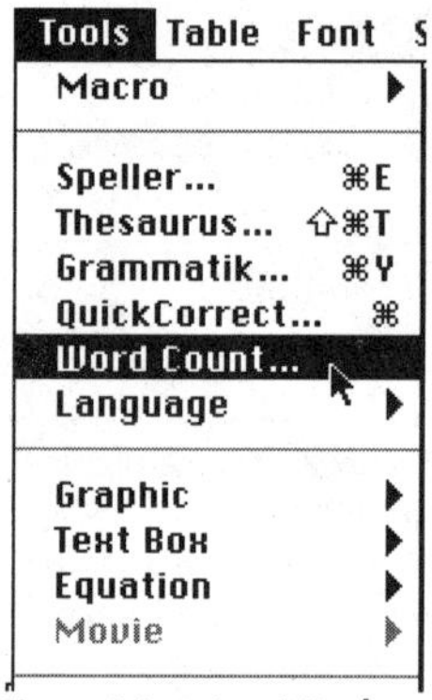

Figure 11: Select **Word Count** from the Tools menu.

To count the words in your document:

1. Click on the document's window to make it the currently active document.
2. Pull down the Tools menu and select Word Count (**Figure 11**).
3. The resulting Word Count dialog box lists statistics for the document (**Figure 12**).
4. Click OK.

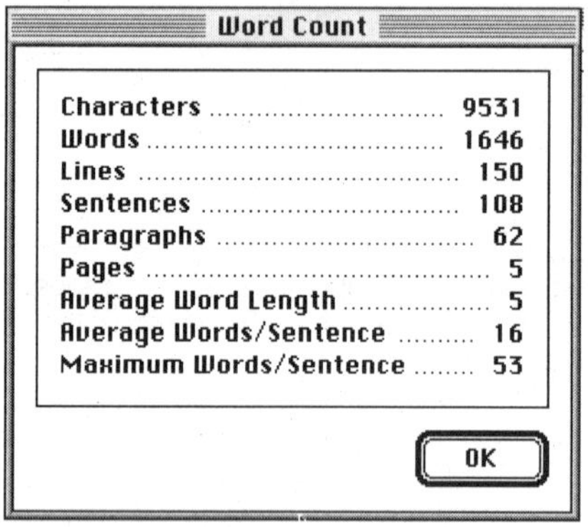

Figure 12: WordPerfect rapidly constructs a statistical picture of your document and displays it in the Word Count dialog box.

Mini-Glossary

Character count	A count of all letters, numbers, and punctuation in a document. Spaces are not counted.
Word count	A count of all words in a document. A word consists of letters, numbers, and punctuation without spaces.
Line count	A count of all of the lines of text within a document.
Sentence count	A count of all words from period to period in a document.
Page count	A count of every page in your document.

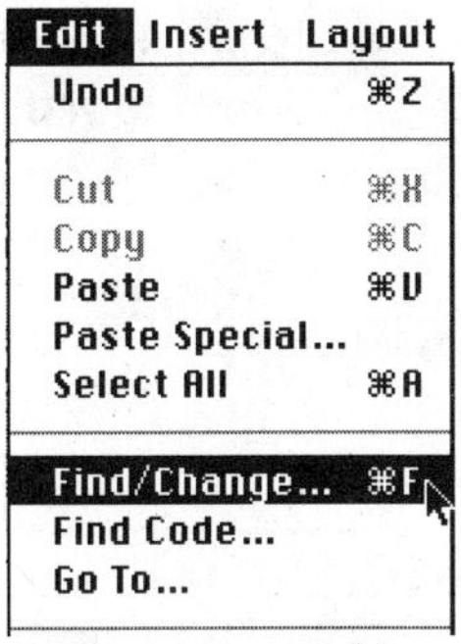

Figure 13: Select **Find/ Change** from the Edit menu.

Shortcuts

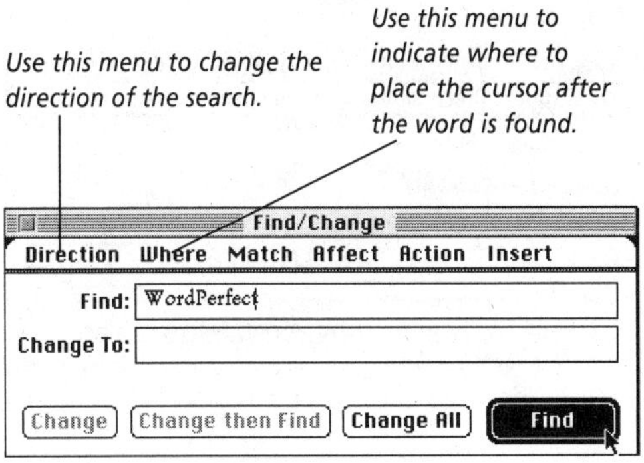

Figure 14a: Type the word (or words) you want to find in the **Find** text box and click **Find**.

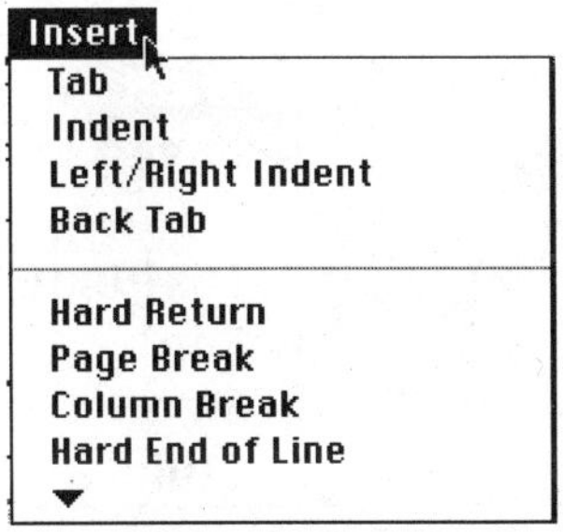

Figure 14b: Use the **Insert** menu to find/ change codes by inserting them in the **Find** or **Change To** text boxes.

Using Find and Change

The Find/Change command is a powerful tool for selectively editing your document without having to slog through each and every line to find the details you are changing. The command lets you find and change text, attributes, formats, and codes, as well as combinations of these three items. You can also write macros (see the previous chapter for instructions) that uses the Find/Change command to automate repetitious editing tasks.

To find text:

1. Move the insertion point to the place in the document where you want to start the search, or select the text you want to use.
2. Pull down the Edit menu and select Find/Change (**Figure 13**).
3. In the resulting Find/Change dialog box (**Figure 14a**), type the text you want to find in the Find text box.
4. *Optional*: If you want to include punctuation or formats in the text box, pull down the Insert menu from the dialog box (**Figure 14b**) and select a code or wild card from the list. You can insert tabs, indents, hard returns, page and column breaks, and end of lines.
5. Click Find.
6. WordPerfect moves to the first instance of the targeted text and highlights it.
7. Click Find again to continue the search, or click the close box to return to your document.

To find and change text:

1. Pull down the Edit menu and select Find/Change (see Figure 13).
2. Type the text you want to find in the Find text box.
3. *Optional*: If the target text could be misconstrued as part of another word and you want to find only independent versions, pull down the Match menu and select Whole Word (**Figure 15**). If you want to find only initial-capitalized versions of the text, type the phrase in the case you want to find in the Find text box, and then select Case from the Match menu.

   If you want to find text in a particular font, size, or style, type the text in that format using the Font, Size, or Style menus or their corresponding buttons on the Font toolbar in the document to make the change or select Font, Size, or Style from the Match menu. If you don't care how the text is differentiated, leave the default in the Match menu as Text Only.
4. Type the text you want to replace the found text with in the Change To text box (**Figure 16**).
5. *Optional*: If you want to replace the targeted text with a specific font, size, or style, type the text in the Change To text box in that font, size, or style or select Font, Size, or Style from the Affect menu (**Figure 17**). If you want to match only the text and do not care about its format or attributes, keep the default Text Only selected in the Affect menu.

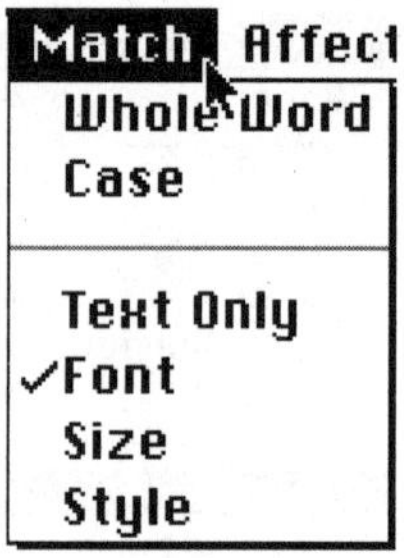

Figure 15: Use the Match menu to edit the word(s) you want to find, including case, font, size, and style to narrow the search criteria.

You can also directly change the words you place in the Find or Change To text boxes to meet your editing needs. The menus will reflect your changes.

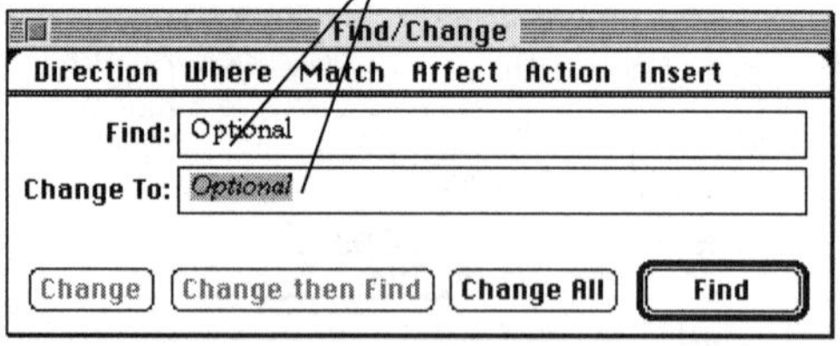

Figure 16: Type the text you want to replace the **Find** text to in the **Change To** text box. You can use the Affect menu to edit the replacement criteria.

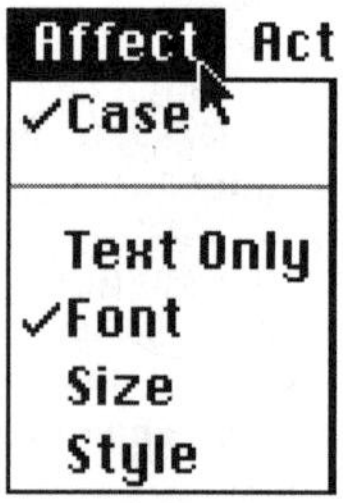

Figure 17: Use the Affect menu to edit the words in the **Change To** text box to meet your replacement criteria.

6. *Optional*: If you want to change all occurrences of the targeted text, click **Change All**.
7. Click **Find** to find the first occurrence of the targeted text.
8. Click **Change then Find** to continue the search and replace task.

   or
9. Click **Change**.
10. You can then type a different item in the **Find** or **Change To** text box and repeat Steps 4 through 7.
11. Click the close box to return to your document.

Tip

You can undo a change by selecting Undo immediately after closing the dialog box. When you select **Undo** from the Edit menu (or press Command+Z), WordPerfect only undoes the most recent **Change** or **Change All** commands.

If you make changes to the fonts, sizes, or styles directly in the **Find** or **Change To** text boxes, these changes are automatically reflected in the selections in the Match and Affect menus.

Use the **Find/Change** command to find double occurrences of hard returns (such as those at the end of and between paragraphs) and replace one hard return with a space to ensure proper paragraph spacing (use the **Insert** menu to insert the appropriate codes in the **Find** and **Change** text boxes).

Sorting Text

The **Sort** command provides an extensive mix of tools for use in organizing your document. This section discusses how to use the **Sort** command to alphabetize text in lists. WordPerfect considers a list to be any set of words separated by hard returns. Thus, lists can consist of side-by-side columns (*see Chapter 9: "Layout" for a description of parallel or side-by-side columns*), a table, or simply a tabbed collection of data.

To sort a tabbed list of data:

1. Select the tabbed list of data you want to sort (**Figure 18**).
2. Pull down the Tools menu and select **Sort** (**Figure 19**).
3. In the resulting Sort dialog box (**Figure 20**), select **Zone** from the **Items** pop-up menu. The other options are used to perform more complex sorts that are beyond the scope of this book.
4. If you are sorting text, select **Alphanumeric** from the **Type** pop-up menu.
5. Count the columns of your data to find the number of the column you want to sort by. Don't get confused by the fact that columns are called *fields* by the Sort program. Type the number of the column you want to sort by in the **Field** text box.

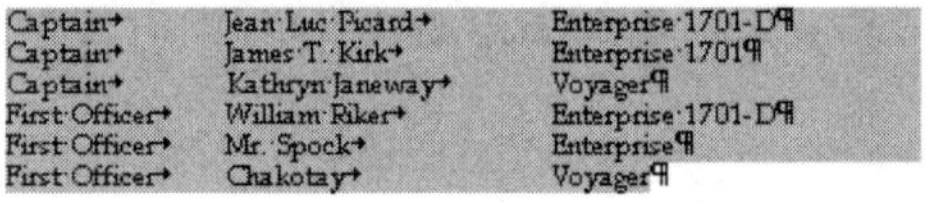

Figure 18: Select the items you want to sort.

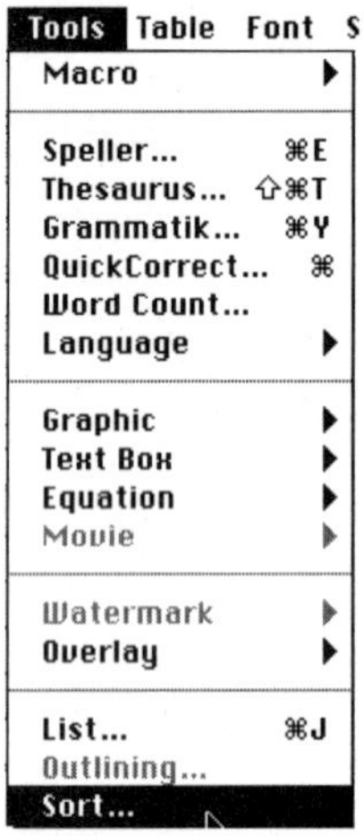

Figure 19: Select **Sort** from the Tools menu.

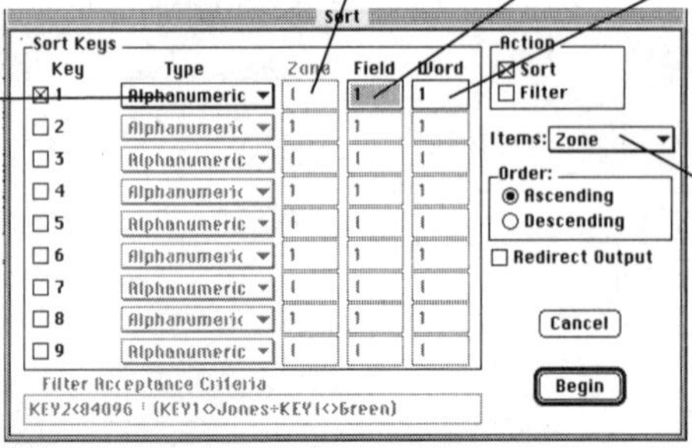

Figure 20: The Sort program uses "fields" to sort by, counting a field as the contents of a column. This method of sorting lets you sort just about any item that you can identify by number.

LISTS 13

IF YOU HAVE been following along in this book, you now have all of the tools to create the internals of a sophisticated document. You can format text, create footnotes and endnotes, number your pages and paragraphs. You may notice that you still have a problem: how do you let your readers know what your document contains? And how can your readers find the information they want quickly and efficiently? Luckily, WordPerfect provides an easy-to-use series of solutions all based on the concept of *lists*. The List command is very versatile, since it groups information contained in your document in several different ways.

This chapter discusses four major uses of lists:

- **Tables of Contents.** WordPerfect lets you create an automatically updatable Table of Contents consisting of up to five hierarchical levels based on the selections you make in the List dialog box.
- **Other Types of Lists.** WordPerfect lets you generate other types of lists, such as Lists of Figures, Tables, or Authorities (stuff lawyers like to use in their documentation).
- **Indexes.** WordPerfect lets you create lists of topics with page numbers identifying their locations in the document.

Creating Tables of Contents

The most basic use of the List command is the creation of a Table of Contents (in shorthand, a *TOC*). To create a Table of Contents, follow three steps:

- Locate where you want the TOC to appear in your document and what it should look like.
- Mark which entries should appear in the TOC and in what hierarchical level.
- Generate the TOC.

To designate the appearance and location of the Table of Contents:

1. Place the insertion point where you want the Table of Contents. Be sure that no text is selected.
2. Pull down the Tools menu and select List (**Figure 1**).
3. In the List dialog box (**Figure 2**), select Define Table of Contents from the Type pop-up menu.
4. In the Attributes section, select how many hierarchical levels you want to use in the Max Level pop-up menu.
5. Select a numbering style for each level by selecting the level number in the Level Format pop-up menu and then choosing a numbering style from the Page Numbers pop-up menu.
6. Click Define.
7. WordPerfect inserts a place holder in the spot you indicated with your insertion point (**Figure 3**).

Shortcuts

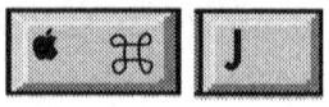

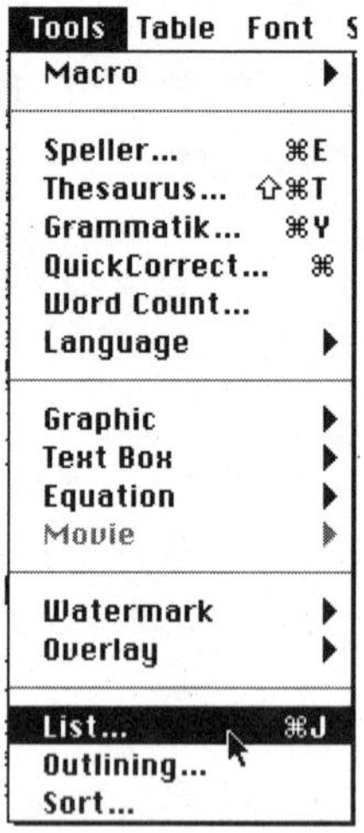

Figure 1: Select **List** from the Tools menu.

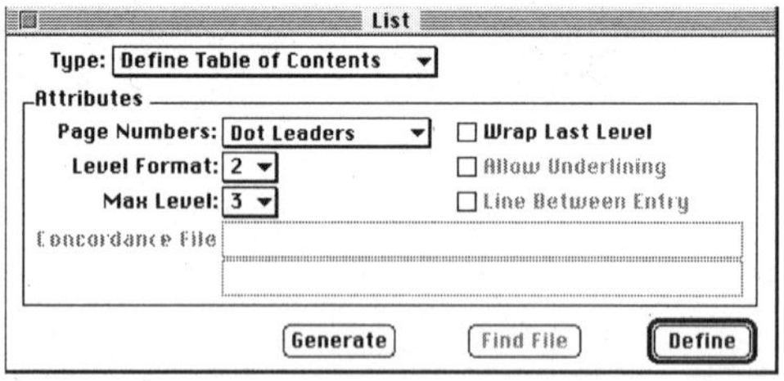

Figure 2: Select **Define Table of Contents** from the **Type** pop-up menu of the List dialog box.

Figure 3: WordPerfect inserts a Table of Contents place-holder at the location of your insertion point.

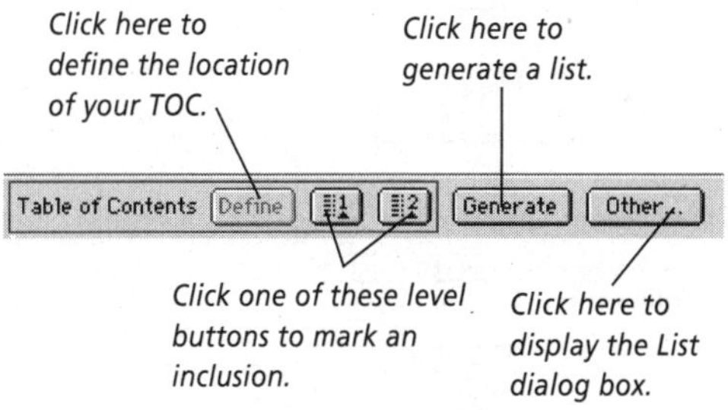

Figure 4: Use the TOC section of the List toolbar to define, mark, and generate your list.

Figure 5: Select an option to define how your Table of Contents pages will be layed out and numbered.

Tip

You can use the List toolbar to perform all three functions required to create a Table of Contents. If the List bar is not displayed, click its button on the Control bar. (*See Chapter 2: "Basics," for a description of how to use the Control bar.*). In the **Table of Contents** area of the List toolbar displayed in **Figure 4**, click the **Define** button to define the location of the Table of Contents and click the **Other** button to open the List dialog box to define the style of the Table of Contents.

WordPerfect offers five different numbering styles for page number displays in your Table of Contents. **Figure 5** displays the Page Numbers pop-up menu options. Each option is explained in the table below.

LIST LAYOUT

If you select this option...	*The list looks like this...*
(No Numbers)	Text
Follows Entry	Text 2
() Follows Entry	Text (2)
Flush Right	Text 2
Dot Leaders	Text 2

Creating a Table of Contents

To mark entries for the Table of Contents:

1. Select the item you want to include in the Table of Contents.
2. Pull down the Tools menu and select List (see **Figure 1**).
3. Pull down the Type pop-up menu and select Mark for Table of Contents (**Figure 6**).
4. In the Attributes section, select the hierarchical level where you want the text to appear from the Level pop-up menu.
5. Click Mark.
6. WordPerfect marks the selected text as a Table of Contents inclusion (**Figure 7**).
7. Repeat Steps 2 through 5 for each entry.

Shortcuts

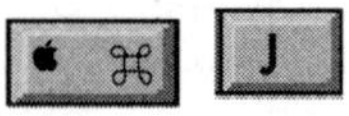

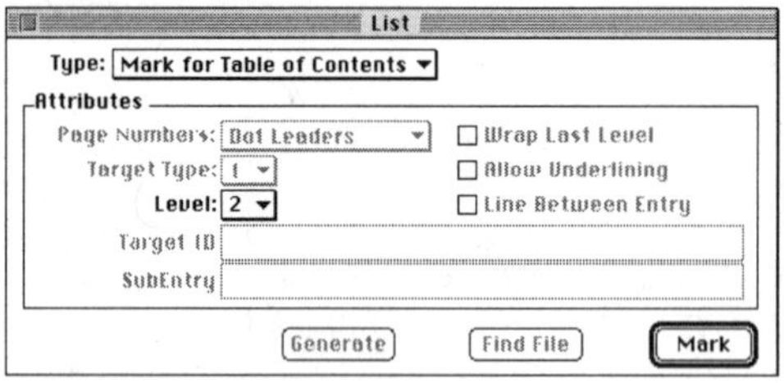

Figure 6: Select **Mark for Table of Contents** from the Type pop-up menu on the List dialog box to mark an inclusion.

Tip

Be sure that **Show ¶** is selected in the Edit menu so that you can see the Table of Contents marks.

To mark your text for inclusion in the Table of Contents using the toolbar, select the text and then click the level button you want to apply on the List toolbar's Table of Contents area.

The List dialog box is modeless, meaning that you can move it out of the way to select new text for inclusion, yet clicking on the dialog box to make it the active window lets you easily mark the new selection. Switch back and forth from dialog box to document to mark all of your entries.

Include the Table of Contents Mark in the Style definition for your headings by using the List command while in a Style window; you only have to apply the style to apply the List command to text.
See Chapter 6: "Styles" for a description of how to create a style.

Figure 7: Marked entries display two tiny arrows at their baselines.

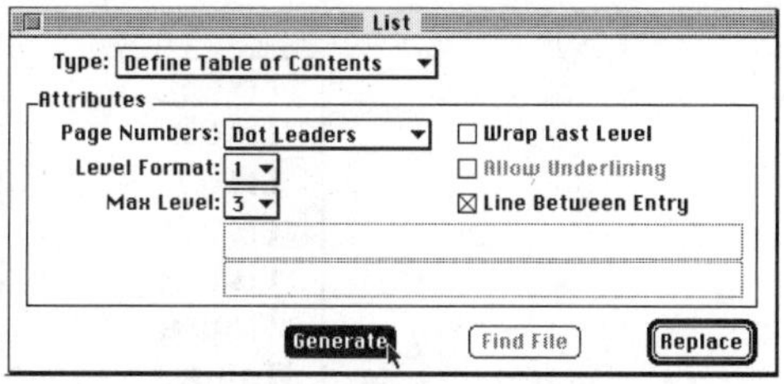

Figure 8a: Click **Generate** to create the actual Table of Contents. (You can also use the **Generate** button on the List toolbar for the same purpose.)

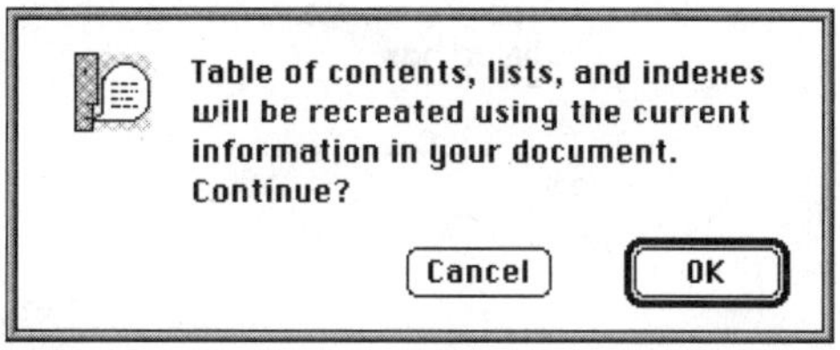

Figure 8b: The **Generate** command both updates and creates lists.

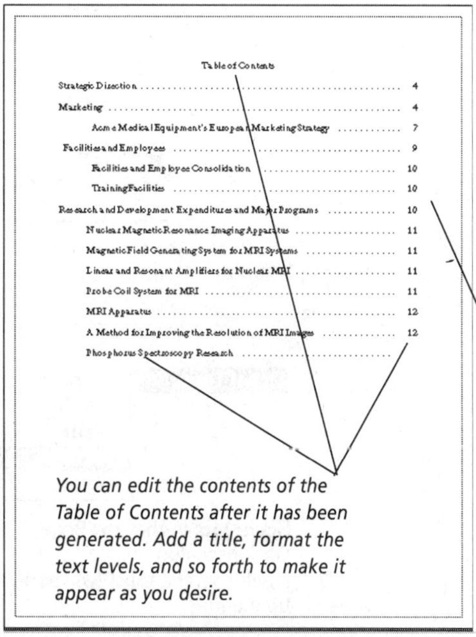

Figure 9: WordPerfect replaces the TOC marker with the actual Table of Contents.

To generate the Table of Contents:

1. Open the List dialog box (see Figure 2).
2. Click Generate (**Figure** 8a).
3. WordPerfect displays an alert box (**Figure 8b**) requesting your approval to update all existing tables, cross-references, lists, and indexes. Click OK.
4. WordPerfect places the Table of Contents (**Figure** 9) at the place holder created in the Definition portion of the process.

Tip

You can also click the **Generate** button on the List toolbar to generate the Table of Contents. Any time you want to update the Table of Contents (or any other list), click **Generate**.

Using the List Dialog Box to Create Other Tables

The List dialog box lets you create other types of tables to assist you in organizing your document for easier use. You can use the dialog box to create Figure Tables, Table Tables, Lists of Authorities, and so forth. These lists are created in the same three-step fashion as you used to create the Table of Contents: define, mark, and generate.

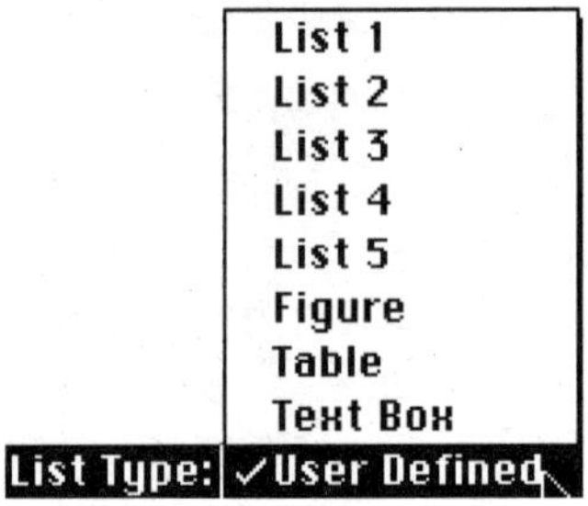

Figure 10: Select the type of list you want to generate from the **List Type** pop-up menu on the List dialog box.

To define the type of list and where it's located in your document:

1. Place the insertion point where you want the list to appear.
2. *Optional:* Type a title for the list and press Return (or Enter, depending on the type of keyboard you are using).
3. Pull down the Tools menu and select List (see **Figure 1**).
4. In the resulting List dialog box (see **Figure 2**), pull down the Type pop-up menu and select Define Lists.
5. In the Attributes selection, pull down the List Type pop-up menu and select what kind of data you want to include in the list (**Figure 10**).

   There are four types of data you can delineate:

   - Figure titles
   - Table titles
   - Text box captions
   - User defined

   In addition, you can define your own inclusions by selecting one of five generic list box types (entitled List 1, 2, and so forth).

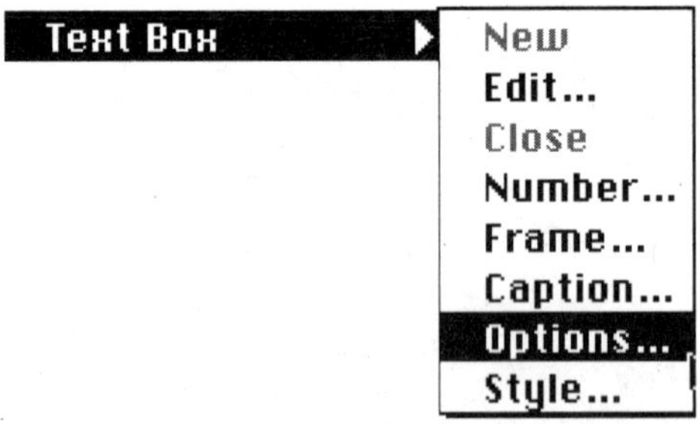

Figure 11a: Select **Options** from the tool you want to use, in this case Text box.

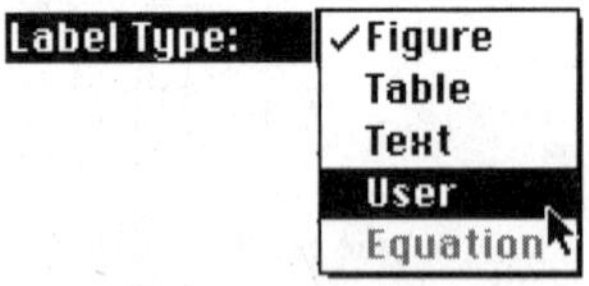

Figure 11b: In the Text Box Options dialog box, select a label from the **Label Type** pop-up menu.

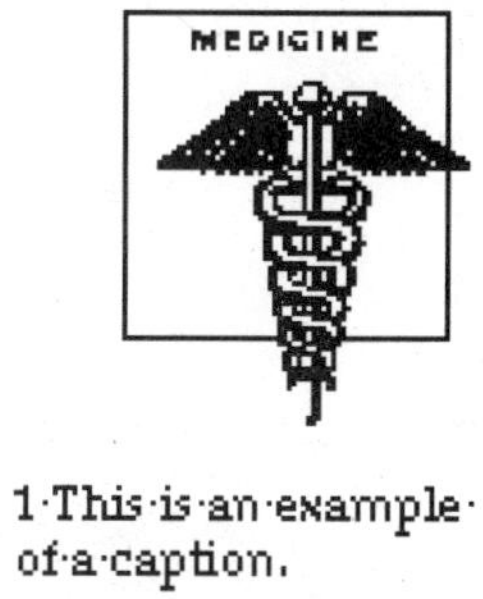

Figure 11c: Text and Graphic boxes require captions and labels if you want to include them on lists.

6. Select other options within the Attributes selection to define the line spacing and page numbering you want to use.
7. Click Define.
8. WordPerfect inserts a place marker to indicate where the list will appear.

Tip

Creating lists is a little more difficult to accomplish than simply creating a Table of Contents because the feature is so versatile. Basically, to create a list you have to give WordPerfect the ability to identify which item in your document is "listable." You do this by labelling the item. All boxes, be they graphics, text boxes, tables, or QuickTime movies, must be labelled as well as captioned to appear in a list. In addition, to include a table in a list, place the table in a text box, and then label and caption the text box. *(See Chapters 8: "Graphics" and 9: "Layout" for information on using text boxes and captions.)*

Labelling boxes

Labels tell WordPerfect which list to assign an item. You can mix and match box types within a single list by giving all of the contents of a single list the same label.

To label an item: Select the **Graphic**, **Text Box**, or **Movie** pop-up menu from the Tools menu and select **Options** from the pop-up menu that fits your needs. For example, if you want to select text boxes for labelling, choose **Options** from the **Text Box** pop-up menu (**Figure 11a**). In the resulting Text Box Options dialog box, select a label from the Label Type pop-up menu (**Figure 11b**). Note that you use the Label Type menu to apply a label to group items for inclusion in lists. To include different types of text boxes (such as, equations, tables, graphics with text, simple text, and so forth) in the same list, label them all with the same "User" label, then you can select the "User Defined" option in the List dialog box. You can also create specific lists of just equations, just simple text box captions, and so forth, by applying a specific Figure, Text, or Table label, as is appropriate for the type of item you are labelling and the type of list you are creating.

Captioning boxes

After you have labelled your boxes, you must create a description or title for the box for inclusion in the list (**Figure 11c**). You do this by creating a caption using the **Caption** command on the Graphic, Text Box, Movie, or Equation pop-up menu on the Tools menu. *(See Chapter 9: "Layout" for a description of how to create a caption.)*

Edit the caption to indicate if the Figure or Table number should appear in the list. The caption's contents will appear in the list exactly as it appears on the page.

To indicate entries for the list:

Just as you had to mark entries for the Table of Contents, so do you have to tell WordPerfect which items to include in your list. Because you can include more than one type of item in a single list, the process of indicating which items to include is tricky. You must use any of three different methods to indicate inclusions, depending on what you want to include. The following bulleted list describes how to use captions, marks, and labels.

- Simple Text items can be marked in the same manner as you did for the Table of Contents by using the List dialog box's Mark button.
- Any item you want to list as a "graphic" needs to be captioned (*see the Tip on page 209 and Chapter 9: "Layout," for a guide on how to apply a caption*). You can set up the caption to automatically apply the proper descriptive label to your graphic (be it a figure or a table) by using the Style command on the appropriate pop-up menu.
- Anything you want to call a "table" in the List Type pop-up menu must be enclosed in either a text or graphic box. It also needs to be captioned and labelled as a Table in the Label pop-up menu on the appropriate Options dialog box (to be found on the Text Box, Graphic, Movie, or Equation pop-up menus).
- Any item you identify as a text box in the List dialog box must have a caption.
- Anything you apply the "user defined" list type to requires both a caption and a label.

You can also use the List command within a Style window to add the list marks as a style. Then apply the "list" style to a selection to automatically apply the marks.

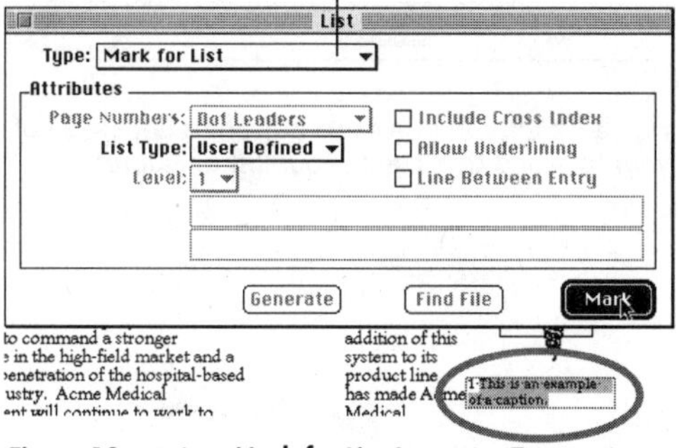

Figure 12a: Select **Mark for List** from the **Type** pop-up menu and click **Mark** to mark selected text.

Select a list type that corresponds to the label you applied to your list items on the Label dialog box or to the type of list you want to build and the type of data you are using.(See pages 203 and 204 for a discussion of the requirements.)

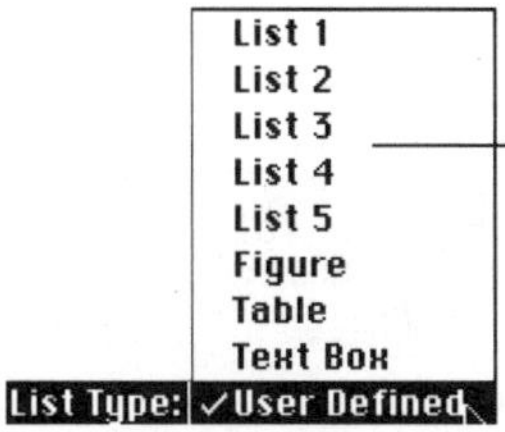

Figure 12b: Select the type of list you want to build from the pop-up menu on the **Attributes** area of the List dialog box.

To mark a list inclusion:

1. Select the text you want to include in the list.
2. Pull down the Tools menu and select List (see **Figure 1**).
3. Select Mark for List from the Type pop-up menu (**Figure 12a**).
4. Select an option from the List Type pop-up menu on the Attributes section of the List dialog box (**Figure 12b**).
5. Click Mark.
6. Repeat Steps 1 through 5 to mark any other list items you want to include in that list.

Tip

If you have built captions and/or labels for text box, tabular, or graphic inclusions, you do not have to mark them prior to generating the list.

Deleting List marks

You can remove marks by selecting **Show Codes** from the Edit menu. Place the insertion point inside the marked item you want to unmark. The cursor will move to the appropriate codes. Click the cursor until the black bar is directly behind the first toggle code. Press Backspace or Delete (depending on your keyboard). Both codes (mark on and off) will be deleted.

To generate the list:

1. Open the List dialog box.
2. Click Generate (**Figure 13**).
3. WordPerfect displays an alert box (see **Figure 8b**) requesting your approval to update all existing tables, cross-references, lists, and indexes. Click OK.
4. WordPerfect places the list (**Figure 14**) at the place holder created in the Definition portion of the process.

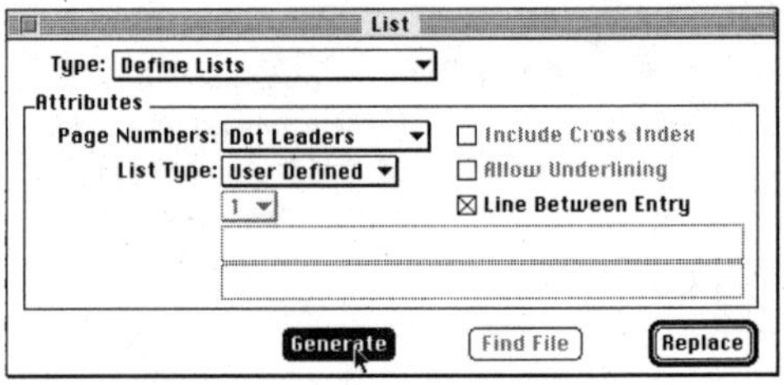

Figure 13: Click the **Generate** button to update all of your lists, and thus create your List of Figures.

Figure 8-1: This is caption 1 .... 1¶
¶
Figure 8-2: This is caption 2 .... 1¶
¶
Figure 8-3: This is caption 3 .... 2¶

Figure 14: This is an example of a List of Figures—a text box list.

Creating an Index

An *index* is a specialized list that consists of topics and the pages where they are found. You treat index entries like any other list item; thus you must mark the entry, define the index' location and style, and finally generate the index. The index feature lets you create two levels: an entry and a subentry. You use the Tab key to toggle back and forth between the two levels.

To mark entries for the index:

1. Select the text you want to include in an index entry. Be thinking of whether you want the entry to contain other entries (be an Entry) or refer to another entry (be a Subentry).
2. Pull down the Tools menu and select List (see **Figure 1**).
3. In the resulting List dialog box, select Mark for Index from the Type pop-up menu (**Figure 15**).

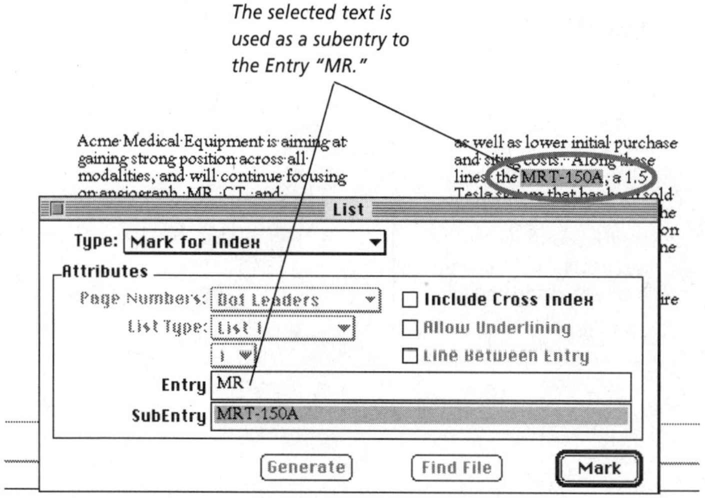

Figure 15: Press the Tab key to move an **Entry** into the **Subentry** text box.

4. When you mark the text using the **Mark for Index** option on the **Type** pop-up menu (see **Figure 15**), your marked index text is placed in the **Entry** text box. If you want the selection to remain an Entry item, press Tab to move your insertion point to the **Subentry** text box where you can type a subentry item that is related to the Entry.

   or

5. If you want the selection to be a Subentry, type an entry-level item in the **Entry** text box. As you type, your original marked index text is moved to the Subentry text box.
6. *Optional:* If you want to reference another item in the index, click the **Include Cross Index** check box. WordPerfect creates two entries for the Entry and Subentry topics, reversing their orders so that they appear two places in the index (**Figure 16**).
7. Click **Mark**.
8. Repeat Steps 1 through 7 for each index item.

> **Tip**
>
> Index entries are case sensitive, so be sure to type Entries and Subentries exactly as you want them to appear in the document, using capitalization carefully.

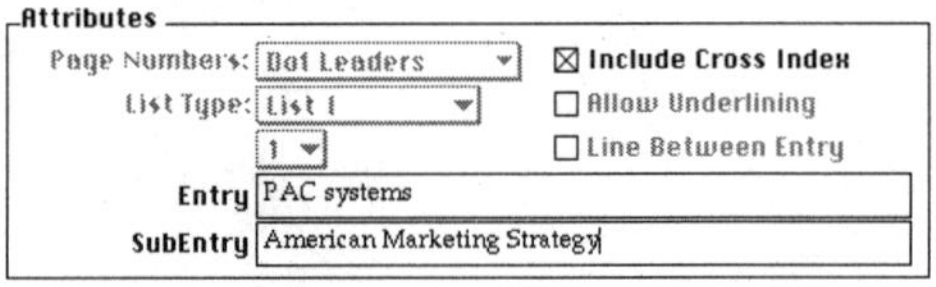

Figure 16: When you select the **Include Cross Index** check box, two entries are generated: one that says *"Entry, Subentry"* and the other that says *"Subentry, Entry."*

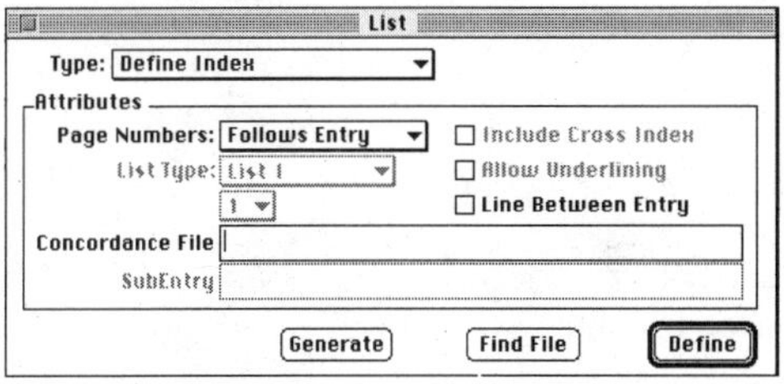

Figure 17: Select **Define Index** from the **Type** menu to define the location and layout of the index.

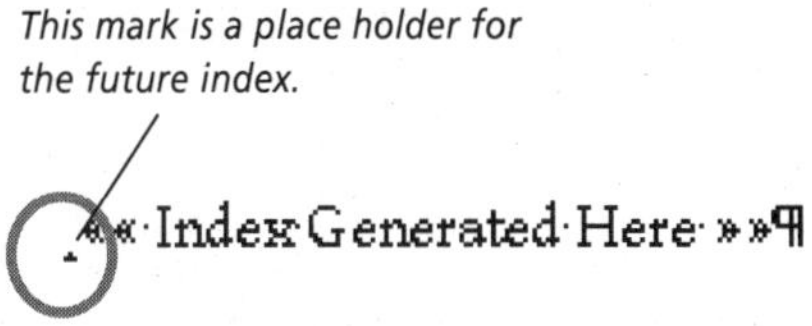

Figure 18: When you click **Define**, WordPerfect inserts a place holder at your insertion point.

To define the location and style of the Index:

1. Move your insertion point to the end of your document. You can press the End key on an extended keyboard to automatically move to that spot.
2. Type a title for the index and press Return.
3. Pull down the Tools menu and select List (see **Figure 1**).
4. In the resulting List dialog box, select Define Index from the Type pop-up menu (**Figure 17**).
5. Select a numbering style from the Page Numbers pop-up menu.

   (See the Tip on page 199, for a description of what the five options mean.)
6. Click Define.
7. WordPerfect inserts a place holder at your insertion point (**Figure 18**).

To create the Index:

1. Open the List dialog box.
2. Click **Generate**.
3. WordPerfect displays an alert box (see **Figure 8b**) requesting your approval to update all existing tables, cross-references, lists, and indexes. Click **OK**.
4. WordPerfect places the index (**Figure 19**) at the place holder created in the Definition portion of the process.

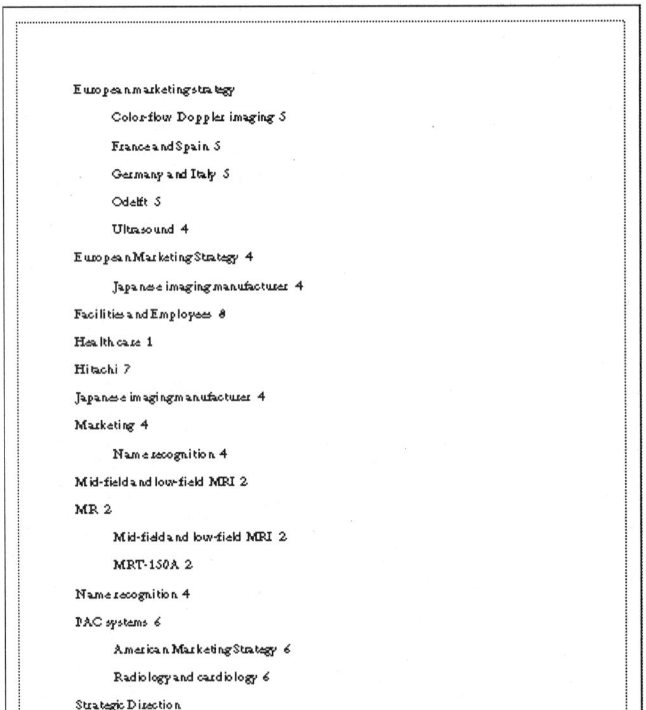

European marketing strategy
Color-flow Doppler imaging 5
France and Spain 5
Germany and Italy 5
Odelft 5
Ultrasound 4
European Marketing Strategy 4
Japanese imaging manufacturer 4
Facilities and Employees 8
Health care 1
Hitachi 7
Japanese imaging manufacturer 4
Marketing 4
Name recognition 4
Mid-field and low-field MRI 2
MR 2
Mid-field and low-field MRI 2
MRT-150A 2
Name recognition 4
PAC systems 6
American Marketing Strategy 6
Radiology and cardiology 6
Strategic Direction
electronics and energy development 1
Ultrasound 2, 4

Figure 19: When you click **Generate** on the toolbar or dialog box, WordPerfect creates your index.

EQUATIONS 14

EQUATIONS ARE SPECIAL text that express mathematical, logical, or scientific expressions in symbols. Because equations are symbolic, they use special line and word spacing, Greek letters, numbers, fractions, and so forth that are very difficult to type using the standard Document Editor or Graphics Editor tools. WordPerfect provides an environment to create and edit equations (although, sadly, it does not solve them), called the Equation Editor.

The Equation Editor consists of a special menu, Button bar, and tool palette. This chapter introduces the Equation Editor and explains the functions of its tools.

$$M_n(t) = E \exp\left\{ \frac{Sn - np}{\sqrt{np\,(1-p)}} t \right\}$$

$$= \prod_{i=1}^{n} \mathrm{E} \exp\left\{ \frac{X_i - p}{\sqrt{np(1-p)}} \mathrm{t} \right\}$$

$$= \exp\left\{ -\frac{npt}{\sqrt{np(1-p)}} \right\} \left\{ q + p \exp\left[\frac{t}{\sqrt{np(1-p)}} \right] \right\}^{n} \quad q = 1-p,$$

WordPerfect provides the Equation Editor window and its buttons and tools with which you can construct and edit complex formulas.

The Equation Editor Window

Like the Document Editor and Graphics Editor, the Equation Editor consists of a window containing a new Button bar containing commonly used formatting commands, a screen to create and edit equations, and a tool palette used to generate the components of your equation. **Figure 1** displays the Equation Editor window.

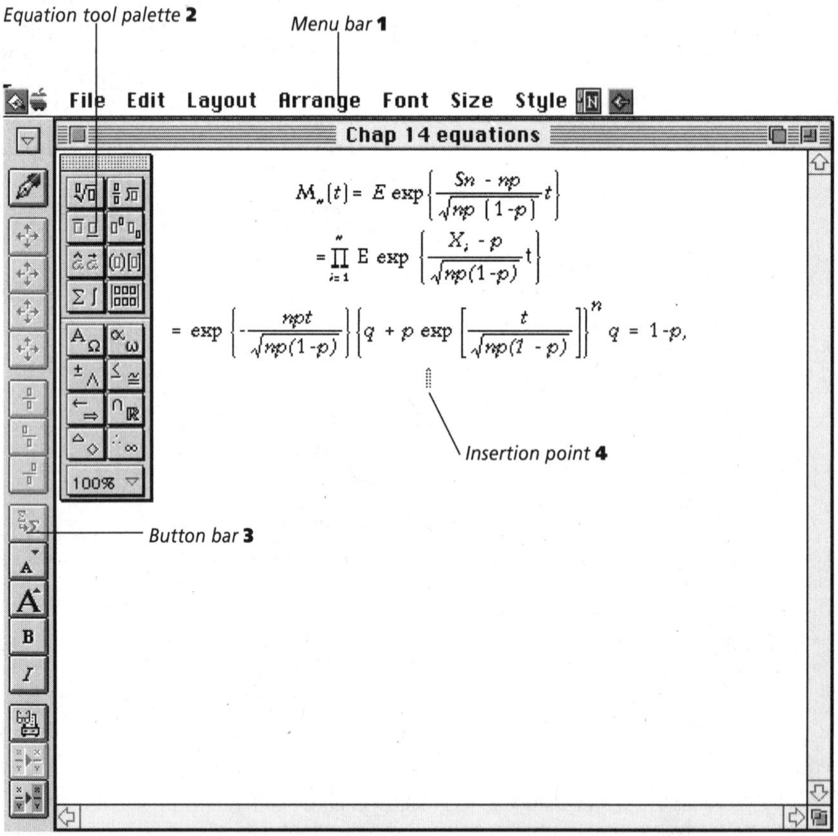

Figure 1: Navigating the Equation Editor window.

The Equation Editor Explained

1 *Menu bar*

The Menu bar of the Equation Editor contains additional commands specific to the Equation Editor, such as Insert Equation, Close Equation, Typesetting, Line Spacing, Select In/Out, Align, and Move.

2 *Equation tool palette*

The tool palette contains 16 pop-up menus containing operators, Greek letters, brackets, mathematical symbols, arrows, diacritical marks, and limiters. Select tools to draw the components of the equation.

3 *Button bar*

The Button bar contains a series of buttons that provide access to commands located on the Menu bar, as well as other Equation tools not found on the menus. The Button bar can be positioned like the Button bars on the Graphics Editor and Document Editor so that it can be easily accessed while keeping the screen clear for your work.

4 *Insertion point*

Type the variables using the keyboard, then select tools from the tool palette to insert brackets, square root symbols, limiters, and so forth, as needed to complete the equation.

The Equation Button Bar Explained

Figure 2 displays the Equation Editor Button bar. Use the Button bar to perform common tasks, such as formatting the equation, increasing/decreasing the font sizes you are using in the equation, moving a selection, moving in between levels in the equation, inserting bold-faced text or italicized text, and so forth.

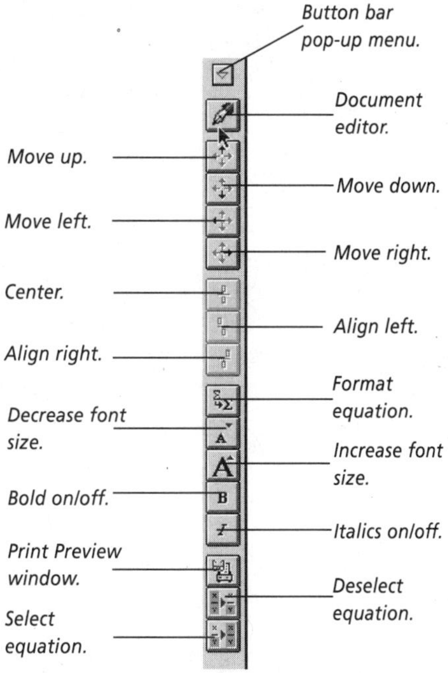

Figure 2: Use the Button bar to quickly access common equation commands.

The Equation Tool Palette Explained

Figure 3 displays the tool palette used to insert mathematical, scientific, electronic, or logical expressions and symbols into your equation.

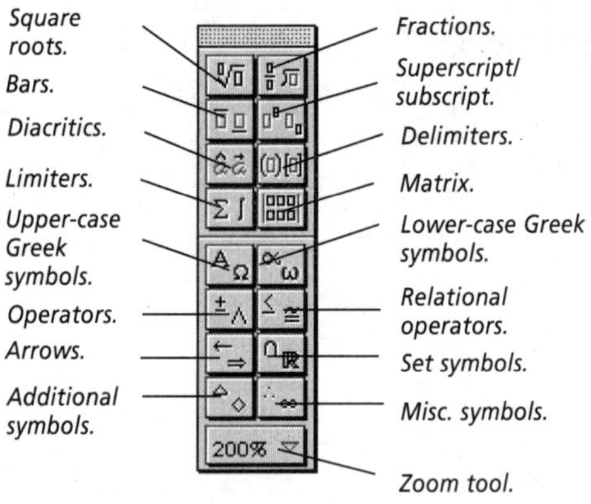

Figure 3: Use the Equation tool palette to create mathematical, scientific, or logical expressions.

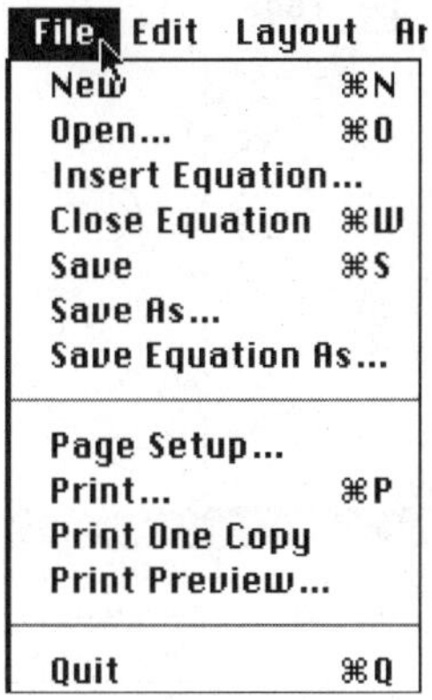

Figure 4: The **File** menu.

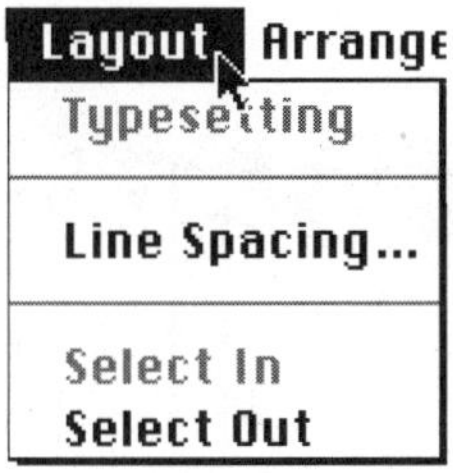

Figure 5: The **Layout** menu.

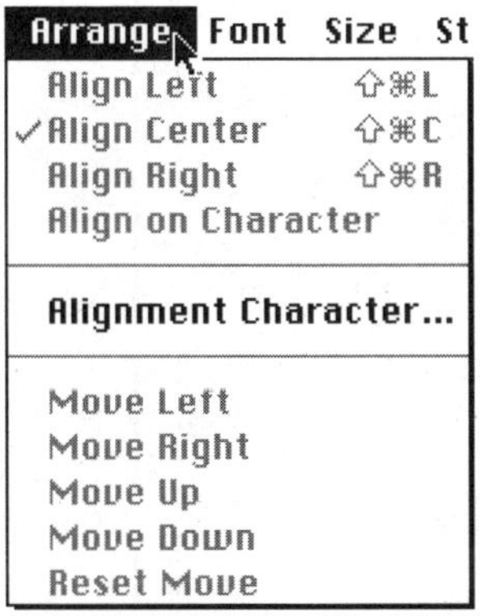

Figure 6: The **Arrange** menu.

The Menu Bars Explained

The following pages describe those Menu bars that change when you invoke the Equation Editor window. Three menus change to accommodate the commands used strictly in the Equation Editor: File, Layout and Arrange.

The File menu

The File menu (**Figure 4**) contains three added commands: The Insert Equation command is used to insert an equation into the Equation Editor from a previously saved file. The Close Equation command is used to close the Equation Editor window and return to the Document Editor. Third, the Save Equation As command is used to save the equation in a separate equation file.

The Layout menu

Use the additional commands located on the Layout menu, shown in **Figure 5**, to format the current equation in standard equation style (for example, align equal signs, center numerators and denominators in fractions, and so forth) and align the spacing of lines in the equation to accommodate non-standard symbols, superscripts and subscripts, and fractions. Two other new commands select and deselect portions of the equation one structure or level at a time.

The Arrange menu

Figure 6 displays the contents of the Arrange menu. This menu appears only in the Graphics and Equation Editor windows and contains different commands for both windows. In the Equation Editor, the Arrange menu performs alignment and moving functions.

To open the Equation Editor window:

1. Place the insertion point in the paragraph where you want the equation.
2. Pull down the Tools menu in the Document Editor and select New from the Equation pop-up menu (**Figure** 7).
3. In the resulting Equation Editor window (**Figure** 8), use the Equation tool palette and Button bar to type the equation.
4. Pull down the File menu and select Close Equation (**Figure** 9).
5. The equation is inserted into your document inside a text box (**Figure** 10).

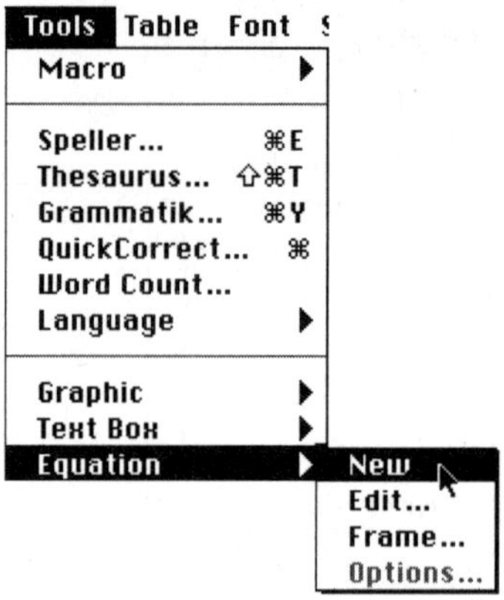

Figure 7: Open the Equation Editor window by selecting **New** from the Equation pop-up menu.

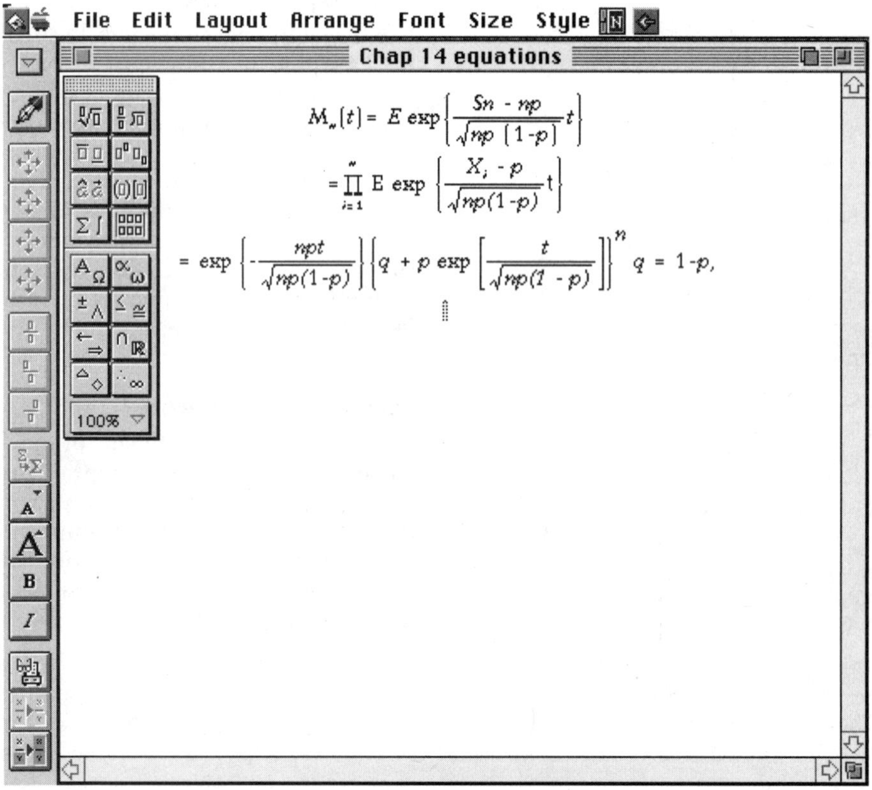

Figure 8: Type the equation, using the Equation tool palette and Button bar to assist you in inserting symbols, operators, and other mathematical constructs.

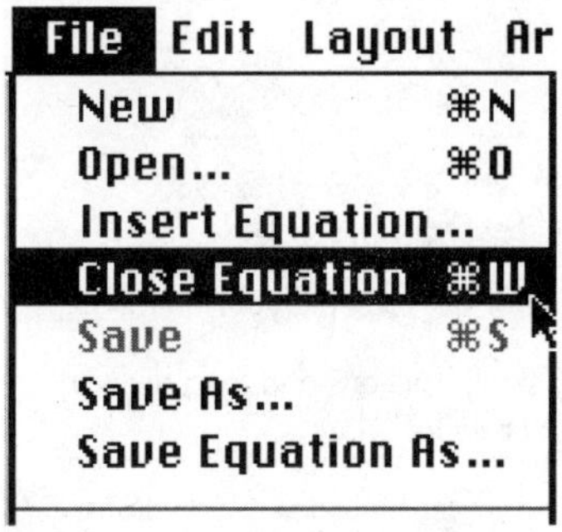

Figure 9: Close the Equation Editor to insert the equation by selecting the **Close Equation** command.

Tip

You can open the Equation Editor to edit an existing equation by double-clicking the equation in the Document Editor. Close the Equation Editor by either clicking the close box or by selecting the **Document Editor** button on the Button bar.

Because equations are inserted into your document in text boxes, you can perform any formatting to the equation as you can to a text box. For example, you can change the fill or border of the equation box, add a frame (use the **Equation Frame** command on the Tools menu to insert a Frame), or add a caption to the equation box. *(See Chapter 9: "Layout," for a description of working with text boxes.)*

$$\sum_{d=0}^{N}\binom{N}{d}\frac{\Gamma(a+b)}{\Gamma(a)\Gamma(b)}\frac{\Gamma(a+d)\Gamma(N+b-d)}{\Gamma(N+a+b)}=$$

Figure 10: The equation is inserted into your document in its own text box.

Equation Tools Explained

To Use This...	Choose This Tool...	To Do This...
Square Root		Insert a square root or nth root into your equation.
Fractions		Insert normal and small fractions and long division expressions into your equation.
Bars		Insert lines over and under functions in equations.
Delimiters		Insert brackets, parentheses, and other vehicles that serve as fences in an equation.
Super/Subscript		Add scientific notion to equations using super- and subscript alignment.
Diacritical Marks		Insert diacritical marks (for example accents, umlauts, and diacritics) to the left of the insertion point.
Limits		Insert integral, product, and summation symbols.
Matrix		Insert a matrix by dragging the cursor across and down the matrix to specify the number of rows and columns in your grid. Use the Other option to specify a different number of rows and columns.
Greek symbols		Insert upper case and lower case Greek letters into equations.
Standard Operators		Insert basic operators, such as +, -, *, and so forth into equations.
Relational Operators		Insert relational operators, such as greater than or less than, into your equations.
Symbols	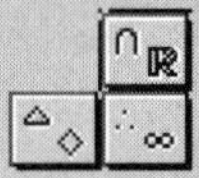	Insert set theory symbols, such as union, and other set symbols into equations. Additional tools insert other symbols, including electronic symbols, and other miscellaneous symbols such as infinity and delta.

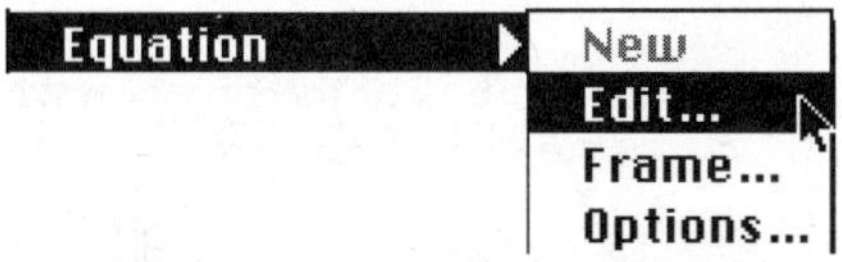

Figure 11: Select **Edit** from the **Equation** pop-up menu to open the Equation Editor to edit an existing equation when you don't know where the equation is in your document.

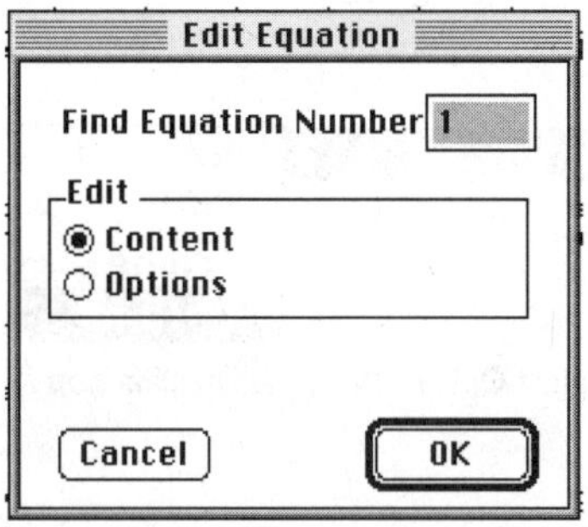

Figure 12: Select **Content** to edit an equation or **Options** to display the Equation Options dialog box (*see the task on page 220*). Type a new number in the text box to locate another equation.

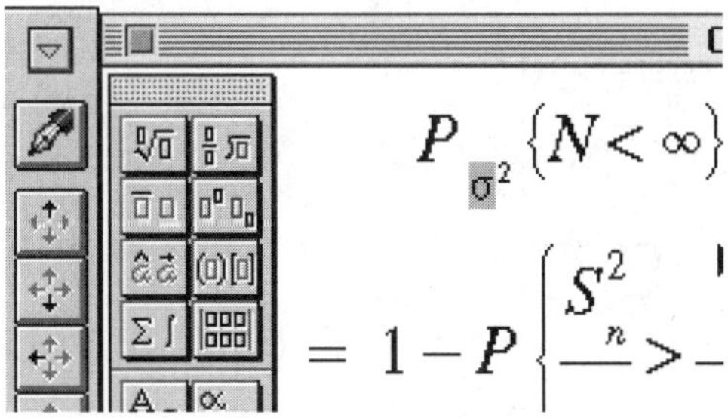

Figure 13: Select an equation component that you want to edit and either type a new character, select another tool from the palette, or press Backspace (or Delete) to erase it.

To edit an equation:

1. Select the equation you want to edit.
2. Pull down the Tools menu and select Edit from the Equation pop-up menu (**Figure 11**).
3. In the resulting Edit Equation dialog box (**Figure 12**), select the radio button option that fits your needs. In this case, since I want to edit the equation itself, I select Content. You can edit another equation by typing its number in the Find Equation Number text box.
4. Click OK.
5. When the Equation Editor window opens, as shown in **Figure 13**, select the component of the equation you want to change by clicking it.
6. Type new text or insert a new symbol, operator, or other tool from the tool palette.

   or
7. Press the Backspace or Delete key (on an extended keyboard) to delete the selection.

Tip

You can also double-click the equation you want to edit to open the Equation Editor window.

You can navigate around the equation in two ways: click the mouse where you want to insert the next component, or press the Tab key to move to the next level in the current structure (for example from the numerator to the denominator in a fraction).

To change the Equation Editor's options:

1. Select the text box of the equation that you want to set up (**Figure 14**).
2. Pull down the Tools menu and select Options from the Equation pop-up menu (**Figure 15**).
3. In the resulting Equation Options dialog box (**Figure 16**), select the options you want to use.
4. When you are done, click the OK command.

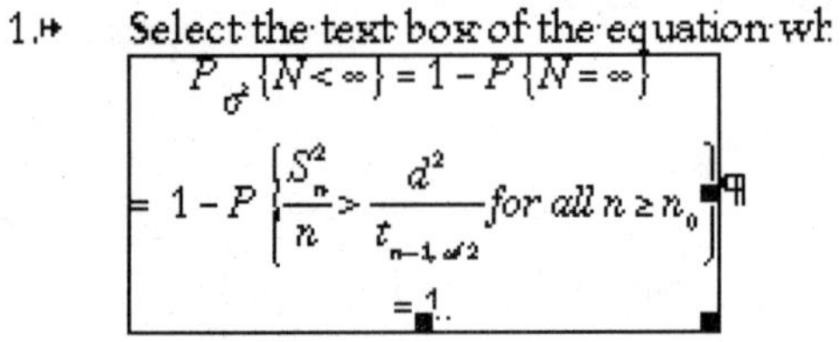

Figure 14: Select the text box of the equation to evaluate the selected equation's options.

Figure 15: Select **Options** from the **Equation** pop-up menu.

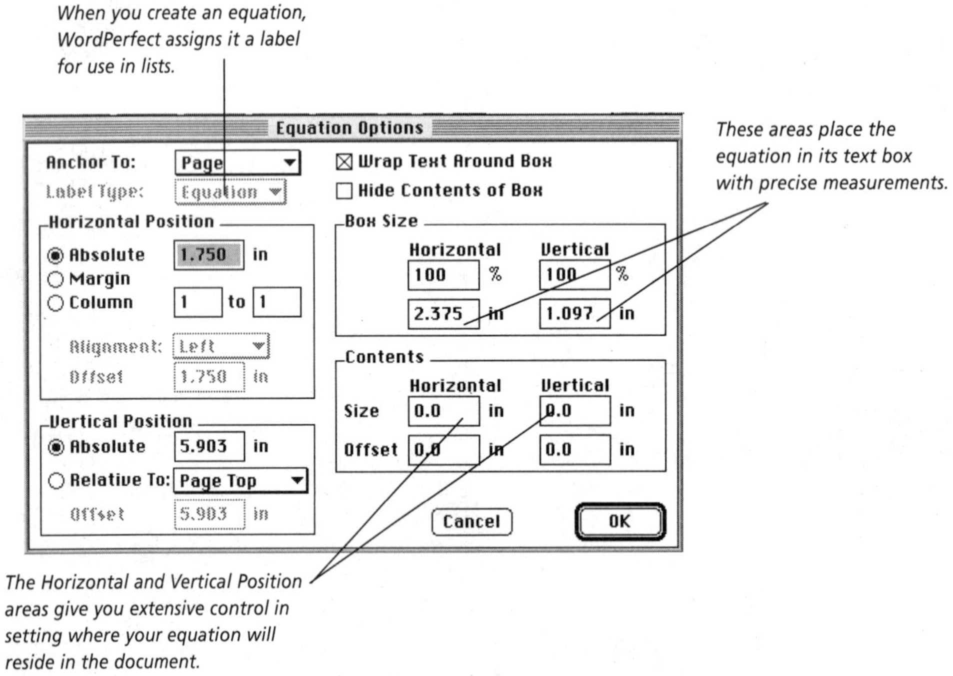

Figure 16: Use the Equation Options dialog box to set anchors and labels for your equation text boxes, as well as position and space the equation and its text box on your page.

CUSTOMIZING 15

THROUGHOUT THIS BOOK, I have alluded to WordPerfect's ability to customize its menus and toolbars to fit your specific working style. Chapter 15 is dedicated to the description of the Preferences window and its eleven buttons that customize different portions of the program.

In addition, this chapter describes how to customize the Button bars using the **Edit** and **New** commands on the Button Bar pop-up menu.

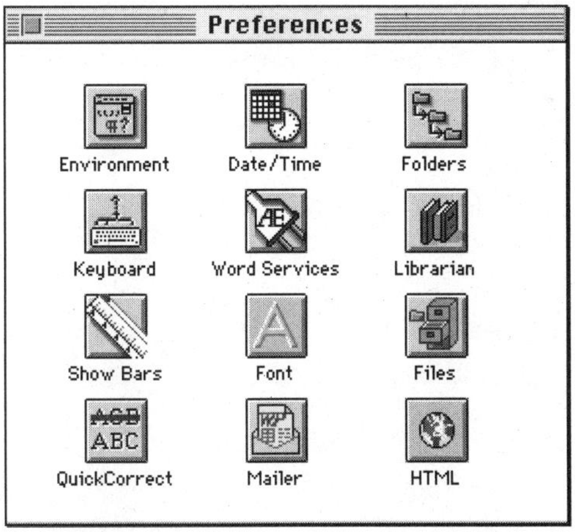

WordPerfect's Preferences window provides you with dialog boxes to customize almost every aspect of the program.

Using the Preferences Window

The Preferences window is your entry into the world of personalization. Yet some of the buttons are more difficult or arcane to use than others. Let's review which buttons I have already described and which are not applicable to a book of this size.

I have already described the uses of the **QuickCorrect** button (*see Chapter 11: "Shortcuts"*) as well as the **Date/Time** button (*see Chapter 4: "Formatting"*).

The **Files, Folder, Word Services,** and **Mailer** buttons generate changes to the way WordPerfect saves documents and mail merges, and are thus beyond the scope of the book.

Customizing buttons examined

The following Preferences buttons and their resulting dialog boxes are described in detail in this chapter.

- **Librarian.** This dialog box lets you retrieve, rename, move, and/or save resources, such as Button bars or Document Styles. Resources can be saved in two places: with your document or in a "public" library, such as the Library (USA) library (you'll learn more about this library later in this chapter).
- **Environment.** This dialog box lets you set when and what files you want backed up on a regular basis. The dialog box also lets you set foreground and background colors for the screen (background) and text (foreground) on color monitors, as well as set the color of the highlight bar.

  The Environment dialog box also provides a series of six menus to set the formatting environment. You use the Environment dialog box to define how many paragraphs are affected by a change in format, whether fonts will be displayed in their actual font on the Font menu, and so forth.
- **Font.** This dialog box lets you change the default font from Geneva 12 point to whatever standard you want to use.
- **Show Bars.** This dialog box lets you set up which toolbars are initially displayed in WordPerfect when you open a document. The Show Bars dialog box also lets you determine if the Status bar will be initially displayed.
- **Keyboard.** This dialog box lets you customize how keyboard shortcuts are applied to commands, macros, special keys, and so forth. You can assign keystrokes to various portions of the program via the Assign button.
- **HTML:** The HTML dialog box lets you assign font type, size, style, and color formatting to Hypertext Markup Language (HTML) tags used to create World Wide Web pages. You can also select the Web browser you will use to export your Web page on to the Internet.

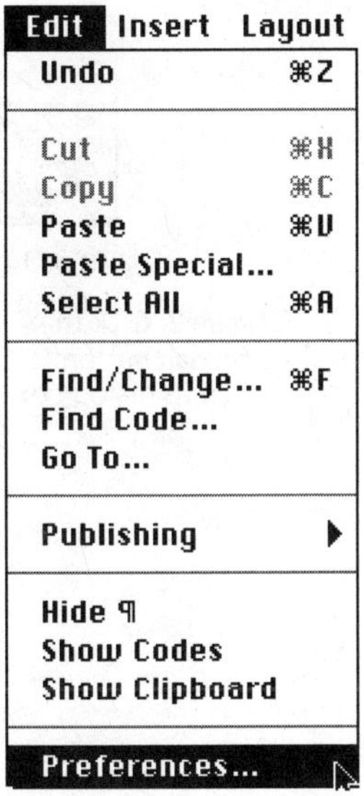

Figure 1a: Select **Preferences** from the Edit menu to change your defaults.

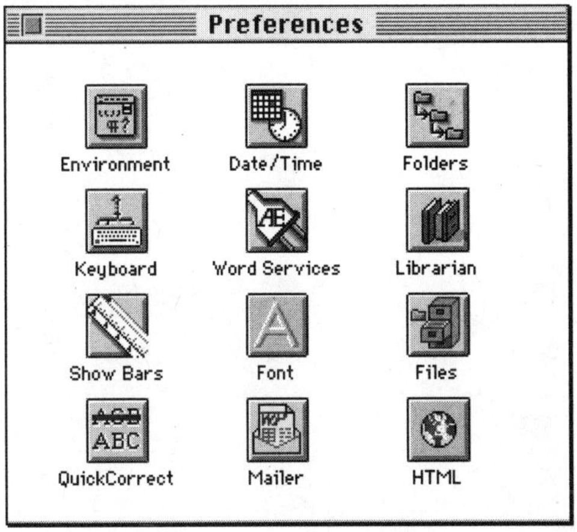

Figure 1b: Select a button from the **Preferences** window to open a dialog box and change your default settings.

To invoke the Preferences window:

1. Pull down the Edit menu and select Preferences (**Figure 1a**).
2. In the resulting Preferences window (**Figure 1b**), select the button of the category you want to edit.

Using the Librarian

WordPerfect provides the ability to share formats and scripts of character maps, keyboard layouts, macros, Style sheets, and Button bars (collectively called *resources*) via a centralized repository called a *library*.

Use the Librarian button on the Preferences window (**Figure 2**) to access your libraries.

Although WordPerfect comes with a few pre-built resources, you can create your own (*see Chapter 11: "Shortcuts" for a description of how to record a macro, Chapter 6: "Styles" for a description of how to create Styles, and the rest of this chapter for other ways to create your own customized resources*).

Figure 2: Click the **Librarian** button to open its dialog box.

Working with libraries

There are two places where document resources are stored: libraries and documents. Both storage areas have implications for how secure and accessible your writing tools remain.

- If you save your resources with the document, only that document can use those resources.
- If you save your resources in a library, those users and documents sharing the library can access the resources.

You can create libraries with different levels of accessibility (depending upon how many users can invoke them via their Librarians.) An example of an extremely open library is the Common Library that comes with WordPerfect. You can place this library filled with group-based resources on to your server for use by your workgroup members.

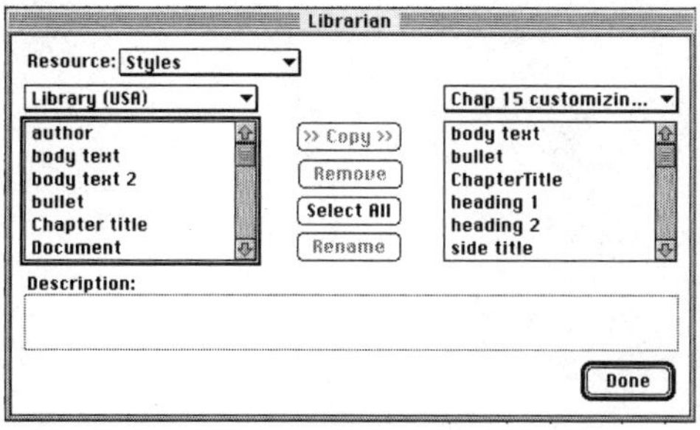

Figure 3a: Use the Librarian dialog box to copy resources from one library to another library or to a document.

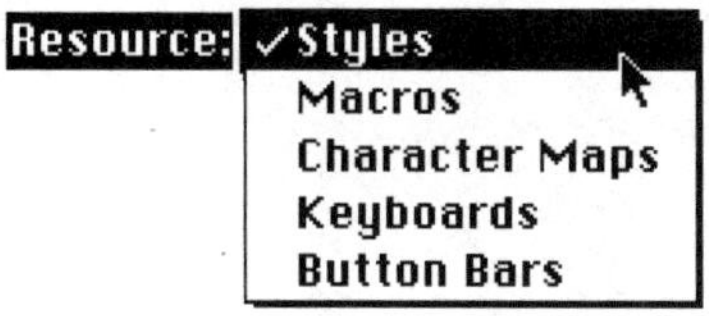

Figure 3b: Select a resource type from this pop-up menu to change the display of resources you want to manipulate.

A private library that resides on your Mac is the Library (USA) library. Library (USA) is a special library created when you first open WordPerfect. This library is the repository for WordPerfect's required resources, such as the pre-built Styles, Normal, Document, Text Box, Caption, and so forth, as well as pre-designed Button bars for the Graphics Editor, Equation Editor, and Document Editor windows.

To change the resources that appear as a default in your document:

1. Open the Preferences window.
2. Click the Librarian button (**Figure 2**).
3. In the resulting Librarian dialog box (**Figure 3a**), select a resource type from the Resources pop-up menu (**Figure 3b**). In this case, I am changing the Styles that appear with my document.

4. Select the *source* library (a library to copy from) on the left-hand pop-up menu.
5. Select the *target* library (a library to copy to) from the right-hand pop-up menu (**Figure 3c**).

   Note: Typically, you copy from the Library (USA) library to your currently open document. (The document's name appears as a default on the right-hand pop-up menu.)
6. Select an item from the right-hand list box.

   Hint: To select more than one item, hold down the Shift key while selecting. You can copy, remove, rename, or select all of the items in either list box by clicking the appropriate button.
7. Click Done to return to your document.

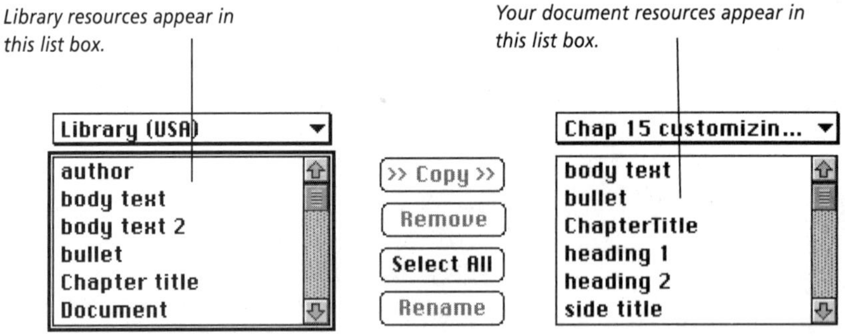

Figure 3c: Select the resources you want to change and click the appropriate button to copy, delete, or rename library or document resources. The buttons work in either direction, depending on the list box location of your selection.

Changing Your Environment

You can make WordPerfect's working environment (menus, screens, Button bars, toolbars, and so forth) operate in a manner that meets your working style by invoking the Environment dialog box.

Figure 4: Click the **Environment** button to change the default settings for WordPerfect's general behavior.

To change your working environment:

1. Open the Preferences window.
2. Click the Environment button (**Figure** 4).
3. In the resulting Environment dialog box (**Figure 5a**), select a backup method and timing option from the Backup area.
4. Select screen color options from the Screen Colors area by selecting new colors from the three pop-up color palettes (**Figure 5b**). The default is a white background color (screen), a black foreground (text), and whatever color you have selected in the Color dialog box on the Control panel pop-up menu on the Apple menu to indicate selected text.

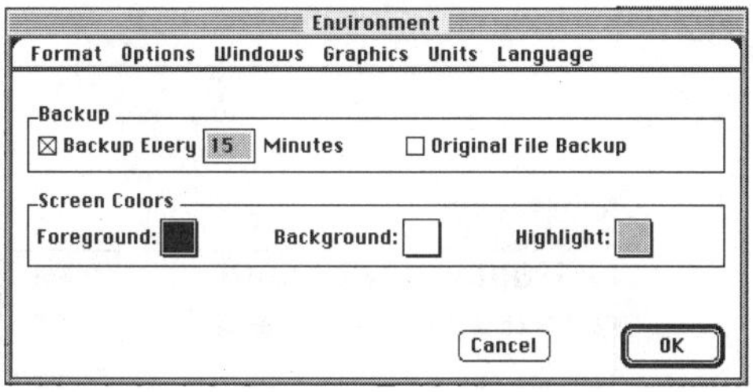

Figure 5a: Use the Environment dialog box to change the defaults for how WordPerfect formats, saves, and displays data.

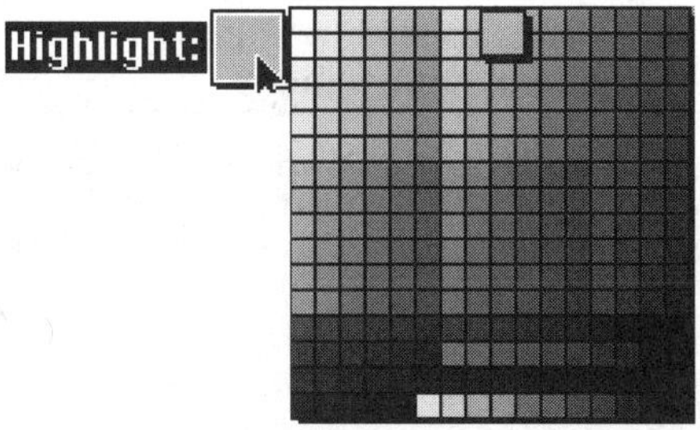

Figure 5b: Select a color from the three palettes in the **Screen Color** area: **Foreground, Background**, and **Highlight**.

5. *Optional:* You can change how formatting affects paragraphs of text by pulling down the Format menu (**Figure 5c**) and selecting a new Paragraph option. The default is Paragraph, although you can change the selection to Single Paragraph to ensure that WordPerfect formats each paragraph individually and not from the insertion point paragraph to the end of the document.
6. *Optional:* You can display fonts in the Font menu with their actual appearance by pulling down the Options menu and selecting Graphic Font Menu (**Figure 5d**). This option is the default.
7. Click OK.

Figure 5c: Use the **Format** pop-up menu to change the Paragraph, Character, and Ruler behavior of WordPerfect.

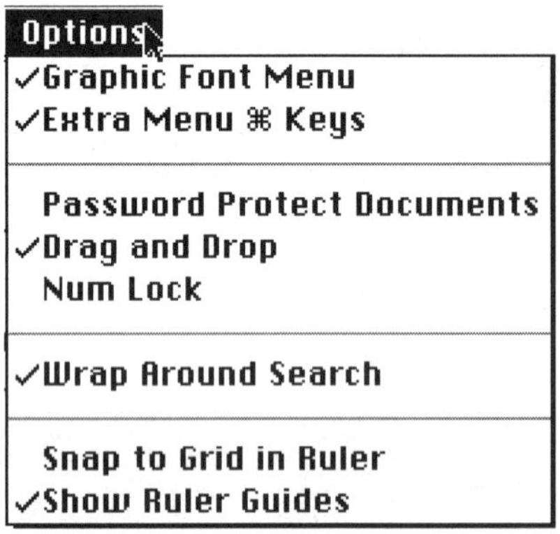

Figure 5d: Use the **Options** pop-up menu to adjust how WordPerfect handles the display of fonts, menu items, files, and the Ruler.

Tip

There are many other default settings that you can change by selecting their options from the **Options, Windows, Language,** and **Format** menus. For example, you can map unknown fonts to related fonts that are already loaded into WordPerfect by selecting **Font Mapping** from the **Format** menu. You can remove extra Return codes from the tops of pages by selecting **Dormant Return** from the **Format** menu. WordPerfect will remember your window locations when you select **Remember Window Locations** from the **Windows** menu. All of these options are turned on by default. Experiment selecting and deselecting the items on each menu to fit your exact needs.

Figure 6: Click the **Font** button to display the Font dialog box where you can change the default font and size.

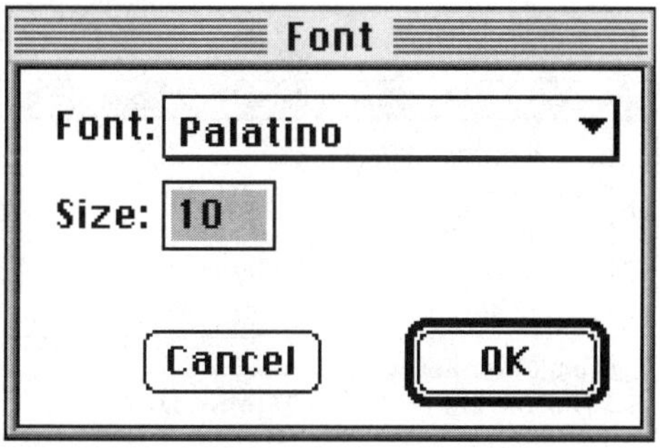

Figure 7a: Select a font from the **Font** pop-up menu to change the default font.

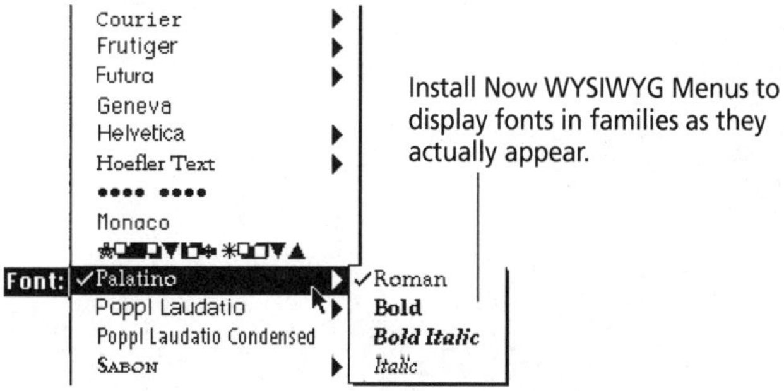

Figure 7b: All of your installed fonts are displayed on the Font pop-up menu.

To change the default font in all documents:

1. Open the Preferences window.
2. Click the Font button (**Figure 6**).
3. In the resulting Font dialog box (**Figure 7a**), pull down the Font pop-up menu and select another font from those listed (**Figure 7b**).
4. *Optional:* Type a new font size in the Size text box.
5. Click OK.

To show or hide toolbars when you open a WordPerfect document:

1. Open the Preferences window.
2. Click the Show Bars button (**Figure 8**).
3. In the resulting Show Bars dialog box (**Figure 9**), select the check boxes next to the Ruler bars you want to display and deselect the check boxes of those toolbars you want to hide.
4. *Optional:* You can opt to display the Button bar and Status bar, or not, by selecting or deselecting their check boxes in the Show Other Bars area of the dialog box.
5. Click OK.

Figure 8: Use the **Show Bars** button to change how many toolbars are displayed when you first open a document.

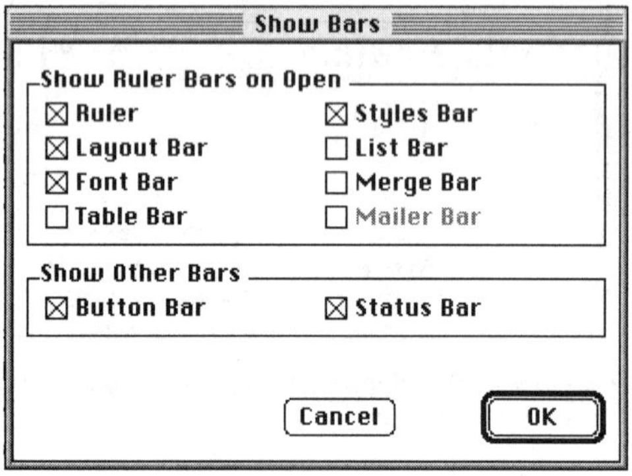

Figure 9: The Show Bars dialog box lets you select which toolbars are displayed automatically when you open a document. You can also opt not to display the Button bar or Status bar automatically.

Tip

The toolbar display options take effect immediately, but do not change your currently active document if it is open. The next time you open a document, the new toolbar arrangement is displayed. Use the **Control bar** to turn toolbars on or off as needed. *See Chapter 2: "Basics" for a description of the Control bar and its use.*

Figure 10: Use the **Keyboard** button to open the Keyboard dialog box.

To set up keystroke assignments for WordPerfect commands:

1. Open the document to automate its Styles or macros with keystroke shortcuts.

   or

2. If you want to add command keystroke assignments, you can open Keyboard without having a document open.
3. Open the Preferences window.
4. Click the Keyboard button (**Figure 10**).
5. In the resulting Keyboard dialog box (**Figure 11a**), select the resource you want to add to the keyboard from the Type pop-up menu (**Figure 11b**).
6. In the resulting Type list box on the left-hand side of the dialog box, select a command, macro, Style, and so forth, that you want to automate.

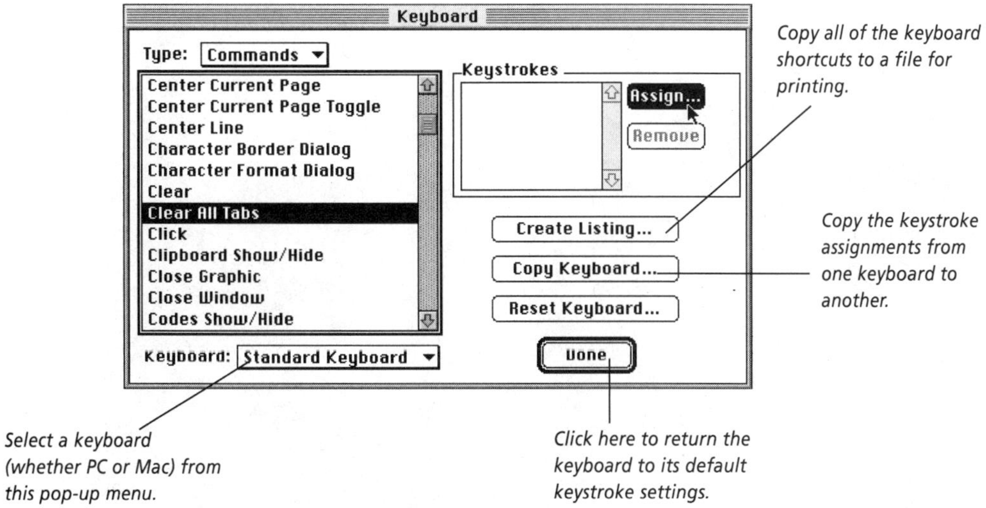

Figure 11a: The Keyboard dialog box lets you set up keystroke shortcuts for resources.

7. If the resource already has a keyboard assignment, the keystroke combination is displayed in the **Keystrokes** list box. Click **Remove** to delete the current assignment. Click **Assign** to assign an additional keystroke combination.
8. In the resulting Assign Keystroke dialog box (**Figure11c**), type a keystroke combination. If the combination is already assigned to another command, that resource name is displayed in the **Assigned** text box. The keystroke you typed appears in the **Keystroke** text box.
9. Click **Assign** to approve the keystroke combination, or type another combination until you are satisfied.
10. Repeat steps 5 through 9 to assign keyboard combinations to other resources.
11. Click Done.

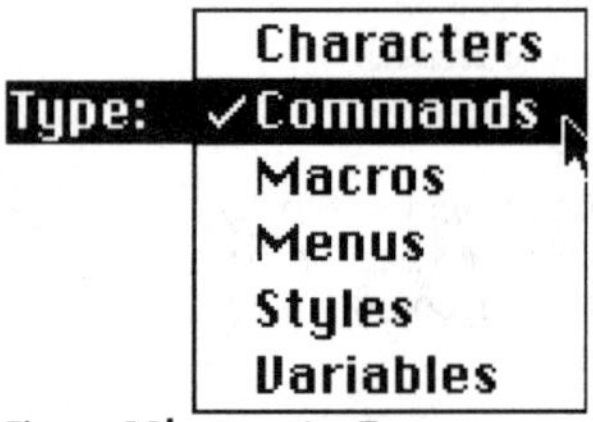

Figure 11b: Use the **Type** pop-up menu to select resources to assign keyboard shortcuts to.

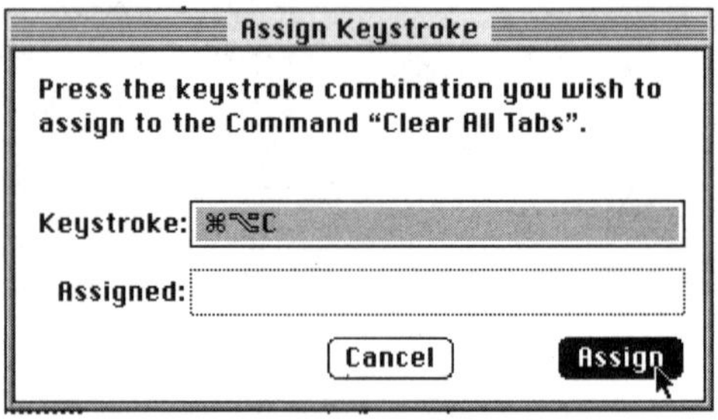

Figure 11c: Use this dialog box to assign keystrokes.

Setting Up Your Document To Create a Web Page

The World Wide Web is so popular because it provides an environment that separates the structured world of UNIX-based *servers* from the free-form world of personal computer *viewers*.

Internet servers only accept documents in ASCII or Text format. Yet, when you view the Web page on your screen, it appears fully layed out and formatted. The connection between the data as it resides on the server and how it is viewed lies in HTML.

The originators of the Web knew that there had to be a way to indicate the parts and formatting of the document so that it could be properly interpreted and displayed on anyone's computer, regardless of what browser or operating system was being used to see the document.

HTML consists of a series of tags that tells the Web viewer what type of formatting to apply to each paragraph of the page document. Note I said "what type of formatting" and not the actual fonts, styles and layouts to display. HTML are text tags that tell the browser (also sometimes called the viewer) how to associate its formatting preferences with the identified Style listed on the tag. Each computer's viewer can set its own formats for these tags, so each computer views the document slightly differently.

The Preferences window in WordPerfect 3.5 has a new button that lets you set how you want HTML tags to display information on your computer so that you can see the results of your tagging efforts on the screen as formats are applied.

The HTML button opens the HTML Preferences dialog box. This Preferences box lets you select formatting options for each tag and set the browser software you will use to export and view your handiwork. *See Chapter 16: "Internet" for a discussion of how to generate Web pages using HTML.*

To set HTML tag formats:

1. Open the Preferences window (See **Figure 1**).
2. Click the HTML button (**Figure 12**).

Figure 12: Click this button to set the formatting of the HTML tags used to create World Wide Web pages. See Chapter 16: "Internet" for a description of how to use the tags.

> **Tip**
>
> WordPerfect 3.5 comes with the new Netscape browser which requires that you own an Internet account with a local Internet server. You can also assign a browser from a commercial gateway such as e•World's or American Online's browser, using their accounts to export and view your work.

3. In the resulting HTML dialog box (**Figure 13a**), pull down the Tag pop-up menu and select the tag whose criteria you want to format from those listed (**Figure 13b**).
4. *Optional:* Use the Font, Size, Style, and Color pop-up menus to change the formatting of the tag.
5. *Optional:* Click the Choose Browser button to open the Choose Browser dialog box. Find another browser on the Finder list box and click Attach.
6. When you return to the HTML dialog box, click OK.

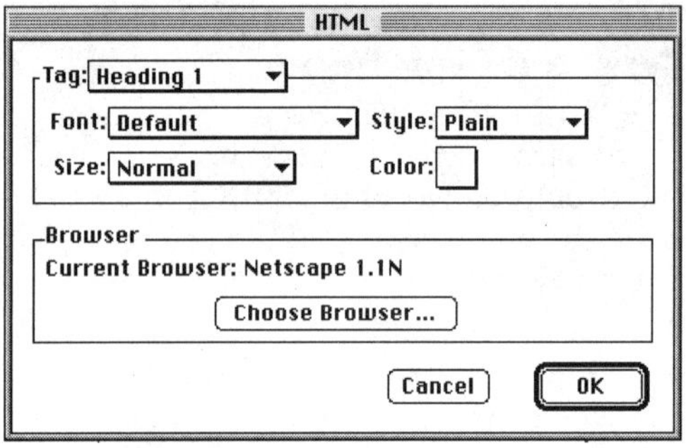

Figure 13a: Use the HTML dialog box to set up tag formatting and select a browser.

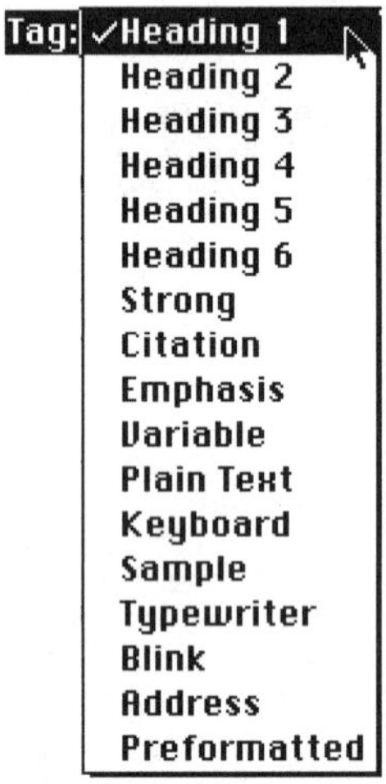

Figure 13b: Select a tag to format from the **Tags** pop-up menu.

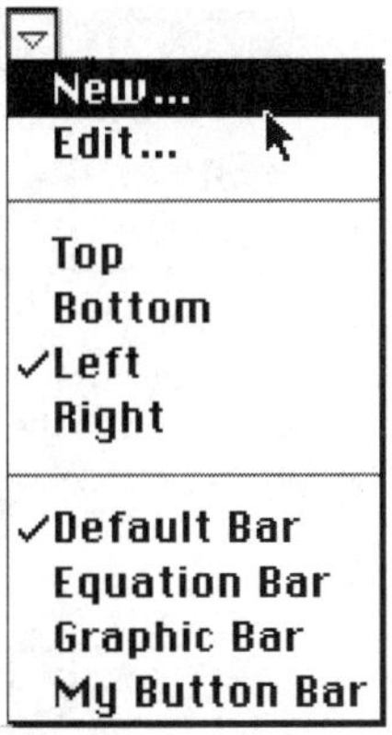

Figure 14: Select **New** from the **Button bar** pop-up menu.

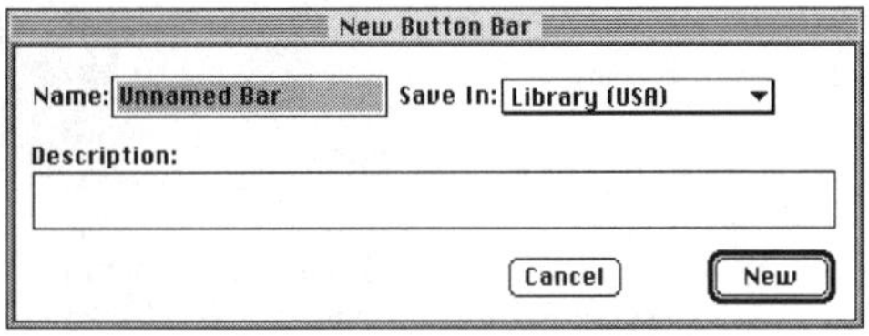

Figure 15: Type a name for the new Button bar in the **Name** text box.

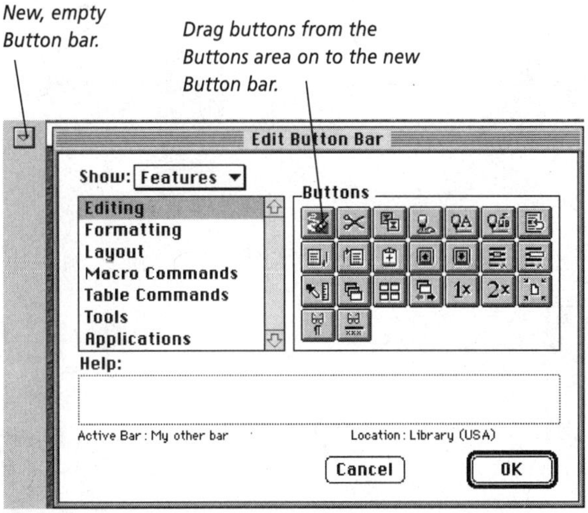

Figure 16a: Use the Edit Button bar dialog box to place buttons on the new Button bar.

Using the Button Bar Pop-Up Menu

The Button bar pop-up menu (*see Chapter 2: "Basics" for a description of the Button bar*) controls where the Button bar is displayed on the screen, as well as which buttons are displayed on which Button bar. The following pages describe how to create a new, customized Button bar, and how to add and subtract buttons from the new bar.

To create a new Button bar:

1. Pull down the Button bar pop-up menu and select New (**Figure 14**).
2. Type a name for the new Button bar in the Name text box (**Figure 15**).
3. *Optional:* Select a library location where you want to save the new Button bar configuration information from the Save In pop-up menu. The default is the universal library called Library (USA).
4. Click the New button. A blank Button bar replaces the existing Button bar and WordPerfect displays the Edit Button bar dialog box (**Figure 16a**).

5. *Optional:* Change the category from which you want to take buttons by selecting a new type from the Show pop-up menu (**Figure 16b**).
6. Select a type of button from the left-hand Directory list box.
7. Double-click on a button to place it on the Button bar. WordPerfect places it next in line on the bar.

   or

8. Select and drag a button on to the Button bar in the location you want it (**Figure 17**).
9. Click OK.

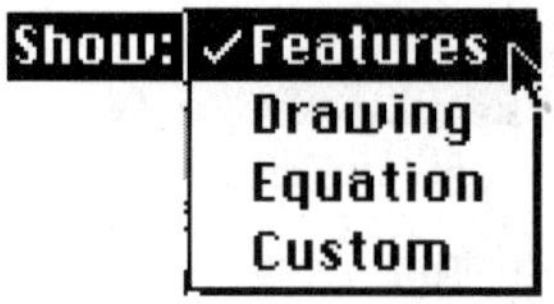

Figure 16b: Use the **Show** pop-up menu to change the type of button you want to add to the new Button bar.

Figure 17: Drag the button from the Edit dialog box on to the new Button bar.

> **Tip**
>
> To remove a button from a Button bar, drag the button off of the bar. You cannot place buttons back on to the Edit Button bar dialog box, but you can click the dialog box's **Cancel** button to undo your change.

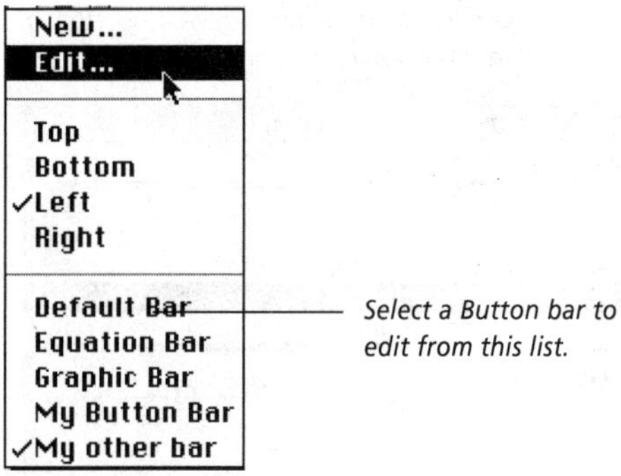

Figure 18: Select **Edit** from the Button bar pop-up menu.

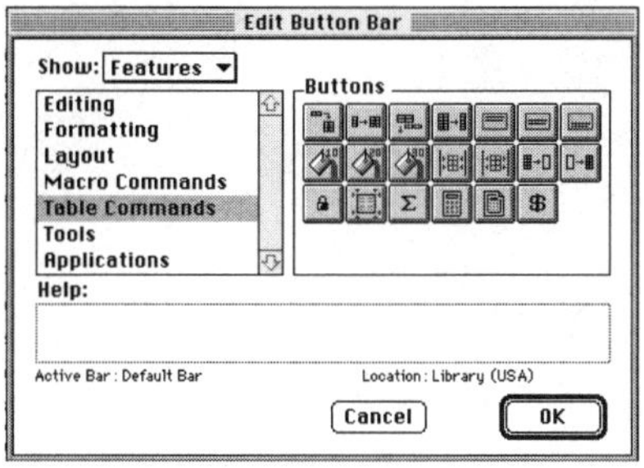

Figure 19a: Use this dialog box to create custom buttons and add buttons to existing or new Button bars.

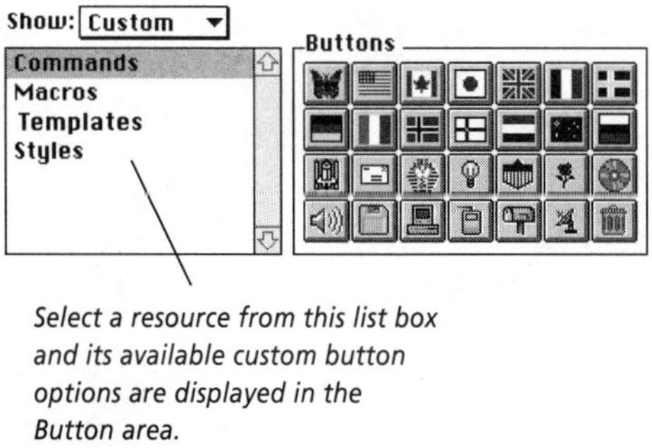

Figure 19b: Double-click a button to display its associated Assignment dialog box for that button.

To create custom buttons:

1. Pull down the Button Bar Control pop-up menu and select the Button bar on which you want to place the new button.
2. With the specified Button bar displayed, pull down the Button Bar pop-up menu again and select Edit (**Figure 18**).
3. In the resulting Edit Button bar dialog box (**Figure 19a**), pull down the Show pop-up menu and select Custom (**Figure 19b**).
4. Select the type of command you want to create a button for from the Show list box. The Button list box for that function is displayed.

5. Double-click on a button. The Assign dialog box is displayed (**Figure 20**). Note that the Assign Command dialog box varies based on the function you selected in the Show list box in Step 4. You can assign Commands, Stationery, Macros, and Styles to buttons.
6. Select an item from the Assign list box.
7. Click Assign.

"Command" is the resource you selected in the Show pop-up menu.

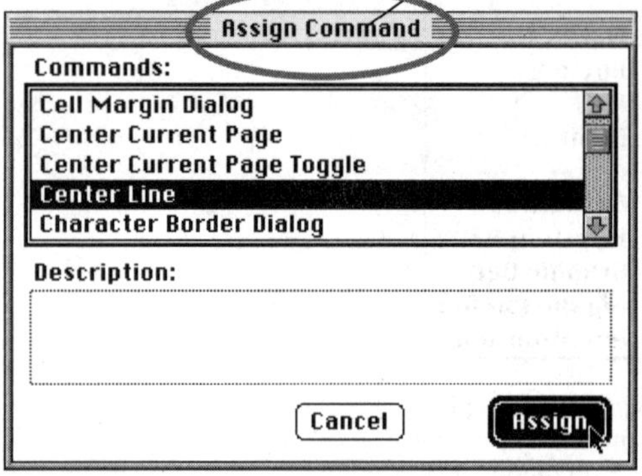

Figure 20: Select an option from the list box, in this case a command from the **Commands** list box, and click **Assign**.

Tip

If you edit the default Button bar and want to return to the original version, just display another Button bar. Select Preferences from the Edit menu and display the Librarian dialog box by clicking the Librarian button in the resulting Preferences dialog box. Remove the default Button bar from the library. Quit WordPerfect and then restart it. WordPerfect will reconstruct the default version.

INTERNET 16

EVERYONE BY NOW has heard of the "Information Superhighway." The big question is, "How do I get on?" and "What do I do as a professional once I'm there?" Although WordPerfect cannot answer the question of what you want to be when you grow up, it can provide access to the Internet (or Net) as this conglomeration of computers, networks, phone lines, and satellites is called; WordPerfect provides the tools to actually interact with the Internet once you are there.

The Internet, as mentioned above, is a collection of mainframe, mini-, and microcomputers that act as database repositories and traffic cops for a vast network of phone lines, optical fiber connections, and satellite linkages.

Welcome to the Web

Because the Net is actually a vast (millions and millions at last count) collection of computers and a vehicle for their communication, finding your way around can be a nightmare unless you have a map. Luckily, entrepreneurial computer programmers have developed vehicles that help you find your way around the Net. These access methods include: e-mail subscriptions (called *Lists*) that broadcast text to multiple people all at once; *newsgroups* in which you can send messages back and forth to set addresses; services that let you download and upload files; and lastly, the *World Wide Web* (or *Web* for short), a graphics-based linking mechanism that connects these disparate worlds into a unified and navigable whole.

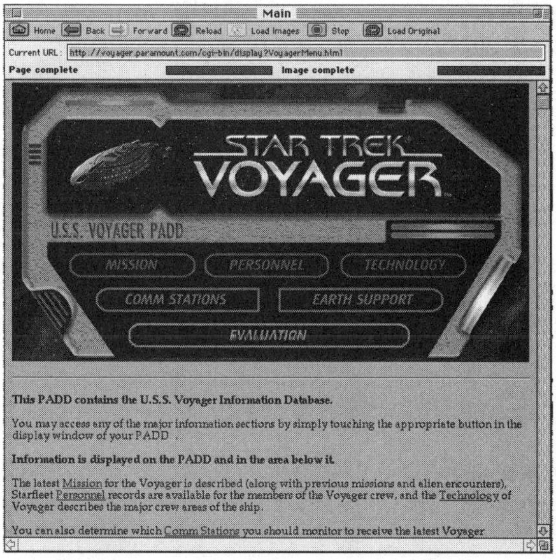

WordPerfect 3.5 provides a series of tools to navigate and interact with the World Wide Web.

The Web is the most graphical way to locate information in the Internet. It relies on graphic maps, buttons, WYSIWYG formats, and special clickable areas of text to help you navigate around the Net. The reason that the Web works so well is that what you see on your screen is not what the Internet server has to store or transmit, so more data can be presented than would ordinarily be easily sent over telephone lines. The difference between the straight ASCII text and computerese addresses that the server uses and what you see is taken up by the tool that your computer uses to interpret and display the data it is sent. The software that performs the interpretation is called a *viewer,* or *browser*.

Browsers are supplied by commercial network services that serve as gateways to the Internet, such as Apple's e•World, CompuServe, or America Online; or by the actual Internet server community such as your university, a government office, or a commercial business. In addition, there are some commercial Internet servers that let you enter the Internet for a fee if you provide the browser. WordPerfect 3.5 provides the Netscape 1.1 browser for this purpose.

The World Wide Web Explained

Servers on the Internet download data a page at a time. Pages of data are connected together via *hyperlinks*. The Web uses an index system based on visual cues that let you select where you want to go next on the Internet by clicking these special areas in the text. Clicking can send you across the United States, or even across the globe. The Web links sites as disparate as Berkeley, California and the Louvre Museum in Paris with the click of your mouse. The first page

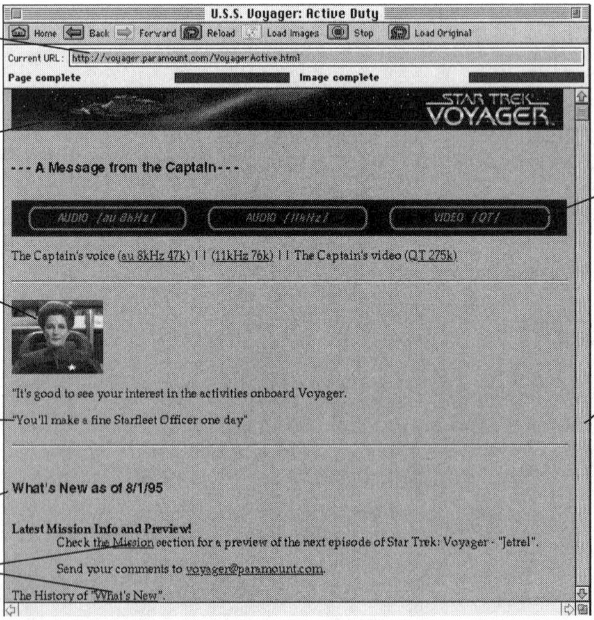

Figure 1: A home page on the Web offers many graphical ways to interact with the Internet.

of text you are sent acts as the table of contents for the document, and therefore is called the *home page.* (Home pages are also called *sites* or *Web pages* just to confuse you.) Each time you click on a hyperlink, the server downloads the page you indicate. It knows which page to jump to because of an address buried in the hyperlink. The home page lets you view movies, or provides a way to easily download sounds, documents, or graphics with the click of a mouse (**Figure 1**).

Understanding URLs

Each page of data on a server has its own storage location. To find a Web site or any other database on the Internet you have to know its address or it has to have keys or anchors programmed into it (namely, the hyperlink) that locate its address for a browser. The address specification used by the Web is called a *Uniform Resource Locator* (*URL*). For example, a good primer on how to write Web pages is located on the Web at:
http//www.ncsa.uiuc.edu/General/Internet/www/HTMLPrimer.html.

What a mouthful. Luckily, modern browsers locate URLs by letting you click on that hyperlink. When you click this anchor, the browser identifies its URL and then takes you to that site.

The Web and WordPerfect

WordPerfect provides three tools that let you use the Internet and the Web to great advantage. Two of these tools are described in this chapter.

- **Netscape browser.** The Netscape browser along with an Internet access provider, gets you on the Internet. Netscape is not discussed in this book because it is not a WordPerfect tool.
- **Bookmarks.** Bookmarks are tools that let you mark text, graphics, movies, or other items within your document, and using hyperlinks, create connections between your document and another item of information, such as marked text in another document, or even data at a Web site. Clicking on a hyperlink within your document automatically jumps you to the site of its connected Web page. The beauty of this system is that you can reference a piece of data such as a stock market quote, financial information, computer hardware descriptions, and so forth and take your reader directly to the site of the information with the click of a mouse.
- **HTML toolbar.** WordPerfect provides an automatic way to apply a collection of styles, called Hypertext Markup Language, or HTML, to your document. HTML tags define the formatting and contents of your document for the Internet, and thus lets you publish your own Web pages.

Creating Hyperlinks in Your Document

The BookMark command is used to create cross-references to other areas in your document or another document. Each bookmark is given a name. After marking your text with a bookmark, use the name to jump to the marked text it identifies. Bookmarks serve as anchors to your document which you can join to outside information sources via hyperlinks. For instance, you can use the BookMark command's components to link your document's text to macros that collect data from other sources, as well as update a page number by referencing another portion of your document. When using the bookmark's hyperlinks to identify an Internet address, you can jump to a Web site, enabling your reader to research further about a topic mentioned in your document.

To create a bookmark:

1. Select the text you want to mark.
2. Open the BookMark toolbar if it is not already open by clicking BookMark on the Control bar (**Figure 2**).
3. Click Mark (**Figure 3a**).
4. In the resulting BookMark dialog box (**Figure 3b**), type a name for the bookmark in the BookMark Name text box and click OK.
5. *Optional*: Click OK to accept the name automatically assigned to the bookmark. (This name is the actual text you selected.)
6. The bookmark name is displayed at the bottom of the BookMark pop-up menu on the toolbar (**Figure 4**).

Figure 2: Click **BookMark** on the Control bar to display the BookMark toolbar.

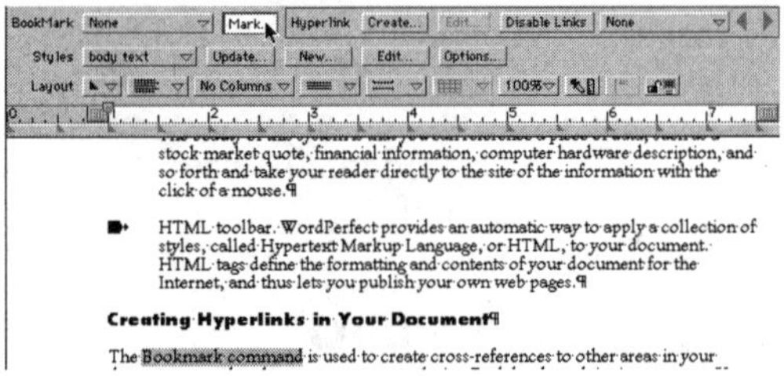

Figure 3a: Select your reference text and click **Mark**.

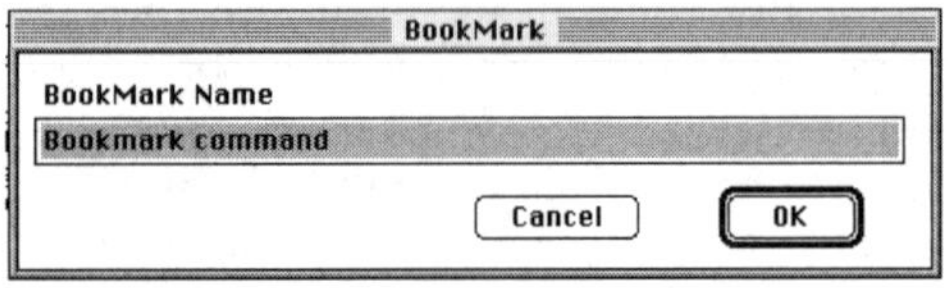

Figure 3b: Either accept the automatic name for your bookmark or type a new name in the text box.

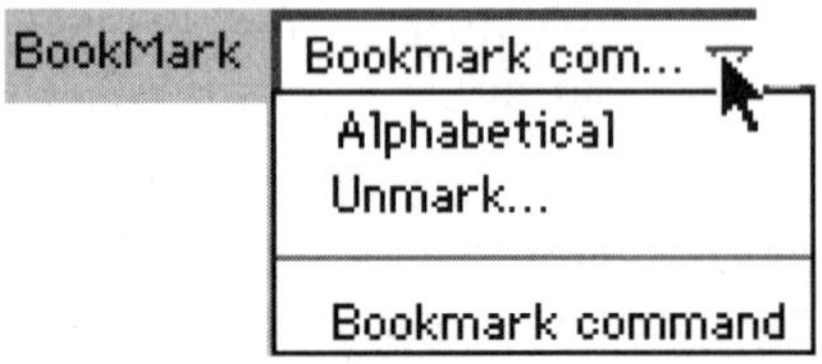

Figure 4: The new bookmark is listed at the bottom of the **BookMark** pop-up menu on the BookMark toolbar. Selecting the bookmark automatically jumps you to the marked reference in your document.

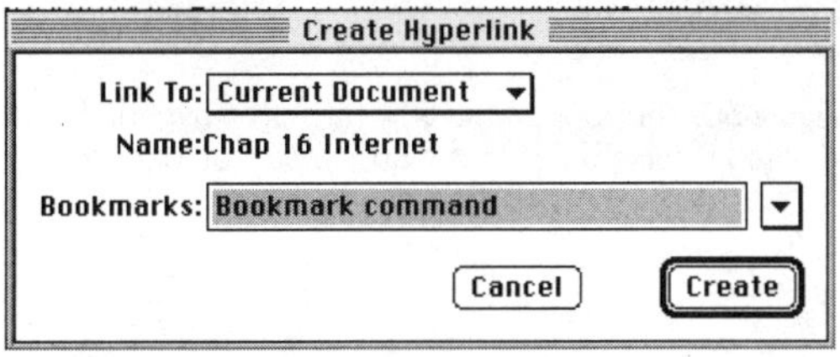

Figure 5a: The Create Hyperlink dialog box provides support for four types of hyperlinks and changes to accommodate their disparate connection requirements.

Figure 5b: Select a link type from the pop-up menu. You can create links to other areas in your document, another document, an Internet Web site, or to a macro.

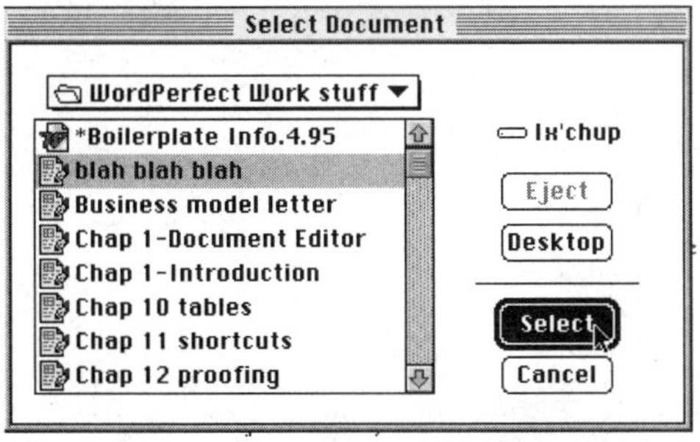

Figure 5c: When you select the **Other Document** option, the Select Document dialog box is displayed. Select a document and click **Select** to add the document's name to the **Name** area of the Create Hyperlink dialog box.

Tip

You can select documents on your computer and across a network. If you want to jump to a Web site, you must know the URL of the site and type its address in the Address text box. WordPerfect only accepts URLs. If you want to link to a macro, WordPerfect will ask you to select the macro's name from a list box and then displays the name in the Create Hyperlink dialog box.

To create a hyperlink:

1. Open a WordPerfect document and select the text or object (such as a graphic or QuickTime movie) you want to use as the hyperlink anchor.
2. Open the BookMark toolbar if it is not already open by clicking BookMark on the Control bar (see **Figure 2**).
3. Click Create.
4. In the resulting Create Hyperlink dialog box (**Figure 5a**), select Current Document, Other Document, Internet Address, or Macro from the Link To pop-up menu (**Figure 5b**).
5. If you select Current Document, the dialog box displays the name of the current document. If you wish to create a link to another document, WordPerfect displays the Finder directory dialog box (**Figure 5c**) and asks you to select the document to which you want to connect your anchor.
6. *Optional*: Select a bookmark name from the BookMark Name pop-up menu, or type a name in the text box. The bookmark is only used for links to current or other documents.
7. Click Create.

To remove a hyperlink from a document:

1. Click Disable Links on the BookMark toolbar (**Figure 6a**). The button changes to read "Enable Links." Click again to turn on your bookmarks and hyperlinks.
2. Select the hyperlinked text you want to delete.
3. The Hyperlink Create button changes to read "Remove" (**Figure 6b**). Click Remove on the BookMark toolbar.

Figure 6a: You can temporarily turn off a hyperlink by clicking **Disable Links** on the BookMark toolbar.

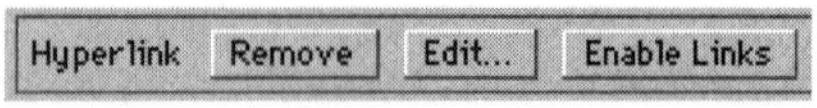

Figure 6b: Click **Remove** to delete a hyperlink.

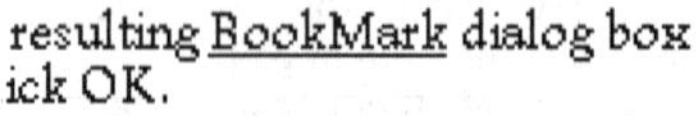

Figure 7: Bookmarks and hyperlinks are indicated by different formatting, such as the default blue underlined version, shown above.

Tip

The hyperlink is displayed as colored and underlined text **(Figure 7)**. When you enter a bookmark name in the **BookMark Name** text box in the Create Hyperlink dialog box, WordPerfect will take you to the specified mark whenever you click on the hyperlink text (**Figure 8**). It does not matter if the mark is in another document, WordPerfect will take you to that bookmark in the other document as well. If you do not specify a bookmark, WordPerfect takes you to the top of the specified document. This is a useful way to open another document without having to resort to the Open dialog box or Finder.

You can specify the formatting of hyperlinks by selecting the **HTML** button of the Preferences dialog box (located on the Edit menu). *See Chapter 15: "Customizing" for a description of how to set hyperlink preferences.*

When you link to an Internet address, clicking the anchor automatically opens the browser. **Note:** You must first establish a connection to your Internet server prior to invoking the browser or it cannot enter the Web.

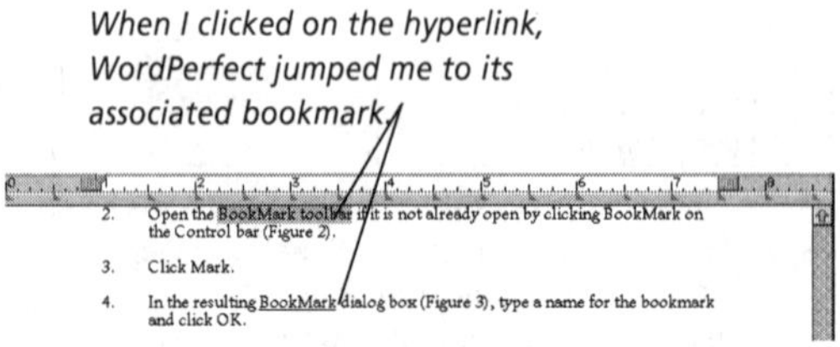

Figure 8: An example of a hyperlink between two bookmarks in a single document.

Using HTML To Create Web Pages

Documents published on the Internet must be saved in plain text format (also called ASCII) to be legible to UNIX, the language of the Internet. Therefore, none of the formatting and WYSIWYG features of WordPerfect work on the Web. How do you convey formatting on the Web? Formatting is indicated on the Web through the interpretation of specialized style tags. These tags, called HTML, tell the Internet that it is dealing with a Web page and tells the browser how the page should be displayed on the computer screen. Each browser interprets the codes embedded in the HTML tags based on the format and layout settings assigned by you in the browser's preferences dialog box (the settings capabilities of the browser will vary depending on the browser you use).

Creating a Good Web Page

Although there is no set way to create a Web page, because HTML lends itself so easily to graphics (such as buttons, graphic lines, bulleted lists, and so forth), you should try to make your page as simple and graphically oriented as possible. Use buttons, bullets, and headings to lead your readers to your hyperlinks. Include plenty of links, because it is this browsing ability that makes the Web so intriguing.

There is one caveat to including graphics with your document. All graphics have to be converted to a format that can be read by your browser. This means that all graphics must be converted to either GIF (from CompuServe), X bitmap (BMP), or Joint Photographic Experts Group (JPEG). You can purchase converters (such as DataViz' MacLink Plus Translators) or download them from bulletin boards (such as the GIF converter from CompuServe). Adobe Acrobat Portable Digital Format (PDF) files also can be directly linked to your home page.

WordPerfect's HTML toolbar will apply basic HTML codes to your document tagging text that you want marked as paragraphs, headers (up to six levels), titles, and areas you want to single out for emphasis (such as quotes or messages). You can set how the tagged text will appear on your screen in the HTML preferences dialog box (accessed from the **Preferences** command on the Edit menu). The browser used to read your home page actually performs the translation from tag to format and so its preferences determine how the header, title, and so forth appear on that computer. The tag simply indicates that it is the style you want applied to that particular set of text.

The beauty of WordPerfect's HTML engine is that you do not have to know HTML to use it. You use English to indicate your formatting selection and WordPerfect applies the appropriate HTML tag to your selection. The codes are displayed on your screen as another type of WYSIWYG formatting (such as bold, italics, color, and so forth), but is interpreted by the browser as an HTML tag. Therefore, you will not see actual HTML (such as <H1> for Heading 1, <P> for paragraph, or <title> for a header).

To generate HTML tags:

1. Open the document you want to convert to HTML.
2. If the HTML toolbar is not open, click its button on the control panel (**Figure 9a**).
3. Select the text or paragraphs in the document you want to assign a tag to.
4. Click the appropriate button on the HTML toolbar. Click the Header button to assign the text as a title. Use the Heading pop-up menu (**Figure 9b**) to select a heading level format, or the Style pop-up menu (**Figure 9c**) to apply specialized formats for emphasis such as bold, italic, and so forth.
5. *Optional*: Select any quotations in your text and click the Quote button to insert appropriate indentation and punctuation tags.

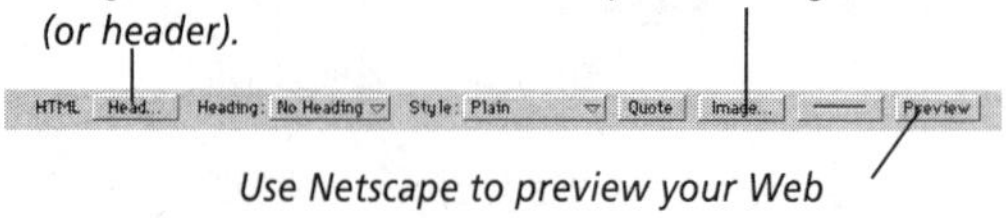

Figure 9a: Use the HTML toolbar to assign tags to your document.

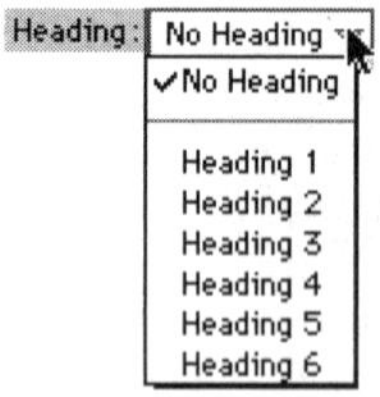

Figure 9b: Use the **Heading** options to assign hierarchical structure to your text.

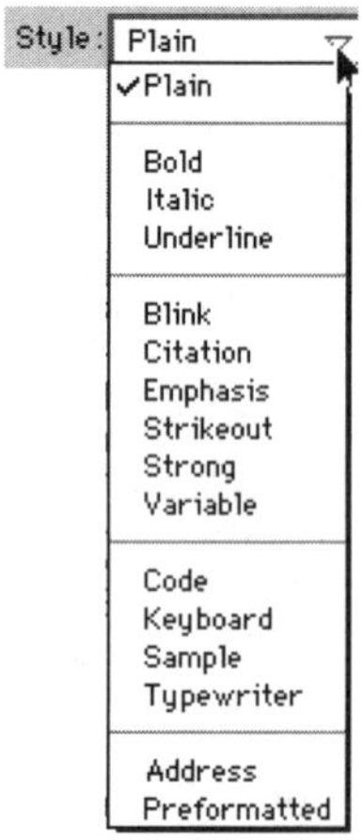

Figure 9c: Use this pop-up menu to assign other formatting options, such as those regularly available on the Fonts and Layout toolbars in WordPerfect.

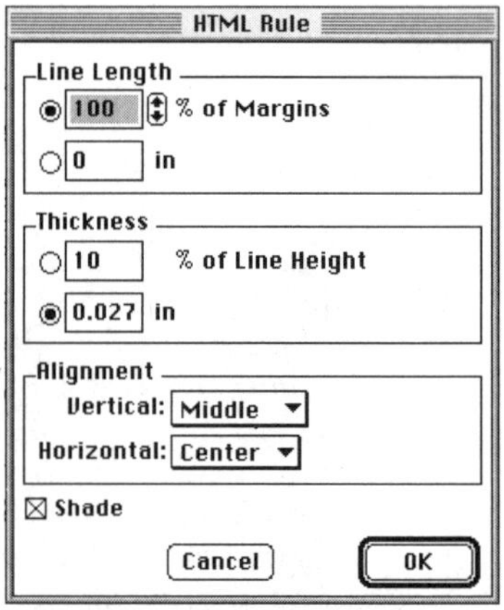

Figure 9d: Use this dialog box to set the formatting of lines.

Tip

HTML documents can display the bulleted or numbered lists created using WordPerfect's Bullets and Outline buttons and commands. The bookmarks and hyperlinks described above are also translated into the HTML document and serve as jump off points in the same fashion as they did in standard documents. Use the Internet Address option on the **Link To** pop-up menu to identify other Web sites that you want your page to link to.

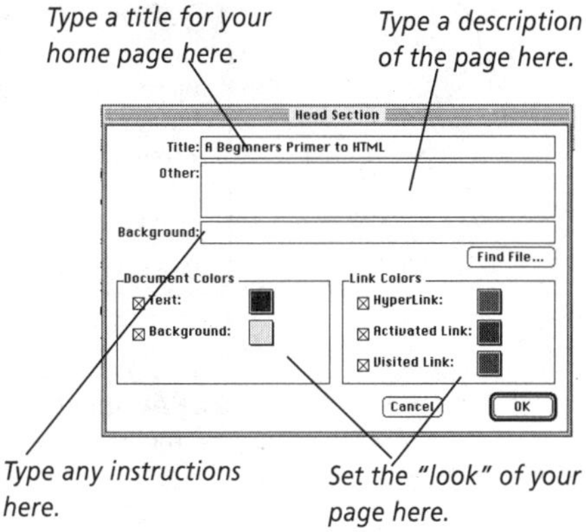

Figure 10: Use the Header dialog box to set up the look and feel of your page.

6. *Optional*: Add lines to your page by clicking the line button. Double-click the line to display its dialog box (**Figure 9d**). You can make it a three-dimensional line if the recipient browser accepts that format for the line tag. Use the HTML Rule dialog box to set the line length, its thickness, its distance from the text, and alignment. Remove the line by selecting the 0 thickness radio button. Click **OK**.

Tip

The following table lists descriptions for the basic tag elements available on the HTML toolbar.

Head	Use this button to create a title for your Web page. The Header dialog box (**Figure 10**) lets you add an image identifying the Web page's originators or purpose. These images can also serve as hyperlinks taking your visitor to other Web sites. The Head Section dialog box also lets you set the background image or colors of your page. You can use Adobe PhotoShop background images, such as wallpapers or screens to enhance your document by clicking the Find File button and attaching the image. Add a description of the page and how it is used by typing your text in the Other text box.
Heading	You can apply heading tags to make your document easier to follow. Headings indicate new topics. WordPerfect provides six heading level formats on its Headings pop-up menu (see **Figure 9b**). Heading 1 is the most prominent heading format and should be used to indicate the top-most topic in your hierarchy.
Style	This pop-up menu (see **Figure 9c**) provides the paragraph and character tags that add emphasis formatting to your document. Because you cannot use standard styles, these tags apply the same bold, italics, outline, and so forth that you would apply using Style Sheets and the Layout tools in WordPerfect.
Quote	This tag indents quotations to set them off from regular text.
Image	Use this button to add graphics to your page. Because not all browsers allow you to view graphic images, this button also lets you type text that will be displayed by these browsers instead of the graphic. You can also indicate whether the graphic will be used as a hyperlink map directing you to other Web pages. The HTML Image dialog box also scales the graphic and aligns it to the text on the page.

To preview your Web page:

1. With the HTML document open, click the Preview button on the HTML toolbar (see **Figure 9a**).
2. WordPerfect opens the browser tool and displays the interpreted Web page.
3. Click the close box to return to your document.

To export your HTML document:

1. Open the document to which you have applied HTML tags.
2. Pull down the File menu and select **Save As** (**Figure 11**).
3. In the resulting Save As dialog box (**Figure 12a**) select **HTML Export** from the **Format** pop-up menu (**Figure 12b**).
4. Type a name in the **Save Document As** text box.
5. Click **Save**.
6. Use your browser (such as Netscape) to upload the saved HTML document to the Internet server. Ask the Network Administrator for specific instructions on how to upload and register the Web page on that server.

Tip

Be sure to save your HTML document under a different name than the WordPerfect version so that you have a backup.

To publish your document, you must reserve disk space and an address on an Internet server linked to the Web. There are many commercial Internet servers, as well as universities, private companies, and Government offices that sponsor such gateways. You can also use public accesses, such as those at libraries. This disk space and address is the URL for your Web page.

Figure 11: Select **Save As** from the File menu.

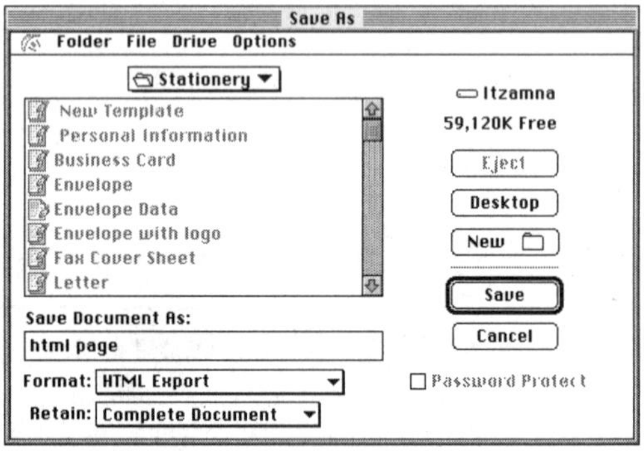

Figure 12a: Use the Save As dialog box to save the document under another name.

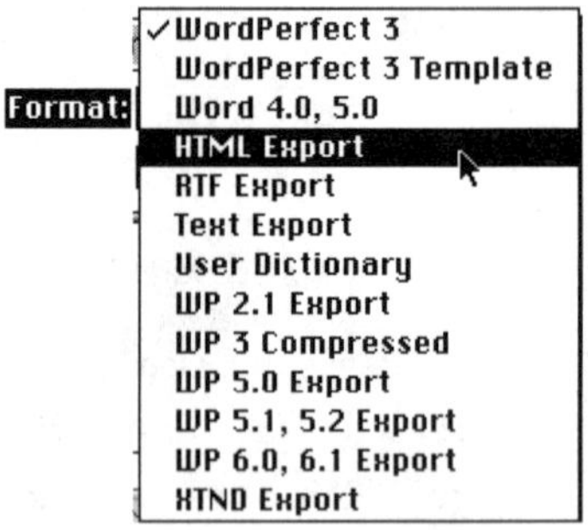

Figure 12b: Select **HTML Export** from the **Format** pop-up menu to indicate how WordPerfect should process its contents.

Appendix A: Glossary

active table cell
The cell that contains the insertion point. The active cell is also indicated by a gray vertical line in the Ruler bar.

anchor
The act of attaching an object (graphic, text box, equation box, and so forth) to either a page, character, or paragraph (the default is character). When you anchor an object, it moves with the item it is anchored to, rather than staying on the page where you placed it (unless you anchored it to the page).

antonym
A word that means the opposite of another word.

arrow cursor
The cursor changes to a left-facing arrow when you pass the cursor over a button on the Button bar, the Ruler, or any toolbar. The left-hand arrow also appears after you select text to enable you to drag and drop the text to another location.

attributes
Those elements of style that help to define how a character appears on the page. Examples include bold, 10-point size, and Normal tracking.

blinking cursor
This cursor is always located in front of text you type to indicate where the next text will appear.

buttons
Three-dimensional icons representing specific features in a program. Click the cursor on a button to perform a task.

character count
A count of all letters, numbers, and punctuation in a document. Spaces are not counted.

codes
Tokens or markers that control how documents will appear on the screen and when printed. Codes can be viewed in two places, either directly in the document in the case of paragraph markers and spaces; or in a special window called the Code Window. There are two types of codes, "universal" that carry information about the formatting of paragraphs or pages, and "toggled" that carry information about the attributes and are usually seen in twos that turn the code on and off (one before the item being coded and one after).

column
The vertical arrangement of cells in a table.

document
The basic place where you do your work in WordPerfect. The term file and document are used interchangeably.

drawing object
The graphic components of a drawing. Objects can be manipulated or grouped together to form graphics.

Encapsulated PostScript (EPS)
Graphics created using the PostScript page description language. EPS graphics are actually generated at your PostScript laser printer, and thus cannot be displayed on the screen by WordPerfect, although they can be imported into the program and printed on the laser printer.

formatting
Those elements that define how a page of text appears. Examples include margins, indents, alignment, and so forth.

grouped objects
One or more drawing or text objects that have been locked together so that they can be manipulated as a single unit.

gutter
This is the space between the right margin of a column and the left margin of the next column. You can change this white space by adjusting the margins of your columns by either dragging the Ruler margin markers or using the Column Format dialog box. The default spacing for evenly-spaced margins is 0.25-inch gutters.

handles
The small, solid rectangular boxes that are displayed when you select a graphic or text box. These handles, also called "resize handles," are what you drag to enlarge or reduce the size of the box or object, or when you want to crop the object.

hanging indent
A type of indent where every line of a paragraph is indented except the first line.

homonym
A word that sounds the same as another word but has another meaning.

I-beam cursor
The I-beam appears on the desktop when you are typing text. Use the I-beam to guide you where to type and where to insert text.

icon
A pictorial representation of a command. Click or double-click the cursor on an icon to perform that function it symbolizes. Icons are used to represent applications, documents, folders, and volumes, as well as specific features within a program. If you are running System 7, you can also drag a document icon on top of its associated application's icon to open and display its contents.

line count
A count of all of the lines of text within a document.

orphan line
A single line of a paragraph that is left alone at the bottom of a page.

page count
A count of every page in your document.

row
Parallel columns are broken into rows, consisting of the column at the left margin and working across the page to the last column on the right margin. A set of columns can have a single row or multiple rows.

sentence count
A count of all words from period to period in a document.

set
When you use the Columns pop-up menu to change the number of columns, you create a "set." Sets exist from the first appearance of new column type on a page to a hard column break that signals the insertion of a new column format. Everything you do to format your columns is done to the column set.

synonym
A word that has a similar meaning to another word.

table row
The horizontal arrangement of cells in a table.

table cell
The space that contains a unit of data within a table. Cells can hold numbers, text, graphics, endnotes, or equations.

text object
Boxes containing text that can be manipulated like a graphic object. For example, you can resize, rotate, and move the box along with its text or edit its textual contents. See Chapter 9: "Layout" for more information about text boxes.

tools
Button icons located on bars used as shortcuts to perform WordPerfect commands.

word count
A count of all words in a document. A word consists of letters, numbers, and punctuation without spaces.

widow
A single line of a paragraph left by itself at the top of a page.

Appendix B: Keyboard Shortcuts

Navigating Shortcuts

Move to beginning/end of line	⌘+Shift+Left arrow/Right arrow, ⌘+Keypad 4 (with Number Lock on and an extended keyboard)
Move to the top of the page	Home key
Move to the end of the document	End key
Move to next/previous screen	⌘+Down arrow/Up arrow or Keypad + (plus)/Keypad - (minus)
Move to next/previous page	Option+Down arrow/Up arrow
Number Lock on/off	Shift+Number Lock key
Select a character	⌘+Shift+Right arrow/Left arrow
Select to the end of a line	⌘+Shift+Right arrow
Select to the end of the document	Shift+End key

File menu

New...	⌘+N
Open...	⌘+O
Close	⌘+W
Save or Save As...	⌘+S
Print	⌘+P
Print Preview...	⌘+Shift+P
Quit	⌘+Q

Edit menu

Undo	⌘+Z
Cut	⌘+X, F2
Copy	⌘+C, F3
Paste	⌘+V, F4
Paste Special...	⌘+Shift+V
Paste Attributes	Shift+F4
Paste Text	⌘+F4
Select All	⌘+A

Find/Change...	⌘+F
Find Next	⌘+G
Find Previous	⌘+Shift+G
Go To...	Option+F13
Show/Hide ¶	Option+F1
Show/Hide Codes	⌘+Shift+K, Option+F2

Insert menu

Page Break	⌘+Return
Column Break	⌘+Shift+Return
Indent	Option+Tab, F5, ⌘+Shift+I
Left/Right Indent	⌘+Option+Tab, ⌘+F5
Back Tab	Shift+Tab key
Symbols...	Option+F4
Text Date/Time	⌘+Shift+D

Layout menu

Hide/Show Ruler	⌘+R
Hide/Show Ruler bar	⌘+Option+R
Hide/Show Button bar	⌘+Option+B
Margins...	⌘+M
Paragraph borders	⌘+F7
Character borders	F7
Column borders	Shift+F7
Page borders	Option+F7
New Header/Footer...	⌘+Shift+H
New Footnote	⌘+Shift+F
New Endnote	⌘+Shift+E
Page Numbering...	Option+F8
Line Numbering...	Shift+F8
Hyphenation...	⌘+-(dash)

Tools menu

New Macro	⌘+F9
Edit Macro	Shift+F9
Run Macro	⌘+Shift+X, F9
Speller...	⌘+E
Thesaurus...	⌘+Shift+T

Grammatik...	⌘+Y
Word Count...	Option+F3
New Graphic	⌘+F1
New Text box	⌘+F2
List...	⌘+J
Outlining...	⌘+Shift+O

Table menu

Calculate Table	⌘+Option+=(equal sign)

Style menu

Insert Redline	F14
Insert Strikeout	F15
Superscript text	⌘+Option+.(period), ⌘+F14
Subscript text	⌘+Option+,(comma), ⌘+F15

Layout bar

Paragraph layout...	⌘+F8
Center a line	⌘+Shift+Q, Option+F5
Align center	⌘+Shift+C
Align right	⌘+Shift+R
Align left	⌘+Shift+L
Align justify	⌘+Shift+J
Center text on a page	⌘+; (semi-colon)
Columns...	⌘+K
Append to the Clipboard	⌘+Shift+A
Copy Ruler	⌘+F3
Duplicate text without Clipboard	⌘+D
Insert a hard return	Shift+Return key, Return key
Insert a hard space	⌘+Shift+Spacebar
Insert a soft hyphen	⌘+-(dash)
Insert non-breaking hyphen	⌘+Shift+-(dash)

Font bar

Font, size, or style options...	⌘+H
Size up or down one point	⌘+Shift+> or <
Plain text	⌘+T
Convert text to lowercase	Option+F15
Convert text to uppercase	Option+F15

Convert text to small caps	Shift+F14
Use Smart Quotes	Shift+F3, ⌘+Shift+'(apostrophe)

Styles bar

New Styles...	⌘+F10
Edit Styles...	Option+F10
Style Options...	F10
Update a style	Shift+F10

Extended Table bar

Auto sum	Shift+Option+S

List bar

Build index and lists	Option+F11
Mark index	Shift+F11
Mark TOC Level 1	F11
Mark TOC Level 2	⌘+F11

INDEX

Index

D

M

Q